Shmirath Halashon

Rabbi Yisrael Meir HaCohen Kagan

Rabbi Shraga Silverstein (Translator)

Copyright @ 2014 by Shraga Silverstein

Table of Contents

Introduction From the Publication Staff 6
Preface 7

Part One Chapter I 15
Part One Chapter II 19
Part One Chapter III 23
Part One Chapter IV 25
Part One Chapter V 30
Part One Chapter VI 33
Part One Chapter VII 36
Part One Chapter VIII 39
Part One Chapter IX 42
Part One Chapter X 45
Part One Chapter XI 47
Part One Chapter XII 53
Part One Chapter XIII 55
Part One Chapter XIV 58
Part One Chapter XV 60
Part One Chapter XVI 64
Part One Chapter XVII 67

The Gate of Understanding Chapter I 70
G. U. Chapter II 73
G. U. Chapter III 76
G. U. Chapter IV 79
G. U. Chapter V 82
G. U. Chapter VI 84
G. U. Chapter VII 88
G. U. Chapter VIII 91
G. U. Chapter IX 94
G. U. Chapter X 96
G. U. Chapter XI 99
G. U. Chapter XII 102
G. U. Chapter XIII 105
G. U. Chapter XIV 109
G. U. Chapter XV 112
G. U. Chapter XVI 115

G. U. Chapter XVII	119
The Gate of Torah Chapter I	123
G. T. Chapter II	127
G. T. Chapter III	132
G. T. Chapter IV	136
G. T. Chapter V	141
G. T. Chapter VI	146
G. T. Chapter VII	149
G. T. Chapter VIII	155
G. T. Chapter IX	159
G. T. Chapter X	163
Conclusion Chapter I	166
Conclusion Chapter II	168
Conclusion Chapter III	170
Conclusion Chapter IV	173
Conclusion Chapter V	175
Conclusion Chapter VI	177
Conclusion Chapter VII	181
Part Two Chapter I	185
Part Two Chapter II	188
Part Two Chapter III	192
Part Two Chapter IV	195
Part Two Chapter V	197
Part Two Chapter VI	199
Part Two Chapter VII	201
Part Two Chapter VIII	203
Part Two Chapter IX Bereshith	205
Part Two Chapter X Noach Vayetze	208
Part Two Chapter XI Vayeshev	209
Part Two Chapter XII Vayeshev II	215
Part Two Chapter XIII Shemoth	219
Part Two Chapter XIV Beshalach Mishpatim	222
Part Two Chapter XV Tetzave	223
Part Two Chapter XVI Tazria and Metzora	225
Part Two Chapter XVII Kedoshim - Behar	229
Part Two Chapter XVIII Beha'alothecha	231

Part Two Chapter XIX Shelach 233
Part Two Chapter XX Korach 238
Part Two Chapter XXI Chukath 240
Part Two Chapter XXII Tetze 243
Part Two Chapter XXIII Tavo 245
Part Two Chapter XXIV 247
Part Two Chapter XXV 248
Part Two Chapter XXVI 250
Part Two Chapter XXVII 253
Part Two Chapter XXVIII 256
Part Two Chapter XXIX 257
Part Two Chapter XXX 261

Part Two Conclusion Chapter I 266
Part Two Conclusion Chapter II 272
Part Two Conclusion Chapter III 273
Part Two Conclusion Chapter IV 274

Postscript By the Translator 275

Introduction From the Publication Staff

The Chafetz Chaim needs no introduction, nor does his work Shmirath Halashon.

Neither does Rabbi Shraga Silverstein shlita, prolific author and translator whose name goes before him Le'shaim Ule'tiferes.

I am overwhelmed, humbled, and honored that I was chosen to be a part of the publication of the Chafetz Chaim's works Sefer Chafetz Chaim and Shmirath Halashon in English. My heart beats with the feeling of that which I know is always true, but is sometimes hard to keep in our consciousness, that I am working directly for the Aibershter in His efforts to disseminate the works of the Holy Chafetz Chaim.

On behalf of the whole publication staff, I wish Rabbi Silverstein and his Rebbetzin to be able to see the fulfillment of their dreams in Harbatzas HaTorah and Mussar, and Rov Nachas De'Kedusha from their children and grandchildren and all their family with Baryus Gufa U'Nehora Me'Alya.

Hakatan B. R.

Jerusalem Shevat 5774

Preface

It is written (*Mishlei* 21:33): "One who guards his mouth and his tongue guards his soul from troubles." In order to understand why Scripture specified guarding the mouth and the tongue for prevention of trouble to the soul, more than any other things that the complete man must guard in the days of his life (see the commentaries on the *pshat* [the plain meaning]). And I, too, will contribute my share of what the L-rd has given me. And hereby we shall also understand (*Psalms* 34:13-14): "Who is the man who desires life, who loves days to see good? Guard your tongue from evil and your lips from speaking deceit."

The reason for Scripture's singling out just these things seems to be this: It is known that every man has 248 physical organs and 365 physical sinews, as it is written (*Iyyov* 10:11): "With skin and flesh did You clothe me and with bones and sinews did You cover me." Now Scripture mentions skin and flesh and sinews and bones, and calls them only "clothing" and "covering" — "You clothed me"; "You covered me." Whom did He clothe if not the soul that is in his midst — "the essential man." And every organ of the soul is clothed from above with a bodily organ which corresponds to that organ as a garment to the body. And corresponding to *this*, the Holy One Blessed be He gave us 248 positive commandments and 365 negative commandments. And they are also distributed among the organs. For there is a mitzvah depending on the hand and a mitzvah depending on the foot. And so with all the other organs, as stated in the book of *Charedim*. And when a man fulfills a mitzvah in this world with a certain organ, in the world to come the light of the L-rd reposes on that organ, and it is that light which vivifies that organ. And so, with each and every mitzvah. It emerges, then, that when a man fulfills the 248 positive commandments, then he is the "complete man," who is sanctified to the L-rd with all of his organs. And this is the intent of what is stated in the section of *tzitzith* [fringes] (*Bamidbar* 15:40): "And you will do all My mitzvoth and you will be holy to your G-d." But if, G-d forbid, he be lacking one of the 248 positive commandments, which he has "cast behind his back," and which he did not repent of, there will be a defect in his soul in the world to come in the organ corresponding to that mitzvah. And this is the intent of *Berachoth* 26a: "(*Koheleth* 1:15): 'The crooked cannot be made straight' — This refers to one who omitted the *Shema* of the evening prayer or the *Shema* of the morning prayer, or the *Amidah* of the evening prayer or the *Amidah* of the morning prayer.'" And when a man is careful not to transgress the negative commandments of the Torah, he draws down the light of sanctity upon the sinews of his soul. And if he is not careful, they will be — G-d forbid — defective, as is explained at length in the book, *Sha'arei Kedushah*, Chapter I.

And from this one can reflect how he must be heedful of all the 613 mitzvoth with all his strength in the days of his life. For it is they [the mitzvoth] that extend his life eternally in the organs and sinews of his soul. As it is written (*Vayikra* 18:5): "And you shall keep My statutes and My judgments that a man shall do and live in them." It is not written "And he shall live *because* of them" [but "*in* them,"] to teach that the light of the mitzvah itself is his life in the world to come — just as one wishes to be perfect in all of his limbs in this world, so that he not be blemished in his very smallest organ.

And [this holds true] especially in the area of guarding one's tongue. For if he permits, G-d forbid, his soul to be in the category of speakers of *lashon hara* in this world, and, as a mater of course, does not prevent his ears, too, from always hearing *lashon hara* and *rechiluth* and accepting it, (also, so that he will have later what to talk about; for this is the trait of the talebearer, to go and hear in one place and sell this "merchandise" in another place, as a merchant with his wares [viz. *Torath Cohanim* and Rashi's commentary on *Chumash*]), then he will have damaged his faculties of speech and hearing, and will certainly be punished in his soul, correspondingly, in the world to come, in these two faculties themselves, speech and hearing.

[This is the language of the GRA (R. Eliyahu of Vilna) on the verse (*Mishlei* 13:13): "He who neglects a thing will be hurt by it, and the fearer of a mitzvah — he will be complete." "For there are 248 organs in a man, and, corresponding to them, 248 positive commandments. And likewise, every thing derives its vital strength from the mitzvoth. And, therefore, anyone who neglects any matter of mitzvah hurts himself. For he is thereby deprived of the vital strength of that matter. But one who fears forsaking any mitzvah and seeks to fulfill every thing [(of mitzvah)] will be complete in all of his organs."]

And we may also say that this is the intent of the verse (*Devarim* 32:5): "[In the transgressions that they have committed,] they have corrupted [themselves], not Him," [G-d forbid], as it is written [*Iyyov* 35:6]: "If you have sinned, what have you done to *Him*." The intent [of the verse in *Devarim*] is as he [the GRA] explains — that through their sins they become blemished in the end. [see Rashi on "*banav mumam*" ("His sons, their blemish")]. That is, if any mitzvah becomes expendable in his eyes, G-d forbid, then the organ corresponding to that mitzvah becomes blemished in the end, as we have written in the name of the GRA.

For in the *issur* of speaking *lashon hara* and *rechiluth* that he speaks with his mouth he transgresses "You shall not go talebearing among your people," most of which [sin] inheres in the mouth. And in hearing *lashon hara* and accepting it, he infringes on the transgression of (*Shemoth* 23:1): "You shall not bear a false report." [viz. *Sefer Charedim* on the negative commandments dependent on the ears, and what I have copied of his words in Principle X of the *Be'er Mayim Chayim*.] And it is known that these [(speaking and hearing)] are the major faculties of the "form" of man and of his perfection, even in this world. (This is well known from the ruling of Chazal that a deaf-mute [*cheresh*], who does not hear and does not speak is [legally] comparable to a *shoteh* [one who is mentally deficient] and to a minor, in all matters. And, in *Bava Kamma* 85b: "If one rendered another a *cheresh* he pays him the [legal] worth of an entire man"; for from now on he is not [legally] worth anything.) How much more so is he (i.e., "the counterpart of mouth and ear") rendered defective (for sins by those organs)] in the world to come. And even if we say that he will not be lacking entirely in these faculties, (for did he not also employ them in his lifetime in words of Torah and holiness?) in any event, they will certainly be defective, for he damaged them while yet living and did not repent. And this is known to all who have understanding — that even in this world, if, G-d forbid, a man's faculty of speech and hearing is impaired, even if — with great effort — he can still speak and hear, this greatly grieves him in his lifetime, and he will be more greatly shamed by this lack than if he were affected, in his other organs; for these are man's prime faculties and he will also not be able to conceal their loss. How much more so, in the higher world — how much will his soul grieve there before the eyes of all! Even if no punishment were inflicted upon the man of *lashon hara* at all, but only his speech and hearing were impaired, how much shame would he suffer because of this! For there it is known and recognized by all that his speech and hearing impairment *there* is due to his being a man of *lashon hara* and strife in this world.

And it is known that if one is addicted to this sin [of *lashon hara*, G-d forbid, it is very difficult to find any cure for him, as Chazal have said, that in the next world all are healed, except "a man of *lashon hara*." If so, his soul will suffer great shame eternally thereby [see the ed of Chapter V, on Miriam.]

And this, [*lashon hara*] is more likely to result in "the troubles of one's soul" [see introductory paragraph] than anything else. For by this, its [the soul's] perfection is undermined more than by anything else, (it being called "the soul of *man*" by virtue of the power of speech inherent in it [see Rashi in *parshath Bereshith*.]) And this is the intent of "One who guards his mouth and his tongue [in this world] guards his soul from troubles [in the next world]." And this is the intent of King David, may peace be upon him, in singling out this trait [of guarding one's tongue], for this is of great benefit for eternal life [see what we shall write below, the L-rd willing, in chapters IV and V.]

And, in truth, every Jew wishes to observe the Torah in perfection and to omit nothing of it, as it is written (*Isaiah* 60:21): "And Your people are all righteous." But the reasons which cause people to be lax in the holy trait of guarding one's tongue are many. We shall explain them, G-d willing, below at length; but the chief reasons are three:

a) deficiency of knowledge — not knowing which speech is in the category of *lashon hara*, wherefore we wrote the first two parts of the book *Chafetz Chaim*.

b) Intensification of the *yetzer* [the evil inclination] in this area [of *lashon hara*], whereby it gathers the power to "prosecute" us, so that our prayers are not accepted above (as we have written below, citing the holy *Zohar*.)

c) lacking the stratagems to escape the *yetzer*, viz. (*Mishlei* 24:6): "For with stratagems shall you make war for yourself [against the *yetzer*]."

For this reason, we have written with the Blessed L-rd's help, this third part [*Shmirath Halashon*], a collection of many *aggadoth Chazal*, from the *Talmud*, the *Midrashim* and the holy *Zohar*, which speak of the great punishment resulting in this world and the next from this bitter sin, Heaven preserve us, and also of the great reward in this world and the next for the guarder of his mouth and his tongue. For this reason we have called the first gate of this part "The Gate of Remembrance," as per (*Devarim* 24:9): "Remember what the L-rd your G-d did to Miriam" [for speaking *lashon hara*]. And there will also be mentioned in it apothegms of Chazal arousing one to this end and reminding him of it.

We have also labored and selected from the words of Chazal, with the help of the Blessed L-rd, various stratagems and counsels on how to rescue oneself (from the mouth of the *yetzer*) from this transgression of the sin of the tongue. Perhaps through these everyone will see to it to become wise in this area and to overcome his *yetzer* and remove from himself all of the hindrances that keep him from this holy trait of guarding the tongue. For this reason we have called the second gate of this part "The Gate of Understanding," as per (*Mishlei* 1:5): "And the understanding one will acquire stratagems." I have also explained in this gate many other holy traits which are also essential for the conduct of "the man who wants life." Through them it will be easier for him to arrive at the gate of guarding the tongue. All of this we have explained in the first two gates of this part.

We have also opened in this part an additional gate, the third gate, "The Gate of Torah," which subsumes all of the gates, as Chazal have said: "He who lacks this [Torah], what has he acquired? And he who has acquired this, what does he lack?" (And it [Torah], too, is of great benefit to the man who wants life. As they have said (*Arachin* 15b): "What is the amendment of the "man of *lashon hara*? If he is a Torah scholar, let him occupy [himself] in [the study of] Torah.") And in it will be explained the greatness of the reward of the man who sanctifies his speech with Torah, and the reward of him who dedicates his sons to Torah, and various other things that branch out of this. And because there will be in this part, with the help of the Blessed L-rd, many things that are essential for a Jew to know and to fulfill, it [this part] is especially beloved of me, and I have given it a name by itself. It shall be called "*Shmirath Halashon*" ["The Guarding of the Tongue,"] as per *Mishlei* 21:23: "One who guards his mouth and his tongue guards his soul from troubles."

And even so, let the dear reader know that even if this book finds favor in his eyes with the help of the Blessed L-rd, let him not think that it is sufficient to know the third part alone. For the first two parts also ("The Laws of *Lashon Hara*" and

"The Laws of *Rechiluth*" are essential for the man who wants life, as stated in *Midrash Mishlei* 1:2): "To know wisdom and *mussar*" — If a man has wisdom, he can learn *mussar* [chastisement]; but if he does not have wisdom, he cannot learn *mussar*." The plain meaning is: If one errs in the *din* itself, no *mussar* can help him. As, for example, if one thinks about something in his business that it is not in the category of theft. What will it avail him to learn all the teachings of *mussar*, to inflame his heart with the greatness of the *issur* of theft, if he holds that what he is doing is not in the category of theft? And the same, in all the other areas of Torah. Therefore, one must learn the *dinim* of the Torah to know what is forbidden and what is permitted [And he must also learn those areas of *mussar* which bring a man to the fear of the Blessed L-rd, in order to spur his soul to fulfill the Torah], aside from fulfilling thereby the mitzvah of (*Devarim* 6:13): "The L-rd your G-d shall you fear." And the same [is true] in *our* area [of guarding one's tongue]. For what will avail him all the *mussar* in the world, which speaks of the gravity of the *issur* of *lashon hara* and *rechiluth* if he has permitted his soul to say that this thing is not in the category of *lashon hara* or that for such and such a man the Torah did not prescribe the *issur* of *lashon hara*? It is, therefore, essential for a man to know which thing falls into the category of *lashon hara* according to the *din*. And in order to overcome his *yetzer* and to fulfill what he has learned, he must see to it to study *mussar*. And that [i.e., *mussar*] is the [heightening of the awareness of the] greatness of the punishment and of the reward that inheres in this area. And another benefit of knowing the *dinim* — on the reverse side — is not to be overstringent with oneself and forbid [oneself from speaking *lashon hara*] where it is a mitzvah to demean someone [i.e., a heretic], so that he not corrupt the public with his deceitful views. [For yet another benefit, see the Preface of the *Chafetz Chaim*.]

I have also found it fit to set down here in the preface my explanation of *Avoth d'R. Nathan* 27:3, so that one can thereby refute his *yetzer* in its argument against him in this area [of guarding one's tongue]. The *Mishnah* there states: "He [R. Yochanan ben Dahavai] used to say: 'Do not distance yourself from a trait that has no end and from a labor that has no completion.' To what can this be compared? To one taking water from the sea and spilling it on the shore. The sea was not emptied and the shore was not filled — at which he gave up in despair — upon which he was told: 'Empty one! Why do you despair? Every day take your wage — a dinar of gold!'" I explained that the "trait" referred to is the one we are speaking of. It is well known that the *yetzer* entices a man to distance himself from the trait of guarding his tongue and learning the details of this *din*. It sys to you: "What do you gain by learning and probing this thing? Will you be able to reach its end and guard your mouth all the days of your life? Would that you could hold out for one or two days! And even in this small amount of time, would you be able to do all that you *had* to do? Are you not a government official and don't you have dealings with hundreds of people? Turn back and don't begin [to cultivate] this trait at all. For it is a trait that has no end in time or in substance. For it includes all times and seasons that a man goes through in his lifetime and all of the affairs between a man and his neighbors!" And [in refutation of] this came the *tanna*, R. Yochanan ben

Dahavai and taught us in his terse reply that, in truth, things are not so, that one should *not* distance himself from a trait that has no end.

And we shall explain our words in more detail with the help of the Blessed L-rd. As to the contention of the *yetzer* that the thing [i.e., guarding one's tongue] will not last more than a day or two, let him answer: Even if it were as you say, should one be lax in this? Don't you know that if someone walked on the seashore (be he who he may, even a very rich man; how much more so, a poor one,) and he saw the sea cast up precious stones and pearls, would he be lax in picking them up because he could do so for only a few hours, or, at most, for a single day? This might be so for cheap, worthless things, but not for precious stones and pearls, where each moment that he picks them is worth more than a hundred days of picking paltry things!

So, in our case. Do we not know what the GRA has adduced in the name of the *Midrash*? That for every moment that a man muzzles his mouth [against speaking *lashon hara*], he merits the secreted light, which no angel or [heavenly] creature can visualize. Observe that the *Midrash* does not speak of a month or a week or a day or an hour — but a *moment*! And this is the intent of (*Mishlei* 2:4): "If you seek it as silver; if you search for it as hidden treasure, etc." A man must conduct himself in seeking the eternal reward as he would in seeking silver and searching for hidden treasure. And this is the intent of the *tanna*: "Do not distance yourself from a trait that has no end." That is, a man should reckon as a merit and as a "find" for his soul *anything* that he finds of it [i.e., of the hidden treasure].

And all this, even according to the words of the *yetzer*, that the agreement and the acceptance that he reaches in his heart for the future will last for only several days. But if we delve more deeply into these things, we will find that the *yetzer*'s contention is false to begin with. For it has already been proved in the crucible of experience that if one wants to work on this, then the longer he habituates himself to it, the easier it will be to maintain it. For he will be aware of it whenever he utters something unbecoming, as opposed to his earlier state where he felt nothing because of the inclination of his nature for all the things that he desired. And with a little spurring of his soul, he will keep back from forbidden speech, having divested himself of this force of habit.

But as to this question of fixing within one's soul this habit of guarding his tongue, it seems clear to me that one should conduct himself as follows: First he must see to it to be expert in all of the details of the laws of guarding one's tongue and reviewing them thoroughly to the end of becoming expert in them, to know which manner of speech is subsumed in the category of "guarding." By doing so there will as a matter of course fall away from him the major part of his former habit. Thenceforward, even if he only establishes a fixed time for this every week, this, too, will aid him greatly, all according to the nature of the man and of his affairs. For there are some men who must always examine themselves, every day as to how and where they stand in respect to their faculty of speech.

And even if some time transpires in which, for some reason, one cannot spur himself to this, or in which he sometimes finds himself defeated in this by the *yetzer*, still, he must not allow himself to despair of ever attaining it. For if he strengthens himself further and arouses himself to this guarding, he will emerge the victor and will conduct himself accordingly all of his days. This is Chazal's intent in (*Berachoth* 5a): "Let one always incite his good *yetzer* against his evil *yetzer*, etc." This "incitement" consists in his always waging war with him, as we have written.

I heard in the name of a certain Gaon that being asked by someone how to arouse himself to concentrate if, nearing the end of his prayer, he found himself not to have concentrated for most of it, he (the Gaon) replied: "To what may this be compared? To a little girl standing in the marketplace with a great basket of vegetables to sell and being accosted by someone who begins to grab things from the basket. She panics and is at a loss how to act — until a certain wise man standing at a distance calls out to her: 'What are you waiting for? Until he grabs it all? He is grabbing — you grab too! Everything that you grab will be yours!'" And thus, precisely, is it with prayer. The *yezter* overpowers a man and casts upon him indolence and vagrant thoughts, thus preventing him from concentrating upon many blessings. You, too, "grab," and spur yourself on with all of your strength to concentrate on the blessings that yet remain before you.

And thus, precisely, is it in our instance. The *yetzer* bested you today in the area of forbidden speech. Stand up and strengthen yourself against him tomorrow to defeat him. And even if, G-d forbid, he bests you again, notwithstanding this, return and strengthen yourself again against him to wage war with him. And the Holy One Blessed be He will certainly help you, too, to emerge victorious; for "one who comes to purify himself is abetted (from on High.") In sum: A man should spend all of his days warring with his *yetzer*, this being the intent of Chazal in "Let one always incite, etc." And this, in effect, is the intent of the verse (*Koheleth* 10:4): "If the spirit of the "ruler" rises up against you, do not abandon your position."

As to the *yetzer*'s second contention — "Since you cannot observe the *din* completely, it is best to distance yourself from this [(guarding your tongue)] altogether" — you can answer: "Would I allow myself to conduct my business in this way?" For example, If someone saw me running with alacrity to "make a deal" to support myself and he asked me: "Why are you running? Do you think that by doing so you will become the wealthiest man in the whole world, like Ploni?" would I not certainly answer him: "Because I will not become like him should I 'hide my hand in the dish' and not support myself?" And if this is so with the transitory body, what should I answer for the affairs of the [eternal] soul? Because I cannot observe this trait in all its details and aspects, by means of which I could rise to eternal heights of exaltedness and holiness — [as we find in the holy *Zohar*, *Parshath Chukath*, that one who guards his mouth and his tongue merits being clothed with the holy spirit, and also shining eternally in the secreted light that no angel or [Heavenly] creature can visualize, as Chazal say and as we find in *Reshith Chochmah* in the name of Maharam Kordovero of blessed memory, that Rav

Shoshan was shown secrets in a dream in which he saw that every hair of his beard shone with a torchlike luminescence, the result of his abstinence from idle speech] — should I, therefore, forebear from guarding my soul by guarding my mouth with all my might and not being G-d forbid, of the class of "the speakers of *lashon hara*" and the like, of those evil classes of which Chazal state that they do not behold the presence of the *Shechinah*? It is this that King Solomon, may peace be upon him, intended when he wrote (*Koheleth* 9:10): "All that your hand finds to do with your strength — do!" To teach us that even if it enters one's mind that he will not have the strength to complete the mitzvah in all of its details, in spite of this, he should do everything that he *can* do. And along these lines Chazal have said on *Devarim* 4:41: "Then Moses would set apart three cities," that Scripture apprises us of this [to teach us] that even though the three cities across the Jordan could not serve as cities of refuge until those in the land of Canaan had been designated, and he knew that he would not enter Eretz Yisrael, in spite of this Mosheh Rabbeinu, may peace be upon him, said: "Everything that it is in my power to do, I will do," as Rashi explains there. All this we have written, with the help of the Blessed L-rd, in explanation of what is stated in *Avoth d'R. Nathan*, that one should not distance himself from "a trait that has no end." As to "a labor that has no completion," this applies to [the study of] Torah, as indicated by the analogy adduced there.

And know that what we have written in this book as to the great need of guarding oneself from the sin of *lashon hara*, applies to one who is still in the class of "your fellow." But as to those who deny the Torah of the L-rd, even one letter thereof, and those who mock the words of Chazal, it is a mitzvah to publicize their deceitful views before all and to demean them, so that men not learn from their evil ways, as explained in the *Chafetz Chaim* Principle VIII, *halachah* 5.

Part One
The Book of Remembrance
Chapter I

*In this chapter it will be explained why Scripture
was so stringent in respect to this sin.*

It is written (*Psalms* 34:13): "Who is the man who wants life, who loves days to see good? Guard your tongue from evil." The commentators have explained that "who wants *life*" refers to eternal life in the world to come, and "who loves *days* to see good" refers to this world, which is only "days" relative to eternal life. Now, on the face of it, this is cause for wonder. Why does Scripture single out this sin in particular for "guarding against"? Has the Torah not prescribed for us 248 positive commandments and 365 negative commandments, about *all* of which the Blessed L-rd has told us (*Devarim* 30:15): "See, I have set before you this day, the life and the good ... which I command you this day, to love the L-rd your G-d, to walk in His ways, and to keep His mitzvoth, and His statutes, and His judgments, etc."?

And according to what we wrote in the introduction to the *Chafetz Chaim*, concerning the many negative and positive commandments that he is wont to transgress through this bitter sin, as opposed to the case with the other sins of the Torah, the expression "Who is the one who wants life ... Guard your tongue ... Depart from evil, etc." is found to be very apt. For King David, may peace be upon him wished to intimate in general terms that we must guard ourselves from the sins against man and his neighbor and also from the sins against man and his Maker. And in the category of sins between man and his neighbor King David, may peace be upon him, counseled the man who wants life to guard his tongue from evil in all its details, so that as a matter of course, he will be circumspect in all.

And this stands to reason. For when one habituates himself to be careful with his tongue, never to speak demeaningly of his friend, even if he causes him no harm; how much more so will he be careful not to cause him to lose his livelihood thereby, and also not to "whiten his face" with his evil talk, and also not to foment strife through his tales, all this being "evil" in the tongue, and the same with similar negative and positive commandments, as mentioned in the introduction. He certainly will also be watchful in the area of robbery and theft. For has he not already taken it upon himself to be watchful even not to cause him any harm or to demean him by his speech? How much more so [will he not harm him] actively. And if so, in the long run, he will be clean of all the sins between man and neighbor.

And after that, Scripture states: "Depart from evil," relating to the category of sins between man and his Maker. This is followed by "and do good," relating to the 248 positive commandments. [Guarding oneself from sins between man and his neighbor ("Guard your tongue, etc.,") comes first because they include both — transgressing the will of the L-rd, who commanded against it, and also wronging his neighbor thereby.] And the opposite, G-d forbid: If he does not guard his tongue from evil, there multiply in him many transgressions and extremely grave sins which issue from this sin, as explained in the preface. And guarding one's tongue is the root and source of the sins between man and his neighbor and also of some of the sins between man and his Maker, as has been explained there. However, according to the words of Chazal (*Arachin* 15a and 16b) and other places where we have expatiated upon the demeaning nature of this sin and the greatness of its punishment (as we shall show through their holy words in the chapters that follow, G-d willing), it emerges that the sin itself, in its very nature, is extremely severe aside from what issues from it. It, therefore, devolves upon us to explain why this particular sin is more severe than the other severe sins in the Torah.

This can be explained, with the help of the L-rd, in various ways. [See what we have written above in the introduction.] It is written in *Yerushalmi Peah* 1:1 that just as the reward for Torah study is over and against all of the mitzvoth, so is the punishment for *lashon hara* over and against all of the transgressions. It is found, then, that just as Torah study is the greatest of all of the mitzvoth, so is *lashon hara* the severest of all of the sins. The reason, basically, is this: Just as with the elements that the blessed One has implanted in this world — fire, wind, water, and earth — the spiritual element is far stronger than the material so that the material is almost nothing compared to it, as we see plainly that when fire gets the upper hand over a material substance it destroys it, and, likewise, when the element of wind gets the upper hand, it can split mountains and break rocks, as it is written (I *Kings* 19:11): "And a great, strong wind, splitting mountains and breaking rocks," so is the thing with the "higher elements," such as *tzitzith*, *lulav*, *shofar*, and all the mitzvoth. Just as through them great things are worked in the higher worlds, and through them, too, a man is sanctified to the L-rd, as it is written (*Numbers* 15:40): "And you shall do *all* My mitzvoth and you shall be holy to your G-d," still, there is no comparison between them and Torah study, as we find in *Yerushalmi Peah* 1, that all of the mitzvoth are not comparable to one word of Torah. The reason is that all the mitzvoth are combined with matter. So that, for example, it is impossible to fulfill the mitzvah of *tzitzith* without donning a garment, which is material. And the same with *succah* and *lulav*, and thus with all of the mitzvoth. Not so with Torah study, which inheres in the faculty of speech, which is an abstract, "spiritual" faculty alone. For this reason its higher workings are awesome, wherefore the study of Torah is "over and against all." The reverse is true of *kilkul* ["damage"]. For with all of the organs through which he sins, because they are material, the *kilkul* wrought by them is not so [relatively] great. Not so, with the sin of *lashon hara* and *rechiluth*, which works purely through a spiritual agency, wherefore its *kilkul* in the higher worlds is awesome. Its punishment, therefore, correspondingly, is "over and against all."

And now we shall explain, with the help of the L-rd, what we projected in the beginning, to detail how many *arurin* he who does not guard himself against this evil trait beings upon himself.

(1) Aside from all the aforementioned negative and positive commandments, he transgresses (*Devarim* 27:24): "Cursed be he who smites his neighbor in secret," which refers to *lashon hara*, as we find in *Sifrei* and in Rashi's commentary on *Chumash*.

(2) He also transgresses (*Devarim* 27:18): "Cursed is he who misleads the blind man on the way," it being known that the intent of Scripture is to curse one who places a stumbling-block before another so that an *issur* be committed by him, as in the negative commandment (*Vayikra* 19:14): "And before the blind man do not place a stumbling-block," which we have already explained (Negative Commandments 4) as also falling into this category.

(3) And if (G-d forbid) this matter becomes *hefker* [inconsequential] to him, so that he does not take it upon himself to guard himself from it, he transgresses further a third *arur* (*Devarim* 27:26): "Cursed is he *who does not fulfill* the words of this Torah to do them," which is understood as his not accepting it upon himself to fulfill the entire Torah. And he is called a "*mumar* [heretic] in respect to one thing" because of this — gratuitously transgressing this grave *issur*, regarding this article of the Torah of the L-rd as *hefker* — being like any other "*mumar* in respect to the entire Torah." Therefore, his sin is too great to forgive. We have thus enumerated three *arurin* which are often attendant upon this evil trait.

(And if, G-d forbid, the *lashon hara* were against his father and mother, he also transgresses a fourth *arur* (*Ibid* 16): "Cursed is he who demeans his father and his mother," which we have already explained above (Positive Commandment 14) in the *Mekor Hachaim* and in the *Be'er Mayim Chayim*.)

The following *Gemara* (*Shevuoth* 36a) is well known: "'*Arur*' connotes 'curse,' 'banishment,' and 'oath,'" Therefore, everyone who knows himself to be remiss in this bitter sin, must fear for his soul, lest (G-d forbid) he be "banished" by Heaven because of this (as is written in *Charedim* regarding one who demeans his father and mother).

And yet other evils stem from the bitter sin of *lashon hara*, such as the base trait of cruelty and that of anger, which is a grave sin, as *Chazal* dilate upon in *Shabbath* (105b). And very often it leads to levity and to other evil traits of the kind. Therefore, form all the words of this introduction, from which we can understand the greatness of the harm wrought by *lashon hara* and *rechiluth*, the Torah has explicitly delineated this *issur*, assigning to it a distinct negative commandment (viz. *Vayikra* 19:16): "Do not go talebearing among your people" more than any of the other evil traits, as we have written in the beginning of our introduction; and the Introduction is hereby completed.

And I would ask my friend, the reader, to constantly read and reread this introduction, for it certainly is of greater avail for the future in this regard than anything else. For it is culled from the *Rishonim*, whose words are pure and holy, burning like flames. And, of a certainty, they have guarded themselves form this base trait to its very end, wherefore their words make a deep impress on the hearts of their readers. And let the reader also know that I have not selected the negative and positive commandments fortuitously, but I carefully probed and expounded the 613 mitzvoth, and much did I toil until the Holy One Blessed be He helped me find those [commandments] relevant to our subject.

And so that it not be cause for wonder in the eyes of the reader, since the *issur* of *lashon hara* is so great, as is that of verbal wronging, why do we find many times in the *Gemara* that one *amora* seems to be taunting his colleague. To this, too, I "opened my eyes," and because of this I copied the responsum of the *Chavoth Yair* that appears at the end of the book. And, in the book itself, I also resolved many [seemingly contradictory] citations, a little here, a little there.

Chapter II

More on this Subject

And there is yet another reason for this. It is known that in accordance with a man's ordering of his traits in this world is the corresponding arousal of this trait in the world above. If it is his way to overlook offenses and to deal with men with the traits of lovingkindness and mercy, he thereby arouses, above, the trait of mercy, and the Holy One Blessed be He is merciful to the world because of him. And "from the fruits of a man's mouth, his soul will be sated." And he, too, will merit the mercies of the Holy One Blessed be He, and his offenses will be forgiven, as Chazal have said (*Shabbath* 151b): "All who are merciful to men are granted the mercies of Heaven," and (*Yoma* 23a): "All who overlook offenses to themselves have their [own] offenses overlooked [by Heaven.]" As stated in the *Zohar, Parshath Emor*: "We learned: 'The deed above is awakened by the deed below. If a man does a deed appropriately below, lovingkindness is awakened above, and it reposes [itself] on that day, and it [the day] is crowned by lovingkindness for his sake. And if a man conducts himself mercifully below, he arouses mercy on that day, and it is crowned with mercy for his sake. And then, that day stands for him to be a defense at the time that he needs it, etc. By the same measure that a man measures with, he is measured by. Happy is he who shows a "kosher" deed below. For on that deed depends everything, to arouse its [heavenly] counterpart thereby.'"

And if it is his trait in dealing with people never to forego anything that is his and never to be merciful to them, he intensifies thereby, above, the attribute of *din* against the world and also against himself. For by the measure that a man measures with he is measured by, and none of his deeds will be overlooked. And this is the intent of Chazal (*Bava Metzia* 30b): "Jerusalem was destroyed only because they set their ways on the *din* of Torah." Now did they not have many sins, as indicated in Scripture? But according to the foregoing, it is clear. If they had overlooked offenses, the Holy One Blessed be He would have pardoned them accordingly. But they had set their ways not to forego anything for their friends beyond the parameter of *din*, wherefore the Holy One Blessed be He was exacting with them likewise.

And if one speaks *lashon hara* against his friend and arouses *din* against him, he arouses thereby, above, "prosecution" against Israel, and he thereby gives Satan power to prosecute Israel, as stated in the holy *Zohar, Parshath Pekudei*: "There is a certain spirit that stands over all those 'men of *lashon hara*,' and when men are roused with *lashon hara*, or when that one man is roused with *lashon hara*, there is roused up that unclean, evil spirit above called "*sachsucha*" [contention], and it comes to repose upon that arousal of *lashon hara* initiated by men, and it thereby causes the awakening of *lashon hara*, the sword, and slaughter in the world. Woe to those who arouse that power of evil and do not guard their mouths and tongues and are not fearful of this, not knowing that on the lower awakening depends the higher awakening, both for good and for evil, etc. And all [of these] are prosecutors to arouse that great serpent to prosecute the world. And all because of that lower arousal of *lashon hara*."

And when we reflect but a little upon this awesome thing, we understand immediately why the Holy One Blessed be He is more severe with this sin than with all others, to the point that He refuses to associate with the man of *lashon hara* at all to rescue him from his troubles, as will be adduced, please G-d, below in the name of the *Sifrei*, and as is written in the *Zohar, Parshath Shelach*: "R. Shimon said: 'The Holy One Blessed be He pardoned all, except *lashon hara*.'" For it is known that the love of the Holy One Blessed be He for His people, Israel, is exceedingly great, as Scripture states (*Jeremiah* 31:19): "Is not Ephraim a dear son to me, or a child that I dandle, etc.?" When a man has a dear son or a child that he dandles, and he sees that he is not acting properly, still, he "covers up" for him in his great love for him. And even though he chastises him at times, it will be with compassion and pity. But if some men come to him once or twice and tell him about his sons' waywardness, how he argues and wrangles with people for nothing, how he shames and insults everyone, then certainly he will grow angry with him and beat him and shame him for this. And who caused all this? The teller. The same is true in our case. The Holy One Blessed be He, in His great love for Israel, even though He knows all that is done in secret and in the open (as it is written [*Jeremiah* 23:24]: "Will a man hide himself, etc.?"), still He will not arouse Himself against them to do them evil, as it is written (*Numbers* 23:21): "He has seen no iniquity in Jacob" [see Rashi there]. But, if the accuser comes to Him and tells Him of this, He must give him some kind of answer [just as "the kingdom of the earth" must respond when someone cries out before them over some injustice done to him.] For thus has the King of the world established it, that a man's affairs are mediated through defenders and prosecutors.

Now it is known, that the upper "arousal" is dependent on the lower. Therefore, if the trait of peace is found in Israel, and there are no slanderers among them below, then in the upper world, too, Satan cannot prosecute them — even for the severest sin of all, idol worship, G-d forbid, as stated in *Midrash Shir Hashirim*, that even (G-d forbid) if Israel is idolatrous, but there is peace among them, the Holy One Blessed be He says, as it were: "Satan will not touch them," as it is written (*Hoshea* 4:17): "Ephraim is bound to idols — let him be!" The intent here is that the Holy One Blessed be He has implanted it in Satan that in such an instance [i.e., when Israel are at peace among themselves], Satan cannot touch them at all. And thus have Chazal said (*Yerushalmi Peah* 5:1), that the generation of Achav, even though they were idolators, would go down to war and win, because there was no slander among them. The proof — they did not slander [(to Achav)] Ovadiah, who sustained the one hundred prophets [who were hiding from Achav]. And, as I have written below, (Chapter IV), "measure for measure" is a [guiding] principle in all affairs. Therefore, if one suppresses himself and muzzles his mouth against speaking demeaningly against his friend and arousing strife against him, so, above, the Prosecutor, above, will not be able to open his mouth to speak accusingly. As opposed to a situation where there is slander in Israel below. For aside from the slanderer's arousing prosecution against himself because of his sins (as we shall explain below in the name of Chazal), he arouses the power of prosecution against Israel in general. For through this, Satan comes and prosecutes Israel for *their* sins, and calls for *din* against them; and [the L-rd], as it were, is "compelled" to punish them for this. And who caused all this? The speaker of *lashon hara* below.

[And, in my view, this is the intent of the verse (*Bamidbar* 23:21): "He does not see iniquity in Jacob ... the L-rd his G-d is with him": When does He not see iniquity in Jacob? When the L-rd his G-d is with him. But when there is, G-d forbid, *lashon hara* in Israel, which leads to departure of the Shechinah, as stated in *Midrash Rabbah, Parshath Shoftim*, then, G-d forbid, He *does* probe their deeds.]

And from all this we can understand the greatness of the hatred that the Holy One Blessed be He bears to the "teller." For though the father strikes his son, being compelled to do the teller's will, understanding the thing to be true — in any event, great hatred is aroused in his heart against the teller, recognizing that his motive is not to benefit his son, but to censure him. How much more so is this true in our case. For it is known that the Holy One Blessed be He loves a man more than he loves himself, and He desires only the good of Israel, and that they not be slandered at all. As Chazal have said on *Isaiah* 6:6: "And in his [the angel's] hand, a coal [*ritzpah*]," the Holy One Blessed be He saying to the angel: "Let the mouth be crushed [("*retzotz peh*," like "*ritzpah*")] that slandered My sons." And the speaker of *lashon hara* causes the opposite of all this [(love between G-d and His children)], for which reason he is detested in the eyes of the L-rd.

Now if the man of heart reflects upon the aforementioned holy *Zohar*, and sees with a "knowing eye" what is destined to result from his speech, he will be filled with fear and trepidation [at the thought of] speaking *lashon hara* against his friend. For if a man were told to enter the sanctuary of the L-rd by himself or to send a messenger in his place to stand before the ark of His covenant and prosecute all of Israel and not speak falsehood of them but only what he knows to be the truth, is it not obvious that even the worst man of Israel would not take upon his soul a sin as horrendous as this? And is this not exactly the case with *lashon hara*?, the slander that he utters with his mouth arising before the Blessed One's throne, as stated explicitly in *Tanna d'bei Eliyahu*, Chapter 18: "Just as the wicked speak *lashon hara*, which ascends before the Throne of Honor, etc." And by this he arouses the Great Prosecutor against the children of Israel, as per the aforementioned holy *Zohar*.

From all of this, we can understand the greatness of the punishment exacted for this sin in this world and the next. And, therefore, King David, may peace be upon him, exhorted us that if it is our desire to live eternally in the world to come and to enjoy good days in this world, the beginning of all is to guard our tongue from evil. And how much should we be ashamed and abashed before the Holy One Blessed be He to whom we pray on the Days of Awe: "Silence the prosecutor and let the defender take his place," when we ourselves, through our *lashon hara*, arouse him [the prosecutor] and give him the power to prosecute! May the L-rd repose among us love and brotherhood, peace and friendship!

Chapter III

*In this chapter it will be explained that eternal life and the good
of this world depend on the guarding of our tongue.*

We can give yet another reason for King David's attributing eternal life and the good of this world to guarding one's tongue. For it is known that a man's soul is called "the soul of life," for with it a man lives eternal life. But the holy soul of a man who speaks *lashon hara* departs from him thereby, as stated in the holy *Zohar, Parshath Metzora*.

And in this world, too, he is destined for afflictions, (the fruits of this bitter sin, as stated in *Yerushalmi Peah* 1:1), which are exacted of a man for this sin in this world, the principal [of punishment] remaining with him for the world to come.

And the man who muzzles his mouth against speaking forbidden things merits in the life of the world to come, the light secreted for the righteous, as the GRA wrote in the name of the *Midrash*, that for every moment that a man muzzles his mouth [in this world], he merits [in the world to come] the secreted light, which no angel or [celestial] spirit can conceptualize. That is why King David of blessed memory exhorted us (*Psalms* 34:13): "Who is the man who wants life" [in the world to come] and "to see good" [in this world]? "Guard your tongue from evil."

There is yet another obvious reason for the demeaning nature of this bitter sin: It is known that man's great superiority over all living creatures is G-d's having superadded to him a "speaking soul," as it is written (*Bereishith* 2:7): "And He blew into his nostrils a soul of life and man became *a living soul*," which Onkelos translates "a speaking soul." And this [(superiority)] is so only if he enhances [the world] with the faculty of speech which the Holy One Blessed be He gave him. Not so, if he employs his speech for evil, in which instance he is worse than the beasts of the earth, which, in any event, cause no harm [by their muteness]. And that is why Scripture emphasizes: "Who is the *man* who wants life, etc." For otherwise, [i.e., without speech], he is not a *man*. And this defect [i.e., abuse of speech] is most glaring if he is a Torah scholar, in which instance he is like a great palace with a tannery gutter built into it (as we find in *Derech Eretz* 1).

And the Gaon, R. Refael, in his book, *Marpeh Lashon*, explained this verse, too, with great discrimination, on the basis of what is written in *Chovoth Halevavoth, Sha'ar Hakniyah*, 7: "Many people will come for the day of accounting. And when they are shown their deeds, there will be found in the Book of Merits, mitzvoth which they did not do. And they will say: 'We did not do these!'

And they will be answered: 'They were done by one who spoke of you demeaningly [and they were credited to you.]' Likewise, when their [merits] will be lacking from the Book of Merits of those who spoke demeaningly of them, they [the speakers will ask why they are missing], and they will be answered: 'You lost them when you spoke demeaningly of such and such person.' And, likewise, there will be found in the Book of Liabilities of some, acts which they did not commit, and when they say 'We did not commit them,' they will be answered: 'They were added to your account because of such and such that you spoke about, etc.'" And the same has been written in other holy works.

And, this being so, one who is addicted, G-d forbid, to this evil trait of constantly emptying the arrows of his tongue against his friend will not avail his soul with any wisdom or counsel, even if he habituates his tongue always to Torah and mitzvoth. For as soon as he earns a week or two worth of eternal bliss, through Torah and mitzvoth, he will "find" his friend with the arrows of his mouth and give him his merits forever and take in exchange his [the other's] sins. And then, if afterwards he will earn a few months or years more of eternal bliss, he will find a different man and give them to him! And so, ad infinitum, until the day of his death, G-d forbid. In sum, this man is liable to leave the world bereft of his possessions; that is, the eternal acquisitions of Torah and mitzvoth. And he will be "filled" in exchange with many grave sins of infinite variety, from many people, from each in accordance with the shame and humiliation that have been wrought them at his hand in the days of his life. Therefore, King David of blessed memory exhorted us that the beginning of all is to guard our tongues from evil, and then: "Depart from evil and do good." For by guarding his tongue, then as much of the good that the Holy One Blessed be He has accorded him, whether less or more, in any event, will remain in his hand, and his wealth will not be given to others.

Chapter IV

In this chapter the power of Lashon Hara will be explained

How great is the power of *lashon hara*, which is over and against three grave transgressions, as stated in *Arachin* 15b. And in *Midrash Shocher Tov*: "The school of R. Yishmael taught: 'All who speak *lashon hara* mount iniquity over and against three transgressions: idolatry, illicit relations, and the spilling of blood, it being written here (*Psalms* 12:4): 'the tongue that speaks "*great*" [i.e., slanderous] *things*'; but, in respect to idolatry (*Shemoth* 32:31): 'I pray you — this people has sinned a *great* sin'; in respect to illicit relations (*Bereshith* 39:9): 'And how shall I do this *great* evil?'; in respect to the spilling of blood (*Ibid.* 4:13): 'My sin is too *great* to bear'" — whence [("things" - plural)] it is derived that *lashon hara* is severer than these three sins."

Another explanation: One who kills a man kills only one soul; but one who speaks *lashon hara* kills three: the speaker, the accepter, and the one spoken about. Whence do you derive this? From Doeg, who spoke *lashon hara* about Achimelech before Saul, and the three of them were killed: Saul, who accepted it; Achimelech, who was spoken about; and Doeg, who spoke it. Saul, who accepted it, viz. (I *Samuel* 31:6): "And Saul died, etc."; Achimelech, who was spoken about, viz. (*Ibid.* 22:16): "Die, shall you die, Achimelech"; and Doeg, who spoke it, who was driven out of the world [to come], viz. (*Psalms* 52:7): "G-d also will destroy you forever" from life in the world [to come]. And what caused this? *Lashon hara.*

And it is stated in *Sifrei*, and also in *Arachin* 15a that our forefathers tried the L-rd ten times, and their decree was sealed only for the sin of *lashon hara* alone, as it is written (*Bamidbar* 14:22): "And they tried Me this ten times, and they did not heed My voice," and (*Malachi* 2:17): "You have wearied the L-rd with your words."

And thus have we found in *Midrash Shocher Tov* and in *Yerushalmi Peah* 1:1, that in the days of Achav, even though they served idols, they were victorious in war because there was no *lashon hara* among them. The proof: They did not slander Ovadiah [to Achav] for hiding a hundred prophets in two caves, and no man of them revealed that there was a prophet in Israel aside from Eliyahu, as it is written (I *Malachi* 18:22): "I alone have been left as a prophet to the L-rd" — even though everyone knew of it. For they would give Ovadiah bread and water to Ovadiah to feed them with.

And in the end of the days of Saul, there was slander among them as with Doeg and the Zifim. But there was no idolatry among them as there was in the days of Achav. And there were young children among them who were conversant in forty-nine facets of Torah, [and yet] they went to war and were defeated.

And it [*lashon hara*] causes the Shechinah to depart from Israel, as it is written in *Midrash Rabbah, Parshath Shoftim*: R. Mona said: Everyone who speaks *lashon hara* causes the Shechinah to depart from "below to above." Know this to be so, for what did David say (*Psalms* 57:5): "My soul is in the midst of lions. I lie down (in the midst of) those that send out flames, (those) sons of men, whose teeth are spears and arrows, whose tongue is a sharpened sword." What follows? "Rise above the heavens, O L-rd, etc." David said: "Master of the world, what is the Shechinah doing below? Remove the Shechinah to the heavens!" And thus we find in *Midrash Rabbah, Parshath Tetze*: "The Holy One Blessed be He said: "In this world, because there was *lashon hara* among you, I removed the Shechinah from among you." And, similarly, in *Arachin* 15b: R. Chisda said in the name of Mar Ukva: "[About] one who speaks *lashon hara*, the Holy One Blessed be He said: 'I and he cannot live [together] in the world, etc.'" And Jerusalem was destroyed in the time of the second Temple only because of the sin of the speakers of *lashon hara* and the vain hatred that they harbored [see *Yoma* 9b and *Gittin* 56a and b, in the name of R. Elazar, as explained by Rashi.]

And one who, by his *lashon hara* and *rechiluth*, stirs up strife between good companions and causes quarrels among them, G-d forbid, is abominated because of this before the L-rd. And this sin is more severe than that of pride, lying, spilling innocent blood, etc., as written in *Mishlei* 6:16-20: "These six are hated by the L-rd, and the seventh is the abomination of His soul: haughty eyes, a false tongue, and hands spilling innocent blood; a heart plotting vain thoughts, feet hastening to run to evil; a false witness spouting lies, and the inciter of strife among brothers" — concerning which Chazal have said (*Vayikrah Rabbah* 16): "This ['the inciter of strife'] is 'the seventh,' that is more severe than all.

And more than this we find in the *Midrash*, that the Holy One Blessed be He does not want to associate at all with a man of *lashon hara* to rescue him from his troubles. And there is no remedy for a man other than to guard his tongue from evil and to hide himself always from sitting in the company of men who speak demeaningly of their friends.

And this is the language of the *Midrash* and *Sifrei Zuta* [adduced by *Yalkut, Parshath Tetze*]: "The Holy One Blessed be He said: 'From all the troubles that come upon you I can rescue you. But from *lashon hara* [slander]? Hide yourself and you will not be hurt!' An analogy: A rich man who loved a villager went to visit him. There was a mad dog there who bit everyone. The rich man said to his beloved: 'My son, if you are in debt to anyone, I will pay your debt, and don't hide from him. But if you see a mad dog, hide from him. For if he bites you, I don't know what I can do for you.' Thus says the Holy One Blessed be He (*Iyyov* 5:19): 'From six troubles shall He rescue you … but from the lash of the tongue — hide!'" See the aptness of these words of Chazal, who compared one afflicted by this sin to one bitten by a mad dog. For, in truth, both are alike. As stated in *Yoma* 84a: "One bitten by a mad dog has no cure." And about *lashon hara* they have also said that there is no remedy for one who is habituated to this sin, G-d forbid, viz. (*Arachin* 15b): "If he has already slandered, there is no remedy for him."

How apt is this analogy of our sages of blessed memory. For when we reflect upon it, we find in it all the signs described by our sages of blessed memory, in *Yoma* 83b, of a rabid dog — wherefore there also rests upon him [the slanderer] the spirit of uncleanliness that reposes on that dog. This is what the *Gemara* says there: "The Rabbis taught: 'Five things were said of a rabid dog: His mouth hangs open; his spittle drips; his ears hang down; his tail hangs down on his hindquarters; and he walks on the sides of the public thoroughfare. Others say: He also barks without being heard … One who rubs against him is in danger of dying. One who is bitten by him dies. 'One who rubs against him is in danger of dying': What is the remedy? Let him doff his mantle, throw it before him, and run.'" We shall now explain: "His mouth hangs open" — This is also the way of the man of *lashon hara*. His mouth is always open to speak against anyone he meets, child or adult. "his spittle drips" — Because a foul spirit reposes upon him, and the power of anger and audacity implanted in him intensifies itself within him [(*Beitzah* 25b): "Three are audacious. The most audacious of the animals is the dog"], [he wants] to swallow anything that he chances upon, wherefore his mouth [always] drips spittle, especially so, in that his mouth is [always] open, and there is no restraint for it. This is the way of the confirmed speaker of *lashon hara* — to vent his anger at whoever he wants to. And there is in this, something [even] more apt. Just as it is the way of a rabid dog to drip spittle, the mucous of the dog, which is certainly repulsive — especially that of a rabid dog — [it follows that] wherever he was, even for a few moments, there is recognized, even after he has left that spot, the dripped spittle of his constantly open mouth. And this is the way of the man of *lashon hara*. His mouth hangs open like the mouth of this dog. And he raises his stench wherever he goes, and he leaves an impression on that spot.

There are yet three more signs of a rabid dog. His ears hang down, etc. That is, the rabid dog, aside from his bite being extremely dangerous, as mentioned by Chazal, has a great desire to bite anyone who comes before him. And so that people not hide from him because of the great danger owing to the evil spirit reposing upon him, as written there, he hides and conceals himself in every possible way, and suddenly he pounces upon the person and bites him. That is why he walks (and does not run) on the sides of the public thoroughfares and not on the thoroughfares themselves facing the people [(for that is where people walk, viz. *Bava Kamma* 60b: "A man should not walk along the sides of the roads, etc.")], so that people should think that he is going slowly on his way. And because of this, his ears also hang down. For it is well known that the Holy One Blessed be He has given a dog an acute sense of hearing to help him protect his master and himself from danger. And so, this dog, who wants to attack everyone, walks along the sides of the road with his ears dragging, so that he appears to everyone as going his own way and not wanting to hear anything on his sides. And that is why his tail also hangs down on his hindquarters, unlifted. All this to show everyone that he is quiet and secure and has no desire to rouse his senses to attack the people at his sides. And some say that he also barks without being heard. All because of the same reason, so that everyone think that he is the very best of dogs, and will not guard themselves from him at all. And all of these things he does through the agency of the evil spirit that rests upon him. And thus, exactly, is the man of *lashon hara*. Aside from always probing the houses of the city in order to have what to relate thereafter in the marketplace, he is versatile in changing. For when he is adversely publicized as one who goes peddling [his tales] from one to the other and becomes like a thorn in the eyes of the people of the city, and everyone guards himself against him, he walks on the sides of the public thoroughfare, enwrapped in silence, as if nothing concerns him, in order to spy out everything going on in the city — secret and otherwise. And, correspondingly, when he tells his *lashon hara* and *rechiluth* [talebearing], he does so deceptively, as if speaking in pure innocence, not telling the whole story, but intimating — whereby his interlocutor "figures out the rest." And his ears drag, and his tail hangs between his legs. There also applies to him what was said about the aforementioned dog. That is, even though there burn in his midst all the senses of feeling, and, especially, that of hearing, to hear of everything that is done in the city and to run and peddle it from one to the other — in spite of this, in public, he appears to the eye of the beholder as one who suppresses all of his feelings, is equable to all, and wants to hear nothing of what is done among people — all, so that the people of the city not guard themselves against him and everything be revealed to him. "And others say: He also barks without being heard." For in his *lashon hara*, he wounds in secret (as do those writers of wrongs [called "*paskevilim*"], about whom it is written (*Devarim* 27:24):"Cursed be he who smites his neighbor in secret.") — all so that his neighbor will be unable to guard himself against him and he will be able to attack him, like the aforementioned dog. Therefore, there reposes upon him the same spirit of uncleanliness that reposes upon a mad dog, and the *Sifrei* refers to him as "one bitten by a dog." For upon him, too, there reposes the spirit of uncleanliness. [The end of the comparison is self-explanatory. See the end of Chapter 16.]

And what need is there for me to elaborate on the greatness of this sin, when they have already said that he [a speaker of *lashon hara*] is like one who transgresses the five books of the Torah and a denier of the Deity, G-d forbid. For this is the language of the *Midrash Rabbah* (16:1): "R. Yehoshua b. Levi said: Five "*toroth*" are written in the *parshah*:

(*Vayikra* 13:59): "This is the Torah of the plague-spot of leprosy";

(*Ibid.* 14:54): "This is the Torah for all plague-spots of leprosy";

(*Ibid.* 14:2): "This shall be the Torah of the leper";

(*Ibid.* 14:32): This is the Torah for him with a plague-spot of leprosy";

(*Ibid.* 14:57): "This is the Torah of leprosy" ["*hametzora*," (acronym for)] "*hamotzi shem ra*," ("one who spreads a false report") — to teach you that one who speaks *lashon hara* transgresses five books of Torah.

And Chazal have said in *Arachin* 15b: "R. Yochanan said in the name of R. Yossi b. Zimra: If one speaks *lashon hara*, it is as if he would deny the Deity, as it is written (*Psalms* 12:5): 'Who have said: "With our tongue will we be mighty, our lips are with us. Who is L-rd over us?"' The reason is as they have written in the books of *Yereim*: It is known that one who wants to speak *lashon hara* looks all around to make sure that the one he wants to talk about is not there, as if the Eye above did not see, G-d forbid, as Chazal have said about a thief [(who steals at night)]. And in *Midrash Tanchuma, Metzora* 2: "[The sin of] *lashon hara* is grave; for one does not utter it until he denies the Deity."

Therefore, one who has a brain in his head will see to it always to spur himself and to fight the war of the L-rd with his *yetzer* not to be ensnared in this great, bitter sin.
And then, happy is his portion in this world and in the world to come.

Chapter V

In this chapter there will be explained the punishment of men of *lashon hara*.

How great is the punishment of the man of *lashon hara*, who brings upon himself plague-spots because of his speech and becomes thereby a "confirmed" leper, as stated in *Arachin* 15b: "If one speaks *lashon hara*, plague-spots come upon him, as it is written (*Psalms* 101:5): 'He who slanders his neighbor in secret, him shall I confirm [as a leper].' Resh Lakish said (*Vayikra* 14:2): "This shall be the law of the *metzora* [the leper]" — the law of the *motzi shem ra* [the slanderer]."

And see how stringent the Torah was with the uncleanliness of the *metzora*, which is more severe than the uncleanliness of a *zav* and a *keri* [(types of genital discharges)] and dead-body uncleanliness, his not being permitted to come [even] into the camp of Israel, as it is written (*Vayikra* 13:46): "Solitary shall he sit; outside the camp [i.e., the three camps] is his dwelling."

And it is stated there (*Arachin* 16b): "Why did the Torah single out the leper for 'Solitary shall he sit'? He [(by his slander, for which he was stricken with leprosy)] separated between a man and his wife, between a man and his neighbor; therefore, the Torah writes 'Solitary shall he sit, etc.' And R. Yehoshua b. Levi said: "Why did the Torah single out the leper for bringing two birds for his cleansing? (*Ibid.* 14:4). The Holy One Blessed be He said: '*He* committed an act of prattling' [i.e., slander]; therefore, let him bring a sacrifice of 'prattlers' [i.e., 'chirpers']."

And we learn in *Sifrei* (*Devarim* 24:8): "Be heedful of the plague-spot of leprosy, etc.," followed by (*Ibid.* 9): "Remember what the L-rd your G-d did to Miriam, etc." What is the rationale of the juxtaposition? We are hereby taught that she was punished only because of *lashon hara* [(Miriam having slandered Moses because of the Kushite woman that he had taken.)] Now does this not follow *a fortiori*? viz.: If Miriam, who had spoken thus only of her younger brother, was punished, then one who speaks thus of someone greater than he, how much more so [should he be punished!] Another interpretation: Now, if Miriam, who, when she spoke, was heard by no one but the Holy One Blessed be He alone, as it is written (*Numbers* 12:2): 'And the L-rd heard,' was punished thus, how much more so, one who speaks demeaningly of his friend in public!"

And they also expounded (in *Vayikra Rabbah* 16) the verse (*Koheleth* 5:5): "Do not allow your mouth to cause sin to your flesh" — do not speak *lashon hara* with your mouth to punish all of your flesh with this sin. The Rabbis applied this verse to Miriam: "Do not allow *your* mouth" — you, Miriam, as it is written

(*Numbers* 12:10): "And, behold, Miriam was leprous, [white] as snow." (*Koheleth*, Ibid.): "that it was an error" — as it is written (*Numbers* 12:11): "wherein we [(Aaron and Miriam)] have erred and wherein we have sinned." (*Koheleth, Ibid*.): "Why should G-d be angry at your *voice*?" — at the *lashon hara* you have spoken against Moses, as it is written (*Numbers* 12:9): "and the anger of the L-rd burned against them, and He departed." (*Koheleth, Ibid*.): "and [He shall] destroy the work of your hands." R. Yochanan said: "With her mouth she sinned, and all her limbs were smitten, as it is written (*Numbers* 12:10): 'And the cloud departed from the tent, and, behold, Miriam was leprous, [white] as snow.' This is the intent of: "Do not allow your mouth to cause sin to [destroy] your flesh" … (*Mishlei* 21:33): 'He who guards his mouth and his tongue guards his soul from troubles.'"

And we learn in *Devarim Rabbah*: "R. Chaggai said: Plague-spots come only for *lashon hara*. The Rabbis said: Know this to be true, for Miriam the *tzaddeketh*, because she spoke *lashon hara* against Moses her brother, plague-spots came upon her, as it is written (*Devarim* 24:9): 'Remember what the L-rd your G-d did to Miriam on the way when you went out of Egypt.' And this is the intent of the verse (*Psalms* 50:20): 'You sit and speak against your brother; against your mother's son you utter slander.' R. Yehoshua b. Levi explained: "If you have taught your tongue to speak against your brother from your father, but not from your mother, in the end, "against [even] your mother's son you will utter slander." For whoever presumes to speak [slander] against him who is greater than he, causes evil to himself, plague-spots drawing near to him. And if you do not believe this, Miriam the *tzaddeketh* is the paradigm for all the speakers of *lashon hara* — 'Remember what the L-rd your G-d did to Miriam, etc.' R. Shimon said: Now if with Miriam the *tzaddeketh*, who did not intend to speak *lashon hara*, but who spoke for the good of her brother, this [was the result], then those evildoers, whose intent it is to speak *lashon hara* against their neighbors to cut off their lives, how much more so will the Holy One Blessed be He cut off their tongues, as it is written (*Psalms* 12:4): 'The L-rd will cut off all the slippery [i.e., slanderous]lips.'"

We also find that the spies, because of the sin of *lashon hara*, died an unnatural death, as it is written (*Sotah* 35a) (*Bamidbar* 14:37): "And they died, the men who had uttered an evil report of the land, etc." R. Shimon b. Lakish said: "They died an unnatural death." And it is stated there in the *Gemara*: "We are hereby taught that their tongues descended to their navels, and worms left their mouths onto their tongues, and from their tongues they descended to their navels."

And, in *Arachin* 15a: "Come and see how great is the power of *motzi shem ra*. Whence is this derived? From the spies, viz.: Now if when one utters a false report about trees and stones, this [is the result], then if one utters a false report about his friend, how much more so!"

From all this we can learn the greatness of the punishment [for *lashon hara*], one being punished for it by plague-spots and by other [dire] punishments. And, G-d's measure of reward being [proportionately] greater than his measure of punishment, we can understand how great is the reward of him who guards himself against this sin.

Chapter VI

More on this subject

And let this not be cause for wonder in your eyes, that we find many who speak *lashon hara* and have no plague spots. We find an answer for this in the *midrash* of Chazal on the verse (*Mishlei* 21:23): "He who guards his mouth and his tongue guards his soul from troubles [*tzaroth*]" — (like "*tzara'ath*," plague-spots).

I have seen part of the explanation of this matter in the book, *Nachal Kedumim*, viz.: It is well known that all of G-d's punishment of a man is for his good, so that he be cleansed of his sins, and, sometimes, that he repent. Therefore, when the Temple stood and we had a Cohein who cleansed, if a man stumbled into the sin of *lashon hara*, the Holy One Blessed be He would bring upon him the punishment of plague-spots. And even so, He did not bring it immediately upon his body, but upon the beams of his house. And he himself would have to come to the Cohein and say to him that there appeared to him something like a plague-spot in the house. And the Cohein would exhort him to repent — "My son, plague-spots come only for *lashon hara*, etc.", as we find in *Torath Cohanim* — so that he should exert himself thereby to depart from the sin. And if he did not take this to heart, the Holy One Blessed be He would punish him yet further in this manner, as explained by Rambam at the end of the laws of *tzara'ath*-uncleanliness: "House *tzara'ath* is not in the order of nature, but was a sign and wonder in Israel to warn them against *lashon hara*. If one spoke *lashon hara*, the beams of his house would undergo a change. If he repented, the house would be cleansed, and if he persisted in his wickedness until the house were knocked down, the leather appurtenances in his house on which he sat and reclined upon would undergo a change. If he repented, etc. And if he persisted in his wickedness until they were burned, his skin would undergo a change, and he would become a leper. And he would be separated [from others] and exposed [as a leper] by himself, so that he not take part in the converse of the wicked, which is levity and *lashon hara*, etc."

And there was great benefit in this punishment. For when he saw the greatness of his punishment and his disgrace, his having to sit solitary outside the [three] camps always, not being allowed to come even to the camp of Israel, and constantly proclaiming his grief to the populace so that they should pray [to the L-rd] to have mercy upon him (viz. *Moed Katan* 5a), and (*Vayikra* 13:45): "and 'Unclean! Unclean!' shall he cry," then, as a matter of course, he would be extremely humbled by his sin and would take it upon himself for the future to take great care against this bitter sin and to conciliate the one he spoke [*lashon hara*] about. And the Holy One Blessed be He in His [great] lovingkindness would send a cure for his *tzara'ath*, and the Cohein would go outside the camp to see if the plague-spot had healed, as it is written (*Vayikra* 14:3): "And the Cohein shall go outside the camp, and the Cohein shall see, if the plague-spot of leprosy is healed, etc.", and then he would proceed according to the whole order written in the *parshah* concerning sprinkling and shaving, and afterwards, he [the Cohein] would bring his sacrifices for him.

And when he came afterwards to his house, when he saw the great lovingkindness that the L-rd had done with him, having healed him of his *tzara'ath*, he certainly would do all that he had undertaken when he was outside the camp, and he would conciliate all those he had spoken *lashon hara* about. And through this he would be healed completely of this plague-spot and also of this sin. For his punishment and disgrace would atone for him for the past, and, as to the future, he would exert himself with all his strength not to come to [commit] this sin again.

And all this, when the Temple stood, as opposed to our situation today, in our many sins, when we have neither Temple nor sacrifices, nor cleansing Cohein, so that if the Holy One Blessed be He brought plague-spots on his body, he would remain in his uncleanliness forever, it being impossible for him to cleanse himself from it. Therefore, the uncleanliness of the plague-spot that came through this sin would remain in his soul alone and would not project from his soul outwards. And this is the intent of the *midrash* [brought in *Yalkut, Parshath Metzora* in the name of R. Yannai]: "He who guards his mouth and his tongue guards his soul from troubles [*tzaroth*]" — from the *tzara'ath* of his soul. For the plague-spot of *tzara'ath* is fixed in the soul.

Therefore, the man who is habituated to this sin, G-d forbid, must mourn always for his soul. For even though the Holy One Blessed be He "covers up" for him in this world and does not reveal his disgrace to all, in any event, after his death, when the soul leaves the body, the "pollution" of his *tzara'ath* will be revealed to all. And so long as the scum of this pollution remains in his soul, certainly, the afflicted one will not enter the sanctuary of the L-rd in Gan Eden, and he will have to remain solitary above, outside the camp of Israel, in the place of the "external elements" [impurities] if he did not repent as required.

And also, while yet alive, when his soul rises on high, all those words of *lashon hara* that he spoke during the day rise with it, and all of the holy ones separate themselves from it because of this. And there is no greater disgrace than this to the soul, as the *Zohar* states in *Parshath Tazria*: "It is written: 'He who guards his mouth and his tongue guards his soul from troubles.'" For if his lips and his tongue speak evil things, these words rise above. And when they rise, all proclaim: "Remove yourselves from the vicinity of the *lashon hara* of Ploni. Make way for the coming of the mighty Serpent!" And then his holy soul flies far away from him and cannot speak, as it is written (*Psalms* 39:3): "I was dumb in deep silence. I was stilled from good." And this soul rises in shame and great suffering and is not given a place as before. And of this it is written: "He who guards his mouth and his tongue guards his soul from troubles." This is its language in short.

And I have found another answer to the aforementioned question in the book *Davar Shebikedushah* called *Sefer Hakaneh*, viz.: "See and understand that whoever utters *lashon hara* is judged [i.e., punished] by *tzara'ath*." Rabi said to him: "If so, all of Israel should be lepers, for because of the sin of *lashon hara*, Israel was exiled, etc." He answered: "Poverty is equivalent to *tzara'ath*, and he becomes impoverished and beholden to men." That is, through this, his pride, the major cause of *lashon hara*, will depart from him, as Rabbeinu Yonah wrote in the *Sha'arei Teshuvah*, and as will be explained, please G-d, below. And he also will be afraid to speak *lashon hara* of them for fear that the thing will become known and they will not be benevolent to him.] (See there, too, another awesome statement on this subject.) And thus is it adduced in *Tikkunei Zohar*, that this sin leads, G-d forbid, to poverty. Therefore, he who would live a good life will guard himself.

Chapter VII

*In this chapter it will be explained how one harms himself
by this [lashon hara] in many respects.*

Come and see further how great is the punishment of this bitter sin. For by speaking *lashon hara* and *rechiluth* he loses the little Torah that he has. As per *Midrash Shocher Tov* 42 (*Koheleth* 5:5): "'Do not allow your mouth to cause sin to your flesh.' This speaks of *lashon hara*, etc. 'Why should G-d be angry at your voice?' — at that voice which you uttered with your mouth and spoke *lashon hara* against your friend. 'And [He shall] destroy the work of your hands' — the little Torah that you have in your hands will go lost." And it is obvious that the intent of the *midrash* is as written in the holy books, that one who speaks *lashon hara* against his friend causes his merits that have accrued until now to be taken from him and given to his friend.

And because of this, his prayer, too, is not accepted. As stated in the holy *Zohar, Parshath Metzora*: "If one has *lashon hara* in him, his prayer does not come before the Holy One Blessed be He, because a spirit of uncleanliness has reposed itself upon him. Once he repents and takes it upon himself to return [to the L-rd], what is said of him? (*Vayikra* 14:2): 'On the day of his cleansing, he shall be brought to the Cohein.'" (And this explains the Torah's writing "And 'Unclean! Unclean' shall he call." Chazal understand this as his having to apprise the populace of his suffering, so that they pray [to the L-rd to grant] him mercy. And it is because his [own] prayer is not acceptable above, that the Torah revealed this counsel to us specifically in respect to *this* sufferer.)

And his holy soul, too, departs from him because of this, as written above in Chapter III in the name of the holy *Zohar*.)

In this [(the following)], too, this sin is graver than other sins: For in other sins, in that limb by which he commits the sin, he draws down upon himself the spirit of uncleanliness. Not so, with *lashon hara*. With *that* sin he draws down upon *all* of his limbs the spirit of uncleanliness, and he renders them unclean, as it is written in the holy *Zohar, Parshath Metzora*: R. Chiyya said: "If one speaks *lashon hara*, all of his limbs are rendered unclean, and he is to be quarantined, because his evil speech ascends and awakens the spirit of uncleanliness upon him, and he becomes unclean. One who *comes* to become unclean is *made* unclean [from above]." (As Chazal say in *Yoma* 39a: "A man makes himself unclean below — he is made unclean from above"). The lower world "triggers" the upper world. The reason is obvious: Speech is not a specific part of a man as his other limbs are, each one being of benefit in itself. But it is the generality of man and his completeness. And that is why, when he perfects himself by occupying himself with Torah, all of his limbs are amended. For it reposes upon them a spirit of holiness to vivify them and to sustain them in this world and the next. As Chazal have said: "If one's head ails him, let him study Torah, as it is written, etc. If his throat ails him, let him study Torah, etc. If his whole body ails him, let him study Torah, as it is written (*Mishlei* 4:22): 'And to all his flesh it is healing.'" And the opposite, G-d forbid — by forbidden speech, he harms and defiles all of his limbs, and each and every limb falls from its eminence through this. And what advantage is it to them that their master lives and speaks if only to render *din* and accounting!

Also, in defiling his mouth, he renders defective the words of holiness that he utters afterwards, as it is written in the holy *Zohar, Parshath Pekudei* 263: "And in that evil spirit [of his *lashon hara*] there reside several other arousers of *din*, which are appointed to take hold of the evil, filthy, speech which issues from a man's mouth; and afterwards, when he utters holy words — woe unto him and woe unto his life! Woe unto him in this world and woe unto him in the world to come! For those unclean spirits take that unclean speech, so that when he afterwards utters holy words, they come forward and take that unclean speech and defile thereby that holy thing, so that it does not accrue to the merit of the speaker, and, as it were, the power of holiness is attenuated."

And, similarly, in *Shabbath* 119b: "The world endures only by the breath of the mouths of the young students." R. Pappa asked Abbaye: "What about mine and yours?" He answered: "The breath of the mouth that has sin is not like the breath of the mouth that has no sin." Even though their complete dedication [to Torah] and the holiness of their Torah was extremely exalted, notwithstanding this, because sometimes (as they saw it) some inappropriate speech became intermixed with their words [of Torah], their faculty of speech fell from the level appropriate for it, so that it [their Torah] was not comparable to the [untainted] breath of the mouths of the young students.

And see, my brother, a wondrous thing in "the breath of the young students." Even though there is no holiness of thought or cleaving to the L-rd in their speech, the world endures by this breath of their mouths. To what may this be compared? To a poor man who found a rare, precious stone of uncommon powers, to be found only on the crowns of kings. His finding it becomes known to the king, who rewards him with great wealth. Now the poor man who found it, even though he cannot, with his wisdom, conceive of the special properties of the stone, notwithstanding this, the great good of the stone itself and the grandeur of its light bring him all this great good — that he acquires special distinction in the eyes of the king. The very same is true with the Torah of the living G-d. One who wishes to achieve holiness through it does not require great preparation in order to do so; for it itself is holy and exalted beyond measure. And when a man speaks in it, he cleaves to its holiness, as it is written (*Jeremiah* 23:19): "For whenever I speak in it

[Torah], I remember Him even more" [see *Nefesh Hachaim*]. And a man must just take heed not to do the opposite; that is, not to dim its light by his [tainted] speech. This is the intent of R. Pappa's words to Abbaye: "What about mine and yours?" That is, our Torah in itself is holier than the Torah of the young students, for [in *us*] it is [accompanied] by holy thought. And Abbaye answered: "The breath of the mouth, etc.," i.e., the defect [of tainted speech] overrides the [holiness of Torah], as we explained.

And now, let us see: If in the "cedars of the Levanon" of the past, whose thoughts always cleaved to the Holy One Blessed be He with fear of the L-rd and His mitzvoth, and whose speech was always in great holiness and purity (and if, by chance, an inappropriate word sometimes became intermixed with it, they immediately afterwards repented as necessary) — with all this, this one word undermined the holiness of their speech in general, if so, what should we, the "moss of the wall" do, whose constancy in Torah is, even without this, on a very low level, in our many sins — what shall we do if we yet sully our mouths, G-d forbid, with words of *lashon hara*, *rechiluth*, levity, contention, and the like? What holiness can repose on such learning, learned afterwards with such a mouth?

And from this we can understand the greatness of our weakness in Torah and mitzvoth, in our many sins. For do we not plainly see that everyone, always, sets his thoughts on his business or his trade, to enlarge and expand it, and also to remove from it any possible cause of loss? And it would not occur to anyone of common sense to destroy with his own hands the business that he lives from. But when we look at the [really] desired end, the very opposite is the case! For not only does our *yetzer* intensify itself in us each day to increase sin and offense; but we also create reasons and causes through which there will be undermined, G-d forbid, the "surviving remnant," the little Torah and prayer that yet remains with us.

May the L-rd spare our eyes from seeing falsehood, and make us worthy of recognizing the greatness of the holiness of Torah. And through this may our souls be healed and its [the Torah's] words be sweeter in our mouths than honey, as it is written (*Psalms* 19:11): "They are more desirable than gold and much fine gold and sweeter than honey, etc."

Chapter VIII

In this chapter there will be explained the greatness of its punishment in this world.

He also diminishes his stature as a human being thereby [(by speaking *lashon hara*)] until he emerges "worse than a dog," as Chazal have said (*Pesachim* 118a): "One who speaks *lashon hara* ... deserves to be thrown to the dogs, it being written (*Shemoth* 23:1): 'You shall not receive a false report,' which is read as you shall not *spread*, which is preceded by (*Ibid.* 22:30): '...to the dog shall you throw it.'" The rationale is obvious, as written by the Maharal of Prague: "For the dogs guarded themselves when necessary, from 'sharpening their tongues,' as it is written (*Ibid.* 11;7): 'And against all the children of Israel, a dog shall not sharpen its tongue' — and *he* [(a human being)], whom the L-rd accorded understanding and knowledge could not restrain his *yetzer* from this [(*lashon hara*)] — wherefore he is 'worse' than a dog."

It is stated in *Arachin* 15b: R. Chisda said in the name of Mar Ukva: "All who speak *lashon hara* deserve to be stoned, it being written in one place (*Psalms* 101:5): "Him [(the speaker of *lashon hara*)] shall I *cut off*," and, in another (*Eichah* 3:53): "They *cut off* my life in the pit, and threw a *stone* at me."

We also find in *Arachin* 15b: R. Yehoshua b. Levi said: "If one speaks *lashon hara*, his sins mount unto the heavens, viz. (*Psalms* 73:9): "They set their mouths in the heavens and [(i.e., when)] their tongues run on the earth." And it [*lashon hara*] is over and against the three grave sins, as mentioned above in Chapter IV. And just as *it* is over and against, so is its *punishment*, as we find in *Yerushalmi Peah* 1:5 and in *Semag*, that for four things punishment is exacted of a person in this world, and the principle is left for him for the world to come. They are: idolatry, illicit relations, and blood-spilling, and *lashon hara* over and against all. And, likewise, we have written above in Chapter VI in the name of *Sefer Hakaneh* that for the sin of *lashon hara* he is smitten with poverty.

And we find also in *Tanna d'bei Eliyahu* 16: "Those who smite in secret '[i.e., speakers of *lashon hara*] and desecrators of the Name in the open and those who cheapen their friends with words, and those who instigate quarrels will, in the end, be like Korach [and his congregation] of whom it is written (*Bamidbar* 16:33): "And the earth covered them up."

And sometimes the punishment for the sin of *lashon hara*, the gravest sin of all, is *askarah* [diphtheria], the gravest death of all, as Chazal have said (*Berachoth*

8a): "Nine hundred and three types of death were created in the world ... *askarah* is the gravest of all." A sign is given here for all who enter the world, that their punishment is indicative of their sin, as stated in *Shabbath* 33b: The Rabbis taught: "Why does this death (*askarah*) begin in the intestines and end in the mouth? R. Yehudah b. Ilai answered: "Though the kidneys counsel, the heart deliberates and the tongue formulates, it is the mouth which consummates [the *lashon hara*]."

And, more than this, we find in *Midrash Aggadath Bereshith* 20: "In time to come, all will be healed, but the serpent will not be healed. And just as there is no cure for the serpent, there is no cure in time to come for one who speaks *lashon hara* against his friend, as it is written (*Koheleth* 10:11): "If the serpent bites, [it is because] there is no charm [against him]; so, there is no advantage [i.e., cure] for the man of the tongue."

And we learn also in *Pirkei d'R. Eliezer*: "Anyone who speaks *lashon hara* against his friend in secret has no cure, as it is written (*Psalms* 101:5): 'He who slanders his neighbor in secret, him will I cut off [forever].' And it is stated elsewhere (*Devarim* 27:24): 'Cursed be he who smites his neighbor in secret.' Come and see [what happened to] the serpent. Because he spoke *lashon hara* between the Holy One Blessed be He and Adam and his wife, the Holy One Blessed be He cursed him (*Bereshith* 3:14): 'And dust shall you eat all the days of your life.'" (That is, just as it is written there "all the days of your life," the intent being that he not be cured even in the days of the Messiah, as stated in *Berachoth* 12b: "the days of your life" — this world; "*all* the days of your life" — to include the days of the Messiah" — so, here, he [the speaker of *lashon hara*] has no cure forever.) And I have seen also in the holy books that if one speaks *lashon hara*, his sustenance diminishes, like that of a serpent [i.e., "And dust shall you eat, etc."]

And it is obvious that if one habituates himself to this sin, his punishment for this (through poverty, penury, and the like) will also be constant, in lieu of the "confirmed leprosy" wherewith he should have been afflicted because of this, as explained in Chapter V.

From all of this, the severity of his punishment should be clear. For punishment is exacted of him in this world and he is punished with constant suffering and impoverishment, and sometimes also with death, G-d forbid.

And it is not enough that the speakers of *lashon hara* cause *themselves* to be smitten, but the whole world is smitten by their sin in this manner, that their sustenance is thereby diminished. As stated in *Ta'anith* 7b: R. Shimon b. Pazzi said: "The rains are withheld only because of the speakers of *lashon hara*, etc." And *lashon hara* also causes death, the sword and slaughter in the world, as we wrote above in Chapter II in the name of the holy *Zohar*.

Therefore, one who desires his own life and the life of the world should guard his tongue from evil. And he shall enjoy good both in this world and the next.

Chapter IX

In this chapter there will be explained the abjectness of his lot because of this [sin of lashon hara] in the next world.

In the preceding chapters there has been described the punishment of the speaker of *lashon hara* in this world. And now we shall explain the greatness of his punishment in the world to come.

Chazal have explained that the class of slanderers is one of four classes who do not behold the Shechinah, viz. (*Sotah* 42b): "R. Yirmiyah b. Abba said: Four classes do not behold the Shechinah: the class of flatterers, the class of liars, the class of scoffers, and the class of slanderers ... The class of slanderers, viz. (*Psalms* 5:5): 'For You are not a G-d that desires wickedness; evil will not sojourn with You.' You are righteous, O L-rd; evil will not sojourn in Your dwelling place.'" This section deals with the sin of *lashon hara*, as Rashi explains there. And the speaker of *lashon hara* is even *called* "evil," as we find in *Aggadath Mishlei* on the verse (*Mishlei* 12:20): "There is deceit in the heart of plotters of evil" — R. Chamma b. R. Chanina said: "One who speaks with his friend and eats and drinks with him and speaks *lashon hara* against him, the Holy One Blessed be He calls him 'evil,' etc."

He is also judged in the fourth level of Gehinnom for this sin, as stated in *Midrash Hane'elam* on *Ruth*.

Consider the greatness of their punishment. Because of the greatness of their sin, it is almost impossible for Gehinnom to cleanse them of it, as explained in *Tanna d'bei Eliyahu* 18: "Just as the wicked speak *lashon hara*, which ascends until the Throne of Glory, so, angels descend from the mouth of the Omnipotent One and take those evildoers and cast them into the [nethermost] depths of Gehinnom. At that time, Gehinnom responds and says to the Holy One Blessed be He: 'Master of the universe, I cannot punish them as much as they deserve to be punished, and the whole world cannot punish them enough. Did this speaker of *lashon hara* not sin from the earth until the heavens? But first send Your arrows from above, and then they will get from me coals of the broom bush from below, as it is written (*Psalms* 120:3-4): 'What will He give you and what will He add to you, you tongue of deceit? Sharpened arrows of the Mighty One, together with coals of the broom bush.' 'the Mighty One' is none other than the Holy One Blessed be He, as it is written 'the G-d who is great and mighty, etc.'" (We find the same in *Arachin* 15b.) And how much must the man of heart strengthen himself and stand guard against this bitter sin, in reflecting upon this awesome punishment, which the great prison house of Gehinnom itself is powerless to inflict unless it also be assisted from above!

    And all that a man speaks with his mouth, all is written down above, as we find in the *Midrash Rabbah, Tetze* 6 on *Koheleth* 5:5: "Do not allow your mouth to sin against your flesh, etc." What does this mean? When the mouth speaks *lashon hara* it sins against the body, causing it to be smitten. Thus: 'to sin against your flesh' — the mouth sinning against the flesh. What is the intent of 'Do not say before the angel: "It is a mistake"?' Do not say: 'I shall go and speak *lashon hara* and no one will know.' The Holy One blessed be He says: "Know that I am sending an angel, and he will stand at your side and write down all that you are saying against your friend." As stated by the GRA in his book, *Alim Litrufah*: "He will bring all into judgment; all talk, and not even small talk will be lost. Therefore, I exhort you to train yourself as far as possible to sit alone, for the sin of the tongue encompasses all, as our sages of blessed memory have said: 'These are the things … and *lashon hara* against all.' And what need is there to elaborate on this sin, which is greater than all? Our sages of blessed memory have said: 'All of a man's toil is with his mouth' All the mitzvoth and learning of a man do not suffice for what he utters with his mouth. (*Chullin* 89a): 'What is a man's craft in this world? Let him make himself mute and close his lips like two millstones, etc.' And every "slinging" [of the soul after death], all (comes from) the breath of idle words. For every vain utterance, he [i.e., his soul] must be slung from one end of the world to the other. All this, for superfluous talk. But for forbidden talk, like *lashon hara* and levity and oaths and vows and quarrels and curses, especially in the house of prayer and on Sabbaths and festivals — for this, one must descend deep into Sheol. And it is impossible to conceive of the greatness of the suffering and the anguish that one must undergo for one utterance. And not even one word is left unwritten. [Heavenly] informers accompany each man at every moment and write down each and every word. (*Koheleth* 10:20): 'For a bird of heaven will carry the voice, and the winged one will tell the thing.' 'Do not allow your mouth to sin against your flesh, and do not say before the [recording] angel that it is a mistake,' etc."

    And he himself afterwards becomes a "chariot" to the unclean "shell" called "*lashon hara*," as it is written in *Sefer Charedim* 3:4. And know further that the Kabbalists have written (*Sefer Charedim* 7) that the man of *lashon hara*, after his death, is reincarnated in inanimate matter, in the stones of the field. "And sometimes the man of *lashon hara* is reincarnated as a dog."

    And, likewise, one who is accustomed to eat unkosher meat or to feed it to a Jew. And this is intimated in the Torah, it being written (*Shemoth* 23:1): "And men of holiness shall you be to Me, and flesh torn in the field you shall not eat. To the dog shall you throw it," after which it is written (*Ibid.* 23:1): "You shall not spread a false report." It emerges, then, that the verse of "To the dog shall you throw it" is found between these two sins — eating *treifah* [torn flesh] and speaking *lashon hara*, to teach us that for these two sins, a man may be reincarnated as a dog. And this is what King David, may peace be upon him, intimated in (*Psalms* 22:21): "Rescue from the sword, my soul; [rescue] from the dog, my soul," followed by "I will speak Your name to my brothers, etc." That is, I do not use my tongue to speak *lashon hara*, to be punished therefor by this dreadful reincarnation, but I use it to praise You and to exhort Israel, that they should fear You and praise You. And know that the Kabbalists have said that even though when a man is reincarnated in the form of another man he is unaware of his prior state, still when he is reincarnated as an animal or as a bird, he is aware of his prior state and suffers terribly at having descended from heaven from the form of a man to the form of a beast. Therefore, every man should fear and tremble and be soft of heart while he yet lives, while he yet has free will and knows his G-d, so that He forgives his sins and removes His wrath from him. And when his soul leaves him he will rest in peace and repose in His shade in Gan Eden. For He is gracious and merciful and abundant in lovingkindness. And (*Berachoth* 34b): "In the place where penitents stand, absolute *Tzaddikim* cannot stand." Until here, the words of the *Sefer Charedim*, in short.

Chapter X

*In this chapter there will be explained the
greatness of the quality of guarding one's tongue,
whereby one sanctifies his faculty of speech.*

Now we shall explain the greatness of the merit of one who guards his mouth and his tongue from speaking forbidden things. First, he amends and sanctifies thereby the distinctive "tool" of the Jew, which is speech. So that all the words that he speaks thereafter in Torah and in prayer ascend to the source of its root on high. For not in vain did Chazal compare this [faculty] in many places to a "tool of the trade" [see Rashi, *Bamidbar* 31:8], to teach us that just as a tool is necessary for the making of new, beautiful vessels, [so is it with the "tool" of speech]. Even if one be the king's craftsman, the greatest of all the artists, whose intellect is extremely subtle, and who can conceive of the finest way of fashioning vessels, still, he cannot make them without tools. And, more than this, even if he has the tools, but they are defective and damaged, and he is "pressured" to make some vessels, there will be recognized through them the defect and the imperfection of the tools, inside and outside, because he will not be able to smooth them [the vessels] out correctly and they will remain like formless blocks of wood, unfit for use even by commoners; how much more so, for a king. But that craftsman whose tools are polished and shined as they should be — the vessel that he fashions with them will emerge perfect and beautiful. It is exactly the same with the faculty of speech given to the Jew for the service of the awesome King (blessed be His name) for Torah and prayer, and for blessing, glorifying, praising, and exalting Him. For it [(this faculty)] is the great tool whereby the complete man can build heaven and earth, as it is written (*Isaiah* 51:6): "And I have placed My words in your mouth to plant the heavens and to lay the foundations of the earth." And this is to be understood literally. For with the words of holiness that a man speaks here in this world before the blessed L-rd, there are created on high holy worlds and angels, who will afterwards be protagonists for and defenders of his soul.

And the quality of the worlds and the angels created through his Torah and mitzvoth depend on several factors:

1) his mind-set at the time. That is, his having readied himself at that time with all his powers to fulfill his task according to the Torah, in all of its requisite parts and details.

2) his tools, by which his Torah is fashioned. That is, the tools of speech (and, likewise, in respect to the mitzvah, the tools required to execute it.) For if they are beautiful and elegant, being used always for the good, and the power of their

sanctity being thereby strengthened, they will have the power to draw down the higher sanctity and great light on whatever he is doing. But if he renders defective and unclean, G-d forbid, his faculty of speech through *lashon hara, rechiluth*, levity, and falsity, and the like, and he does not repent, and then he speaks with his mouth words of Torah and prayer, what power will they have to draw down on that Torah and prayer the higher sanctity after his "tools of utterance" have been rendered defective and unclean in and of themselves?

And Chazal have said (*Shabbath* 119b): "The breath of the mouth that has sinned is not like the breath of the mouth that has not sinned." ["the breath of the mouth that has sinned":] That is, he who has sinned only sometimes, by chance, as we have explained in Chapter VII. How much more so if the breath of his mouth is habituated to sin every day and every hour. And all this, even if his mouth sins in other forbidden things; how much more so, in the *issur* of *lashon hara* and *rechiluth* by which he certainly undermines the prayer that he prays after this; and it does not ascend unless he undertakes to repent of this, as we explained above in Chapter VII in the name of the holy *Zohar*. And we can say that this is the intent of the verse in *Koheleth* 7:13: "See the act of G-d. For who can straighten out what he has made crooked?" That is, set your eyes and your heart on the G-dly things, the holy sanctuaries and the celestial lights created by you on high by your Torah and your mitzvoth — that they be created in perfection, by all the preparations needed for this and also by "clean tools," as explained above. For who can straighten out what he has made crooked? This is, if you damage them, G-d forbid, they will remain forever defective and damaged, and this will cause you eternal worry and constant grief in remembering that it was your slothfulness that caused all this. For they [(the heavenly edifices)] are not like the buildings of this world, which, if one damages them, another builder can repair them. Not so, with the desired [eternal] end. As stated by the *tanna* in *Avoth* 1:13: "If I am not for myself, who is for me?" And this is the intent of the verse "For who can straighten out what he has made crooked?"

What follows from all we have said is that by guarding his tongue according to the *din*, a man merits sanctifying his faculty of speech, and, thereby, his Torah and his prayer will be accepted on high.

Chapter XI

In this chapter there will be explained the greatness of the reward for guarding the tongue in this world and the next, and also the quality of peace.

In the guarding of the tongue there are also many holy qualities:

1) being rescued through it from all of the punishments attendant upon this sin [of *lashon hara*].

2) being secure through this of what one has gained of the desired end, that he will not henceforward lose it. (For in not guarding his tongue, he is in danger of losing all, G-d forbid, as explained above in Chapters III and VI in the name of the *Midrash*.)

3) being called "a man," as it is written (*Psalms* 34:3): "Who is the *man* who desires life, etc." For lacking this quality, he is only in the class of an "unspeaking animate object." And in *Midrash Shocher Tov* we find (*Isaiah* 57:20): "'And the wicked are driven as the sea' — Just as the sea spews all its mire on the shore, so do the wicked spew their mire on their lips."

4) Because he suppresses himself from "prosecuting" and seeks merit with all his strength, so, above, the ministering angels argue his cause, as we find in *Midrash Mishlei*.

Also, through this he merits being "clothed" with the Holy Spirit, as written in the holy *Zohar*: "Whoever guards his mouth and his tongue merits being clothed in the Holy Spirit."

He also brings himself to eminence in this world, as it is written in *Mechilta, Parshath Mishpatim* on *Shemoth* 32:30: "And flesh torn in the field you shall not eat. To the dog shall you throw it" — to teach us that the Holy One Blessed be He does not withhold reward from any creature, as it is written (*Shemoth* 11:17): "And to all the children of Israel a dog will not sharpen its tongue." Now is this not a *kal vachomer* [i.e., Does it not follow *a fortiori*]: If it is so [i.e., that He does not withhold reward] from an animal, how much more so from a human being!

Also, for all the time that he guards his tongue, he merits great eminence in Gan Eden, as the Gaon Rabbeinu Eliyahu has written in the name of the *Midrash*, that "for every moment that a man muzzles his mouth, he merits the secreted light that no angel or creature can visualize."

Also, he is rescued thereby from Gehinnom, as we find in *Midrash Tanchuma*: "The Holy One Blessed be He said: 'If you wish to rescue yourselves from Gehinnom, distance yourselves from *lashon hara* and you will merit this world and the next.'"

There is another great and holy quality that branches out from guarding one's tongue — that is the quality of peace. It is known that by guarding one's tongue, one removes envy from himself, and all will love him and share their secrets with him and never speak against him — measure for measure, as it is written in the *Arizal*.

And, the converse — If one speaks evil of his friend and demeans him things will come to such a pass that they will demean him, too, aside from his punishment in the world to come. And thus have I seen it written in the name of the early authorities, and they have found an intimation [in Scripture] for this (viz. *Vayikra* 24:20): "As he imputes a blemish to a man, so shall it be imputed to him." And, more than this, he comes to be despised and reviled even in the eyes of those to whom he spoke the *lashon hara* and the *rechiluth*. As Chazal have said: "False witnesses are despised [even] by their hirers." Also, each one of the listeners suspects him, saying to himself; "Now he spoke against my friends before me; and now he will go and speak before my friends against me."

And it is found that it [(guarding one's tongue)] leads to peace [*shalom*]. And the greatness of peace is already known. As Chazal have said: "Even if there be, G-d forbid, the sin of idolatry in Israel, but there is peace among them, the Holy One Blessed be He tells Satan not to touch them." And if one accustoms himself to speak well of his friend, he merits that the Holy One Blessed be He calls him by His name — "Shalom!" As it is written (*Judges* 6:24): "And he called it [(the altar)] 'the L-rd - *Shalom*.'" And if he does the opposite, G-d forbid, he is called "*Ra*" ["evil"]. As Chazal have said: "If one speaks with his friend and eats with him and drinks with him and speaks *lashon hara* against him, the Holy One Blessed be He calls him '*Ra*,' as it is written (*Mishlei* 12:20): 'There is deceit in the heart of the plotters of *ra*.' And if one does not eat and drink with him and does not deal with him [i.e., if he has acquired no favors from him] and [still] he speaks well of him, the Holy One Blessed be He calls him 'Shalom,' viz. (*Ibid*.): 'And for the counselors of *Shalom* there is joy.'"

In order to explain somewhat the quality of peace, I shall adduce some of the apothegms of Chazal on this subject. This is from *Ma'aloth Hamiddoth*: "Know, my sons, that peace is among the highest qualities, it being one of the names of the Holy One Blessed be He, as it is written (*Judges* 6:24): And he called it [(the altar) 'the L-rd-*Shalom*.'" Wherever peace is found, fear of Heaven is found. Where there is no peace, there is no fear of Heaven. Great is peace before the Blessed One, our sages of blessed memory saying in the *aggadah* (*Yevamoth* 65b, *Bava Metzia* 87a): "Great is peace, even Scripture prevaricating to maintain peace between Abraham and Sarah. For whereas she said (*Bereshith* 18:12): 'And my lord [Abraham] is old,' G-d transmitted this to Abraham as (*Ibid.* 13): 'And I [Sarah] am old.'" Similarly (*Ibid.* 40:16-17): "and they had it reported to Joseph: 'Your father commanded before he died: "So shall you say to Joseph: 'Forgive, I pray you, the offense of your brothers and their sin, for they accorded you evil.'" Now nowhere do we find Jacob commanding any such thing at all, for he entertained no apprehension whatever of Joseph's conduct. My sons, come and see how great is the power of peace, for the Holy One Blessed be He said that even foes should be approached with peace as it is written (*Devarim* 20:10): "When you draw close to a city to wage war against it, call out to it for peace." Great is peace, for it consummates the priestly benediction, as it is written (*Numbers* 6:26): "And He shall repose peace upon you." Great is peace, for it is the consummation of prayer, as it is written (*Psalms* 29:11): "The L-rd will give His people strength; the L-rd will bless His people with peace." And what is more, in the day of Israel's consolation, the first report shall be of peace, as it is written (*Isaiah* 52:7): "How comely upon the mountains are the feet of the herald, announcing peace!" My sons, come and see how great is the power of peace, for the Holy One Blessed be He said that even foes should be approached with peace, as it is written (*Devarim* 20:10): "When you draw near to a city to wage war against it, call out to it for peace." It was stated of R. Yochanan b. Zakkai that no one ever preceded him in greeting, not even a gentile in the marketplace. And our sages of blessed memory have stated (*Avoth* 4:15): "Extend greeting to all men." What is meant by greeting "*all* men"? Even if you see that he is ill disposed towards you, extend greeting to him; for if you do so, you will cause him to love you. What is more, even if he will not condescend to make peace with you, the Holy One Blessed be He will deliver him into your hand and humble him beneath you, as it is written (*Devarim* 20:1): "And if it [the city] does not make peace with you, but wages war against you, then you shall besiege it, and the L-rd your G-d will deliver it into your hand…" And so we find with David, may peace be upon him, that he pursued peace with Saul, as it is written (*Psalms* 120:7): "I am for peace, but when I speak, they are for war." Not only was Saul not appeased, but he pursued David to do him injury, and the Holy One Blessed be He delivered him into David's hand in the cave and in the encampment. And even so, it never entered David's heart to do him wrong. For one must love peace and pursue peace, as it is written (*Ibid.* 34:15): "Seek peace and pursue it." Seek it with your friend and pursue it with your enemy. Seek it in your place and pursue it in other places. Seek it with your body and pursue it with your money. [Sometimes one must be liberal with his money to seize upon the "stronghold of peace."] Seek it for yourself and pursue it for others. Seek it today and pursue it tomorrow. And do not despair, saying: "I will never achieve peace," but pursue it until you do achieve it. And what is the pursuit of peace? Thus have our sages of blessed memory said (*Sanhedrin* 110a): "This is speaking peace at a time of dispute and sacrificing one's honor for the general good, as was done by

Moses, as it is written (*Numbers* 16:25): 'And Moses arose and he went to Dathan and Aviram...,'" and suspending one's affairs to make peace between a man and his wife, a man and his neighbor, and a teacher and his student — even to the extent of arranging a meal for two to make peace between them.

Come and see how great is the power of peace. For in the beginning of the creation of the universe the Holy One Blessed be He employed Himself in the creation of an instrument of peace, as it is written (*Bereshith* 1:3): "And G-d said: 'Let there be light' — and there was light." And how do we know that light is peace? For it is written (*Isaiah* 45:7): "He fashions light and creates darkness; He makes peace and creates evil." On this basis, our teachers of blessed memory ruled (*Shabbath* 23b): "As between a candle for his house and wine for *kiddush*, to sanctify the Sabbath [if he can afford only one], a candle for his house takes precedence because of the peace of his household." What is more, our sages enacted many ordinances in pursuit of the paths of peace, viz. (*Gittin* 59a): "They declared the following in pursuit of the paths of peace: 'The Cohein reads first [in the Torah], then the Levite, then the Israelite, because of "the paths of peace."'" An *eruv* [a halachic enabling device] is placed in an old house, because of "the paths of peace." The pit nearest the irrigation canal is filled first because of "the paths of peace."'" And so is it written (*Proverbs* 3;17): "Its [Torah's] ways are ways of pleasantness and all of its paths are peace." And thus did our sages of blessed memory say in the *aggadah* (*Bamidbar Rabbah* 15:13, *Tanchuma Beha'alothecha* 11): "There are thirteen things that the Holy One Blessed be He loved, and of all of them, He "doubled" [in profusion of love], only "peace." They [(the thirteen)] are: Cohanim, Levites, Israel, Sanhedrin [the high court], the first-born, the offerings of the tabernacle, the sacrifices, the oil of anointment, the Land of Israel, Jerusalem, the Temple, the kingdom of the house of David, and the silver and the gold. The Cohanim — (*Shemoth* 28:41): "And they shall be priests *unto Me*." the Levites (*Numbers* 3:41): "And I shall take the Levites *unto Me*." Israel — (*Shemoth* 19:6): "And you [Israel] shall be *unto Me* a kingdom of priests." Sanhedrin — (*Numbers* 11:16): "Gather *unto Me* seventy men." The first-born — (*Shemoth* 13:2) "Sanctify *unto Me* every first-born." The offerings of the tabernacle — (*Ibid*. 25:2): "And they shall take *unto Me* an offering." The sacrifices — (*Numbers* 28:2): "You shall heed to sacrifice *unto Me* in its appointed time." The oil of anointment — (*Shemoth* 30:31): "The holy oil of anointment shall this be *unto Me* for your generations." The Land of Israel — (*Ibid*. 19:5): "For *unto Me* is all the land." Jerusalem — (I *Kings* 11:36): "The city that I have chosen *unto Me*." The Temple — (I *Chronicles* 17:12): "He shall build *unto Me* a habitation." The kingdom of the house of David — (I *Samuel* 16:1): "For I have seen in his sons a king *unto Me*." The silver and the gold — (*Chaggai* 2:8): "*Mine* is the silver, and *Mine* is the gold." But, of all of these, none was doubled [in profusion of love] but "peace," as it is written (*Isaiah* 27:5): "Or let him take hold of My strength. He shall make peace *unto Me*; peace shall he make *unto Me*." Great is peace, which takes precedence to praise of the Blessed One Himself. For when Yithro came to Moses, immediately (*Exodus* 18:7): "And each made inquiry of the other's peace," whereas only afterwards (*Ibid*. 8): "And

Moses related to his father-in-law all of the miracles that the Holy One Blessed be He had wrought for Israel." What is more, for all of the mitzvoth that the wicked perform in this world, the Holy One Blessed be He gives them their reward in this world — such as wealth, property, years, honor, and the like — except peace, which He does not give them, as it is written (*Isaiah* 57:21): "There is no peace, says my G-d, for the wicked." And, what is more, the Holy One Blessed be He gives peace as a reward to the righteous, as it is written (*Ibid.* 32:17): "And the reward for righteousness shall be peace…" What is more, it is with peace that He draws near to Him converts and penitents, as it is written (*Ibid.* 57:19): "He creates the utterance of the lips: 'Peace, Peace,' for the far and the near, says the L-rd, and I will heal him." Great is peace, for in regard to all of the journeyings in the desert it is written "And they journeyed and they rested," journeying in strife and resting in strife. But when they came to Mount Sinai, they made one great "resting," as it is written (*Shemoth* 19:2): "And Israel rested *there*, before the mountain." (*Vayikra Rabbah* 9:9): "The Holy One Blessed be He said: 'The time has now arrived for Me to give Torah to My children.'" For as long as they are at peace with one another, the Shechinah is among them. And thus is it said (*Devarim* 33:5): "And He was a King in Yeshurun when the heads of the people were gathered, together with the tribes of Israel." When does the kingdom and the Shechinah of the Blessed One abide in Israel? When they are all gathered together as one. Come and see how great is the power of peace; for it is through the power of peace that the world endures. For thus have our sages of blessed memory said (*Avoth* 1:18): "On three things does the world stand: on judgment, on truth, and on peace, as it is written (*Zechariah* 8:16): 'Truth and a judgment of peace shall you judge in your gates.'" What is more, when there is peace among men, there is blessing in their fruits, as it is written (*Ibid.* 12): "For as the seed of peace, the vine shall give its fruit, and the earth shall give its produce, and the heavens shall give its dew, and I shall bequeath all of these to the remnant of this people." And thus is it written (*Psalms* 147:14): "He makes peace on your borders and sates you with the fatness of wheat." Our sages have said (*Vayikra Rabbah* 9:9): "Great is peace, for if one erases one letter of G-d's name, he transgresses a negative commandment, as it is written (*Devarim* 12:3): 'And you shall wipe out their [the idols'] name from that place,' followed by (*Ibid.* 4): 'You shall not do so to the L-rd your G-d.' Yet to make peace between a man and his wife, the Torah says (*Numbers* 5:23): 'And the Cohein shall write these curses [containing G-d's name] in a book and erase them into the bitter waters.' The Holy One Blessed be He says: 'Let My name, which was written in holiness, be erased by the waters.'" And Chazal have said further (*Vayikrah Rabbah* 9:9): "Great is peace, for all of the goodly blessings and consolations that the Holy One Blessed be He convokes upon Israel conclude with "peace." The *Shema* — "He spreads a canopy of peace." The *Amidah* — "He makes peace." The priestly blessing — "And He shall repose peace upon you." "Therefore, my sons, be circumspect in this trait — to love peace and to pursue peace. For there is no end to the reward for loving peace and pursuing peace." Until here, the language of *Ma'aloth Hamiddoth*.

And this mitzvah is one of those things whose fruits a man eats in this world, with the principal remaining for the world to come, as we find in the first chapter of *Peah*. And we can also see its great importance from the following (*Ta'anith* 22a): "R. Beroka Choza'ah was standing in the marketplace of Bei Lefet in the company of Eliyahu. He asked Eliyahu: 'Is there anyone in this marketplace who is assured of the world to come?' Eliyahu: 'No.' … In the interim, two others passed by, of whom Eliyahu said: 'These are assured of the world to come.' R. Beroka went to them and asked them: 'What do you do?' They answered: 'We are jesters. When we see a man who looks sad, we make him merry.'" For this, too, is a great mitzvah, to relieve one of his suffering and of his worries, and is in the class of "And you shall love your neighbor as yourself." And one thereby affords great pleasure to the Holy One Blessed be He. As when one has a son in a different city, who is steeped in worry and suffering. Certainly, the father hopes that there will at least be found there someone to console him and to "speak to his heart" and give him support so that he not grow sick from his many sorrows. And we are "sons" to the L-rd our G-d. Our sages have compared this thing itself to charity. [continuation of above Chazal:] "or if we see two men quarreling with each other, we exert ourselves and make peace between them."

Chapter XII

In this chapter there will be explained the guarding of oneself against accepting lashon hara *and* rechiluth

And know further that one who desires to merit the quality of peace must guard himself also against the accepting of *lashon hara* and *rechiluth*. For aside from the punishment itself (Chazal having said (*Pesachim* 118a): "If one accepts *lashon hara*, he is fit to be thrown to the dogs, it being written (*Shemoth* 23:1): 'Do not bear a false report,' preceded by (*Ibid.* 22:30): 'To the dog shall you throw it'"), one further comes through it to vain hatred, quarrels, and contention. For since he accepts the thing at the outset as true, that Ploni spoke against him or did this and this to him, it is almost impossible for him afterwards not to cause his friend suffering or to quarrel with him because of this. And in the end, this results in their becoming great foes, each one wanting to "swallow the other's blood," and rejoicing in his misfortune.

And all of this resulted from acceptance, his acceptance of the speaker's words at the outset as absolute truth. If he had followed the way of the Torah, he would not have come to this. For when someone comes to him and tells him what Ploni did or said to him, he should have thought: Perhaps the thing is an outright lie, or perhaps he added something that changed the complexion of the thing entirely. Or even if he added nothing, perhaps he did not relate the entire thing as it was, but left out several words. Or perhaps he varied his intonation, and thereby entirely changed things. Or perhaps he should have thought of something in defense of the one spoken of, that he did what he did unwittingly, or the like. And [if he had proceeded thus], as a matter of course, things would not have come to quarreling and contention and vain hatred.

But, in such matters, the *yetzer hara*, who desires a man to accept *lashan hara*, comes to him and entices him, making him think: How can I suspect him of relating something that never happened, an outright lie? Or, how can I suspect him of adding some falsehood and transgressing "From a thing of falsehood shall you distance yourself?" You, likewise, answer him: It is better that I suspect this speaker of having told me a falsehood than to believe what he told me. For if you saw a man wearing *sha'atnez* or shaving the edges of his head or his beard and then coming to you and telling you about one of your friends that he spoke *lashon hara* about you, you certainly would not accept it as the truth, but you would say to him: Get away from me! I shall not believe you about my friend! If the other negative commandments of the Torah mean nothing to you, then certainly the *issur* of lying is permissible to you! And is it not exactly the same in our case? For even if his words are the truth, has he not transgressed a negative commandment of the Torah

— (*Vayikra* 19:16): "You shall not go talebearing!" For this is an extremely great *issur* and applies even if what is said is true, as explained in all of the *poskim*. If so, he is also to be suspected of inventing an outright lie, or, in any event, of mixing what he is saying with an element of falsehood and thereby changing the entire complexion of the matter.

And great is the merit of the man who does not accept *lashon hara* even against a plain Jew. How much more so must he take care not to accept it if spoken against a man of eminence, in which instance his merit is even greater. As we find in *Tanna d'bei Eliyahu* 7: "And so, in an instance of good. If one does a mitzvah, good is decreed upon him until four generations.... It was said about Yeravam ben Yoash that he was a man who deferred to the prophets. For this reason those peoples that the Holy One Blessed be He did not deliver into the hand of Yehoshua bin Nun nor into the hand of David, king of Israel, He delivered into the hand of Yeravam ben Yoash, as it is written (II *Kings* 14:25): 'He [Yeravam] restored the boundary of Israel from Levo Chamath until the sea of the plain, etc.' Now what was so special about Yeravam ben Yoash that he restored the boundary of Israel? Was he not an idolator? But because he did not accept *lashon hara* against Amos [the prophet ...], it is, therefore, written, 'He restored the boundary of Israel, etc.' From here it is deduced that 'merit' devolves from the meritorious and liability from the culpable. And by this measure He conducts Himself with all of Israel wherever they find themselves and with all of the idolators and with all the families of the earth."

And know, my brother, that if one guards himself from the acceptance of *lashon hara* and *rechiluth*, his Torah and his mitzvoth will remain intact. But if he does not do so, he is very liable to have deducted from him many hundreds and thousands of mitzvoth, such as answering "*Amen*," "*Amen, Yeheh Shmeih Rabbah*" and learning Torah. For it is known that it is the nature of the scoffers and the speakers of *lashon hara* to tell their tales to whoever want to hear them, even in the synagogue or in the house of study at the time of Torah learning and in the midst of *Kaddish* and the repetition of the *Amidah* and the reading of the Torah. But if one is known in the city as not giving ear to *lashon hara* and *rechiluth*, they [the scoffers, etc.] will prevent themselves from speaking it, even to others, if they see him standing in their midst, lest he brand them as speakers of *lashon hara* in their presence. How much more so, will they not speak it to him himself.

And know further that he who wishes to be perfectly free of the sin of accepting *lashon hara* and *rechiluth*, should constantly reprove the members of his household [in this regard] and apprise them of the greatness of the reward for one who is careful of his speech, and, the opposite, the greatness of the punishment, for one who is not, so that they not fall through their speaking into the snare of *lashon hara*. (See *Chafetz Chaim*, Part One, Principle VIII:4 and Part Two, Principle VI:5)

Chapter XIII

*In this chapter it will be explained that by this sin [lashon hara]
he transgresses and causes his friend to transgress*

How much must a man reflect to beware constantly of this bitter sin! For this sin is committed by two. *He* sins and he causes his neighbor to sin. For through him his neighbor also comes to violate the *issur* of listening to *lashon hara* and accepting it, among other *issurim* explained in the introduction to the *Chafetz Chaim*. And if he [the first] did not speak [*lashon hara*] to him, he [the second] would not come to sin of himself. And Chazal have already said: "Worse is he who causes another to sin than one who kills him. For the second removes him from this world, while the first removes him from this world and from the world to come."

See, my brother, how solicitous the Torah was of the welfare of one's neighbor, so that even if one sees something belonging to his friend lying in a place where it might go lost, he is obligated not to ignore it, but to return it to him, even if it is worth only a *perutah* [a small coin], in which instance he can derive but little enjoyment from it and his friend is completely unaware of it. Now if the Torah commanded us to be so solicitous of our friend's *possessions*, which concern him in this temporal, ephemeral world, how much more so must we be solicitous of his *soul*, which endures with him forever]! And how much more so must we take care not to destroy his soul and affect him eternally!

Now lest your *yetzer* entice you, causing you to think: "Now does not my friend, who listens to all these stories of mine, *not* regard this as harmful — and the proof is that he does not hate me because of this, but, to the contrary, 'beams upon me' because of this" — I shall provide you with a parable [to dissuade you from thinking so]. To what might this be compared? To a thief who disguised himself as a dignitary, and, meeting a passerby, spoke to him as an old acquaintance whom he was glad to see and persuaded him to accompany him to an inn, where he would treat him. At the inn, he says to the passerby: "How happy you have made me after so many years of not seeing you! I have never been happier than today. Tell the innkeeper to give us the finest that the house has to offer, and I will foot the bill." After they eat, the thief absconds and the wayfarer, left to himself, is accosted by the innkeeper, who says to him: "You took the food from me and it is not my business to know who helped you eat it and who fooled you."

Now all the time he ate with the thief, he felt no hatred for him. To the contrary, he regarded him as one of his lovers, his having provided him with all of this for nothing. But when the time came to pay for everything, how much anger and hatred did he bear against him! So is it, my brother, in our case. In this world the listener does not "feel" the *lashon hara* that he is hearing from you and the contamination wherewith you have infested his soul. To the contrary, he considers you his lover in that you relate all of your affairs to him. But all of this obtains so long as the "inn" is open and the innkeeper serves on credit. But when he comes to the next world before "the One who tells a man all of his converse," and finds the ledger open, where there is written all of the things which he has heard and which he has spoken because of your evil companionship, and he will have to render *din* and accounting for everything and undergo great punishment for everything — how much more so if you have caused him to be written down above, G-d forbid, because of you in "the company of the wicked" — as stated in the will of R. Eliezer Hagadol: "My son, do not sit in the company of those who speak demeaningly of their friends, for when their words rise above, they are written down in a book, and all who were present there are written down as "a company of the wicked" — how much anger and bitterness will he bear against you because of this!

And more, if he habituates himself, G-d forbid, to this grave sin, and becomes a "man of *lashon hara*," it is known that it is the way of a man like this, who speaks demeaningly, constantly, of his friend, to assemble people to him and to defend his words until they are enticed to accept his *lashon hara*. And, sometimes, they also become thereby bearers of *lashon hara* against that man and against others. Now if we stop to consider the greatness of the sin of this man of *lashon hara*, words do not suffice. For aside from corrupting himself, he also corrupts all those who "walk in innocence" and who are enticed by his wicked words. For through him they become accepters of *lashon hara* and speakers of *lashon hara*. And sometimes much falsehood and levity is intermixed in what they relate, so that they also become part of the class of liars and scoffers. And certainly, all those who join this wicked company will be punished in the end. As Chazal have said (*Makkoth* 5b): "Scripture has punished accessories of transgressors." And they have also said: "*Lashon hara* kills three: the speaker, the accepter and the object [of the *lashon hara*]." And all of them [the speakers and the receivers] will be inscribed above as "a wicked company," as Chazal have said. Therefore, aside from the great punishment which will be exacted of him in the world to come, his punishment in this world is that he is not given an opportunity to repent. As Chazal have said (*Avoth* 5:18): "If one causes many to transgress, he is not given the opportunity to repent." Therefore, take great care, my brother, have pity and compassion on your soul and on the souls of the other people of Israel, and cease creating companies for Gehinnom by your wicked ways.

And how good and right it is to conduct oneself as I have heard, that a certain sage counseled his friend not to stand any time in the summertime on the holy Sabbath after the third meal near the synagogue or the house of study to tell anything to anyone. For the [men] become three, and three [become] four, five, and six — until in the end there is a large company. And each one tells of his dealings of the week past; and it is impossible that this not lead to *lashon hara* and levity.

And all of this results from the act of the first. Therefore, the wise man should "keep his eyes in his head" [i.e., he should anticipate results].

And one who was remiss in this until now and caused many to transgress in this and wished to amend his soul — it is known what Chazal have said: "*Tzaddikim*, in that which they have sinned they are reconciled." Therefore, first of all, he must habituate himself, against his original nature, to avoid sitting in the company of [wicked men]. As the *Shelah* has deduced from what is intimated in (*Vayikra* 19:16): "Do not *go* talebearing among your people." And he must also see to it to benefit the many and to reprove them and spur them to Torah and mitzvoth, and to bring peace between one man and another.

Chapter XIV

In this chapter there will be explained distancing oneself from hearing forbidden speech

One must take extreme care to habituate himself to heed the exhortation of Chazal (*Kethuvoth* 5a): "The Rabbis taught: 'One must never allow his ears to hear idle talk, for they are 'burnt' first of all the organs.'" That is, just as with a natural fire, if it enters a house, the place that it enters first is first to be burnt, so with the potent spiritual fire, the fire of Gehinnom, which is created by the *tumah* ["uncleanliness"] by which a man defiles his ears, that organ which is first to be defiled is readied to be seized upon immediately by the heavenly punishment, the fire of Gehinnom. Therefore, as it concerns forbidden speech, the ears are the fist organs involved in the *issur*, and, consequently, are defiled immediately. And through them the [forbidden] speech enters afterwards into the heart and defiles it (if he accepts it and believes it) by the *issur* of *lashon hara*. For he transgresses thereby "You shall not bear a false report," which is "heart-centered." (And so, likewise, with other things that are contrary to the Torah.) This, as we find in *Sefer Charedim*, in respect to negative commandments which are contingent upon the heart. For this reason, the ears are "readied" first to receive the fire of Gehinnom. And this certainly applies to hearing *lashon hara* against one's friend, where the sin is exceptionally great.

Therefore, if one recognizes men who are scoffers or speakers of *lashon hara*, he must be especially careful not to enter their company, even if he does not abet them at all, lest he be punished through them, as we have written many times in the name of Chazal. And according to what we see today, in our many sins, the *issur* of *lashon hara* having been blatantly violated, it befits everyone whose heart has been touched by fear of the L-rd not to sit in the company of men unless he knows them to be heedful of forbidden speech [as was the practice of the men of Jerusalem, as we find in *Sanhedrin* 23a]. For in most instances it is found that such company leads to *lashon hara*, *rechiluth*, and other [forms of] forbidden speech.

And, in truth, one who has an understanding heart, should flee the company of "street-corner men" as one flees fire. For why should he enter the company of men whom he will afterwards be obligated to reprove for their forbidden speech? For if he heard their words and neglects to rebut them, he, too, will be punished, as it is written in *Sha'arei Teshuvah* 197: If a man hears others speaking *lashon hara* or he hears "all mouths speaking foulness," or he sits in the midst of scoffers, who shame Torah and mitzvoth, and knowing them to be "defiers and despisers," who, if he reproves them, will not heed his words, wherefore, he puts his "hand to his mouth" — he, too, will be punished. For he will not have answered "the fools according to their folly," so that men may come to say of him that he, too, is like them and acquiesces in their words. How much more so is he obligated to answer and rebuke them to accord honor to the Torah and the mitzvoth which they have scorned and scoffed at, and to be jealous of the honor of the clean and the righteous whom they have spoken against. This is one of the reasons for which it is incumbent upon a man to leave the company of the wicked; for he will be punished for hearing their evil words and refraining from answering them. And this is explicitly stated by Solomon (viz. *Proverbs* 24:1-2)."

And see, my brother: If ten men are standing together and one of them is arrested for a certain offense that he was suspected of, and he is taken to court and tried, and he does not confess — and the other nine are also taken into custody for questioning in his case — though they consider themselves guiltless and have been remanded only to bring the first one's guilt to light, still their heart quakes within them and they are filled with remorse at having been "caught" in the company of the first, who is the cause of all this trouble. Then, afterwards, when with the help of the L-rd, they leave in peace without harm, they take great care not to be in his company again, lest the same thing happen to them. How much more so in our instance, when we know that in the world to come there will be punished both speaker and hearer and all who were with them in this evil company (viz. Chapter XIII in the name of *Pirkei d'R. Eliezer*) — how much more so must one flee this; and, when the *yetzer hara* entices him to join their company, to reflect: "It is enough for me that I must stand [in judgment] in the next world for my *own* sins. Why should I suffer punishment there for the sins of others!" In this way, the *yetzer* will be subdued.

Chapter XV

*In this chapter there will be explained the greatness of the sin of machloketh
[dissension, quarrel,contentiousness]
and the greatness of its punishment,
and also that it leads to other grave issurim*

From all of our elaborating until now on the greatness of the punishment for *lashon hara* in this world and the next, it should be understood how much we must distance ourselves from the sin of *machloketh*. For aside from the sin itself, which is a grave one, as we shall explain, it is a potent cause of other grave sins, namely: vain hatred, *lashon hara*, *rechiluth*, anger, verbal wronging, "whitening of the face" [in shame], revenge, bearing a grudge, vain curses, undermining a person's livelihood, and, sometimes, even desecration of the Name, G-d forbid, an extremely grave transgression. And it is also common to come through this to the sin of flattery, whereby one gains adherents for his quarrel, as we find with Korach, as Chazal have said (*Sanhedrin* 52a) on the verse (*Psalms* 35:16): "Because of the flattery of the quaffing of a draught, he has ground his teeth against me" — Because of the flattery they accorded Korach for the drinks that he plied them with, the plenipotentiary of Gehinnom ground his teeth against them." And *machloketh* also leads to levity, to mock the opposing party and thereby draw adherents to one's counsel. And all this was the conduct of the first man of *machloketh* — Korach, as we find in *Midrash Rabbah, Korach*. And it is known that the punishment for levity begins with suffering and ends with destruction, as Chazal have said. And more than this. It is found that when the *yetzer* entices one to strengthen the *machloketh* and to draw men to his counsel, and he fears lest they turn away from him and leave him by himself, the *yetzer* entices him to create a strong bond [of unity] by means of an oath. All this we find in the *Midrash* and in the *Gemara* in respect to Korach, Dathan, and Aviram. And see, my brother, how much blindness there is in this. For the oath is close to being a vain one, their having sworn to transgress a mitzvah [See *Yoreh Deah* 236:2, and the *Shach* there, section 4]. And even if he fulfills his oath, it still does not leave the category of "a vain oath" [See 238:5]. And the severity of the punishments for a vain oath is well known, the Holy One Blessed be He not absolving one for this, as it is written (*Shemoth* 20:7): "The L-rd will not absolve one who takes His name in vain" [See *Shevuoth* 39a]. I have written all of this only to show to all the great "blindness of the eyes" that inheres in this. And even if in the beginning he does not intend such evil, still, in the end, he will not be absolved of the aforementioned transgressions, as should be clear to anyone with a knowledge of the world.

And the *yetzer hara* has one stratagem in this area whereby he can ensnare even the "perfect man." And that is to instill him with anger and [a quest for] triumph, and then all obstacles will become a smooth path for him. For the *yetzer hara* will then show him many *heterim*. And aside from permitting him to speak *lashon hara* and *rechiluth* and *ona'ath devarim* [verbal wronging] and to "whiten one's face" [with shame], his *yetzer* will spur him further [to believe] that it is forbidden to pity such persons [i.e., his opponents] and that it is a mitzvah to pursue them in all ways.

Now if we came to explain the great harm of *machloketh*, the time would end and the subject would not end, as the Rambam writes in his will: "Prophets have prophesied and wise men have ratiocinated and elaborated on the harm of *machloketh* and have not reached its end." But I shall adduce some apothegms [on the subject] in short, so that the thinking man can reflect in general on the sin of *machloketh*.

This is the language of the *Midrash Rabbah* on *Korach*: "R. Berechiah said: 'How severe is *machloketh*! For the upper *beth-din* punishes only from twenty years and above, and the lower *beth-din* from thirteen and above; but in the *machloketh* of Korach, one-year-old infants were swallowed up in the depths of Sheol, as it is written (*Numbers* 16:27): '…and their wives and their sons and their infants… (*Ibid.* 33): …went down — they and all that was theirs, alive into Sheol.'"

Our Rabbis taught: "Four are called 'wicked': one who raises his hand against his friend to strike him (even though he does not strike him), one who borrows and does not repay, one who is brazen-faced, and is not ashamed before one who is greater than he, and a man of *machloketh*, as it is written (*Ibid.* 26): 'Depart, now, from the tents of these wicked men' [Korach, Dathan, and Aviram]."

And if so, how much should one be ashamed of himself when he knows in his soul that he is the cause of the *machloketh*. For if one's friend calls him "wicked," even between the both of them [i.e., not in public], where he is not put to [public] shame because of this, still, he will pursue him to his very life because of this. How much more so, this one, who caused himself to be called wicked because of this [*machloketh*] — how much shame and humiliation will be his lot above thereafter, when his [formerly] good name is bruited thus above in the Heavenly assembly before thousands of thousands and tens of ten thousands of holy encampments! As the holy books write, all of a man's affairs are proclaimed and publicized above in the presence of all [aside from his punishment for the *machloketh* itself]. And this is the intent of (*Avoth* 2:13): "And do not be [called] wicked in your own presence."

And Satan himself provokes men of *machloketh*, as we find in *Gittin* 52a: "There were two men whom the Satan was wont to provoke to argument every Sabbath eve. Once, R. Meir chanced to be there and he prevented them [from quarreling] for three Sabbath eves, until he made peace between them, at which they heard Satan saying: 'Woe unto that man [i.e., unto me] whom R. Meir evicted from his house!'"

And, in *Yalkut Korach*: "Come and see what *machloketh* does. For '*machloketh*' acronymically (without the *vav*) is '*M*akkah' [a blow], '*C*haron' [wrath], '*L*ikui' [defect], '*K*'lalah' [a curse], '*T*achgith' [destruction (*klayah*)] to the world." And according to the greatness of the eminence of the man of *machloketh*, so will be his punishment (as we find in *Tanna d'bei Eliayhu* 18). And, therefore, it is written in *Parshath Korach* (*Numbers* 16:2): "…chiefs of the congregation, designates of the time, people of name" — to emphasize the greatness of their sin.

Chazal have said (*Reishith Chochmah, Sha'ar Ha'anavah* 4): "In three instances the Holy One Blessed be He overlooked idol worship; but He did not overlook *machloketh*. First, in the generation of Enosh, when men began to serve idols, as it is written: 'Then they began to call [idols] in the name of the L-rd.' But, because there was peace among them, the Holy One Blessed be He allowed them a hiatus. In the generation of the flood, however, because there was *machloketh* among them, so that they stole and plundered from each other, the Holy One Blessed be He did not relent, as it is written (*Ibid*. 6:"13): 'Because the earth was filled with violence by them, etc.' Second, in the generation of the desert when the Jews came to make the golden calf, the Holy One Blessed be He forgave them; but when they lapsed into *machloketh*, the Holy One Blessed be He did not overlook it. For wherever you find 'and they protested' [*vayalinu*] of *machloketh*, you find a great smiting, the most extreme instance being the Korach rebellion. Third, the image of Micah. Because there was peace among them, they were given a grace period, as it is written (*Judges* 18:30): 'And the children of Dan set up the image; and Yehonathan, the son of Menasheh, he and his sons were priests to the tribe of Dan until the day of the captivity of the land.' But when the tribes contended with the tribes of Judah and Benjamin, and there was no peace among them, they became scourges to each other. When the one sinned, the Holy One Blessed be He would bring the other upon him and exact payment from him, as it is written (II *Chronicles* 13:17): 'And Aviyya and his people slew them with a great slaughter, so there fell slain of Israel five hundred thousand chosen men.' And when the tribes of Judah and Benjamin sinned, the ten tribes came and exacted punishment of them, as it is written (*Ibid*. 28:6): 'For Pekach, the son of Remalyahu, slew in Judah a hundred and twenty thousand in one day.'" We are hereby taught that men of *machloketh* become instruments of destruction, one to the other.

Grave is *machloketh*, for it places one's life in danger. For the quarrel between the shepherds of Avram and those of Lot led them to separate from each other, as a result of which Lot went to Sodom and was almost destroyed along with them.

Grave is *machloketh*, for it leads to stripes, as it is written (*Deuteronomy* 25:1): "If there be a quarrel between men…" Peace does not come from a quarrel. (*Ibid*. 2): "And if the wicked one incur the penalty of stripes…" What caused him to receive stripes? The quarrel.

Grave is *machloketh* for it leads to death, as it is written (*Exodus* 21:22): "If men grapple and strike a pregnant woman…" (*Ibid.* 23): "And if there be death [in the woman], then you shall give a life for a life." What caused this? The quarrel.

And our sages have said (*Derech Eretz Zuta* 9): "If there is *machloketh* in a household, in the end it will be destroyed. If there is *machloketh* in a synagogue, in the end it will be disbanded. What is more, in the end it will be laid waste. If there is *machloketh* in the city, there is bloodshed in the city. Two Torah scholars who live in the same city and, similarly, two courts in the same city, if there is *machloketh* among them, they are destined to expire. Furthermore, a contentious court is the destruction of the world. Know this to be so, for so long as there is peace in the lower tribunal, there is peace in the higher tribunal, as it is written (*Amos* 9:6): 'He builds His chambers in the heavens.' When? (*Ibid.*): 'when His bond is founded upon the earth." That is, when Israel are united in one bond and live in peace with one another.

Chapter XVI

In this chapter there will be explained the greatness of the punishment of one who argues with his Rabbi

The sin of *machloketh* obtains even if one argues with another who is equal to him in status. How much more so, G-d forbid, if he argues with a Torah scholar, even if he is not his Rabbi. How much more so if he *is* his Rabbi, is his sin great and his wickedness redoubled. For it is well known that the way of men of *machloketh* is to shame by words those who oppose them. And the greatness of the punishment of one who shames a Torah scholar is well known from what is stated in *Sanhedrin*, Chapter *Chelek*, and is ruled in *Yoreh Deah* 234:6, that one who shames a Torah scholar is in the category of (*Numbers* 15:31): "For the word of the L-rd he has despised. That soul shall be utterly cut off; its sin is in it." And even in our day, if he be but fit to rule [on *halachah*] and toils in Torah, he is called a Torah scholar. And if one shames him, even in general matters, and even not in his presence, it is a grave sin and he is liable to *nidui* [excommunication] because of this (as we find in *Yoreh Deah* 246:7 and in the *Shach* section 68.) And there is also no cure for his illness, as we find in *Shabbath* 119b: "R. Yehudah said in the name of Rav: 'If one shames a Torah scholar, there is no cure for his illness.'" And the destruction of Jerusalem also is attributed to this sin, as we find there: "Jerusalem was destroyed only because Torah scholars were shamed there, as it is written (II *Chronicles* 26:16): 'And they shamed the angels of G-d [i.e., the Torah scholars], and scorned His words and mocked His prophets until the wrath of the L-rd rose against His people, without cure.'" They have also said (*Berachoth* 19a): "R. Yehudah b. Levi said: 'All who slander a Torah scholar after his death descend to Gehinnom.'"

And (*Sanhedrin* 101a): "R. Chisda said: 'If one argues against his Rabbi, it is as if he would argue against the Shechinah, viz. (*Numbers* 26:9) ["who strove against Moses and Aaron with the congregation of Korach] when they strove against the *L-rd*.'" And R. Chamma b. Chanina said: "If one quarrels with his Rabbi it is as if he would quarrel with the Shechinah, viz. (*Numbers* 20:13): 'They are the waters of Merivah (contention), whereby the children of Israel strove with the L-rd' [in striving with Moses].'" And, along the same lines: "R. Chaina b. Pappa said: 'If one rails against his Rabbi, it is as if he would rail against the Shechinah, etc.' ... R. Avihu said: 'If one arraigns his Rabbi, it is as if he would arraign the Shechinah, etc.'" And the four levels that the *Gemara* mentions below are meant to apprise us that even thinking alone [against one's Rabbi] is also a great *issur*.

And how foolish are those people in whose eyes it is a light matter to argue with the Rabbi and the *beth-din* of the city and to shame them, not fearing the great punishment awaiting them for this in the world to come, as we have explained. And also in this world they will not escape sore judgment because of this. Come and see what we find in *Midrash Rabbah, Parshath Pinchas* on the verse [*Vayikra* 19:32]: "And you shall honor the face of the *elder*," (which refers to a Torah scholar), as we find in *Kiddushin* 32b: "What is the intent of 'And you shall honor'? That you not stand in his place, nor sit in his place, nor contradict his words, etc. For one who does not conduct himself thus with his Rabbi is called 'wicked' before the L-rd, and his learning is forgotten, and his years are shortened, and in the end he becomes impoverished. As it is written (*Koheleth* 8:13): 'And it shall not be well with the wicked one, and he shall not prolong days, like a shadow, because he does not fear G-d.'" Now this *Midrash* applies even if he does not fear him as he should. How much more so if he draws upon him *machloketh* from the men of his city, in which instance he will certainly be doubly punished.

And the man of *machloketh* is, indeed, to be wondered at. If another would hurt his son a little, even unintentionally, he would vent his wrath upon him. How much more so if he hurt him intentionally and caused him to be bedridden. Even if he recovered, he [the father] would publicize him as a cruel man and he would not be quiet until he had repaid him in kind, and in his heart he would bear him eternal hatred because of this. Yet when he himself brings all this suffering upon his sons because of his [shaming of Torah scholars] (even, possibly, to the point of their dying, G-d forbid, as we wrote above in Chapter XV in the name of the *Midrash*, that even infants at the breast may be punished because of this sin of their fathers [See also *Tanna d'bei Eliyahu* 21]) — he himself does not pity them at all! To the contrary, it is in keeping with his trait [of contentiousness] to hint to the men of his household to abet him in his *machloketh*. As we find with Dathan and Aviram, that they went out and stood in front of their tents — they, their wives, their sons, and their little ones, as Scripture says (*Jeremiah* 7:18): "The sons gather the wood and the fathers light the fire." This is only because the *yetzer hara* blinds his eyes and transforms all the holes and pits before him into a straight path.

Come again, my brother and I will show you the greatness of the power of the *yetzer* inherent in the trait of *nitzachon* ["triumph"]. For when one enters the abyss of *machloketh*, then, even if he sees with his own eyes that he is walking on a way of pitch darkness, leading to Gehinnom, still, he would rather go the way of Sheol than give up the *machloketh*. This is an inheritance to them [the men of *machloketh*] from their forefathers, Dathan and Aviram, the fathers of all the men of *machloketh*. And they themselves said so explicitly, as we find in *Midrash Rabbah, Parshath Korach*: "We would rather stick to our words than escape the *din* of Gehinnom." Therefore, my brother, have compassion on your soul and those of your sons and daughters, and keep yourself from *machloketh*.

And even if one has already entered the *machloketh* and it is difficult for him to separate from his other friends, still, he should attempt with all of his strength to rescue himself from them. As was done by On ben Peleth who, in the beginning, was of one mind with the men of the *machloketh*, as written in the Torah, and who, in the end, freed himself from them, as stated in *Perek Chelek, Sanhedrin*. And, therefore, he was not punished along with them. And he would not pay heed to the words of his *yetzer* and its claims that it would not befit him to stop in the middle and not consummate the triumph. For it is better that one be shamed in this world before a few individuals and not be shamed in the world to come before all of the heavenly assembly. And Chazal said (*Eduyoth* 5a): "Better that one be called a fool all of his days than be wicked for one moment before the L-rd."

Chapter XVII

In this chapter there will be explained the greatness of one's distancing himself from abetting machloketh (even if by doing so [i.e., abetting it] he helps his father and his mother) and striving with all his strength to pursue peace.

One must also take care not to be among the abettors of *machloketh* so that he not be punished among them when their appointed time comes, as Chazal have stated (*Makkoth* 5b): "Scripture has punished the abettors of transgressors as the transgressors themselves." And in *Midrash Parshath Korach* we find: "Come and see how severe is *machloketh*. For if one abets *machloketh*, the Holy One Blessed be He destroys his remembrance, as it is written (*Numbers* 16:35): 'And a fire went forth from the L-rd and consumed the hundred and fifty men, the presenters of the incense.'" And, in *Sanhedrin* 110a: "Rav said: 'All who persist in *machloketh* transgress a negative commandment, viz. (*Numbers* 17:5): "And he shall not be like Korach and like his congregation."' R. Assi said: 'He deserves to contract *tzara'ath*.'" (And see above, Chapter VI, what is written in the name of *Sefer Hakaneh*, that sometimes the Holy One Blessed be He transforms the punishment of *tzara'ath* to poverty, so that he becomes dependent upon others.)

And the man of heart must reflect always upon what Chazal have said in *Midrash Rabbah Parshath Emor* 27 on the verse (*Koheleth* 3:15): "And G-d seeks [i.e., stands up for] the pursued." R. Huna said in the name of R. Yosef: "G-d always 'seeks' the pursued." You find a *tzaddik* pursuing a *tzaddik* — "And G-d seeks the pursued"; a *tzaddik* pursuing an evildoer — "And G-d seeks the pursued." R. Yehudah said in the name of R. Yossi b. Nahora: "The Holy One Blessed be He always claims the blood of the pursued from the pursuers." R. Elazar said in the name of R. Yossi b. Zimra: "It is also so with sacrifices. The Holy One Blessed be He said: 'An ox flees a lion; a goat flees a leopard; a lamb flees a wolf — Do not sacrifice before Me [animals] from the pursuers, but from the fleers.'" And if so, one must give thought to distancing himself from abetting *machloketh*, from taking one side over another, since, in the final analysis the Holy One Blessed be He claims their blood from his hand. And instead of emerging "the victor" and gaining honor thereby, in the end he will be seen in his shame, being punished by either *tzara'ath* or poverty. But if one guards himself from *machloketh*, he is honored by men, as it is written (*Mishlei* 20:3): "A man's honor is abstention from a quarrel." And Chazal have said: "Now if a man is honored by suppressing a quarrel which is his own, how much more so [is he to be *censured*] for intervening [and taking sides] in a quarrel which is not his own. And thus is it written (*Mishlei* 26:17): 'As one who seizes a dog's ears is he who grows wrathful over a quarrel that is not his.'" And even if a party to the *machloketh* is his relative, even his father, even so he should take great care *not* to accord him the honor of joining him, even if his father commands him to do so (as ruled in *Yoreh Deah* 240:6, that if one's father tells him to transgress even a Rabbinical enactment, he is not to be heeded; for both son and father are obligated to honor the L-rd — how much more so in respect to the grave sin of *machloketh*!)

As we find with the sons of Korach, that because they were not drawn after their father, even though this caused him great shame, they escaped his fate. As we find in *Yalkut Parshath Korach*: "This is as Scripture writes (*Psalms* 1:1): 'Happy is the man' — the sons of Korach; 'who did not walk in the counsel of the wicked' — who did not walk in the counsel of their father, as it is written (*Numbers* 16:26): 'Depart now from the tents of these wicked men'; 'and in the way of sinners they did not stand,' as it is written (*Numbers* 17:3): 'the censers of these sinners.'" And, in *Yalkut*: "What merit was there 'in the hands' of the sons of Korach that they were rescued [from his punishment]? When they were sitting with Korach, their father, they saw Moses and lowered their faces to the ground, saying: "If we stand up for Moses our teacher, we will be spurning our father, whom we have been commanded to honor. And if we do not stand, it is written (*Vayikra* 19:32): 'Before the hoary head shall you rise' — Better that we stand before Moses our teacher, even though we are thereby spurning our father.'" At that time, they moved their hearts to repentance. About them David said (*Psalms* 45:2): 'My heart has stirred with a good thing.'" From this we learn that if one is not drawn after his father's counsel in his *machloketh*, he will not be ensnared in his net.

And even if one sees that the *din* is with his father, he should see to it to quiet the quarrel and not to strengthen it against the opposing party. For aside from the mitzvah of promoting peace, he should reflect that he might be mistaken in his assumption because of the love implanted in a man's heart for his father, whom he loves as himself. As we find in *Sifrei* (*Devarim* 13:7): "'Your friend who is as your soul' — this is your father." And a man cannot perceive *himself* as being in the wrong.

And all this, when he is powerless to protest and to quiet the quarrel. But if the son finds favor with his father and is able to quiet the quarrel and keeps silent, he is punished because of this. As we find in *Tanna d'bei Eliyahu* 21: "And a man should not look on when he sees his parents engaging in idle talk [(i.e., *lashon hara* and the like, and, how much more so, *machloketh*, which subsumes all)], and remain silent. And if he does, both he and they do not live out their days and years. And, likewise, it is a mitzvah for every man to make peace between the sides. And this [(making peace)] is one of those things whose fruits a man eats in this world, with the principal remaining for the world to come, as we find in *Peah* 1. And even if he sees that the *din* is not in accordance with one party and that they deserve to be punished for the *machloketh*, but he is able [to suppress it], even so, he should make every effort to make peace between the sides. And he should not be lax in doing so even if he is the most eminent man in Israel, as we find (*Numbers* 16:25): "And

Moses arose and went to Dathan and Aviram [to make peace]." And Chazal have said (*Sanhedrin* 110a): "From here we derive that it is forbidden to persist in *machloketh*."

And in the *Midrash* we find: "Because Moses went to the [tent] entrance of Dathan and Aviram, he merited rescuing four *tzaddikim* from the entrance of Gehinnom: the three sons of Korach and On ben Peleth." And it is written (*Psalms* 34:15): "Seek peace and pursue it," concerning which Chazal have said: "Seek it for your loved one and pursue it with your foe. Seek it in your place and pursue it in other places. Seek it with your body and pursue it with your possessions. Seek it for yourself and pursue it for others. Seek it today and pursue it tomorrow."

The intent of the *Midrash* in "and pursue it tomorrow" is: Let one not despair of making peace, but let him pursue it today and also tomorrow and also the day after until he attains it. For even the stoutest of cart ropes, if it is constantly worn down, will weaken and snap in the end. Here, too. Even if one does not succeed the first or second time, let him not abandon this holy trait [of pursuing peace]. And even if his efforts do not succeed at all with the parties to the *machloketh* themselves, the trait of "triumphing" having overpowered them and their eyes having been blinded to the truth, still, this will deter the "outsiders," who are not parties in the *machloketh*, but who have been drawn into it by the evil counsel of the parties involved, and will save them from bitter punishment, as in the instance of Moses our teacher, may peace be upon him.

The Gate of Understanding

Chapter I

In this chapter there will be explained the Talmudic apothegm
"What is the proper craft of a man in this world?"

We learned in *Chullin* 89a: "R. Yitzchak said: (*Psalms* 58:2): '*Haumnam eilem*, righteousness shall you speak; with justness shall you judge the sons of men': What is [the proper] craft [*umanuth* (similar to *hauman*)] of a man in this world"? Let him make himself as an *ileim* [mute]. Scripture's purpose in referring to this as a "craft" is to teach us several different things:

It is well known that if one who is not a craftsman would want to fashion a vessel, even if he can easily visualize its fashioning in all its details, still, its actual making will be difficult for him, for his hands are not yet used to this. As opposed to a craftsman, who is habituated to this from youth. The same is true with the trait of silence. Even though anyone who has sense can perceive that this trait is very desirable, for one is protected thereby from all of the *issurim* that come through speech and without it he is prey to various pitfalls, as we shall explain below, still, if one resolves to exercise this trait only when he is compelled to do so because of mitzvoth of the Torah, such as [to keep himself] from *lashon hara*, *rechiluth*, levity, and other [forms of] forbidden speech, and otherwise he will [permit himself to] say whatever he likes, even what is not essential, then certainly this will not avail, for he will not have habituated his tongue to silence. To the contrary, from his [earliest] youth he will have taught it to say whatever entered his mind. As opposed to one who "trained" his mouth to the trait of silence as a craftsman [trains himself] to his craft, to the point where silence becomes natural to him and speech, unnatural — as with a mute. Then he will be absolutely confident that his tongue will be guarded from evil and that he will not revert to his former folly.

Scripture might also intend thereby to bring one to a great awakening through the ways of fear [of the L-rd]. That is, to have him imagine, G-d forbid, that he were suddenly muted, and none of the doctors of his city could find a cure for him, and a great physician came and cured him of his frightful illness, gratis. Would it not follow that he would thenceforward be his true lover, and that the signs of his love would be manifest on all of his limbs? That is, that he would *run* to fulfill his slightest command, and that, in any event, he would not dare to offend this faithful doctor through his faculty of *speech*, which he restored to him! The same is true in our case. The Blessed Creator exalted man above all other creatures by investing him with a speaking soul wherewith he could merit eternal life through Torah and mitzvoth. So that if a man transgresses with his *tongue* several hundreds of times through forbidden *speech*, it should follow that it [this faculty] be taken from him and that the speaking soul not be returned to him in the morning. But the Holy One Blessed be He in His abundant mercies withholds His wrath from him in the hope that he will repent of his sin. Is this his repayment to the L-rd? That he speak even more against His will through *lashon hara*, levity, and other [forms of] forbidden speech? This is the intent of Chazal in: "What is the craft of a man in this world? Let him make himself mute." Let him constantly remind himself: "For the great abuse of my tongue until now, I should have been rendered mute, if not for the greatness of His lovingkindness to me. How, then, should I sin thereby again?"

[The *Gemara* (*Chullin* 89a) continues: "I might think even in respect to Torah study; it is, therefore, written (*Psalms, Ibid.*): 'righteousness [i.e., Torah] shall you speak.' I might think that [he could do so] even to the point of haughtiness; it is, therefore, written: 'with justness shall you judge the sons of men.'" On the face of it, this is to be wondered at: Why would it occur to us to say that he should be mute to words of Torah? Why was speech created in a man if not to speak in the Torah of the L-rd and of His exalted majesty? And also, the end of the apothegm — "I might think even to the point of haughtiness" — is to be wondered at. For what does this have to do with "muteness"? [The resolution would seem to be as follows:] It is known that one can study Torah in two ways: a) by himself; b) with others. Each way has an advantage and a disadvantage. The advantage of learning by oneself is being protected against forbidden speech — for there is no one to speak to. But there is a disadvantage, that the learning lacks the clarification [that comes from an interplay of minds.] And if he learns with others there is the disadvantage that their company sometimes leads to idle talk, *lashon hara* and levity. But, countering that, there is the great advantage of greater clarification. And this is the intent of the *Gemara*: "I might think even in respect to Torah study." That is, not that he not speak at all in Torah, but that he utilize the trait of "muteness," (which affords greater protection), even for words of Torah, that he not speak even Torah with other men at all, out of fear that he will be drawn by this in the end to forbidden speech, so that he should study only by himself. And, similarly, with other mitzvoth which involve speech, such as prayer and the like. [I might think that] he should not associate with any man, so as not to come to forbidden speech. And the *Gemara* answers: "It is, therefore, written: 'Righteousness [Torah] shall *you* [(plural) speak,' and not 'righteousness shall *he* speak,'" in the singular, as per the introduction ["*eilem*"] — to teach us that he should speak in Torah in company [*chavurah*]. As Chazal have said (*Berachoth* 63b): "A sword upon the 'loners'" — a sword upon 'the foes of Torah scholars' [a euphemism for 'Torah scholars'] who study Torah by themselves. And, what is more, they stupefy themselves." And the same is true of congregational prayer, viz. (*Mishlei* 14:28): "The multitude of people glorify the King."

According to this, the "complete man" is on that exalted level where he must conduct himself as two opposites. That is, in the affairs of the world he must be like a mute and not speak even what is permitted, but only what is essential. And in the area of Torah and mitzvoth he must "expand" speech as far as he can, to study with many and to converse with them in matters of holiness. But, in any event, he must be on guard not to speak with them on any forbidden matter — wherefore the *Gemara* concludes: "I might think that [he could do so] even to the point of haughtiness." That is, when he sees others who are completely irresponsible in their speech and who sully their mouths with *lashon hara*, levity, and other [forms of] forbidden speech, [I might think that] he should hold them to be absolutely wicked, and himself, to he absolutely righteous," it is, therefore, written (*Psalms, Ibid.*): 'with justness shall you judge the sons of men.'" That is he must judge them equably and in [the scales of] merit, assuming that they do not [really] know what *lashon hara* is (and the like, with other [forms of] forbidden speech), and also that they do not know the *severity* of the sin of forbidden speech.]

Chapter II

More on the same subject

Another possible reason for calling this [(guarding of the tongue)] a "craft" is that just as all crafts require study until they are truly learned, so is it with speech. A man may not say to himself; Why belabor myself with guarding my tongue to know all the aspects of its functioning if I can acquire a natural muteness and this can suffice [for all exigencies]! For it is not so. For the proper response changes often according to the circumstances [as explained in *Chafetz Chaim*, Part One, Chapter VIII:5, and in Part Two, in several places]. Therefore it is necessary to learn and to know the categories and particulars of speech in order to know how to conduct oneself properly in the *craft* of that "muteness."

Chazal have also been very specific in their holy language in the term "in *this* world" [("What is the craft of a man in *this* world? Let him make himself mute, etc.")] That is, let a man not think: "I have already been habituated to this ["muting"] for more years than a craftsman to his craft, and I no longer need to devote my eyes and my heart to it so much" — wherefore Chazal have taught us that this is *not* so; but a man must train himself in this craft of making himself a natural mute all the days of his life, as the GRA has written in *Alim Litrufah*: "And until the day of his death a man must chastise himself, not with fasts and mortifications, but by putting a rein to his mouth and his lusts. And this is *tshuvah* [repentance], and this is all the fruit of the world to come, as it is written (*Mishlei* 6:23): 'For a mitzvah is a lamp; and Torah, light, and the chastisements of *mussar* [moral discipline], *the way of life*.' This is [worth] more than all the fasts and mortifications in the world. And Scripture states (*Psalms* 34:13-15): 'Who is the man who desires life, who loves days to see good? Guard your tongue from evil, etc.' And in this way all of his sins will be forgiven and he will be saved from the depths of Sheol, as it is written (*Mishlei* 21:23): 'One who guards his mouth and his tongue guards his soul from suffering,' and (*Ibid.* 18:21): 'Death and life are in the power of the tongue.' Woe unto him who puts himself to death for one particle of speech. And what advantage is there to the man of the tongue?"

And Chazal have said (*Avoth* 1:16): "All of my days I [R. Shimon] have grown up among the sages and I have found nothing better for the body than silence." That is: "I have grown up among the sages and chosen from their comely and holy traits, and the trait of silence was the best of all." Or: "Even though they were learned sages, and their speech was not, G-d forbid, of empty things, still I found that the best thing of all for the *body*, aside from words of Torah, was absolute silence." As far as the stress on "the body" is concerned, the meaning is: A man, though he be wise and perfect in his soul, as were the companions of R. Shimon, still in point of the *matter* "clothing" the soul [i.e., the body], it is almost impossible that all of his words be properly limited — wherefore, silence is best of all. And if in the generation of R. Shimon, whose tongue was habituated to speak in wisdom, so that even if it were not entirely guarded it would not swerve from its path, G-d forbid, still, he said that silence was best of all — what should we, the [mere] "hyssop of the wall" do, all of whose thoughts and speech, from our youth on, are only of vanity and emptiness? If we do not muzzle our mouths with the rein of silence with all of our strength, then certainly the tongue will do as has been its wont from early youth, and the loss [sustained by speaking] will far outweigh the reward.

One who is habituated to silence escapes many transgressions — flattery, levity, *lashon hara*, falsehood, and insult. For if someone shames and insults him, if he answers him, he will get a double portion. And thus does the wise man say: "I hear evil and keep silent." The other: "Why?" The wise man: "If I answer and retort to my shamers, I fear that I will hear insults more biting than the others!" Also, if one cultivates the trait of silence, everyone feels free to share his secrets with him. Since he is not disposed to speaking, he will not reveal them. In addition, he is not given to *rechiluth*. In this connection it is written (*Mishlei* 18:21): "Death and life are in the hands of the tongue." For a man does more [damage] with his tongue than with his sword. For [through scandal] a man can stand here and deliver his friend, who is far from him, to death, whereas the sword kills only at close range. Therefore, a man was created with two eyes, two ears, and two nostrils, but [only] with one mouth, to teach him to minimize speech.

Silence becomes sages; how much more so, fools. (*Avoth* 3:17): "A fence for wisdom is silence." "Silence is the universal cure." And guard your tongue like the pupil of your eye. (*Mishlei* 18:7): "The mouth of a fool is destruction to him, and his lips are a stumbling-block to his soul." And (*Ibid.* 21:23): "One who guards his mouth and his tongue guards his soul from suffering."

And if you are sitting in a company, it is better that they say to you: "Speak. Why are you so silent?" than that you speak and your words be so tedious to them that they say to you: "Be silent!"

And it is written (*Michah* 7:5): "From her who lies in your bosom, guard the doors of your mouth." Scripture has hereby intimated to us that the mouth is like a door. And just as the door of a house has a time to be open and a time to be closed (for if it is always open everything in the house will be lost), so the doors of your mouth have a time to be open — to words of Torah and other essential things, and a time to be closed — to other things.

And a man must know that speech is the "beloved of all the beloved," for through it the form of man is perfected.

Therefore, just as one who has silver, gold, and pearls makes an enclosure within an enclosure to guard them and hides them in his innermost chamber in a special chest, so, even more, must he make an enclosure within an enclosure for his mouth; and that is, through the trait of silence.

Chapter III

In this chapter there will be set
forth various counsels for guarding the tongue

And if he is a man who is by nature depressed and fears exerting himself in this trait of silence, for he *must* speak about the affairs of the world for the sake of his health, in any event, he should accustom himself not to speak about people, whoever they may be (with the exception of those who have left the fold to deny the L-rd and those who mock the words of Chazal; for such as these, it is a mitzvah to demean, as we have written in *Chafetz Chaim*, Principle VII, section 5). And if sometimes it is *essential* to speak about someone he should be extremely terse and not speak at length in order not to come close to an *issur*. And I have heard the about the Gaon, R. Refail of Hamburg that four years before his death he removed from himself the yoke of the Rabbinate, and when people came to him, he asked them not to speak in his house about any person. And, likewise, I have heard about another great man of the generation that he would take great care that there not be heard from his mouth the name of any person. And all, for the aforementioned reason.

Even more so, should he take care not to speak to a shopkeeper about other shopkeepers or with any tradesman about his fellow tradesman. For, in all probability, one tradesman does not love the other and he is very likely to come through this to *lashon hara*. And if one knows that the first harbors hatred against the other, he should certainly not speak to him about the other. And, it goes without saying that he should not praise one to the other, which is certainly forbidden, as Chazal have said (*Arachin* 16a): "Let one not speak in praise of his friend, for from praising him he will come to demeaning him," all of which I have explained in *Chafetz Chaim*, Part One, Principle IX. And it is also highly advisable to avoid with him even speech in general, which is not in the class of demeaning or praising. For in his hatred of the other, he is highly likely to draw the speech in another direction, which will make it easier for him to shoot the arrows of his mouth against him.

And if he must tell him something essential about the other, he should not linger with him in this. For if not so, he will certainly come to *lashon hara*, as with flash powder, which *smells* of fire, it being impossible not to ignite the flame [of *lashon hara*] thereby.

And if he began to speak with Reuven about Shimon, not knowing that Reuven hates him and in the course of his conversation he comes to sense that he hates him and that [continuing to talk] would lead to *lashon hara* — then, if he has no way of leaving him, he should divert the talk to some other matter. Similarly, if he starts talking to someone and feels that when he concludes, he will have been trapped into *lashon hara* or the like, he should gird his soul to battle his *yetzer*, stop in the middle, and change the topic, just as, if in the middle of a meal, he were told that he was eating forbidden food, he would certainly stop eating immediately and spit out even what was in his mouth (as written in *Ya'aroth D'vash*.) And even if he would sometimes come to shame because of this, Chazal have said (*Eduyoth* 7b): "It is better that a man be called a fool all his life and not be an evildoer for one moment before the L-rd." And Ramban has already written in *Sha'ar HaGmul* that one moment in Gehinnom is worse than all the suffering of Iyyov all of his days. And it is known that a person would rather be shamed than endure terrible suffering.

And all that we have written applies only when he has no way to correct matters [between the parties]. But if he [knows that] his words will be heeded and he has the ability to make peace between them, then certainly it is a *mitzvah* for him to hear all that is [transpiring] between them, and there is no *issur* of *lashon hara* in this whatsoever.

Furthermore, he should take great care not to stand in the company of men. And even if he needs something essential, he should not linger there, unless he does not know them to be men among whom there is no forbidden speech. And even if the entire company are good men, and there is found one among them who is a man of malice, he spoils the entire company and it is advisable to leave them, or at least to court silence at that time with all of his strength, as written in *Rosh Hagivah*: "Take heed, my son, of what was said by King Solomon, may peace be upon him (*Mishlei* 23:9): 'In the ears of a fool do not speak, for he will shame the wisdom of your words.' Take heed, then, of a gathering of a hundred men if there is among them one fool or one speaker of levity, especially one who is wise in his [own] eyes, who is the true fool, as it is written: 'The fool is wise in his eyes.' Strengthen yourself and sit in silence and speak of nothing in that gathering. For even if you speak all kinds of wisdom, he will triumph over you, and you will take [only] shame for yourself. For thus has Solomon said (*Ibid.* 11:2): '[The man of] malice comes and shames comes, etc.' And even if you want to speak [privately] with your friend, make sure that you are not heard by that man, even from behind a fence. For this reason it is written 'In the ears of a fool do not speak,' and *not* '*With* a fool do not speak.' This is the voice of experience. I have tried all of this several times at a mitzvah feast and have found it to be true. Therefore, flee, my son, from a gathering like this, for he [the fool] demeans all who are there; or seize silence and be saved."

In sum, if one wishes to merit the trait of guarding his tongue, he should do the opposite of what "the men of the tongue" do, who are wont to walk always in a gathering of men, hoping to hear something they can mock or that they can afterwards "peddle" to others. And they are accustomed always to look for news in the city between man and his neighbor, so that their tongue should not be silenced for one moment in the day. And *he* [who desires to guard his tongue] should do the opposite.

All should be done by stages. First, he should accustom himself not to stand in the company of men and not to "sniff out" news. Afterwards, he should accustom his soul, little by little, not to *want* to hear any news, until, in the course of time, the Holy One Blessed be He will help him acquire the trait of guarding his tongue, as [part of] his nature. So that if he afterwards sees a man transgressing the *issur* of *lashon hara* and the like, his soul will be astounded, for this thing will already have become strange to him by *nature*, as are all of the other *issurim* to all of Israel. This has already been tried in the crucible of experience, that the guarding of one's tongue from evil and one's ears from hearing forbidden things produces hardship for a man for only a few weeks. For afterwards, when the people see that this man refuses to listen to *lashon hara* and levity and other forbidden things, every speaker will stop telling this man things which might be tainted with this *issur* and he will take his wares of *lashon hara* and *rechiluth* to those who desire to take them. For he will see that this man will not accord him honor and glory [by peddling his wares to him], but will see him as a man of *lashon hara* and a mocker. And he will almost not have to guard himself anymore from listening [to such speech], for the men of *lashon hara* themselves, when they are telling some story, will guard themselves against *him*! If he is standing near them, they will not speak, fearing that this hearer will spoil their wares in the eyes of the other "buyers." It [(guarding one's tongue)] will be difficult for a man only in the beginning, to resolve to undertake this faithfully. And all of this is included in the principle of Chazal (*Moed Katan* 5a): "He who assesses his ways in this world merits seeing [the truth], with the help of the Holy One Blessed be He."

Chapter IV

*In this chapter there will be explained the merit of one
who judges his friend in the scales of merit*

One should also accustom himself to judge his friend in the scales of merit, as Chazal have said (*Shevuoth* 30a): "(*Vayikra* 19:15): 'In righteousness shall you judge your friend' — Judge your friend in the scales of merit." And this is one of the things for which one eats the fruits in this world, with the principal remaining for the world to come, as they said in *Shabbath* 127a.

The idea of "the scales of merit" is either to side with the one who is reported to have done or said something, i.e., to say that the *din* is with him, or to say that he was unwitting in what he did or said, or that he did not know the severity of the *issur*, or, even if none of the above possibilities apply, to think that perhaps the speaker left out a certain detail or added a small detail, which slanted the report in his disfavor. And Chazal have stated as a principle (*Avoth* 2:4): "Do not judge your friend until you find yourself in his place."

Come see the episode in *Shabbath* 127b, from which the just man may learn that one must judge his friend in the scales of merit, even if the premise of the merit is farther [from reality than that of liability]: "The Rabbis taught: If one judges his friend in the scales of merit, he, too, will be judged in the scales of merit. Once, a man from upper Galilee went and hired himself out to a man in the south for three years. On Yom Kippur eve, he said: "Give me my wages so that I can go and feed my wife and children." The employer: "I have none." The worker: "Give me land." The employer: "I have none." The worker: "Give me mattresses and pillows." The employer: "I have none." The worker slung his belongings on his back and went home dejected. After the festival, the employer took his [the worker's] wages along with three asses, one laden with food, one with [containers of] drink, and one with all manner of clothing, and he went to the worker's house. After they had eaten and drunk, and he had given the worker his wages, he asked him: "When you asked me for your wages and I told you that I had no money, what did you suspect me of?" The worker: "I thought that a 'good buy' had come your way and that you had used your money for that." The employer: "When you asked me for the animals and I told you that I had none, what did you suspect me of?" The worker: "I thought that you might have hired them out to others." The employer: "When you asked me for land and I told you that I had none, what did you suspect me of?" The worker: "I thought that you might have rented it out to others." The employer: "When I told you that I had no produce, what did you suspect me of?" The worker: "I thought that perhaps you had not tithed it." The employer: "When I told you that I had no mattresses and pillows, what did you suspect me of?" The worker: "I thought that perhaps you had consecrated all of your belongings to Heaven." The employer: "I swear that this is what happened. I vowed [i.e., consecrated to Heaven] all of my possessions because my son Hyrcanus would not study Torah; and when I came to my colleagues in the South, they annulled all of my vows for me. And, as for you, just as you judged *me* in the scales of merit, may the Holy One Blessed be He judge *you* in the scales of merit." And there are adduced further instances in the *Gemara* where the scales of merit are farther [from reality] than those of liability, notwithstanding which they were careful to judge according to the scales of merit.

Now according to the extent of one's habituation to this trait, so will there be diminished from him the sin of *lashon hara*. How much, then, must a man strengthen himself in this trait, to judge every man in the scales of merit. For on this trait or on the reverse, G-d forbid, can easily depend a man's being called a *tzaddik* or a *rasha* [wicked] forever. For it is known that a man's guilt or merit depends upon the majority of his mitzvoth or sins, as Chazal have stated in many places. If the majority [of his deeds] are mitzvoth, he is called a *tzaddik*; and, if sins, he is called a *rasha*. And Chazal have said (*Rosh Hashanah* 16b): "Three books are opened on the day of judgment [(that is the "great" day of judgment at the resurrection [viz. Rashi])]. The absolutely righteous are written down and sealed immediately for eternal life. The absolutely wicked [(that is, those with a majority of sins [viz. Rashi])] are written down and sealed immediately for Gehinnom." Now it is well known that in respect to a man's merits, even if they be as many as the sands [of the sea], if the Holy One Blessed be He conducts Himself with him according to the absolute measure of *din* [judgment], there will remain with him only a miniscule amount. For with many of them he will not have fulfilled them in all the details and aspects relevant to that mitzvah. And even those he did fulfill thus, would not have been fulfilled with the love and the fear and the joy appropriate for the doing of the mitzvah. In sum, if the Holy One Blessed be He were exacting, G-d forbid, as to the doing of His mitzvoth, most would be found blemished, and the remaining mitzvoth would not constitute a minority of a minority of his sins, and he would be called a *rasha* for eternity. But if the Holy One Blessed be He conducted Himself with him according to the attribute of mercy, and sought merit for him in all of his acts, his merits would remain intact. More than this, even if his deeds were counted and he were found to have a majority of sins, if the Holy One Blessed be He would conduct Himself with him according to the absolute measure of mercy, his sins would be diminished. For there would certainly be found many sins which could be attenuated because of his having committed them unwittingly, or for some other reason. In sum, if the Holy One Blessed be He wished to seek merit for a person, there would be no hindrance to His doing so, and if, as a result, some of his sins were diminished, the scale of merit would predominate and he would be called a *tzaddik* for eternity.

Now all of this is dependent on how he has conducted himself all the days of his life with his fellow man. If his way were to judge them in the scales of merit, he, too, will be judged in [the scales of] merit (as in *Shabbath* 127b above). And if his way were to find guilt in people and to speak evil of them, the ministering angels above will speak evil of him, too, as we find in *Midrash Mishlei*. Therefore, a man must know in his soul, while he is still alive, that as he judges his friend, whether for good or for bad, by his words themselves he is determining his own judgment.

Chapter V

In this chapter there will be explained the mitzvah of (*Vayikra* 19:18):
"And you shall love your friend as yourself"

And when we reflect upon this in truth, we find that the fulfillment of the mitzvah of judging one's friend in the scales of merit and the trait of guarding one's tongue depend on the fulfillment of the positive commandment of "And you shall love your friend as yourself." For if one truly loves his friend, he certainly will not speak *lashon hara* against him and he will seek merit for him with all of his strength. For if it happened to *him* that he did something unfitting and people were standing and talking about that thing and he knew of some aspect of merit in himself, whether it were his having acted unwittingly or the like, how much he would desire that there were someone who would speak up for him so that he not be unduly shamed. Exactly this should he do for his friend.

And this mitzvah of loving one's friend applies *before* the act, too, that his friend not come to shame. As when one marries off his son in a different city or when he himself comes to live in a different place, where he is a stranger to its customs. He taxes his brain to find some faithful friend there to apprise him of the customs of that place, and who, if he [the friend] finds him deviating from them in some way, will tell him so privately, so that he will take heed and not be embarrassed in the eyes of the men of the city. Thus, exactly, must he do for his friend. That is, if he sees him "stumbling" in some thing which is not to his credit, even if there is no *issur* in it, he must tell him so, that he not be shamed thereby. [And thus do we find in *Horiyoth* 13a with R. Yaakov b. Korshai and R. Shimon b. Gamliel. And more than this, we find in *Sanhedrin* 11a with several *tannaim* that they drew shame upon themselves to remove it from another. And how much more so if he sees him doing something against the *din*, he certainly must tell him so privately and reprove him for it so that he not fall into evil in the present and in the future; and he fulfils thereby the positive commandment of reproving and also the mitzvah of "And you shall love your friend as yourself."

And this will afford great pleasure to the Blessed Creator, his having perfected His son for His service. But if, G-d forbid, he does not do so, but, to the contrary, goes and shames him because of this before others, what does the Blessed Creator have from this?

To what may this be compared? To one who has a son who conducts himself improperly in some matter and his friend goes, in the eyes of his father, and publicizes this before others. Certainly, he [the father] will take offense and will say "You should have reproved him privately for this and I would have thanked you greatly for doing so, but you should not have gone and publicized him immediately for scorn and shame in the eyes of all. And I perceive that your intent was not concern for the truth. For if it were, it would have been better both for him and for you if you had reproved him for this. But your intent was only to blame and incriminate your friend and rejoice in his misfortune. This is nothing other than meanness of heart!"

So is it exactly with the Blessed Creator vis-à-vis the children of Israel, His holy people. For they are like sons to Him, as it is written (*Devarim* 14:1) "You are sons to the L-rd your G-d." And He rejoices in their good and grieves in their cries and in their shame (viz. *Sanhedrin* 46a). And this one [the friend] goes, in the eyes of the Father, whose glory fills all the world and shames His son before people to no purpose. What pleasure has He from this? And Rambam (*Deoth* 6:3) has adduced a principle in respect to the mitzvah of "And you should love your friend as yourself," that one should be just as solicitous of his friend's possessions and honor as he is of his own. And, as stated by *Tanna d'bei Eliyahu* 27: "Thus did the Holy One Blessed be He say to Israel: 'My beloved son, do I lack anything that I ask it from *you*? And what *do* I ask of you. Only that you love one another and honor one another and fear one another, and that there not be among you transgression and theft and unsightliness, so that you not be rejected forever, wherefore it is written (*Michah* 6:8): 'He has told you, O man, what is good. And what does the L-rd your G-d ask of you, but that you judge rightly, and love lovingkindness, and walk humbly with your G-d.'"

Chapter VI

In this chapter there will be explained the *issur* of revenge and grudge-bearing, and the greatness of the reward of him who guards himself against them

More than this. If it happens that one's friend conducts himself with him improperly in something, in spite of this, he must take care not to avenge himself of him and to bear hatred against him. But he must wipe the thing from his heart and do good to him in all ways, as to all other Jews, as if there were no hatred between them, as it is written: "Do not take revenge and do not bear a grudge against the sons of your people, and you shall love your friend as yourself." Come and see, in the holy *Zohar, Parshath Miketz*, how great is the man who repays bad with good: "Come and see [how] Joseph [conducted himself]. Not only did he not return evil to his brothers, but he accorded them good and truth, as is the way of *tzaddikim* always, wherefore the Holy One Blessed be He has compassion for them always, in this world and in the world to come."

And in order to set one's mind at rest in this, I have thought it fit to introduce an exalted thought here which is rooted in the *Yerushalmi* adduced by Semag, that if one were walking on the road and struck one of his feet with the other and, in doing so, fell to the ground and hurt his body, his face and also that foot — aside from the fact that it would never enter his mind to take revenge of that foot by [desisting] from healing it, he would also harbor no hatred whatsoever against it. For what is the foot and what are his body and his face — they all are one [body], but divided into organs. Rather, he would reason that his sins caused this.

Here, too, if it happened that his friend did not benefit him with a certain good that he asked of him, or even if he grieved or insulted him in some way, he should not avenge himself and harbor hatred against him. For who is his friend and who is he? Both are from one root, as it is written (I *Chronicles* 17:21): "And who is like Your people, Israel, one nation in the land?" And it is written [*Bereshith* 46:27]: "All of the soul of the house of Jacob that came etc." It is not written "souls," to teach us that all the souls of Israel above are reckoned as one soul. It is just that each one is an entity in itself. As with a man in his entirety — even though, as a whole, he is one man, still, he has organs which are "heads" to him, like the head and the heart; and there are those beneath these, like the hand and the foot. And it is also into one rest that all of Israel will gather in the end — under the Throne of Glory — as it is written (I *Samuel* 25:29): "And the soul of my lord will be bound in the bond of life with the L-rd your G-d, etc." It is just that because in this world, where everyone is clothed in his own matter by himself, and because each of his affairs and undertakings is an entity in itself that a man imagines himself to be a distinct person and not "one" with his fellow Jew at all — but this is not so.

And that is why we find many times in the words of Chazal that if one transgresses, G-d forbid, he thereby harms all of Israel, for they [he and all the rest] are like one body. And if one has a great pain in one organ, the other organs, too, even though their pain is not so great, still feel a "vibration" of that pain. As we find in *Vayikra Rabbah* 84: "(*Jeremiah* 50:17): 'A scattered lamb is Israel.' Israel is compared to a lamb. Just as a lamb, if it is hurt in one of its organs, all of them feel it, so Israel — one sins and all feel it. R. Shimon b. Yochai said: 'This may be compared to [an instance of] men sailing in a boat. One of them takes a drill and starts drilling under him. His friends say to him: "Why are you doing this?" He answers: "What business is it of yours? Am I not drilling under *me*?" And they say: "But you are flooding the boat on *us*!"

Therefore, my brother, take great care not to avenge yourself and not to bear a grudge against your brother. For it is yourself against whom you are taking revenge and bearing a grudge! Think only that Heaven is causing all this to happen to you, because of your sins. And what difference does it make whether this suffering comes upon you by the one or by the other? And if I accept all this upon me [resignedly] in truth, all of my sins will be pardoned thereby. As David said to Avishai ben Tzeruyah when he wanted to take revenge on his [David's] behalf, of Shim'i ben Gera, for having shamed and vilified David and cursed him with a dire curse — David did not allow him [Avishai] to do so, saying: "The *L-rd* told him to curse!" And Chazal have said that because of this the Heavenly tribunal designated David to be the fourth leg of the Divine Chariot, as we shall explain at length below, please G-d.

[To set one's mind at rest not (even) to think of taking revenge and bearing a grudge) I have adduced my interpretation of (*Vayikra* 19:18): "And you shall love your friend as yourself; I am the L-rd," viz.: How are we to understand the juxtaposition of "I am the L-rd" with the beginning of the verse? I have said that the intent of Scripture here is to elucidate the beginning of the verse: "You shall not take revenge and you shall not bear a grudge against the sons of your people." ("And you shall love, etc.") For, ostensibly, that is to be wondered at. If one is very pressed for time and he asks his friend to do him a favor, and the latter is in a position to grant the favor and refuses, especially if he grieves him in the process — how can he not take umbrage, and even love him as himself?

I have explained the verse by an apt analogy, viz.: Reuven hated Shimon and stirred up a quarrel with him. Afterwards, Yehudah came along, who was held by Shimon and by all men to be a man of truth and told Reuven: "Shimon, whom you hate, and who you told me is dishonest and despicable — I saw him a few days afterwards with one of the great men of this generation, renowned as a Gaon and a *tzaddik* and a peerless sage. And that Gaon honored him greatly and showed him tokens of love in many ways. You were greatly mistaken in this, my brother." And when Reuven heard this, he was astounded and said: "You have placed a doubt in my heart. It is possible that the truth is with R. Shimon and that only because 'all the ways of a man are *just* in his eyes' that I thought that the *din* was with me — *or* perhaps, in truth the *din is* with me, but this Shimon is a deceiver and "smooth-talked" this great man until he thought him to be an honorable man; but, nevertheless, I will no longer speak [evil] of him because of the doubt you raised in my heart."

A few days after that, Yehudah, whom Reuven holds to be a man of truth, comes to him and says: "I have seen an even more wonderful thing. The man that you told me that you still had doubts about, that he might be a deceiver and dishonest — I saw him afterwards, meeting with the early sages of the generation, and they, too, honored him greatly and showed him tokens of love in the presence of all. And about the great man of the generation that I told you about in the beginning, — you may have thought that Shimon deceived him; but about men like these it is impossible to say this." When Reuven hears this he immediately replies: "You are right. The *yetzer* deceived me in the very essence of the thing." Yehudah continues: "Don't I know about Shimon that he met with the early sages of Israel, R. Meir, R. Yehudah, and Rabbi, who redacted the *Mishnayoth*, and his colleagues, whose company Eliyahu would frequent, as is well known; and they, too, lauded and praised him. And Eliyahu the prophet told these *tannaim* that this R. Shimon was "spoken of on high" and he heard from the mouth of the Holy One Blessed be He that *He* loved R. Shimon.

And when Reuven hears this, he recoils and falls on his face and says: "Woe unto me for what I thought at first, that *I* am the *tzaddik* and he, the *rasha*. For from what I see now, this is not so. For the Holy One Blessed be He, who is the Root of all and knows what is done in darkness and in light, whose work is perfect and all His ways just — when *He* loves a man, certainly His love is not in vain. As far as what passed between me and the honored R. Shimon, I can see this now in several ways. First that the *din* is with him in principle itself, but, because I was personally involved and I did not know Shimon, it seemed to me that truth and rightness was with me, and this is what I consider most likely. Or, it is possible that Shimon was unwitting in what he did and that he sorely regretted it [thereafter], and it is possible that he yet intends to conciliate me. Or, there may be other reasons that I am not acquainted with. In any case, I have greatly sinned in speaking against a man whom the Holy One Blessed be He, Himself, said that He loved, whose soul-root on high must be exceedingly holy and awesome — publicizing him as "dishonest," "despicable" and "deceitful." I greatly regret this and bear no hatred towards him, since the Holy One Blessed be He, Himself is his Lover.

And this is the intent of the verse "You shall not take revenge and you shall not bear a grudge against the sons of your people. And you shall love your friend as yourself — I am the L-rd." If you say: "How can I *make* myself not have anything against him and even *love* him?" the verse itself provides the answer — "I am the L-rd." As per (*Malachi* 1:2): "'*I* have loved you,' said the L-rd," and (*Devarim* 14:1): "You are sons to the L-rd your G-d" — you, too, can love him. And, in truth, the matter is simple. For since a man looks "downwards" at his friend, seeing him clothed in physical matter, he [his friend] is not very significant to him, especially, if he is against him in some matter, in which instance he "nullifies" him completely. Not so the Holy One Blessed be He, who knows, in essence, that the root of the holiness of the soul of Israel is exceedingly great and awesome, as it is written in the holy *Zohar* in several places, that the root of the holiness of the soul of Israel on high is in an extremely awesome sphere, wherefore their eminence and His love for them, accordingly, are extremely great.]

Chapter VII

In this chapter there will be explained the great care one must take of ascribing liability to Israel and his reward for ascribing merit [to them]

In the preceding chapters we spoke about the individual. How much more so must one take great heed not to impute liability to Israel in general, for this sin is very severe. As we find in *Pesachim* 87b on *Proverbs* 30:10 "'Speak not ill of a servant to his master… a generation that curses its father and does not bless its mother.' …Even a generation that curses its father and does not bless its mother — do not speak ill of it to its Master — the Holy One Blessed be He." And see now [the instance of] Isaiah the prophet. When he saw the glory of the L-rd and said (*Isaiah* 6:5): "Woe unto me, for I am lost, for I am a man of unclean lips; and in the midst of a people of unclean lips do I dwell, etc." — because he said "and in the midst of a people of unclean lips," even though his intent in this was not to shame Israel, (for he said this also of himself) but only to say that he was not worthy of seeing the Shechinah, neither in point of *his* deeds nor of those of the people in whose midst he dwelt — in spite of this, see what follows (*Ibid.* 6): "Then one of the seraphs flew unto me [Isaiah] and in his hand was a live coal [*ritzpah*]," concerning which Chazal say that "*ritzpah*" is acronymic of "*retzoth peh*" ["crush the mouth"] that slanders My children." And he died as a result of this, as they say in *Yevamoth* 49b: "[He (Isaiah) uttered the Name and was 'swallowed up' in a cedar.] the cedar was brought and sawed. When it [the saw] came to his mouth, he died, [this, for having said 'And in the midst of a people of unclean lips do I dwell.']"

And so, with Moses our teacher, may peace be upon him, because he said (*Bamidbar* 32:14): "a growth of sinful men," there descended from him Shevuel ben Gershom, who ministered to idolatry, as Chazal have said (*Bava Kamma* 109b, *Yerushalmi* 9:2). And more than this we find with Eliyahu, who, because he said (I *Kings* 19:10): "I have been very zealous for the L-rd … for they have forsaken Your covenant, etc.", he was removed because of this from prophecy and the Holy One Blessed be He commanded him to anoint Elisha in his place, as Chazal state (in *Yalkut Melachim*).

And *Sefer Charedim* 51 states, in the name of the *Midrash* that the intent of the captain who was punished because he had said (II *Kings* 7:19): "Even [if] the L-rd made windows in the heavens, could such a thing happen?" — his intent was that the L-rd could certainly make it happen, but this generation was like the generation of the flood, deserving that the windows of heaven be opened [for *evil*], as there, viz. (*Bereshith* 7:11): "And the windows of heaven were opened." How is it possible that for such an evil generation as this such a great miracle [for good] could happen? And Elisha the prophet answered him that because he slandered Israel, he would see the miracle, but not eat (viz. II *Kings*, *Ibid.*)

And see, my brother, this wondrous allegory in *Tanna d'bei Eliyahu* 7: "The children of Israel are compared to a vineyard, as it is written (*Isaiah* 5:7): 'For a vineyard of the L-rd of hosts is the house of Israel,' concerning which R. Eliezer Haladul said: 'The house of Israel, which is the vineyard of the Holy One Blessed be He — do not look at it [with ill intent]. And if you have looked at it, do not go down into it. And if you have gone down into it, do not derive benefit from it. And if you have derived benefit from it, do not eat of its fruit. And if you have looked, and gone down, and derived benefit from it, and eaten of its fruit, the end of that man [i.e., you] is to be cut off from the world."

And the *Zohar Chadash* 21b states: "R. Akiva said: 'Though one be the greatest *tzaddik* in the world, but he speaks ill of the Holy One Blessed be He or *lashon hara* against Israel, his punishment is the greatest of all. And there was no *tzaddik* as great as Eliyahu in the whole generation, but because he spoke *lashon hara* against Israel, etc.' At that time he sinned greatly against Him. Come and see what is written of him (I *Kings* 19:6): "And he looked, and, behold, at his head was a cake baked on coals [*retzafim*]," the Holy One Blessed be He saying as it were: 'This is what is fit to be eaten by one who speaks *lashon hara* against My children, etc.'" R. Yitzchak said: "Eliyahu did not stir from there until he swore before the Holy One Blessed be He to impute merit to Israel always.' And everyone who acts meritoriously — he [Eliyahu] comes forward and says before the Holy One Blessed be He: 'Such and such did that man do now.' And he does not stir from there until the merit of that man is recorded, etc."

From all of this we can realize the greatness of the care that one must exercise against imputing liability to all of Israel. To the contrary, he must accustom himself always to arouse mercy and to bring their merits to remembrance. And if he does so, he will be beloved and compassionated by the Holy One Blessed be He, as we find in *Yoma* 77a with respect to Gavriel. When he stood outside the Divine curtain and awakened merit for Israel, the Holy One Blessed be He responded: "Who is this that imputes merit to My children?" And they brought him within [the Divine curtain because of this].

We find many references along these lines in *Tanna d'bei Eliyahu*, some in Chapter 19:1, which awaken much merit for Israel, viz.: "L-rd of the world, behold our affliction, fight out battles and let our shame rise before You, what is done to us at every moment. And remember how many householders there are in Israel who have no livelihood, but toil in Torah every day, always. And remember how many paupers there are in Israel whose flesh the idolators draw from them (with taxes), but who toil in Torah every day, always. Remember how many youth there are in Israel, who do not know [the difference between] their right and their left hands, but who toil in Torah all the day, always. Remember how many old men and women there are in Israel, who go early and late to houses of prayer and houses of study, and who long and lust and look for Your salvation every day, always. Remember Your covenant which You made with our fathers, with the three *tzaddikim*,

Abraham, Isaac, and Jacob. And You also wrote for us in Your Torah (*Vayikra* 25:35): 'And if your brother grows poor and his hand falls with you, then you shall uphold him.' (You, too, uphold *us*.) My Father in heaven, remember how many cripples and how many blind ones we have in Israel, who have no food, and, even so, give wages to teachers to teach their children Torah. My Father in heaven, remember Israel, Your eternal acquisitions, as it is written (*Devarim* 32:6): 'Is He not your Father, your Acquirer?' And (*Mishlei* 8:22): 'The L-rd acquired me [in] the beginning of His way,' My Father in heaven, remember how many widows and orphans there are in Israel, who toil in Torah and in mitzvoth every day, always, etc."

And from this every man can learn how much each one in Israel must awaken the mercies of the Holy One Blessed be He for Israel in these things and the like. For today, too, these merits and their like [still] obtain for one who recognizes in our times the depressed condition of Israel — in spite of which there are, thank the L-rd, many learners of Torah and fulfillers of mitzvoth and many upholders of Torah and bestowers of lovingkindness, and givers of charity "in all quarters and corners."

And in *Tanchuma*, on the verse (*Devarim* 16:18): "And they shall judge the people [with] a righteous judgment": R. Yehuda b. R. Shalom said: 'They should "incline" [judgment] and impute merit to them before the Holy One Blessed be He. From whom do we learn this? From Gideon the son of Yoash, in whose days Israel was [steeped] in suffering, and the Holy One Blessed be He sought a man who would impute merit to them and could not find one, the generation being poor in mitzvoth and in [virtuous] deeds. When merit was found in Gideon, who imputed merit to them, immediately the angels appeared to him, as it is written (*Judges* 6:11): 'And an angel of the L-rd came' [to Gideon] ... and (*Ibid.* 14): '...and He said: "Go, with this your strength and save Israel, etc."', with this strength of your having imputed merit to My children, this being the thrust of 'And they shall judge the people [with] a righteous judgment, that they shall impute merit to the generation.'" From all of this, we can understand the eminence of one who "imputes merit," before the Holy One Blessed be He. And he [Gideon] afterwards became the chariot for the light of the holy sanctuary, which was called "the sanctuary of merit," where the merits of Israel were brought to remembrance, as we find in *Sefer Charedim*.

Chapter VIII

In this chapter there will be explained the trait of savlanuth [acquiescence, resignation], in the merit of which one's sins are forgiven

One must furthermore take great heed to accustom himself to the trait of acquiescence, to be resigned to all that happens to him, as we find in *Avoth d'R. Nathan* 41:11: "Teach yourself to accept suffering and to resign yourself to your shame." This will make guarding his tongue much easier for him. For lacking this, he will constantly have to overcome his *yetzer* — not to go and tell others what happened between himself and Ploni or to take heed of how to speak [see *Chafetz Chaim* Part One, Principle X: 13, 14, 15]; and sometimes he will overcome the *yetzer* and sometimes it will overcome him. And even if one shames him to his face, he must not answer at all, but know that all comes from the L-rd because of his sins, and that it is his *sins* which shame him.

And when he accepts the *din* upon himself in truth, certainly the Holy One Blessed be He will "lift his horn" because of this in this world and in the world to come, as we find with King David, may peace be upon him (II *Samuel* 16:7), when Shimi ben Gera cursed him and cast stones upon him and the servants of David wanted to be zealous for his honor because of this. He did not allow them to do so and accepted the *din* upon himself, saying (*Ibid.* 10): "The L-rd has told him to curse," concerning which Chazal have said: "At that time David merited becoming the fourth of the legs of the Divine Chariot."

And, likewise, any man, if he merits [attaining] this trait in perfection, will be accounted in the future among the lovers of the Blessed L-rd and will shine as "the sun coming forth in its strength" As Chazal have said (*Shabbath* 88b): "Those who are shamed but do not shame [in return], who hear themselves abused and do not retort, who serve [the L-rd] out of love and rejoice in afflictions, — of such it is written (*Judges* 5:31): 'And His lovers, as the sun coming forth in its strength.'"

And the commentators explain that three levels are mentioned here:

1) not being ashamed when his friend shames him, but possibly retorting.

2) compelling himself not to retort so as not to draw down upon himself through this even more shaming by his friend.

3) serving out of love and rejoicing in afflictions. That is, his not retorting stems from his loving the L-rd and accepting these afflictions with joy. And when he reaches the third level, he merits all this honor. For this trait comes to a man

from the holiness of his soul and his pure faith in the L-rd that He directs all his ways, as it is written (*Iyyov* 34:21): "For His eyes are on the ways of a man, etc.", and He does all for his good. As we find in *Midrash Tanchuma*: "One should rejoice in afflictions more than in good. For even if a man receives good all of his days, his sins are not forgiven. And how *is* he forgiven? By afflictions. R. Elazar said: "A man must be grateful to the L-rd when afflictions come upon him. Why so? For afflictions draw a man to the Holy One Blessed be He, as it is written (*Mishlei* 3:12): 'Whom the L-rd loves, He chastises.'" If afflictions come upon a man let him suffer them and accept them. Why? For there is no limit to their reward. (*Psalms* 37:7): 'Be silent in the L-rd and hope [*vehithcholel*] in Him.' Hope in the L-rd. If He brings afflictions upon you, do not "kick" at them but accept them as *chalilin* (like "*vechithcholel*"), as flutes [of joy]." And toleration of shame is in the category of afflictions, as mentioned above, "who serve out of love and rejoice in afflictions."

And if a man wishes to cleave to this trait of *savlanuth*, let him reflect always on the punishment for sins in Gehinnom and through *gilgul* [metempsychosis]. As Chazal have said (*Eruvin* 19a) on *Psalms* 84:7: "*ovrei be'emek habacha mayan yeshituhu*": "*Ovrei*" — these are the transgressors [*ovrim*] of the L-rd's will; "*emek*" — Gehinnom is deepened [*ma'amikim*] for them; "*habacha*" — they cry [*bochim*] and shed tears as the well of Shitin [*mayan shel shitin* (into which the remainder of the alter libations was poured)]." And it is known that the fire of the first level of Gehinnom is sixty times more intense than ours; of the second level, sixty times more intense than that of the first level. And thus the punishment redoubles itself in all the [succeeding] levels. And Ramban has already written in *Sha'ar Hagmul* that one moment in Gehinnom is more excruciating than all the afflictions of Iyyov all of his days. And it is also known that the punishment of *gilgul* is more excruciating than the punishment of Gehinnom.

Therefore, if one reflects upon his deeds always and knows that he, too, will not be cleansed on the day of *din* from the awesome punishment, he will certainly accept upon himself with much joy this trait of *savlanuth* and of overlooking his prerogatives in exchange for the aforementioned terrible punishments. (As written in *Sefer Charedim*: "When I hear all those who shame and insult me in public, I put before my vision, scales. In one [balance] I place my sins, and in the other, the shamings and insults, and I see the balance of sins pressing downwards. And I remain silent and vindicate my judgment. And thus I do with all kinds of afflictions in speech or in deed.") For do we not see plainly that a man is ready to accept all kinds of denigration if through this he can prevent the loss of his possessions (as in a conflagration and other sufferings, G-d forbid)? How much more so if he knows that through this [denigration], he will escape severe physical punishment. From all this we can conclude the same *a fortiori* with respect to *savlanuth*, where he is under duress only when he stands near his friend and hears his shame.

We shall explain our words: Even if he were not forgiven through this [*savlanuth*] only for one sin completely, but would only have his punishment [somewhat] attenuated, it would suffice him [to suffer this denigration]. How much more so if he were forgiven completely for one sin. And how much even more so now that we know that he is forgiven for *all* his sins, even those which are called "*pesha*" [offense], (so long as he takes heed not to commit them from now on.) As Chazal have said (*Rosh Hashanah* 17a): "If one forgives slights against himself, all of his offenses are forgiven, as it is written (*Michah* 7:18): 'He forgives transgression and passes over offense.' Whose transgression does He forgive? The one who 'passes over' [i.e., overlooks] offense."

But if one wants the Holy One Blessed be He to forgive him even for his offenses, let him take heed not to take offense at all, even if he knows for a certainty that what his friend did against him was done with malice and treachery, which is called "*pesha*' [offense]e forgive? The one who passes over" [i.e., overlooks] offernse."But, as they have said (*Yoma* 36b): "'*Peshaim*' — these are sins of rebellion." This is their intent in "Whose transgression does He forgive? The one who overlooks offense." (For, in truth, the Holy One Blessed be He forgives him even for his "offenses," as it is written: "All of his *offenses* are forgiven." And Scripture states first (*Michah* 7:18): "He forgives transgression" because of the *order* of the traits of the Holy One Blessed be He. For he [first] forgives transgression and *also* overlooks offense, as it is written in the Torah (*Exodus* 34:7): "He forgives transgression and offense.")

And this trait sometimes avails a man to lengthen his life, even if it were already decreed upon him to die, as in the following instance (*Rosh Hashanah* 17a): "When R. Huna b. R. Yehoshua took ill, R. Pappa went to visit him. Seeing that he was gravely ill, he said: 'Ready his escort' [i.e., funeral shrouds]." In the end, however, he recovered, and R. Pappa was embarrassed to be seen by him. [Later,] R. Huna asked him: "What did you see?" [that prompted you to say what you did? (And R. Pappa answered him.)] R. Huna (in response): "I really *was* designated for death, but the Holy One Blessed be He said [to the angels assigned thereto]: 'Since he is not exacting [in slights to himself], do not be exacting with him.'" Therefore, one must cleave to this holy trait, and it will be well for him, now and in the future.

This, too, shall he see [to do]. Not to take upon himself any appointments, if not for mitzvah matters. For [if he does] he is very likely to stumble into the sin of *lashon hara*. And he should fulfill in himself the dictum of Chazal (*Sanhedrin* 14a): "Be lowly and live." In general, one who wishes to be "complete" in his ways should avoid the company of men as much as he can. And even if he is a businessman, who sometimes must meet with men who are not reputable at all, to do business with them, still, so long as it is not absolutely essential to join them, he should distance himself from them.

Chapter IX

In this chapter there will be explained the trait of bitachon [trust] and the setting aside of times for Torah

This, too, shall he see [to do], to strengthen himself always in the trait of *bitachon*. For aside from its being a holy trait and essential for the fundamental end of [Divine] service, it is also greatly needed for the trait of guarding one's tongue. For it is well known that one is often ill disposed to his friend, and his *yetzer* incites him to go and publicize him as a wicked, unprincipled man for having (as he thinks) harmed his business or having detracted from his honor, and it is very difficult for him to overcome his *yetzer* in these things. But if one reflects upon what Chazal have said, that one cannot touch even a hair of what is set aside [by Heaven] for his friend, and that everyone will be given what was decreed for him by Heaven, both in respect to honor and in respect to possessions, as Chazal have said (*Yoma* 38a): "From here Ben Azzai derived: 'By your name shall they call you, and in your place shall they seat you, and of yours shall they give you, etc.'", his *yetzer* will relax its hold on him.

We shall explain the trait of *bitachon* a little before returning to our subject. David, may peace be upon him, said (*Psalms* 37:3): "Trust in the L-rd and do good, dwell in the land and cultivate faith." First he exhorts man in the trait of *bitachon* ("Trust in the L-rd") and then in the doing of good. For it [*bitachon*] is a strong foundation on which the entire edifice can be built. For example, our holy Torah commanded us to be heedful of Torah study at all times — at least, of the setting of assigned times for Torah study, and, likewise, with the giving of charity, and with other mitzvoth — which, on the surface, would seem to bode a loss for one's possessions. And the *yetzer hara* incites him to think: "What will I do in 'my latter end,' if I do not exert myself more for my business, especially at this time, which is especially auspicious for going here and there, and 'if not now, then when?'" It attempts to divert him by such devices from his assigned Torah times and, also, from the giving of charity. Scripture, therefore, comes to exhort us: "Trust in the L-rd!" For He will certainly recompense you with all that is due you; "and do good" — As a result of this, you will be able to do good. As stated in *Yerushalmi, Sotah* 9: "One was learning and the [potential] buyers called for him to come out and do business with him, and he said: 'I cannot interrupt my study time; if it [my livelihood] has to come, it will come,'" of itself, from the Holy One Blessed be He, even after I have completed my assigned study time.

And this is something that stands to reason. For how is it possible that the Holy One Blessed be He will decrease a man's livelihood, which He has decreed for him on Rosh Hashanah because he did not want to sacrifice his set time for Torah study? And even if it happens that because of his study time he misses his profit for that day he need not worry about it, for there are many options open to the L-rd.

And if not today, He will give it to him on a different day, and he can rest assured that by the end of the time for the sustenance of that year (i.e., until Rosh Hashanah, as Chazal have said), there will certainly be paid him what was decreed for him by Heaven. And all of his increased diligence and exertion will not help him one bit. For certainly he will not add anything [to his "stipend"] by transgressing the will of the Holy One Blessed be He by interrupting his set Torah study time or [his time for] giving money to charity — unless he be one who entirely denies the L-rd and His providence, of whom it is written (*Devarim* 7:10): "And He pays His foes to his face [in this world] to make him go lost" [in the world to come].

And even if he sees that there are some people who entirely neglect their Torah studies and yet succeed in business, let him reflect always upon their affairs, and he will see that very often they run into adversities, such as being set upon by brigands and the like and losing much of their money thereby. And this, because of their having amassed money which was not theirs [viz. (*Jeremiah* 17:11): "One who makes money, but not by just (means) — in the half of his days he shall lose it"], or in a time that was not theirs, but which should have been set aside for Torah study and Divine service. As we find in *Avoth d'R. Nathan* (29:2): "All who nullify words of Torah are assigned 'nullifiers' correspondingly (who come and nullify what they have labored in until now), such as lions, wolves, leopards, tigers and snakes. And brigands and robbers come and belabor him and exact payment of him. As it is written (*Psalms* 58:12): "But there is a G-d who judges the land," measure for measure. Because he nullifies Torah and toils for wealth, he is assigned "nullifiers," who nullify what he has toiled in until now. For even if the lions and the wolves do not kill him, they nevertheless cause him monetary loss, so that he must flee them and abandon his possessions or heal himself from their wounds. And many times great suffering and rare illnesses come to him from Heaven until, in the end, he spends [on doctors] that money that he did not want to give for charity. As they have said: "A house that is not open to the poor is open to the doctor." And this, too, sometimes results from the neglect of Torah study. As Chazal have said (*Berachoth* 5a): "If a man sees afflictions besetting him, let him examine his deeds. If he did examine [them] and did not find [anything to attribute them to], let him attribute [them] to neglect of Torah study."

If so, my brother, why heap up money that is not yours or hold back money that you must give for the cause of the Holy One Blessed be He (i.e., charity,) or steal from the time that you must devote to the Name of the Hoy One Blessed be He and gather at that time money, which, in the end, you will be constrained to return in suffering and trouble [(such as brigandage and illness, G-d forbid)], and to rejoice at having survived them? In sum, the world and its fullness is the L-rd's, and He created all for His honor, as it is written (*Isaiah* 43:7): "All that is called by My Name and which I have created for My glory, etc." And certainly no option is withheld from Him, even in this world in executing His will for better or for worse, wherefore Scripture states "Trust in the L-rd and do good."

Chapter X

This, too, relates to the trait of *bitachon*

And, in truth, when a man reflects upon this, he should be ashamed and humiliated. How should we *not* trust in the L-rd? I shall begin with my explanation of (*Isaiah* 26:4): "Trust in the L-rd forever; for in *Kah*, the L-rd, is the Rock of the worlds." I have explained that "forever" comes to teach us that even in *our* time, when we see some *hester panim* ("hiding of the Divine Countenance"), when the ordinance [of the L-rd] is not so manifest as it was before, in the time of the Temple, wherefore there are found some heretics and rebels against the Holy One Blessed be He, still, one should "trust in the L-rd."

To what may this be compared? To [the instance of] a king, who reigned over several hundreds of provinces and ruled over his kingdom with an abundance of strength and splendor, who had the wherewithal to sustain all the places of his rule and all the princes and appointees under him with an abundance of glory and strength. And afterwards there were found some individuals in one city, very few in number, who, in their haughtiness rebelled against the king. And the matter was reported to the king. And while they were yet deliberating the punishment of the rebels, the king went in the morning to promenade in his garden, where he heard a bird of beautiful form and voice singing and bade one of his attendants to take it immediately on that day and put it in his palace so that he could always enjoy it; and he did so. As he was taking it to the king's palace, it began to sing in a sweet beautiful voice — whereupon one of the fools said: "Beautiful bird, how much I would love to see you [always] and hear your beautiful song, and how great my sorrow when I bring to mind the great sorrow that will befall you. For whence will come your food now that we have heard that there are rebels against the king?" And the king's attendant answered: "You fool, with such a king — who reigns over several hundreds of provinces and numberless treasures — will the bird, whose appearance the king enjoys and whose song he rejoices in, have to worry about the few grains it needs for its sustenance because it is found in the province of a little city where one or two rebels have been found?"

So, upon reflection, is it, exactly, in our case, *a fortiori*, many thousandfold: The Holy One Blessed be He, has created this world, the material world, and the higher world. And it is known that in the higher world many worlds are contained, almost without limit. But, as a whole, they are considered three worlds: the world of formation [*olam hayetzirah*], the world of the angels; above it, the world of creation [*olam habriah*]; and, above all, the world of Splendor [*olam ha'atziluth*], where the splendor of the Blessed One's holiness is found. As Chazal have said: "About this, Scripture states (*Isaiah* 43:7): 'All that is called by My Name [*olam ha'atziluth*] and which I have created for My glory [*olam habriah*, where the Throne of Glory is found] — I have formed it [*olam hayetzirah*, where are found the holy creatures (*chayyoth hakodesh*) seen by the prophet Yechezkel, and all the world of the angels] — I have also fashioned it [this world and all of the spheres].'" And it is known that this world and all of its spheres are as nothing compared to *olam hayetzirah*, for *there* [in the *olam hayetzirah*] are found classes of angels without limit. And in each class are found angels almost without number, as it is written in *Daniel* 7:10: "A thousand thousands serve Him. Ten thousand ten thousands stand before Him," about which Chazal have said (*Chagigah* 13b): "All this, in one class, and the classes are infinite, as it is written (*Iyyov* 25:3): 'Is there a number to His troops?'" And we find in *Tanna d'bei Eliyahu* 31 that 496,000 ten thousands of ministering angels sanctify the name of the Holy One Blessed be He always. From the rising of the sun until its setting, they say: "Holy, Holy, etc." And from its setting until its rising: "Blessed is the glory, etc." And it is known that all of the creations, even the highest of the highest, all require the Divine effluence, as it is written (*Nechemiah* 9:6): "You have made the heavens, the heavens of the heavens, and all their hosts, and You vivify all of them." But the effluence of their sustenance is not like ours. For it is rarefied, spiritual sustenance. As it is written (*Psalms* 78:25): "The food of the mighty did a man eat," concerning which Chazal have said: "This is the 'bread' [i.e., the Divine effluence] that the ministering angels 'feed' upon."

And it is known that the withholding of honor from the Holy One Blessed be He because of the fools who have denied Him or rebelled against Him and said: "What profit [is ours] that we have kept His keeping [i.e., His mitzvoth]?" — such dishonor obtains only in this terrestrial, material world, where "eyes" are those of flesh. But in the higher world, *all* the angels crown the Blessed One's name and proclaim His glory — how He vivifies and leads them. As Scripture states (*Nechemiah, Ibid.*): "And the host of the heavens bow down to You." And (I *Kings* 22:14): "I saw the L-rd sitting on His throne, and all the host of heaven standing before Him, on His right and on His left." (*Isaiah* 6:2-3): "Seraphs were standing above Him ... and one called to the other and said: 'Holy, Holy, Holy is the L-rd of hosts [*tzevaoth*],'" for which reason the Holy One Blessed be He is called "Tzevakoth," as we find throughout the Torah. And when we reflect well, we see in truth that this world is not even like a mustard seed compared to all of the higher worlds. (For there are many worlds on high, as Chazal have said (*Avodah Zarah* 3b) that every day the Holy One Blessed be He soars through all His eighteen thousand worlds, and, especially, in respect to what is explained in the holy *Zohar* in many places.) So that their "rebellion," G-d forbid, is considered naught. And in this world, the Holy One Blessed be He found His people Israel, who are especially beloved by Him — so much so, that they are called "sons" unto Him, viz. (*Devarim* 14:1): "You are sons, etc." And their voice is sweet to Him, viz. *Song of Songs* 2:14: "Let Me hear your voice." How, then, can we not be ashamed of ourselves if we do not trust, G-d forbid, in His name, which vivifies all of the worlds? And of all the angels, of whom there are found tens of thousands of them in each class, not one of the celestial angels, from the time the Holy One Blessed be He created all of the worlds, has descended, G-d forbid, to apprise us that he is lacking some of the

Divine effluence. And it is known that there are angels whose size is several thousand parasangs, as Chazal have said in *Chullin* 91b, that the size of Gavriel was two thousand parasangs, this being deduced from what is written in *Daniel* (10:6) when he [Daniel] saw the angel, viz. "And his body was like [the Sea of] Tarshish," (which is two thousand parasangs.) And there are angels who are much taller, as stated in Chazal (*Chagigah* 13b) about Sandalfon that he was five hundred years "walking distance" taller than his fellows [(The walking distance of an average man is ten parasangs a day.)] And this little man [in *this* world], who is not even [the size of] a mustard seed compared to them — how can he constantly fret and worry: "Whence will come my livelihood and whence will come my help!" When we reflect upon this well, we should be astonished much more about ourselves in this than we are astonished at the fool in connection with the bird! There is nothing left for us to do but to gird ourselves with strength and do His will without worrying at all, just as the King's son need not worry that he will be left without a loaf of bread, as it is written (*Devarim* 14:1): "You are sons to the L-rd your G-d."

And all of our words are included in the [aforementioned] verse, in short, viz. (*Isaiah* 26:4): "Trust in the L-rd *forever*" — even when Jerusalem is in ruins and Israel is in exile, wherefore there are many rebels against the Holy One Blessed be He — even so, trust in the L-rd and He will help you. For the ability is still in His hand as before, and He certainly did also not remove His will completely from the world. For if not so, the creation would have been entirely annulled. For it is known that the Holy One Blessed be He vivifies the whole creation, as they have formulated for us in the blessing of *Yetzer* ["*Yotzer hameoroth*"]: "Who renews in His goodness, every day, always, the act of creation." And, as it is written (*Nechemiah* 9:6): "and You *give* life to all of them [the heavens, etc.]." It is not written "You *gave* life" (as stated in the *Zohar*.) And this is the intent of the ending of the verse (*Isaiah*, *Ibid*.): "For in *Kah*, the L-rd, is the Rock of the worlds." As Chazal have stated (*Menachoth* 29b), that the Holy One Blessed be He created *this* world with the letter "heh" from His name; and the world to come, with the letter "*yod*." And "Rock" [*tzur*] signifies strength. That is, His name, "*Kah*" [*yod-heh*] is, up to this day, the strength of the world. (As we find in *Othioth d'R. Akiva*, that the ends of heaven and earth are sealed with His holy name.) And if He removed His will from them [heaven and earth], they would revert to vacuity and void, as before the creation. From all this we can understand the greatness of the trust that one should put in the Holy One Blessed be He.

Chapter XI

In this chapter there will be explained how the Holy One Blessed be He is a haven for a man because of the trait of trust

And know that guarding the tongue from evil includes guarding it from all aspects of speech that are intended to do harm or to antagonize his friend, such as *lashon hara, rechiluth, machloketh,* cursing, "whitening of the face" [in shame], and wronging with words. One who wishes to merit guarding his tongue must strengthen himself greatly in the trait of trust, as explained in the beginning of Chapter X, so that he not come to harm one who [adversely] affects his affairs, and not come to speak demeaningly of him or quarrel with him or curse him or whiten his face or antagonize him, but trust in the L-rd that He will make up in some other way for the loss that the other causes him. And Chazal have said (*Menachoth* 29b): "All who place their trust in the Holy One Blessed be He — He is a haven for them both in this world and in the world to come." "*All* who place their trust" includes even [an instance] where the "needs of Heaven" are not affected; how much more so when one restrains himself from quarreling with his friend who affected his affairs [adversely], for the sake of Heaven, fearing that he would not be able to hold back, when angry, from speaking things that are improper according to the *din*, wherefore he "overlooks his traits and trusts in the L-rd" and beseeches Him to provide for him in some other way, in which instance the Holy One Blessed be He will certainly be a haven for him in this world, too.

To what may this be compared? To [an instance] of a man whose sons are seated around his table. He hands out portions to each one of them, and one of them snares his neighbor's portion. The robbed son goes to his father and says to him: "Father, I asked my brother to return my portion and he refused. I know that you don't want us to fight or to quarrel, so please give me a different portion." When the father hears this, he kisses him and gives him a different, bigger portion, saying: "You, my son, have found favor in my eyes because of your goodly trait. Your brother, the fool, will keep your portion, and at the next meal I will give you a double portion and he will get nothing."

But if the robbed son had not done this but had quarreled with his brother, and they had fought with each other until he had disgorged what he had swallowed from his mouth, even though the truth is with this robbed one, still, this certainly would be painful to his father and he would hate both of them, saying: "You should have asked me for a different portion, and I would have given it to you gladly, and not fight and quarrel with each other before my eyes over trifles like these."

So, precisely, in our case. The Holy One Blessed be He, who apportions food to all of His creations, as it is written (*Psalms* 136:25): "He gives bread to all flesh," is the Father of Israel and they are His sons, as it is written (*Devarim* 14:1): "You are sons, etc." And He desires their peace and not their quarrel, as we find in *Tanna d'bei Eliyahu* 28: "The Holy One Blessed be He said to Israel: 'My beloved sons, do I lack anything that I ask it from you? And what *do* I ask from you? Only that you love each other and honor each other, etc., and that there not be found among you sin and theft, etc.'" Therefore, if one intrudes himself upon another and he [the second] asks him to stop, and he refuses, and he [the second] comes before the Blessed L-rd and entreats Him to give him a different portion so that he need not quarrel with his friend, he certainly will find favor in the eyes of the Blessed L-rd because of his holy trait, as they have said (*Chullin* 89a) on the verse (*Iyyov* 26:7): "He suspends the earth on nothingness [*b'limah*]." "Because of whom does the world exist? Because of him who muzzles [*bolem* (like *b'limah*)] his mouth in a time of quarrel, because of his trust in the L-rd" — and he receives a double portion.

[And his friend will only lose because of this. For it is known that one who robs his friend is only a fool and an evildoer. For his grant will not increase beyond what was decreed for him on Rosh Hashanah, because of his theft. For in exchange for taking the grant that came or that was destined to come to the hand of his friend, there will be taken from him the grant that was decreed for him on Rosh Hashanah. And the end of the matter will be that the money of [i.e., attained by] the wrong will consume also the "surviving remnant," the "kosher" grant that had already been allotted him. As Chazal have said (*Succah* 29b): "Because of four things a man's property goes lost," one of them being because he divests himself of his own yoke and places it on his friend. And so we find in *Derech Eretz Zuta*, Chapter 3: "If you have taken what is not yours, yours will be taken from you." And he will remain only with the bartering of a kosher grant for one that is forbidden. For he will be destined to give *din* and accounting for every [misappropriated] *p'rutah* [small coin]. As Chazal have said (*Bava Kamma* 119a): "If one steals from his friend the worth of a *p'rutah*, it is as if he has taken his soul." And he also constrains the Holy One Blessed be He to return the theft to its owner. As Chazal have said (*Sanhedrin* 8a): "The Holy One Blessed be He says to the wicked: 'It is not enough that you steal, but you also constrain Me to return the theft to its owner." And all of these things are intimated in our holy Torah, in *Parshath Vayetze*, where it is written (*Bereshith* 32:11-12): "And the angel of the L-rd said to me in a dream: 'Yaakov, … lift up your eyes and see all the rams that go up on the sheep — ringstraked, speckled and grizzled" (As Rashi explains there, the angels would bring them from the flock assigned to the sons of Lavan to that assigned to Yaakov. And lest you ask, how am I permitted to take from the grant of Lavan and give it to you? The angel, therefore, concludes: "For I have seen all that Lavan does to you," that he has changed your wage ten times and taken your grant; therefore I am returning it to you.)]

But if he does not act this way, but always quarrels with his friend over this, even if the truth is with him, still, this thing will not bring pleasure to the Blessed

L-rd, like a father whose sons wrangle at his table because of the portions he has given them.

And if he conducts himself with the trait of trust, he will merit seeing the lovingkindness and goodness of the Holy One Blessed be He, as Scripture states (*Psalms* 31:19): "Taste and see that the L-rd is good; happy is the man who takes haven in Him." As to "*Taste* and see," this is to teach us that just as one who tastes a thing in his mouth recognizes the nature of what is tasted, so, one who in truth possesses the trait of trust recognizes the greatness of the goodness of the Holy One Blessed be He.

Chapter XII

In this chapter there will be explained the Torah's saying that remembrance [i.e., mentioning] of the episode of Miriam is of avail in rescuing one from this bitter sin [of lashon hara]

There is a general way to rescue oneself from this bitter sin and its punishment. And this is what we are taught by the Blessed L-rd in *Parshath Tetze* (*Devarim* 24:8): "Guard yourself against the plague-spot of leprosy, to take great care and to do according to all that the Cohanim teach you, etc.", followed by (*Ibid.* 9): "Remember what the L-rd your G-d did to Miriam on the way when you went out of Egypt." And we learned in *Sifrei*: "Remember what the L-rd your G-d did" — I might think, [remember] in your heart, but 'Guard yourself against the plague-spot of leprosy to take care and to do' already speaks of the guarding of the heart (For the *Sifrei* understands "Guard yourself *in* [lit.], the plague-spot of leprosy" as "*from* the plague-spot of leprosy"; that is, that we not divert our heart from guarding against the sin [*lashon hara*], which leads to it). How, then, am I to fulfill 'Remember'? Mention it with your mouth." The will of the Torah, then, is that we remember the greatness of the punishment of this bitter sin both in the heart and by the mouth in order to avail our souls by this. As Ramban wrote in Mitzvah 7 of his *Mitzvoth*: "We have been commanded to remember by the mouth and return it to our heart, what the exalted L-rd did to Miriam when she spoke against her brother, though she was a prophetess, in order to distance ourselves from *lashon hara* and not be one of those of whom it is said (*Psalms* 50:20): "You sit and speak against your brother; against your mother's son you utter slander." For, in truth, the remembrance of the *issur* and the greatness of its punishment lead to guarding against it, just as the remembrance of the positive commandments leads to their fulfillment, as it is written (*Bamidbar* 15:40): "And you shall remember all the mitzvoth of the L-rd and you shall do them."

And let one not wonder that we actually see people who after the saying of "Remember," and, sometimes, even at the time of its saying, speak *lashon hara*. Where, then, is the assurance of the Torah? But, in truth, is it not written of words of Torah (*Devarim* 32:47): "For it is not an empty thing from you" — If it *is* empty, it is from *you* [i.e., because of you] that it is empty. And there has been fulfilled in us, in our many sins, the words of Isaiah the prophet, may peace be upon him (*Isaiah* 29:13): "Because this people has drawn near. With its mouth and its lips it has honored Me, but its heart is far from Me." For we say "Remember" only with our mouths, but we do not remember at the time of doing. And if a man brought it up to his heart to fulfill the remembrance as the Blessed L-rd has commanded us, it would certainly be of great avail in rescuing us from this sin.

We shall explain in detail this verse ["Remember what the L-rd your G-d did to Miriam on the way when you went out of Egypt"], so that every man of intelligence can see that our words are correct. The holy Torah noted for us in the mitzvah of remembering, four things: 1) "Remember *what*, etc."; that is, what was done. 2) To whom did He did it? To Miriam. 3) In what place did He do it? On the way. 4) When did this occur? When you went out of Egypt. Why does the Torah mention these four specifically? What difference does it make to us that the punishment was *tzara'ath* [leprosy] and not any other punishment? Or whether this happened in the house or on the way? Or whether it happened at some other time and not at the exodus from Egypt?

But the truth is that these four details are essential for "remembering" and there is great benefit in reflecting upon them. And for this reason it is written "Remember what He did." That is, one should remember and reflect upon the greatness of the punishment inflicted upon her because of her speaking against Moses, our teacher, may peace be upon him. And that punishment was *tzar'ath*, an extremely severe punishment, which [illness] it is impossible to cure unless the Holy One Blessed be He conduct himself with him [the leper] above the bounds of nature. As we find in *Midrash Rabbah Vayikra* 16 on (*Vayikra* 14:5): "And the Cohein shall command and he shall slaughter the one bird" — Why does he slaughter one and release the other? To teach us that just as it is impossible for the slaughtered bird to return, so is it impossible [within the bounds of nature] for the plague-spots to return [there being no possible cure in the interim]." And [the degree of] his uncleanliness is extremely severe. For he must sit outside the three camps, as opposed to all the other unclean ones. And he also renders unclean all who enter his tent as mentioned in the verse [(an intimation that all those who keep company with the slandered become unclean, as he is)]. And he is also considered like a dead man, as Chazal have said (*Nedarim* 64b). This explains "Remember *what* He did, etc."

And to *whom* did He do it? To Miriam, who was a great *tzadeketh*, in whose merit the well rose [for Israel], and also a prophetess, as it is written (*Shemoth* 15:20): "And Miriam the prophetess, the sister of Aaron took, etc." And she spoke only against her brother, whom she loved as herself, having risked her life to save him from the water. And she did not speak demeaningly of him, but only likened him to the other prophets (as Rambam writes at the end of *Hilchoth Tumath Tzara'ath*). And she did not speak to his face to shame him, and not in public, but only to her holy brother, in private, her intent being only the betterment of society. And he [Moses] was indifferent to all of these things, as it is written (*Bamidbar* 12:3): "And the man, Moses, was extremely humble, etc." And in spite of all this, all of her good deeds did not avail her, and she was punished with *tzara'ath* because of this.

And in which place was this punishment inflicted upon her? "On the way," her merits not sufficing her to suspend her judgment until they came to camp in some place, where it would not have been so conspicuous. But now that she was punished immediately on the way, as they were walking, as it is written (*Bamidbar*

12:15): "And the people did not journey until Miriam had been gathered in," the greatness of her shame was revealed to all, as it is written (*Ibid.* 14): "Will she not be shamed, etc.?"

And *when* did this happen? When they went out of Egypt, in the beginning of the second year of the exodus, when the greatness of its punishment was not yet known. (As to its being written in respect to Moses our teacher, may peace be upon him, [that his hand became leprous (viz. *Shemoth* 4:6)], it [the leprosy] was immediately removed from him, as it is written (*Ibid.* 4:7): "And, behold, it had resumed its fleshy appearance" — as opposed to what happened afterwards, when they had to enter Eretz Yisrael and this was aborted through the *lashon hara* of the spies. For in this instance the sin was far greater, their having witnessed the punishment of Miriam and not having taken *mussar* [reproof] — wherefore the *parshah* of *Shelach* was juxtaposed with that of Miriam (See Rashi there).

And from all this one can deduce upon reflection, *a fortiori*, that today when we are all like "the hyssop of the wall" compared to Miriam, the prophetess, and when the greatness of the punishment for *lashon hara* is known to all from the episode of Miriam and of the spies — if one does not guard himself against *lashon hara*, even if it be of the [attenuated] type of Miriam (How much more so if he speaks the *lashon hara* with the intent of demeaning his friend and shaming him), he certainly will not be clean of the great punishment of *tzara'ath* or other punishments like it, and he will not be granted a suspension of time. And one who hears, and who fulfills "remembrance" always, in this manner, will certainly be saved from this sin.

As a matter of course, it follows from this that a Jew must know the details of the laws of *lashon hara*, in order to know what to guard against. For lacking this, how will remembering the episode of Miriam avail him if the *yetzer* seduces him [into believing] that this speaking [of his] is not in the category of *lashon hara* or that the Torah did not proscribe the speaking of *lashon hara* against a man like this!

Chapter XIII

*In this chapter there will be explained several bad habits
through which a person comes to the* issur *of* lashon hara
— wherefore he should distance himself from them

All this, [the foregoing,] for one who has not yet habituated himself to this sin, for whom it is [relatively] easy to rescue himself from this bitter sin through these counsels. But if he *is* habituated to it and it is extremely difficult for him to separate himself from it, he must treat this illness of his soul as one who has an illness of the body, which the physician wishes to cure — he seeks the source of the illness to know which dressing to apply. So is it with [the illness of] the soul. One must follow it to its source — Whence did he come to this evil trait? — so that he know how to take care not to succumb to its stumbling blocks again. There are several possible causes of this sin. Their sign is *Kol Gihinnom*: *Ka*'as [anger], *l*eitzanuth [levity], *ga*'avah [pride], *y*eush [despair], *h*efker [abandonment], *o*mer *m*utar [regarding as permitted.] We shall now explain them one by one.

One is sometimes habituated to *lashon hara* because of the abundance of his anger. That is, by nature he is an angry man, who is easily angered by anything. And, at the time of his anger, he cannot restrain himself and says whatever it enters his mind to say. A man like this cannot be counseled to guard his tongue, for whenever his anger gets the better of him, he is out of his mind — unless he sees to it to uproot this evil trait from himself.

Whoever has a brain in his head must flee this evil trait as one flees fire. For he knows in his soul clearly that because of this evil trait he will certainly emerge "liable" on the day of judgment, as it is known, that one who has an abundance of sins [over merits] is in the category of *rasha* [wicked]. And Chazal have said (*Nedarim* 22b): "If one is prone to anger, it is known that his sins are more than his merits, as it is written (*Mishlei* 29:22): 'And the man of wrath is abundant in offense [*pesha*].'" As to "*pesha*" being written, which is rebellion, and worse than *meizid* [malice], this is because at the time of anger, Torah and mitzvoth are entirely meaningless to him. As Chazal have said: "If one gets angry, even the Shechinah is meaningless to him." And our Rabbis of blessed memory have said: "If one tears his garments in his anger or breaks his vessels in his anger or scatters his money in his anger, let him be as an idolator in your eyes. Where is this written? (*Psalms* 81:10): 'Let there not be a foreign god within you.' What is the foreign god within a man's body? The *yetzer hara* of anger."

And this is the language of the holy *Zohar* (*Parshath Tetzaveh*) on the verse (*Isaiah* 2:22): "Leave off from the man *asher neshamah be'apo, ki bameh nechshav hu.*" Here, the Holy One Blessed be He has commanded a man and warned him to guard himself against those men who have inclined their ways from the way of good to the way of evil and who have defiled themselves with that uncleanliness of the *sitra achara* ["the other side"]. And how shall a man know how to distinguish between one he should draw near to and one he should separate from? By his anger itself he can know that man and distinguish him [from the other]. If he guards his holy soul when his anger comes upon him, not to uproot it from its place and repose in its stead a foreign god — that is the man who is worthy, etc. And if he does not guard it, but uproots this celestial holiness from its place and reposes in its place the *sitra achara* ["the other side"], then certainly that is the man who rebels against his Master, and it is forbidden to draw near to him or to befriend him. And this is the intent of (*Iyyov* 18:4): '*Toref nafsho be'apo*,' viz. He tears [*toref*] and uproots his soul *because of his anger* [*be'apo*] and reposes within himself a foreign god. And concerning this it is written: 'Leave off from the man *asher neshamah be'apo*" — whose soul [he tears] in his wrath [*be'apo*], whose soul he exchanges in his wrath [for a foreign god], *ki bameh nechshav hu*. With what [*bameh*] is that man to be distinguished? He is to be accounted a worshipper of idolatry [*bamah*, an altar to idolatry (like '*bameh*'), etc.]"

And Chazal have said (*Pesachim* 66b): "Any man that gets angry — even if greatness has been decreed for him [by Heaven], he is brought down [from that greatness]. "and Chazal have said further (*Nedarim* 22a): "Whoever gets angry — all kinds of Gehinnom prevail over him." The intent is that for each [kind of] sin in itself there is, in Gehinnom, a distinct punishment for that sin. And through the trait of anger a man comes to all the different kinds of sin [as is clear] to one who reflects upon the evil of that trait, to the extent that Chazal have said about him that of a certainty his sins are more abundant that his merits. This is the intent of "All kinds of Gehinnom prevail over him." Therefore, a man must remove anger from his heart and he will be saved from Gehinnom and will merit life in the world to come.

And one is sometimes habituated to *lashon hara* because of *leitzanuth*. That is, by habituating his soul to levity and the company of scoffers, whereby, as a matter of course, he is drawn to mock men and to speak demeaningly of them.

Therefore, if one wishes to cleanse his soul, let him reflect upon the greatness of the *issur* of levity in several respects. For aside from the fact that he [the mocker] sins himself, it [levity] being one of the four things because of which one does not receive the Shechinah, as Chazal have said (*Sotah* 42a), he also causes many to sin, bringing them to multiply mockery. And the punishment of causing many to sin is well known, it not being granted one to repent because of this, as Chazal have stated (*Avoth* 5:18). And, aside from all this, involvement in idle talk, even if it contained nothing forbidden, causes one to lose the time that he could have spent in Torah study and the acquisition of the world to come. And he gives the impression that he scorns the words of the L-rd and the reward of the world to come, as stated in *Sanhedrin* 99a on the verse (*Bamidbar* 15:31): "For he has scorned the word of the L-rd" — R. Nehorai said: ['This refers to] one who could have studied Torah but did not do so.'"

And let one learn from what we see of the prisoners who are brought before the judge for cross-examination. They guard their mouths and do not utter even a single word which might incriminate them. And they also take upon themselves all of the blows and revilings in order not to admit the truth, even though they know that in either event they will not live forever, and that even if they do confess, it is very likely that they will not be executed, only a minority of a minority meeting such a fate. In spite of this, they would rather take all of these sufferings upon themselves because of the possibility of a possibility of thereby lengthening their temporal lives. How much, then, should those people restrain themselves [(from speaking what is forbidden)], who sit in the company of mockers a few hours, without anyone beating or forcing them thereto. And if they restrain themselves from speaking what is forbidden, they merit eternal life, as we find in the *Midrash*, that for every moment that a man muzzles his mouth he merits the secreted light, which no angel or creation can conceptualize; and, conversely, they are punished for every article of speech. As the GRA has written in his holy letter, *Alim Litrufah* "(*Koheleth* 6:7): 'All of a man's toil is for his mouth.' Our sages of blessed memory have said (*Chullin* 89a) that all of a man's mitzvoth and Toroth do not suffice [to offset] what he utters with his mouth. 'What is the [proper] profession of a man in this world? Let him make himself mute and clamp his lips like two millstones, etc.' And all *kaf hakela* ["hollow of the sling" punishments] come because of the breath of the mouth of idle talk. For each article of [such] speech, he must be slung from one end of the world to the other. And all this, with *superfluous* speech. But with *forbidden* speech, such as *lashon hara*, *leitzanuth*, oaths, vows, quarrels, and curses, especially in the synagogue and on Sabbaths and festivals — for these one must descend to the nethermost depths of Sheol. And it is impossible to conceptualize the greatness of the suffering and afflictions that one must undergo for one article of [forbidden] speech. And there is not even one such article which is not written down. Angels accompany each man constantly and do not separate from him and write down each and every article of speech (*Koheleth* 10:20): 'For a bird of heaven will carry the voice and the winged one will tell the word.'" And we have learned (*Avodah Zarah* 18b): R. Katina said: "All who engage in levity fall into Gehinnom."

[It seems apt to explain "*fall*" instead of "*will* fall" according to what the GRA has written on *Mishlei* 1:23 in connection with men of levity: "They have a great lust to speak idle talk and levity even though they have no bodily pleasure therefrom. For with every thing that a man does he is given a spirit from on high. And this spirit does not rest until it does other such things, wherefrom he has pleasure — both in an act of mitzvah or in an act of sin. And this is the intent of *Avoth* 4:2: 'A sin begets a sin and a mitzvah begets a mitzvah.' And the greater the sin, the greater the spirit that it begets, and the more it lusts for more sin. Correspondingly, with a great mitzvah. A spirit comes from a very holy place and lusts greatly for that mitzvah and has great pleasure in that mitzvah. And it is known that the greatest mitzvah of all is Torah study, and, conversely, [the greatest sin of all,] idle speech and levity, which is the opposite of Torah. Therefore, there is more pleasure in idle speech and levity than in all other sins, even though there is no worldly [i.e., bodily] pleasure in this. But [the pleasure arises from the fact that] the spirit of uncleanliness is extremely great, like a 'bubbling spring,' as opposed to the [pure spirit of] Torah, which is [also] a 'bubbling spring.'" And it is known that the spirit of uncleanliness created by the sin, *itself* punishes the doer, after his death, in Gehinnom, wherefore Chazal have said "*fall* into Gehinnom" [rather than "*will fall*"]. For at the very utterance of the levity the great spirit of uncleanliness hovers above him. And he actually *falls* [that is, "*dwells*," as in (*Bereshith* 25:18): 'In the presence of all his brothers, he fell' (i.e., dwelt)] in Gehinnom in his lifetime, G-d forbid, (as written in *Nefesh Hachaim*, Gate One, Chapter 12. And their second apothegm is also to be explained along these lines.)]

And in this world, too, afflictions befall a man because of levity, as it is said there (*Avodah Zara* 18b): "R. Elazar said: 'All who scoff, afflictions come upon them, as it is written (*Isaiah* 25:22): "And now, do not scoff, lest your bonds be strengthened."' Rava said to the rabbis: 'I pray you, do not scoff, so that afflictions not come upon you.'" [And see *Sha'arei Teshuvah* of Rabbeinu Yonah, who wrote that it is forbidden to engage in levity, even adventitiously, by chance. In this regard, the sages had to exhort their disciples, many of whom stumbled in this by chance.]

And also his sustenance diminishes [because of levity], as stated there. And also, all the world is punished because of the scoffer. As stated there: "All who scoff bring destruction to the world."

And even if he does not scoff with them, but just sits in their company, this, too, is an absolute *issur*, as it is written (*Psalms* 1:1): "And in the seat of scoffers, he did not sit." And in *Avoth d'R. Nathan* 30:3, we find: "One who attaches himself to sinners, even though he does not do as they do, receives the same punishments as they do." Therefore, one must distance himself from their class and not sit in their place, so as not to learn from them. But he must sit in the seat of learning, and then he will be happy in this [world] and in [the world] to come.

Chapter XIV

In this chapter there will be explained the cause of lashon hara that originates in the habit of pride

There are some [who are habituated to *lashon hara*] because of pride. That is, considering himself wise and a man above men, all being lowly in his eyes, wherefore his heart prompts him to scoff at his friend. His pride also brings him to envy and hate his friend who is honored in the eyes of the people of the city, because it seems to him that his [own] honor is diminished because of this. He will think to himself: "If not for him, I would be regarded among men as an eminent person." And he will probe hidden things in order to have something to say against him, be it true or false, in order to denigrate his name among people and to show his superiority to him and to diminish his eminence and to humiliate and shame him. And sometimes his pride will bring him into all four classes [who do not behold the Divine Presence]: CHASHMAL [*chanefim*-flatterers; *shakranim*-liars; *mesaprei lashon hara*-speakers of *lashon hara*; *leitzanim*-scoffers]. He will speak demeaningly of his friend, so that he be honored and his friend despised; and he will mock him for not being eminent in his eyes. And he will glory in falsehood, in qualities that he does not possess. And because of his pride, he will flatter evildoers always and not reprove them, so that they not hate him and diminish his honor. Therefore, one who wishes to purify his soul from this bitter sin should reflect always upon the great baseness of pride. For how should a person be proud when the beginning of his existence is a putrefying drop and he is destined for a place of dust, maggot and worm, and his remnant consumes his remnant?

He should also reflect upon the severity of this sin, a negative commandment among the 613 mitzvoth, as it is written (*Devarim* 8:14): "And your heart will swell [with pride] and you will forget the L-rd your G-d," as listed in *Semag*. And Chazal have said (*Sotah* 4b): "One who is haughty of heart is like a server of idols." And the more one thinks to magnify his name in the world, the more it is diminished and his body is spurned by the creations. He should also reflect upon the greatness of his punishment in this world and in the world to come, as they said (*Succah* 29b): "Because of four things the possessions of householders go to waste ... and haughtiness of heart." And they also say (*Sotah* 5a): "All who have haughtiness of heart are in the end deflated." And we also learn there: R. Chisda said: "Whoever has haughtiness of heart — the Holy One Blessed be He says of him: 'He and I cannot inhabit the [same] world.'" And R. Elazar said: "If one has haughtiness of heart, his dust does not stir for the resurrection." And this is measure for measure. For instead of reflecting always that he is destined for a pace of dust, maggots, and work, to still his pride, he did not think thus, but only that the heights of the rocks would be his domain forever and that the spacious heights would be his eternal rest, above all of his contemporaries. Therefore, when his body turns to dust, his dust lacks the power to stir from its place, and all will arise and stand on their feet, and he will remain lying low, beneath the soles of the feet of all the people whom he vaunted himself over while yet in life. And he is also abominated because of this in the eyes of the Blessed L-rd, as it is written (*Mishlei* 16:5): "The abomination of the L-rd are all the haughty of heart."

And when one reflects upon his great poverty in Torah and mitzvoth, he will have nothing to be proud about. As Chazal have said (*Nedarim* 41a): "One who lacks *this* [(Torah)], what has he acquired?" And even if he has some Torah and good deeds, when he reflects upon them in truth, he will find that he has not attained even half and even a third [of the potential] of the wisdom that the Holy One Blessed be He has implanted in his soul.

[And the holy books have provided for this a telling parable, which I think I saw in *Zichru Torath Mosheh*: (To what may this be compared?) To the [instance of] a wealthy merchant who sends two men to a distant country to purchase precious jewels for him. To one he gives for this a thousand golden pieces; to the other, only a hundred, and they waste their money on the way on trifles, until the first remains with only two hundred golden pieces, and the second, with forty. One day, they start quarreling with each other, the first saying to the second: "Can you compare yourself to me? You are a pauper, not possessing even a fourth of what I do?" Another man speaks up, and says to him: "Fool and haughty one, with what should you be proud? Don't we know that the money is not yours and that you are only a messenger to bring merchandise to your sender? And, in truth, you are poorer than the second, over whom you have vaunted yourself. For he owes his sender only sixty golden pieces, which he scattered in his folly, whereas you have scattered eight hundred golden pieces on trifles. What will you say to your sender about such a great sum? Will you not then be covered with shame and humiliation, much more than this poor pauper?" So is it, exactly, in our case. For are we not all messengers of the Merciful One from the upper world to this one, each one to amend his soul and to "polish" it according to the amount of wisdom that the Holy One Blessed be He implanted in it?" Therefore, one should not vaunt himself because of the superiority of his wisdom to that of his friend; for is it not *not* his, but only given to him for the ultimate end. Rather, he should think to himself about how many days and how many years he neglected Torah, and that he will have to give an accounting of his activities for every day of the days of his life.

And this is the language of *Sefer Hapardess* of Maharam Cordovero, the Gate of Sanctuaries 1: "A level above the four holy creatures, is Yofiel, the angel of Torah, with all the keys of wisdom in his hand. And when the soul rises on high, the angel, Deah, [knowledge,] questions it on the wisdom it acquired in this world. And to the extent that it toiled in Torah and pursued it, to that extent will it receive its reward. And if it could have occupied itself with Torah but did not, it pushes it below, under that sanctuary, in shame and humiliation. And when the seraphs under the [heavenly] creature lift their wings and beat them one against the other, they burn that soul until it is burnt, etc. And thus is it judged every day, although it have good deeds, because it did not occupy itself with Torah as is should have."

Therefore, the man of heart must reflect upon this all the days of his life, as it is written in *Tanna d'bei Eliyahu*, that a man should see to it to grasp in his hand what he has learned so that shame and humiliation not overcome him on the day of judgment, when they say: "Arise and set forth the Scripture that you have read and the *Mishnah* that you have learned."]

Chapter XV

In this chapter there will be explained the cause of lashon hara that originates in abandonment [to it] and in despair [of its containment] in the eyes of certain men

And sometimes *lashon hara* originates in despair. That is, the *yetzer* entices them [into believing] that it is impossible for a sociable man to abstain from it unless he separates himself completely from the affairs of the world — and this is impossible. And they rationalize by citing (*Bava Bathra* 165a): "And all [are guilty] of *lashon hara*," wherefore they despair completely of observing this.

And, in truth, this is a great error. For if so, why did the Torah command this [(abstention from *lashon hara*)] by a negative commandment? Is it not known that "the Holy One Blessed be He does not deal despotically with His creatures"? The Torah, then, should have included this only in the class of *middoth* [desirable character traits], like other holy *middoth*, that are addressed only to unique individuals, [and not as a mitzvah]. But certainly the Creator of man put it in the power of each and every Jew that if he only puts his eyes and his heart to his ways he can avoid this [(speaking *lashon hara*)]. As we find in *Sifrei, Parshath Ha'azinu* (*Devarim* 32:4): "He is a G-d of trust, without wrong." That is, He did not create men to be *reshaim*, but to be *tzaddikim*. (For if not so, there is wrong, G-d forbid, in the ordinance of the Blessed One in the punishment that He metes out to them afterwards.) And thus is it written (*Koheleth* 7:29): "G-d made man just and they sought out many [devious] accountings."

And thus is it stated in *Tanchuma, Parshath Bereshith* 7: "G-d made man just" — The Holy One Blessed be He, who is called "*tzaddik* and *yashar* [just]," created man in His image only *to be tzaddik* and *yashar*, as *He* is. And if you ask: "Why, then, did He create an *evil* inclination, of which it is written (*Bereshith* 8:21):'For the inclination of a man's heart is evil from his youth'? *You* say: 'It is evil. Who can make it good?' The Holy One Blessed be He answers: "*You* made it evil. You were a child and did not sin. You grew up and you sinned. [That is, a man *draws* it (the *yetzer*) upon himself by his acts and by his affairs. For the Holy One Blessed be He gave man the power to withstand it and to make it his servant in many areas for the ultimate end, as it is written (*Bereshith* 4:17): "And you shall overcome it." And it is written (*Mishlei* 29:21): "One who indulges his servant from youth, etc." The words lend themselves to much elaboration.] And how many things there are in this world tougher than the *yetzer hara* and more bitter than it, yet you 'sweeten' them. There is nothing more bitter than lupine, yet you exert yourself to soak it and to season it in water seven times until it is sweet, and so with mustard and caper. Now, if the bitter things which I have created, you season to your needs, the *yetzer hara*, which is given into your hands, how much more so!"

And so it is in our case. If a man puts his eyes and his heart to his ways, and resolves to heed the openings of his mouth, that he open it only for what is needed and not for evil and deceit, certainly it will not be withheld from him to do so, and "One who comes to purify himself is aided [by Heaven]." And, as Chazal have said: "If a man [truly] wishes to be a *tzaddik*, the Holy One Blessed be He assigns him an angel which leads him in the way of a *tzaddik*. And if he wishes to be a *chasid*, [saintly], He assigns him an angel which leads him in the way of a *chasid*.

As to Chazal's having stated (*Bava Bathra* 165a): "And all [are guilty] of *lashon hara*," do they not conclude immediately: "Can you say "*lashon hara*"? [i.e., this is unthinkable.] Say, rather, the 'dust' [*avak*] of *lashon hara*." And even in respect to *avak* Maharsha writes [(*Chiddushei Alladoth* 164b)]: "The intent of 'All' is only that if a man does not put his eyes and heart to his speech and only leaves it to its nature, then certainly, *all* will stumble into it, as opposed to theft and illicit relations, which even if he leaves them to their nature he can sometimes rescue himself from for some time. This is not so with *lashon hara*, which is linked to his speaking. But Chazal did not intend to say, G-d forbid, that a man cannot rescue himself at all from *avak lashon hara*." (see the Preface, where we have explained this at length)

And sometimes the cause of habituation to his sin originates in *hefker* ["abandonment"], i.e., his seeing that this thing [i.e., guarding one's tongue] has been "abandoned" by many people in our many sins, and [that *lashon hara*] is not considered a sin at all, so that he becomes weakened in his observance.

A remedy for this is to imagine that he and the people of his city came down with a severe malady, G-d forbid, to the point that all the doctors of the city despaired of finding a cure for it, and it was heard that there had come to the city a great doctor, universally renowned and unrivaled for his treatments of this malady, which restored the hopeless patient to his former state, so that no trace of the malady was visible in him. Would he hesitate to send immediately for this doctor to come and see him in his suffering on his sickbed in the hope that he might cure him of his illness? And if one of his loved ones would ask him: "Why are you more zealous than others?" would he not answer: "Fool, where my life is at stake, I would not look at others even if there were a possibility of a possibility [that I might be saved]! How much more so with this doctor, whom we know, ourselves, from the past and who is universally renowned for his awesome cures of all desperate illnesses, would I abandon my life for the sake of these fools who have no mercy on *their* lives?" And if this is so with the [life of the body], how much more so with the soul! For we know that one who guards his tongue from evil will merit living eternal life in the world to come, as it is written (*Psalms* 34:12-13): "Go my sons … Who is the man who desires life, etc." And who is a more trusted physician than our lord, David, may peace be upon him? And, otherwise, [i.e., if we did not follow his regimen], there is no cure for this illness eternally. And in this world, too, in the end there will come upon him because of this [*lashon hara*] great suffering and pain. How much more so should he pay no heed in this to others!

Chapter XVI

*In this chapter there will be explained lashon hara
which originates in nirganuth [complaining]*

And sometimes the cause of habituation to their sin[(*lashon hara*)] originates in the trait of *nirganuth*, as [in the instance of] the man whose nature it is to complain and to fume and to find fault with his friend always, against his acts and against his words, even though his friend is completely whole-hearted with him and seeks no occasion against him. And he [the complainer] judges all things in the scales of liability and not of merit, and converts every unwittingness to malice and suspects his friend of being motivated by hatred, as it is written (*Devarim* 1:27): "And you grumbled in your tents, and you said: 'In the L-rd's hatred of us He took us out, etc.'" One who is afflicted with this evil trait will never escape the sin of *lashon hara*; for whatever his friend does or says, it will seem to him as if only *he* were intended.

One who wishes to rescue himself from this evil trait will reflect upon the evils involved in this degrading trait and will rescue himself thereby:

Through this, he transgresses "And you shall love your friend as yourself."

And he is also very liable to come thereby to the sin of vain hatred, against which there is an explicit negative commandment in the Torah (*Vayikra* 19:17): "Do not hate your brother in your heart." And the second Temple was destroyed because of this, as stated in *Yoma* 9b. And (*Shabbath* 32b): "Because of the sin of vain hatred, there is great contention in a man's house, his wife miscarries, and a man's sons and daughters die young."

And he also transgresses because of this (*Vayikra* 19:15): "*In righteousness* shall you judge your friend," which Chazal interpreted as judging one's friend in the scales of merit. And in *Sefer Charedim* we find that one who judges his friend in the scales of liability is "the chariot of the shell of uncleanliness" called "Chovah" [(liability)].

And also through this [trait of *nirganuth*]) one is very liable to suspect the innocent, concerning which Chazal have said (*Shabbath* 97a): "One who suspects the innocent is stricken in his body." And [he is] also [liable] to come thereby to the *issur* of wronging [one with] words and "whitening" his face and to the sin of contentio4n, whose punishment is very severe (as mentioned in Gate 1:15.)

Therefore, if one wishes to rescue his soul from the pit, he will distance himself from this very evil trait, and all will be well with him.

And there are people whose habituation to their sin originates in their considering it permitted. That is, the *yetzer* deceives them [into thinking] that this thing is not in the category of *lashon hara* or that the Torah did not forbid speaking *lashon hara* against this [kind of] man, [and that] to the contrary, it is a mitzvah to demean him for this and this reason. And, in truth, almost the majority of people stumble into *lashon hara* because of this failing; that is, the lack of [adequate] knowledge. And there is no remedy for this failing but prior study of all the aspects of the *issur* of *lashon hara* according to the *din*, as we explained in *Chafetz Chaim*, Part One, principle 1:4 and 5.

And, in truth, this remedy is almost the most effective of all. And not only with *lashon hara*, but with every mitzvah that he stumbles in [i.e., that he transgresses] many times, until the *yetzer hara* predominates in this area. And there is nothing new in this [remedy], for it is included in the counsel of "remembering," which is mentioned in the section of *tzitzith*, viz. (*Numbers* 15:39): "And you shall see it [(the purple strand)] and you shall remember all the mitzvoth of the L-rd, and you shall do them," as Rashi explains there. For remembering leads to doing. That is, he should study the *din* that he stumbles in with much concentration on all the details of that *din*, and he should also review it many times. If he does so, the *din* will become fixed in his memory and the power of the *yetzer* in this sin will also be removed from him, as we find in *Midrash Rabbah, Parshath Nasso*: "If you toil much in their [the rabbis'] words, the Holy One Blessed be He will remove the *yetzer hara* from you."

A piece of good advice for guarding the tongue: Even if he has already become habituated to it [(i.e., to a certain kind of *lashon hara*)], G-d forbid, and his *yetzer* has overcome him in this area, so that he himself does not "feel" the *lashon hara* that issues from his mouth, still he should not despair, but he should rest assured that by reviewing the *din* several times, a transformation will take place and the thing [i.e., the *din*] will become fixed in his nature, and, in the end he will "feel" [i.e., he will be sensitive to] every [article of] speech that leaves his mouth; and even if it be only the "dust" of *lashon hara*, he will feel it with his tongue at that time. For the Holy One Blessed be He has implanted in a man the faculty of "feeling" [i.e., sensitivity]. And He has done it in such a way that he feels it more when the "thing" comes in contact with his tongue. (This is similar to what Chazal have said (*Chullin* 17b): "The master examined it [(the slaughtering knife for *kashruth*)] with his mouth.,") And this faculty is of great avail in the learning of Torah, so that when one brings the thing [(what he is learning)] from his mouth to his tongue, its correctness is "tested." As Chazal have said (*Eruvin* 54a) on *Mishlei* 4:22: "For they [(words of Torah)] are life *lemotzeihem*"... to those who *utter* them ['*lemotzi'eihem*'], with their mouths." And the same [phenomenon] holds true for all aspects of speech; but it is only because of his great habituation to superfluous speech and [his tendency] to pay no heed to it that this faculty of his has become greatly weakened. But if he follows our advice (And he certainly will be attentive to what he says from that time on), this faculty of feeling will gradually strengthen itself in him, little by little until it reaches ifs full development.

And, in general, a man should know that so long as it has not become clear to him, according to the *din* that something is *not* in the category of *lashon hara* or *rechiluth* or *machloketh*, he should take heed not to say it, even if the *yetzer* entices him and inclines him to say that there is a mitzvah in this thing and that he will merit the world to come because of it — even so, he should not heed it. For in this way [i.e., by not heeding it], he will certainly be rescued in any event from the *din* [i.e., the punishment] of Heaven. For even if, in truth, the *din* [the law] were *not* with him [(and he *should* have demeaned the other)] and they ask him on high: "Why did you not demean him in this and this matter? Would it not have been a mitzvah to do so?", he could answer: "To me, it was a matter of doubt, so that I had to govern myself by the rule of "sit and do not do" [i.e., "When in doubt, don't."] As opposed to his demeaning the other or entering into *machloketh* with him in an instance of doubt, the yetzer enticing him [into believing] that there is a mitzvah in doing so. What will he do afterwards if it becomes clear to him that he had transgressed the *issur* of *lashon hara* or *machloketh* and had only been deceived by the *yetzer*? How will he answer on high for this? He will not be able to answer that he had spoken thus because of doubt. For, because of doubt, he should not have spoken at all!

[And we can say that this is the intent of (*Mishlei* 21:33): "One who guards his mouth and his tongue guards his soul from troubles." For, on the surface, does he not merit the world to come for this, as it is written (*Psalms* 24:13): "Who is the man who wants life, etc.," the intent being *eternal* life, as the exegetes have written? But, according to what we have said, the verse can be understood as saying that one who guards himself [against speaking] constantly, even when there is a possibility that in his speaking [demeaningly] he might be doing a mitzvah — still, since he guards himself [from speaking demeaningly] because it is not perfectly clear to him [that he may do so], for that reason the verse affirms that the *din* is with him. For, in any event, he certainly rescues himself thereby [(by his remaining silent)] from the 'troubles' of Gehinnom. As opposed to his doing the reverse, where it might be that instead of entering Gan Eden for this, as he hopes, he might enter Gehinnom thereby if it becomes clear that the *din* (in speaking disparagingly of the other) is not with him.]

Until this point we have explained the sign of "*Kol Gehinnom*," the evil traits through which a man is liable to root himself in the trait of *lashon hara* (See beginning of Chapter XIII). Therefore, the man who wishes to heal himself of this sure illness, to which he has become habituated over a long period of time must first examine himself [to determine] which evil trait caused this, and he must root it out of himself. And then he must begin to heal his soul, little by little, habituating himself to the good traits, which we have spoken of in the previous chapters.

Chapter XVII

In this chapter it will be explained that one who punishes his neighbor [even according to the din*] will not go free if he, too, is not free of that sin*

A man should also reflect and know that at the time that he speaks *lashon hara* against his friend, the angels on high also mention *his* sins, as Rokeach wrote in his book, and so we find also in *Aggadath Mishlei*.

He must also etch into his consciousness what is written in *Semak* (283, in the name of Riva), viz. :Even those whom it is a mitzvah to kill, such as one pursuing a male [for sodomy] or a betrothed maiden, or his neighbor, to kill him, the one who kills them must afterwards be [especially] careful of their "dust" [i.e., a similar sin]. For if, G-d forbid, their killer stumbles into a similar sin, the one killed will be accounted to him as innocent blood. The proof is from Yehu, who was punished for the blood of the house of Achav, even though the prophet commanded him in the name of the L-rd to kill them, because he himself had stumbled in the sin of the house of Achav."

And even though he had rendered a great favor to Israel, for Achav had served the Ba'al and the calves, and Yehu had abolished Ba'al worship from Israel and made [their sites] sewers, as Scripture states (II *Kings* 10:27), and he had also found favor in the eyes of the L-rd for having killed Achav (for which the kingdom was given him for four generations as mentioned in Scripture), and Yehu's later idol worship was unwitting, (as written in *Sanhedrin* 102a): "Yehu was a great *tzaddik* ... but he saw the signature of Achiya Hashiloni and erred" — in spite of all this, since there remained in him part of the sin of Achav, he was punished, as is written in the beginning of *Hoshea* (1:4): "And I will remember the blood of Yizre'el (i.e., the blood of the house of Achav, whom he had killed in Yizre'el) on the house of Yehu."

And from the words of *Semak* we learn that the same applies in all similar instances between man and his neighbor. If one punishes his friend with any manner of punishment — by striking [him] or "whitening" his face or by speaking *lashon hara* against him — even if in this, the *din* were in accordance with the shamer or the speaker — still, he must "know in his soul" that if he himself had transgressed in this way in the past or if he will transgress in this way in the future, then the suffering of this man whose face he whitened or against whom he spoke *lashon hara* will be reckoned "innocent blood," and he will be punished for it, just as if he had acted thus against a man complete in the Torah of the L-rd and His mitzvoth.

And because of this the speaker of *lashon hara* against his friend or one who causes him all kinds of suffering will be in [constant] trepidation. For if he reflects well he will find that not long past he himself had transgressed in exactly the same matter or in similar matters. And even if he examined himself closely and did not find [this to be so], still, he should know that after speaking [as he did], if he himself transgressed in this way, he would immediately be punished above for this sin retroactively, for having spoken in this manner against his friend.

And thus is it stated (*Yevamoth* 105b): "R. Chiyya and R. Shimon ben Rebbi were sitting [in the house of study] ... R. Yishmael ben R. Yossi came to them ... In the interim, Rebbi came to the academy [and all had to sit in their places]. These (R. Chiyya and R. Shimon), who were agile, [quickly] sat in their places; R. Yishmael ben R. Yossi, being heavy, had to step [over those who were seated to get to his place], whereupon Avdan called out: 'Who is this that steps over the heads of the holy people!' R. Yishmael: 'I, Yishmael ben R. Yossi, who has come to learn Torah from the mouth of Rebbi!' Avdan: 'Are you worthy of learning Torah from the mouth of Rebbi!' R. Yishmael: 'And was Moses worthy of learning Torah from the Almighty?' Avdan: 'Are you Moses!' R. Yishmael: 'Is your teacher [(Rebbi)] G-d!' ...In the interim, a *yevamah* [a woman slated for levirate marriage] came before Rebbi for *chalitzah* [release from levirate marriage], whereupon he said to Avdan: 'Go and have her examined' [for pubertal signs (to see if she is fit for *chalitzah*)]. At this, R. Yishmael b. Yossi said: [This is not necessary.] 'Thus did father say: "The *man*" is stated by Scripture in the section [on *chalitzah* (*Devarim* 25:7)], but as far as the *woman* is concerned, whether she be grown or a minor [the *chalitzah* is valid].'" Hereupon, Rebbi called Avdan back, saying: 'It is not necessary [to examine her]; the elder [R. Yossi] has already ruled.' As Avdan stepped [over those who were seated to return to his place], R. Yishmael ben R. Yossi said to him: 'Let him of whom the holy people have need step over the heads of the holy people; but how should he of whom the holy people have no need step over the heads of the holy people!' — whereupon Rebbi said to Avdan: 'Remain in your place.' It was taught: 'At that time, Avdan was smitten with leprosy [(the punishment for *lashon hara*)], his two sons drowned, and his two daughters-in-law [(who had been betrothed when minors)] had their marriage annulled."

Now why did the L-rd so order things that "in the interim, a *yevamah* came, etc."? But it is as we have said. For, in the beginning, Avdan demeaned R. Yishmael ben R. Yossi for having stepped over the heads of the holy people. And even though the *din* was not with him [Avdan] in his saying: 'Are you worthy, etc.', for this is unquestionably *ona'ath devarim* ["wronging with words"], still, there was no room here for being so severe with Avdan as to smite him with leprosy if his primary motivation was zealousness for the truth, even though he erred in his manner of speaking. For this reason he was immediately "tested" from "above," so that in the interim the *yevamah* came and Avdan had to leave. And in the midst of this, R. Yishmael ben R. Yossi ruled as he did..." At that time, Avdan was smitten with leprosy, etc." That is, since he, too, was not careful in this [(not to step, etc.)], he was, therefore, punished retroactively for having demeaned R. Yishmael ben R. Yossi. He was also shown that not in accordance with the *din* did he say to R. Yishmael: "Are you worthy of learning Torah from Rebbi?", ruling [wrongly] in his words according to Rebbi's original opinion, that for *chalitzah* a woman [(as opposed to a minor)] is required, wherefore he was punished with leprosy. And also, his two sons drowned, it being known that the punishment of drowning and that of *askara* [diphtheria] are [essentially] the same punishment (viz. *Kethuvoth* 30b); and it is known that the death penalty for *lashon hara* is *askara*, as stated in *Shabbath* 33a.

In sum, let a man see to it to habituate himself in his traits to be of "the good ones" and not of "the wicked ones." And it is the trait of "a good one" to help his friend with all his power and to "cover up" for *his* faults as for his own. And if he sees that another harbors anger against his friend, he will remove it from him with defenses and excuses. And this is wisdom and strength in truth. And "the wicked one" does exactly the opposite. He does evil to his friend and rejoices in his downfall, and he reveals his unwitting faults in public and makes them malicious ones. And he stirs up strife among men, inciting one against the other and vaunting himself in this as having exhibited wisdom and strength thereby. And, in truth, this is not so. As we find in *Midrash Shocher Tov* 52, which speaks of Doeg, who spoke *lashon hara* against David and Achimelech before Saul: "(*Psalms* 52:3): 'Why do you [Doeg] pride yourself in evil, O mighty one!' David said to him: 'Is this strength? Seeing one's friend at the edge of a pit and pushing him into it? Or seeing him on top of a roof and pushing him off it? But who is the mighty one? One who saw his friend about to fall and pulls him by the hand to save him from falling. Or one who sees his friend fallen in the pit and pulls him out of it. And you saw Saul raging at me and you 'passed water on my limbs'? Is this what a man does?'"

And see the greatness of the hatred borne against the wicked. For aside from their being driven away from the table of the King of kings, the Holy One Blessed be He, as we find in *Shabbath* 149b: "You are righteous, O L-rd; evil will not dwell in Your dwelling place" — even at a time when the prophets and the saintly ones implore mercy for Israel, they have no desire at all to implore mercy for the wicked. To the contrary, they intimate in their prayer that they ask nothing at all for the wicked, as it is written (*Psalms* 125:14): "Do good, O L-rd, for the *good ones* and for the upright in their hearts."

And how careful must a man be not to rejoice in the falling of his friend and in his shame, as it is written (*Mishlei* 24:17-18): "When your foe falls, do not rejoice, and when he stumbles, let your heart not be glad. Lest the L-rd see, and it be evil in His eyes, etc." And this sin greatly arouses the power of *din* against a man, and it has the power to actually destroy, as does the sin of *avodah zarah*. For thus do we find in the words of Chazal (*Eichah Rabbah, Pethichta*), that at the time of the destruction of the Temple, when our father Abraham went into the Temple and the Holy One Blessed be He asked him: "What does My loved one in My house?" he asked: "Why have my sons been exiled among the peoples of the world?" And the Holy One Blessed be He answered: "Because they serve idols and rejoice in each other's downfall," the Holy One Blessed be He equating this [second] sin with [that of] idolatry! Let a man, then, always reflect within himself that in view of his sins and his faults, he, too, deserves to be demeaned and shamed — if not for the L-rd's pitying him in the merit of his fathers.

The Gate of Torah

Chapter I

In the chapter there will be explained that Torah study is a *tikkun* [amendment] of the taint of *lashon hara*, and the greatness of the obligation of a man to Torah

There is yet another general *tikkun* distinctive for the trait of *lashon hara*, and that is Torah study, as stated in *Arachin* 15b: "R. Chamma b. R. Chanina said: 'What is the amendment for the speakers of *lashon hara*? If he is a Torah scholar, let him occupy himself with Torah, as it is written (*Proverbs* 15:4): 'The healer of the tongue is the tree of life,' and the tree of life is none other than Torah, as it is written (*Ibid.* 3:18): 'It [Torah] is a tree of life to those who hold fast to it.'" As to its being called "a tree of life" — "Death and life are in the hand of the tongue" (*Ibid.* 18:21). If so, one who speaks *lashon hara* acquires for himself eternal death, wherefore Scripture counseled one who wished to heal his tongue to eat from the tree of life, which is Torah, "and he shall eat [thereof] and live forever."

But he must spur his soul in any event thenceforward to guard himself against this sin, like the man who, by mistake, put poison into his mouth and took antidotes for it. It is only if he does not ingest this poison anymore that the antidote will avail him for the past.

Torah study is also a preventative against one's coming to (speak) *lashon hara*, as they said there (*Arachin* 15b): "What is the preventative against *lashon hara*? If he is a Torah scholar, let him occupy himself with Torah." The reason is obvious, as we find in *Sanhedrin* 99b: "All men are created for toil, viz. (*Iyyov* 5:7): 'For man is born for toil.' I would not know whether for toil of the lips or toil of labor — if it were not written: (*Mishlei* 16:22): 'For he saddles his mouth with it,' which indicates that he was born for toil of the lips. And I still would not know whether for the [lip] toil of Torah or the toil of converse — if it were not written (*Joshua* 1:8): 'Let the book of this Torah not depart from your mouth,' which indicates that he was created for the toil of Torah." The idea is that the nature was given man, when speech was given to him, that the tools of speech do what is theirs without becoming fatigued, unlike the other organs, which man must spur himself to put into operation. Not so, the faculty of speech. And this is the intent of "the toil of the lips." But a man must reflect that this power was given him only to merit Torah. Therefore, it is stated that the preventative of speaking *lashon hara* is only occupying oneself with Torah, for lacking this, he will certainly stumble into forbidden speech. For it is man's nature that his tools of speech not be inoperative (unless he is able to overcome his *yetzer* and make himself "mute," as they say in *Chullin* 89a).

We can understand, according to this, how much we must strengthen ourselves in Torah study, both because of the obligation in itself, as we shall explain below, please G-d, and both because we are rescued thereby from all of the aspects of forbidden speech. How much more so in our time, when the pillar of Torah has fallen — how much more so must one strengthen himself in this, as we find in *Yerushalmi* (*Perek Haroeh*): "R. Shimon ben Yochai says: 'If you see a generation who have become weakened in Torah, arise and strengthen it, and you will receive the reward of all, etc.'" We shall explain a little of the greatness of a man's obligation in Torah and the greatness of his reward in this world and the next.

It is known that Torah study in itself (aside from learning leading to doing) is a positive commandment of the Torah, as it is written (*Devarim* 5:1): "And you shall study them (the mitzvoth) and you shall take care to do them."

And Chazal have said (*Peah* 1:1): "These are the things that a person eats… and Torah study over and against all." And we find in *Yerushalmi* (*Peah*, Chapter 1) that all of the mitzvoth are not comparable to one word of Torah.

And it is written (*Mishlei* 4:2): "For a good taking have I given you; My Torah shall you not forsake." The intent of "good," "My Torah," is as follows: It is known that something that is so significant to a poor man that he calls it "good" may not be significant to one who is not poor; and that something which is significant to *him* may not be significant to one who is very wealthy; and that something which is significant to *him*, may not be significant to a king; and that something which is significant to *him*, (like the conquering of a country) may not be significant to an angel [(It is known that the size of some angels is several thousand parasangs, as stated in *Chullin* 91b)]. Therefore, the verse comes to say: "For a good taking, etc." That is, see and reflect upon the greatness of its [Torah's] good, to the point that it is called "good" by *Me*, who have created all of the worlds, all of which are insignificant to Me — notwithstanding which I have called Torah "good." And it is the secreted treasure with which the Holy One Blessed be He disports Himself at all times, as it is written (*Mishlei* 8:30): "and I [Torah] was His plaything every day." And it is "*My* Torah." Therefore, "do not forsake it."

For, in truth, there is no end to the holiness of the Torah. As Chazal have said, there are six hundred thousand interpretations of every verse of Torah. And in *Midrash Othioth d'R. Akiva* we find that the light of the holy names of the Holy One Blessed be He on high illumines twenty-one thousand ten thousands of parasangs, according to the Name "*E-he-yeh*" [twenty-one in *gematria* (numerical equivalent)]. And Chazal have said in *Yalkut Tehillim*: "R. Elazar said: 'The sections of the Torah were not stated in sequence. For if they were, anyone who read it could resurrect the dead and perform wonders. Therefore, the sequence of the verses remained hidden from them; but it is manifest to the Holy One Blessed be He, as it is written (*Isaiah* 44:7): "'And who, as I, shall read, etc.?'"

And in *Sifrei, Parshath Ekev* we find (*Mishlei* 5:16): "'Then your springs [of Torah] will spread outwards': Words of Torah are compared to water. Just as water lives forever, so, words of Torah live forever, as it is written (*Ibid.* 4:2): 'For they are life to him who finds them, and to all of his flesh, healing.' And just as water raises the unclean one from his uncleanliness, so, words of Torah raise one from uncleanliness to purity, as it is written (*Psalms* 19:10): 'The fear of the L-rd is pure.' [And, just as water purifies a man, though the uncleanliness has spread through all of his limbs, so, Torah purifies a man from the uncleanliness of his sins, even if it has spread throughout him, from the soul of his foot until his head. And just as a man is not purified until the water rises over all of his limbs, and there be nothing intervening between his limbs and the water, so, he must subject all of his body and his limbs, in truth, to Torah, with nothing intervening, as it is written (*Devarim* 6:6): 'And these words shall be … upon your heart']. And just as water restores a man's soul, so do words of Torah restore a man's soul from the way of evil to the way of good, as it is written (*Psalms* 19:8): 'The Torah of the L-rd is complete, restoring the soul,.' And just as water is free for the world, so is Torah free for the world, as it is written (*Isaiah* 55:1): "Ho! all who are thirsty, go to the water [of Torah]." Lest you say: 'Just as water has no valuation, so, Torah has no valuation; it is, therefore, written [to negate this] (*Mishlei* 3:15): 'It is more precious than pearls and all of your desires cannot be compared to it.'"

And man was created only for Torah. For thus have Chazal expounded (*Sanhedrin* 99b): "All men were created for toil, viz. (*Iyyov* 5;7): 'For man is born for toil.' I would not know whether for toil of the lips or toil of labor — if it were not written (*Mishlei* 16:26): 'For he saddles his mouth with it,' which indicates that he was born for toil of the lips. And I still would not know whether for the [lip] toil of Torah or the toil of converse — if it were not written (*Joshua* 1:8): 'Let the book of this Torah not depart from your mouth,' which indicates that he was created for the toil of Torah." And it [Torah] is the mainstay of the life of the soul, as we find in *Sifrei, Parshath Ekev*." R. Shimon says (*Devarim* 4:9): 'Only take heed to yourself and heed your soul exceedingly.' This may be compared to [the instance of] a king who captures a bird and hands it to his servant, saying to him: 'Take care of this bird for my son. If you lose it, do not think that you have lost a one-*issar* (a small-coin) bird, but that you have lost your soul.' And thus is it written (*Devarim* 32:47): 'For it [Torah] is not an empty thing for you [Not in vain do you toil in it; great reward inheres in it]; for it is your life.'"

And the world endures only through Torah, as it is written (*Jeremiah* 33:25): "If not for My covenant, day and night, the statutes of heaven and earth I would not have ordained." And this is the language of the holy *Zohar, Parshath Bereshith* 47a: "Everyone who occupies himself with Torah every day will merit having a share in the world to come, and it will be accounted to him as if he had built worlds. For it was through Torah that the world was built and fashioned, as it is written (*Mishlei* 3:19): 'The L-rd, through wisdom [Torah] founded the earth, etc.' And everyone who occupies himself with it shapes the worlds and sustains them. And come and see: It was with a spirit that the Holy One Blessed be He made the world, and it is with a spirit that it endures, the spirit of those who toil in Torah."

And this is the language of *Parshath Tzav*: " R. Elazar opened and said: (*Isaiah* 51:16): 'And I have placed My words in your mouth, and with the shadow of My hand have I covered you, etc.' From here we learn that if a man occupies himself with words of Torah and his lips murmur Torah, the Holy One Blessed be He hovers over him and the Shechinah spreads its wings over him. What is more, he causes the world to endure and the Holy One Blessed be He rejoices with him as if the heavens and the earth were planted on that day."

And it is written in *Chovath Halevavoth* that it befits a man to reflect that if a book reached him [written by] a king of flesh and blood and he was in doubt as to its meaning because of the nature of the writing or its subtlety, or the profundity of the language, he would grieve greatly until he could understand it and he would set all of his heart and mind upon his understanding it. And if this is the case with a book of flesh and blood, who today is here and tomorrow in the grave, how much more so with the King of kings, the Holy One Blessed be He, who is his life and his salvation, as it is written (*Devorim* 30:20): "For He is your life and the length of your days."

And many men stumble in this sin, expending all of their energy to understand the statutes of a king of flesh and blood, and neglecting to understand the statute of the King of kings, the Holy One Blessed be He. This is similar to what is written (*Daniel* 5:23): "And the gods of silver, and gold, of copper, iron, wood, and stone, which neither see, nor hear, nor know, you have praised; but the G-d in whose hand your soul is and who *His* are all your ways, you have not glorified."

And Chazal have said (*Eicha Rabbah, Pethichta*): "The Holy One Blessed be He 'overlooked' the sin of idolatry, illicit relations, and blood-spilling, but He did not overlook the sin of *bitul* Torah [neglect of Torah study], as it is written (*Jeremiah* 9:11-12): 'Why was the land destroyed?' And the L-rd said: 'Because they forsook My Torah which I set before them.'" And because there are some people who have become indifferent to the sin of *bitul* Torah and who spend all their time on vanity, and who do not consider this a sin at all, and, "transgression leading to transgression," do not support their sons in Torah study, and through this the "eternal mountains" have fallen, I have thought fit to adduce some of the apothegms of Chazal dealing with the greatness of the reward for Torah study both in this world and the next, and, conversely, the greatness of the punishment [for *bitul* Torah], G-d forbid, in the hope that through this they will awaken somewhat to hold onto the Torah of the L-rd.

Chapter II

In this chapter there will be explained the reward for Torah study

Chazal have said (*Sanhedrin* 99b): "All who study Torah for its own sake make peace in the celestial and terrestrial retinues, viz. (*Isaiah* 27:5): 'Or if he but take hold of My stronghold [Torah], he shall make peace for Me [1]; he shall make peace for Me [2].' Rav said: 'It is as if he would build the celestial palace and the terrestrial palace, viz. (*Ibid.* 51:16): "And I have placed My words in your mouth … to plant the heavens and to lay the foundations of the earth."'"

[And according to the words of Rav, the words of the verse (*Psalms* 62:13) are well explained, viz.: "And Yours, O L-rd, is kindness; for You pay a man according to his works." For many ask: "What kindness is there in the L-rd's bestowing good for the fulfillment of his mitzvoth?" But according to this [interpretation of Rav], it is well understood. For it is known that if one would, with his wisdom, invent a machine with which the builders could build a city in one day, and news of this came to the king, he [the inventor] would certainly find favor in his eyes, and he would give him a great gift according to "the king's hand," but it is inconceivable that he would give him those cities that his servants built with this machine and call them by his name as if he himself had built them. But in this case, through the words of Torah that one learns in this world, the creation of heaven and earth is fulfilled, as we wrote above in Chapter I. Now, in truth, did the man himself build these palaces that they should be called by his name? Is it not the Holy One Blessed be He through His power and His strength, who, in His goodness, renews the creation every day and who Himself gives power to the words of Torah that he learned to be the foundation of this thing? And even so, the Holy One Blessed be He accounts it to him as if he himself had built the celestial and terrestrial palaces. And this is Rav's intent in "as if he himself had planted the heavens and the earth."

And it is also possible to interpret the seemingly superfluous "You" [(in the Hebrew)] in the verse ["For *You* pay a man according to his works,"] in the manner of the GRA on (*Mishlei* 10:24): "The fear of the wicked one, *it* will come upon him, and the desire of the righteous, *He* will give." For the transgression that a man commits, *it* itself will punish him, wherefore the punishment has a limit, just as the transgression itself has a limit. But, for the mitzvah, the Holy One Blessed be He pays him, by Himself and in His honor, wherefore the reward is eternal, without limit, just as the Holy One Blessed be He Himself is without limit. And this is the intent of the verse: "And Yours, O L-rd is kindness; for *You* pay a man according to his works." That is, You Yourself pay a man reward for the fulfillment of his mitzvoth, so that there not be a limit to his reward.

(*Sanhedrin* 99b): "R. Yochanan said: 'He [one who learns Torah] also secures protection for the entire world, viz. (*Isaiah* 51:16): "and with the shadow of My hand have I covered you" [and, consequently, the entire world].'" Levi said: 'He also brings the redemption nearer, viz. (*Ibid.*): "and to say to Zion: 'You are my people.'""'

[Torah study is] greater than all the sacrifices, for thus have Chazal expounded (*Rosh Hashanah* 18a): "(I *Samuel* 3:14): 'The iniquity of Eli's house will not be purged with sacrifice or offering forever.' Rava said: 'It cannot be purged with sacrifice or offering, but it can be purged with words of Torah.'" And thus does Scripture state (*Vayikra* 7:37): "This is the *Torah* for burnt-offering, meal-offering, and sin-offering, etc." And they have said (*Menachoth* 110a): "If one occupies himself with Torah, it is as if he sacrificed a burnt-offering, as if he sacrificed a meal-offering, as if he sacrificed a sin-offering, as if he sacrificed peace-offerings."

And this is the language of the holy *Zohar*, *Parshath Shelach* 159a: "If one occupies himself with Torah, it is as if he sacrificed all the offerings in the world before the Holy One Blessed be He. What is more, the Holy One Blessed be He grants him atonement for all of his sins and they set up for him many 'chairs' for the world to come."

And Torah is greater than the saving of lives, as stated by Chazal (*Megillah* 16b).

And through it [Torah study] one merits the world to come, as Chazal have said (*Peah* 1:1): "These are the things ... and Torah study over and against all." And Chazal have said (*Bava Metzia* 85b): "That which is written (*Iyyov* 3:19): 'The small and the great are there [in the next world], and the servant free of his master.' Do we not know that the small and the great are there? — [The intent is] rather, that all who make themselves small for Torah in this world are made great in the world to come, and all who make themselves servants for Torah in this world are made free men in the world to come." And in *Avoth* 6:3: "There is no honor but Torah, as it is written (*Mishlei* 3:35): 'The wise will inherit honor.' Do not desire more honor than your learning and do not lust for the table of kings. For your table [in the world to come] is greater than their table in this world, and your crown is greater than their crown, etc."

And in *Sanhedrin* 100a: "All who blacken their faces in Torah study in this world, the Holy One Blessed be He brightens them in the world to come, as it is written (*Song of Songs* 5:15): 'His countenance is as Levanon, choice as the cedars.'" And, similarly, in *Midrash Rabbah*: "R. Yehudah interpreted the verse as relating to Torah scholars. One verse states (*Ibid.* 11) 'black as a raven,' and another (*Nachum* 2:5): 'Their appearance is like flames, they flash like lightning.'

These are the Torah scholars, who look ungainly and black in this world but whose appearance is flamelike in the next world." R. Tanchum ben Chanilai said: 'All who starve themselves for words of Torah in this world, the Holy One Blessed be He sates them in the world to come, as it is written (*Psalms* 36:9): 'They will be sated with the fatness of Your house.'"

And we find in *Midrash Tehillim* 49:2: "'To the chief musician, to the sons of Korach, a psalm.' This is as Scripture says (*Koheleth* 11:7): 'And sweet is the light, and good for the eyes.' How sweet is the light of the world to come. Happy is the man who has the good deeds to see that light, as it is written (*Judges* 5:31): 'And His lovers [will be] as the rising of the sun in his might.'"

R. Abba said: "How sweet are those things which are compared to light. As it is written (*Mishlei* 6:23): 'For a mitzvah is a lamp, and Torah, light, etc.' Happy is the man who sees the Torah white as snow, for there is no end to its reward. When the Holy One Blessed be He will come to pay Israel the reward of the toilers in Torah and will bestow upon them of the secreted light in its merit — at that time they will say to the peoples of the world: 'We merited [this] because we occupied ourselves with Torah. And you used to say to us: "You are wearying yourselves for nothing." — See its reward!' As it is written (*Psalms* 49:2): 'Hear this [*zoth*] all you people.' And '*zoth*' is the Torah.' (*Psalms*, *Ibid.*): 'Hear, all you dwellers of the earth [*chaled*]' — these are the men who raise rust [*chaludah*] in Gehinnom. And who are they? (*Ibid.* 3): 'Both the sons of "Adam" and the sons of "Ish."' "Adam" — this is Abraham, viz. (*Joshua* 14:15): 'the great man [Adam] among the giants.' Also *the sons* of Adam' — Yishmael and the sons of Ketura. 'Also *the sons* of Ish' — the sons of Noach, who was called *ish tzaddik* (*Bereshith* 6:9). Another interpretation: These are the idolators, who descend to Gehinnom. (*Ibid.*): "rich and poor together" — rich in Torah and poor in Torah. "rich" — Doeg and Achitophel. Even though they were heads of *sanhedrin*, they descended to Gehinnom. "and poor in Torah" — one who can learn but does not learn. Therefore, the sons of Korach said (*Ibid.* 4): 'My mouth shall speak wisdom' — the wisdom of Torah; 'and my heart shall meditate understanding' — the understanding of Torah. (*Ibid.* 5) 'I will incline my ear to a parable' — the parable of Torah."

And this is the language of the holy *Zohar, Parshath Vayeshev* "(*Psalms* 19:8): 'The Torah of the L-rd is whole; it restores the soul': How much should men occupy themselves with Torah! For all who do so will have life in this world and in the world to come, and will merit both worlds. And even one who occupies himself with Torah and does not do so for its own sake [*lishmah*], as is proper, still merits goodly reward in this world and is not judged in the world to come … When his soul is about to depart to return to its place, it [his Torah] goes before that soul and many gates are broken before the Torah until it enters its place and stands [guard] over the man until he arises for the resurrection, and it [his Torah] speaks in his defense."

And this is its [the Zohar's] language in *Parshath Beshalach* 46a: "How beloved is the Torah by the Holy One Blessed be He. For whoever occupies himself with Torah is beloved above and below. The Holy One Blessed be He heeds his words and does not forsake him in this world and the next. And in Torah must one toil, day and night.

And in *Parshath Emor* 89b: "Happy are Israel, whom the Holy One Blessed be He favored above all of the peoples, who, in His love for them, gave them a Torah of truth to know the way of the holy King. And if one occupies himself with Torah, it is as if he is occupying himself with the Holy One Blessed be He. For all of the Torah is the Name of the Holy One Blessed be He, so that if one occupies himself with it, it is as if he were occupying himself with His Name. And if one distances himself from the Torah, he is distant from the Holy One Blessed be He."

And (*Ibid.* 96a): "How fortunate is the portion of those who occupy themselves with Torah every day. Woe unto those who do not occupy themselves with Torah, for they have no portion in the holy Name, and they are not intimate with it in this world and the next. And one who merits it in this world merits it in the world to come, as it is written (*Song of Songs* 7:10): 'He titillates the lips of the sleepers [in the grave].' For though they are in this world, their lips murmur Torah there."

And in *Parshath Shelach* 259b: "The Holy One Blessed be He takes pride in the Torah: 'Walk in My ways. Go and occupy yourselves with My Torah, and I will bring you to good worlds and to celestial heights.' (*Bamidbar* 13:17): 'Go up this (way) in the south,' and occupy yourselves with Torah, and see that it stands before you and that from it you will know Me."

And (*Ibid.* 176): (*Mishlei* 5:19): "'A beloved hind, of excellent favor' — the Torah, the light of all the worlds. How many seas and rivers, springs and fountains issue from you [Torah]! What can I say about you. All depend upon you, the celestial and the terrestrial. 'A beloved hind, of excellent favor,' for the celestial and the terrestrial. Who will merit [wearing] your honor as befits you? And who can utter and reveal your hidden and secret things?"

And in *Parshath Pinchas*: "If one toils in Torah, he merits the opening of many gates before him in this world, and many lights. When he departs from this world, it [Torah] precedes him and goes to all the keepers of the gates and calls out and says (*Isaiah* 26:2): 'Open, you gates, and let the righteous nation enter.' 'Prepare a seat for Ploni, servant of the King.' For there is no rejoicing for the Holy One Blessed be He except in one who occupies himself with Torah — how much more so, one who stays awake at night to occupy himself with Torah. For all the *tzaddikim* in Gan Eden listen to his voice, and the Holy One Blessed be He prides Himself in him."

And he also merits through Torah a holy soul, as it is written in the introduction to the *Zohar, Bereshith*, the fifth pronouncement (*Bereshith* 1:20): "Let the waters swarm a swarming, a living soul." There are three mitzvoth here: one, to toil in Torah; and to occupy oneself with it; and to add to it every day, to perfect his soul and his spirit. For when a man occupies himself with Torah, he perfects another holy soul, etc. For when a man does not occupy himself with Torah, he has no holy soul. And the holy soul above does not repose upon him. And when he occupies himself with Torah, by the murmuring of his lips in it, he merits that living soul and becomes like the holy angels, as it is written (*Psalms* 103:20): 'Bless the L-rd, *His angels*' — these are those who occupy themselves with Torah, who are called 'His angels' on earth, etc. This, in *this* world. As to the world to come, we have learned that the Holy One Blessed be He is destined to make for them, etc."

Chapter III

In this chapter there will be explained that the Torah saves a man from afflictions and from all [other] evils in this world and the next

Come and see how great is the power of Torah, for they have said (*Berachoth* 5b): "All who occupy themselves with Torah .. all of their sins are forgiven, it being written (*Mishlei* 16:6): 'By lovingkindness and truth, [Torah,] sin is forgiven.'"

And they have said further (*Ibid.* 5a): "All who occupy themselves with the study of Torah remove afflictions from themselves, as it is written (*Iyyov* 5:7): 'And the sons of *reshef* will be dispelled by *uf*,' '*uf*' alluding to Torah, as intimated in (*Mishlei* 23:5): 'If you glance away [hata*uf*] from it [Torah], it will be gone,' and '*reshef*,' [alluding] to afflictions, as in (*Devarim* 22:29): 'Wasted by hunger, embattled by *reshef*" ["*reshef*," in that it follows 'hunger,' also denoting afflictions]. And, in *Tanna d'bei Eliyahu*: "If you see afflictions coming against you, run to words of Torah, and, immediately, the afflictions will flee, as it is written (*Isaiah* 26:20): "Go my people; enter into your chambers [of Torah], etc.'"

And sometimes Torah saves him even from death at the hands of Heaven, as we find in *Midrash Rabbah Kedoshim*: "If he went astray in the transgression of … what shall he do to live? If he were accustomed to learn one page, let him learn two; and if one chapter, let him learn two, etc."

And the Torah also saves him from all the evils of this world and the world to come, as we find in *Tanna d'bei Eliyahu Zuta* 17: "Torah protects a man all the years that he is in the grave, as it is written (*Proverbs* 6:22): 'In your walking, it [Torah] will guide you] — in this world; 'In your lying down, it will protect you' — in the grave, during death; 'and when you awake, it shall speak for you' — in the world to come." The explanation is as we find in the holy *Zohar*: "When you lie in the grave, Torah will protect you from the *din* of *this* world. And when you awake, it shall speak for you. In the world to come, when you awake after death, it will speak for you. That is, it will speak good for you on behalf of your body, so that it awake first for eternal life, as it is written (*Daniel* 12:2): 'These for eternal life, etc.,' because they occupied themselves with eternal life, i.e., Torah. And all those words that one uttered in studying Torah in this world will stand before the Holy One Blessed be He and speak out, and they will not be silenced.

And in *Avoth* 3:6 we find: "If one takes upon himself the yoke of Torah, there are removed from him … and the yoke of [earning] a livelihood." Their speaking of "taking upon himself the yoke of Torah" rather than of "*learning* Torah" implies that this is so *only* if he takes upon himself the *yoke* of Torah, not to grow lax in it by any means — like an ox under the yoke, as they have said (*Avodah Zarah* 5b):

"It was taught in the school of Eliyahu: 'Let one always make himself as an ox for the yoke and as an ass for the burden for [the sake of] words of Torah.'" And then, even if the burden of the yoke of earning a livelihood were upon him already it is removed from him. How much more so will the L-rd "arrange" things so that it not be put upon him [in the first place].

And the Torah also protects a man to rescue him from the *din* of Gehinnom even though he sinned — *a fortiori*, from the instance of Elisha Acher. For they said (*Chagigah* 15b): "When Acher died, they said: 'Let him not be judged [(to descend to Gehinnom)], for he occupied himself with Torah, and let him not come to the world to come because he sinned [(in heresy)].'" And we find in *Aggadath Mishlei*: "There is no charity that saves from the *din* of Gehinnom, but only Torah alone." [And we learned:] "The fathers of the world answered: 'Since you have been caught in the net of judgment, there is nothing you can do but sit and occupy yourselves with Torah, for it [alone] atones for sin.'" They have also said (*Chagigah* 27a): "The fire of Gehinnom does not prevail over Torah scholars — *a fortiori* from [the instance of] a salamander, which, since it is generated by fire, one who anoints himself with it, is not affected by fire. How much more so, Torah scholars, whose entire body is fire, viz. (*Jeremiah* 23:29): "'Is not My word thus like fire?' says the L-rd?"

Also, from the *Great Din*, of which it is written (*Malachi* 3:19): "For, behold, the day is coming which will burn as an oven" — one who occupied himself with Torah is destined to be rescued, as we find in *Midrash Tehillim*: "In time to come, the Holy One Blessed be He will take the sun out of its case and judge [i.e., punish] with it the wicked, and heal with it the righteous, as it is written (*Ibid.* 20): 'And there shall shine for you, fearers of My name, the sun of charity with healing in its wings, etc.'" R. Yehoshua said: "The Holy One Blessed be He did charity with all who enter the world by not having placed it [the sun] in the first firmament. For if he had placed it there, there would be no shade for anyone under it, as it is written (*Psalms* 19:7): 'And there is no hiding from His sun.'" But in time to come, who *is* hidden from His sun? He who occupies himself with Torah, as it is written afterwards (*Ibid.* 8): 'The Torah of the L-rd is complete.'" And the verse (*Malachi* 3:19): "For, behold, the day is coming which will burn like an oven" is, likewise, followed by (*Ibid.* 22): "Remember the Torah of Moses, My servant."

Torah [study] is also (one) of the mitzvoth whose fruits are eaten in this world with the principal remaining for the world to come.

They have also said (*Avodah Zarah* 19b): "Whoever occupies himself with Torah, his possessions prosper," "Whoever occupies himself with Torah, the Holy One Blessed be He takes care of his needs."

From all this we can understand the greatness of occupation with Torah. And Chazal have already said: "The Holy One Blessed be He has in His world only the four ells of *halachah* alone." That is, the [ultimate] end of the will and the desire of the Holy One Blessed be He in His world is only the man who occupies himself with *halachah*, whose space is four ells.

And he who lacks the time to learn Torah continuously is obligated, in any event, to set times for Torah. For thus have Chazal said (*Shabbath* 31a): "When a man is brought to [Heavenly] judgment, he is asked: 'Were you honest in your [business] dealings? Did you set aside times for Torah study?'" And even if he is poor, he must set aside times, as they have said (*Yoma* 35b): "A poor man and a rich man come for judgment. The poor man is asked: 'Why did you not occupy yourself with Torah?' If he says: 'I was poor,' he is asked: 'Were you any poorer than Hillel the Elder?' It is said of Hillel the elder, etc.'" And so is it ruled in *Yoreh Deah* 246: "Every man of Israel is obliged to study Torah — whether he be poor or rich, healthy in body or afflicted, a youth or very old — even a beggar, even a married man with children — he is obligated to set aside times for Torah study, by day and by night, as it is written (*Joshua* 1:8): "'And you shall study it day and night.'"

And the "setting aside of times" means setting a *specific* time, which he does not depart from for any reason — even if he stands to profit greatly by doing so (viz. *Shulchan Aruch, Orach Chaim* 155).

And not in vain has Torah been compared to bread, as it is written (*Mishlei* 9:5): "Come and eat of my bread" [i.e., Torah]. This is to teach us that just as bread feeds the heart, as it is written (*Psalms* 104:15): "And bread, the heart of man shall feed," and if one does not eat bread for one or two days his heart weakens; and, how much more so, if he does not eat bread for a week, his heart weakens greatly, and it is difficult for him to regain the strength that he lost by this — so is it exactly with Torah study, which feeds the holy soul of the Jew. If he does not learn for some days (how much more so, a full week), it is greatly weakened, wherefore he must take great care not to miss the set time for even a day. And, aside from the fact that this undermines the second and third day after this (for it is very likely that he will not learn on them either, as Chazal have said: "If you leave me [Torah] for a day, I will leave you for two days") and it is very difficult for him afterwards to overcome his *yetzer* anew and to set times for Torah — but even those days that he *does* learn, if the set time is not constant, the holy spirit does not repose to its full extent upon that learning. This, as opposed to a constant set time, in which a great and awesome holiness reposes upon each study session. Therefore, if because of some very pressing exigency he must cancel his set time, it shall rest upon him exactly as a debt, which he must make haste to repay in this twenty-four hour period, as we find in *Eruvin* 65b about R. Acha bar Yaakov, that he would "borrow" in the daytime [from his set time (for his livelihood)] and "repay" at night (see Rashi there).

And the holy *Zohar* (296) expands upon the reward of one who sets times for Torah, (and the opposite, G-d forbid): "The fourth sanctuary, etc. The thirty-two others are set aside for those who occupy themselves in Torah continuously, non-stop, day and night. And the others, beneath them, for all those who set specific times for Torah. And all are appointed to punish those who are able to occupy themselves with Torah but do not."

And one who takes care to study [words of] Torah and to place them upon his heart merits loving the Blessed L-rd, as we find in *Sifrei* on (*Devarim* 6:6): "And let these things that I command you this day be upon your heart," viz.: "From (*Ibid.* 5): 'And you shall love the L-rd your G-d with all your heart,' I would not know *by what means* one comes to love the Holy One Blessed be He; it is, therefore, written (5): 'And let these things [(words of Torah)] … be upon your heart.' For by these you come to recognize the Holy One Blessed be He and to cleave to His ways."

Chapter IV

In this chapter there will be explained the greatness of the punishment of one who separates himself from Torah

And in *Avoth* 6:2 we find: "R. Yehoshua b. Levi said: 'A heavenly voice goes forth from Mount Chorev and proclaims: "Woe unto the creations because of the shame of Torah, etc.!"'" And, in *Zohar Chadash* it is stated that the destined day of judgment, viz. (*Malachi* 3:19): "For, behold, the day is coming which will burn like an oven" — this is the day on which Moses, our teacher, may peace be upon him is destined to 'claim the shame of Torah,' as we find in the *Mishnah*: 'Woe unto the creations, etc.'" For, in truth, it is a great shame to the Torah, whose holiness is rooted above all of the worlds, that the sons of man, molded from matter, founded in dust, separate themselves from it!"

And in *Ma'aloth HaTorah* it is written: "One should take it to heart that if it were granted a lowly man to serve a great, awesome king with the same service that all the dignitaries of the kingdom performed, he would certainly experience infinite joy even though he received nothing for his service. And he certainly would not *refuse* the service of the king! How much more so should one rejoice for having merited to learn the holy Torah that all the celestial angels constantly disport themselves with, and that all the *tzaddikim* in Gan Eden occupy themselves with. How much more so, should he not keep himself from it! And Chazal have said that when a man occupies himself with Torah, all the angels who have been created by the breath of his mouth surround him in a circle as far as the eye can see — and he in its midst!

"We can infer from this the punishment of one who forsakes the Torah, about whom Isaiah has written (*Isaiah* 1:28): 'And the forsakers of the L-rd shall perish!' Woe to that shame! Woe to that humiliation! What will he do on the day of visitation? Is there an end to his punishment? According to the greatness of the reward [of one who studies it] is the greatness of the punishment of one who separates himself from it!

"And he should imagine the following: If a great and awesome king saw a man wallowing in filth, smitten and surrounded by all kinds of afflictions and sore illnesses, and lacking everything, and this man found favor in the eyes of the king and he commanded that all the filth be washed from him and healed all of his illnesses until he became healthy and whole in all of his limbs, and clothed him in kingly garments and adorned him with many precious jewels and pearls and gave him all of his treasures and commanded that all the governance of the kingdom be by his hand, and gave him his daughter as a wife and raised him over all the princes and the servants of the king, until he commanded all the great ones of his kingdom to serve him in royal garments according to all that he desired — and, behold, while he was clothed in these kingly garments and adorned in jewels, and all the dignitaries of the kingdom walked before him, leading him with lanterns — at that time, he saw children frolicking in the mud and picking stones to play with, and he envied them and did as they did and cast off all his costly clothes, and spurned all the delights that he had just enjoyed, and abandoned all the dignitaries that walked before him, and rolled in the filth and sullied himself in it as before — would there be an end to this man's punishment for having despised the honor of the king and his ministers, the doers of his will, and sullied his kingly garments, etc.? The analogy is self-explanatory: How much more so is punishment destined and readied for the forsakers of Torah, who separate themselves from it to gambol in the dust of the vanities of this world!"

This enables us to understand (*Berachoth* 5a): "If it is possible for one to study Torah and does not do so, the Holy One Blessed be He brings upon him sore afflictions which sully him, as it is written (*Psalms* 39:3): "I was dumb with silence, silenced from good [i.e., Torah] and my pain [i.e., my afflictions] sullied me." This is measure for measure. Because he shamed the Torah and made it like an unwanted vessel, he, too, was shamed before all.

Chazal have also said (*Berachoth* 63a): "All who are lax in Torah study will lack the strength to withstand a day of affliction, viz. (*Mishlei* 24:10): 'If you grow lax, in a day of affliction your strength will be straitened.'" And we find in the holy *Zohar* on this verse: "When a man grows lax in Torah and walks in ways that are not *kasher*, how many foes are readied for him to be prosecutors against him in a day of affliction! And even the man's soul, which is his power and his strength, will become his enemy, as it is written '*tzar cochecha*' ["Your strength (i.e., soul) will become your foe"]. What is meant by 'you have become lax'? You have loosened your hand from holding fast to the Holy One Blessed be He. And how can a man hold fast to the Holy One Blessed be He? By holding fast to the Torah one holds fast to the "tree of life" and gives strength to the Shechinah and many defenders stand up for him to mention him for the good, etc."

We further find in *Avoth* (3:8): "R. Meir says: 'If one forgets a single thing from his learning, Scripture accounts it to him as if he is liable for his soul, as it is written (*Devarim* 4:9): "Only take heed to yourself, and heed your soul exceedingly, lest you forget, etc."

Also, through this [(laxity in Torah study)] the idolators grow in strength over Israel, as we find in the *Midrash* (*Eichah Rabba Pethichta*) on the verse (*Isaiah* 5:24): 'As straw [Esav] will consume a tongue of fire [Jacob].' When will the straw consume the fire? 'When they [Israel] despise the Torah of the L-rd their [Israel's] root will be like rot.' The 'merit of the fathers' will not avail them."

We find further in the *Midrash* (*Eichah Rabbah Pethichta*): "(*Bereshith* 27:22): 'The voice is the voice of Jacob' — So long as the voice of Jacob "chirps" in the houses of prayer and the houses of study the hands of Esav will not prevail over him. But if the voice of Jacob, etc."

And, in *Midrash Eichah*: "When does the kingdom of the idolators make a decree against Israel and succeed in it? When they [Israel] cast words of Torah to the ground, as it is written (*Daniel* 8:12): 'And a time will be set for the [end of] the daily offering and it [(the idolatrous kingdom)] will throw truth to the ground and it will achieve and prosper.' "Truth" is Torah, as it is written (*Mishlei* 23:23): 'Buy truth and do not sell it!' And it is written (*Hoshea* 8:3): 'Israel has forsaken truth; the foe will pursue it.' And "good" is nothing other than Torah."

And (*Shemoth* 17:1): "And they journeyed … and they encamped in Refidim," after which it is written (*Ibid.* 8): "And Amalek came." This is expounded by Chazal as: [Amalek attacked them] because their hand "weakened" ["*rafu yedeihem*" (like "*refidim*")] in Torah.

And in the holy *Zohar* on *Shemoth* 5:17: "'You are lax, lax' — You are lax in Torah; therefore, (*ibid.* 9): 'Let the work be heavier upon the men' — with taxes and assessments."

And [(by neglecting Torah study)] he especially injures *himself*, as Chazal have said: "Whoever forgets one item of his learning brings bout exile to his sons, as it is written (*Hoshea* 4:6): 'And you have forgotten the Torah of your G-d — I, too, will forget your sons.'"

And a man's sons also die young because of this sin, as Chazal have stated (*Shabbath* 32b).

He is also judged [i.e., punished] in Gehinnom for this sin, as Chazal have said (*Bava Bathra* 79a): "Whoever separates himself from words of Torah falls into Gehinnom, as it is written (*Mishlei* 21:16): 'The man who wanders from the path of wisdom will rest in the congregation of *refaim*' [the shades], "*refaim*" being nothing other than Gehinnom."

And in the holy *Zohar, Parshath Vayikra*: "R. Shimon said: 'Happy are those men of soul, those men of Torah, the sons of the service of the Holy King. Woe unto those sinners, who do not merit to cleave to their Master and do not merit Torah. For all those who do not merit Torah, merit neither spirit nor soul, and their cleaving is to sore judgments. One such as these has no portion in the holy King, has no portion in holiness. Woe unto him when he leaves this world. For he will be revealed to those evil hosts, creatures of *chutzpah* [audacity], hard as dogs, messengers of the fire of Gehinnom, who will have no mercy on him, etc."

And he is also rejected by the L-rd, as stated in *Avoth* 6:2: "Whoever does not occupy himself with Torah is called *nazuf* ['rejected']."

And, in the holy *Zohar*: "How much must men heed their ways and fear the Holy One Blessed be He. For one who does not toil in Torah and does not occupy himself with it is called "rejected" by the Holy One Blessed be He, is distant from Him, and the Shechinah does not repose itself upon him. And those "watchers," who walk with him, remove themselves from him. And, what is more, they call out before him: 'Remove yourselves from Ploni, who is not zealous for the honor of the King. Woe unto him, for he has been forsaken by the celestial and the terrestrial beings, and he has no portion in the way of life!" But when one occupies himself with Torah and, in the service of his Master, toils in Torah, how many "watchers" are readied around him to watch him, and the Shechinah reposes itself upon him, and all call out before him and say: 'Give honor to the image of the King, give honor to the son of the king. He is "watched" in this world and in the world to come. Happy is his portion!'"

And also because of this [(neglect of Torah study)] conflagrations are found in the world, as Chazal say (*Shevuoth* 39a): "All houses in which words of Torah are not heard at night are consumed by fire" — and it is known that all of Israel are 'guarantors, one for the other.'"

And Rabbeinu Yonah has written in *Iggereth Hatshuvah* that "when men finish their work and their dealings and go to their houses or idle on the [street] corners or speak idle talk, their evil is very great and their sin exceedingly severe, for they [thereby] shame the Torah. For if they believed that there is no end to its reward, why would they not turn their feet to the house of study to learn? Does not a man rush to work knowing that all is vanity? And how can he forget the life of the world to come and not devote a day or an hour to learning? And let him not say: 'There is yet time to do for the L-rd, to learn Torah, and to occupy oneself with mitzvoth and *tzedakoth*.' He is guilty! He has sinned greatly against the L-rd! And Chazal have said on the verse (*Bamidbar* 15:31): 'For the word of the L-rd he has despised, and His commandments he has broken. Cut off shall be that soul; its transgression is in it,' that if it is possible for one to occupy himself with Torah but he does not do so, he shames the word of the L-rd. Therefore, every man is obligated to set aside a place in his house in which to learn *halachoth* or Scripture, each according to his ability. And when he is finished with his dealings or with his work, he must turn in there to study. And by doing so, he will "do wonders" for his soul, to rescue it from the pit. And he must reflect upon his end and consider his latter end, as Chazal have said: 'Consider three things and you will not come to transgression, etc.' And it is fitting that one find himself a *pashut* or a half [(types of coins)] to give charity for every day he fails to go to the house of study or to a place where he has one of the holy books to learn from."

[I have heard about a prosperous businessman who separated himself completely from the world's vanities to occupy himself completely with the Torah of the L-rd, day and night. And his brothers and family members banded against him to get him to return to "normal," but he would not pay heed to them and they despaired of him.

When his old acquaintances asked him how he had gotten himself not to be swayed by his family's outcry, he answered: "I reflected upon the words of Chazal (*Shabbath* 83b): 'Torah endures only with one who "kills himself" over it, etc.'" That is, [one should imagine] that he has already died, and had completed all of his affairs, and, with them, his life. And he were brought to judgment before the King of kings, the Holy One Blessed be He, for all of the things for which he had spent his life in vanity, and emerging "guilty" in the Heavenly *din*, he screamed: "Woe unto me, for the wickedness of my acts and of my affairs!" If in the midst of all this he were permitted to return immediately to this world and to repent, he certainly would not hesitate for a moment, and would not incline his ear at all to hear of the business of his house.

If so, let a man bethink himself of his sins, and [imagine] that he should have died already, and that if after his death the Holy One Blessed be He had done him the great lovingkindness of permitting him to repent, he certainly would not hesitate to do so for even one moment. If so, what "harm" has the Holy One Blessed be He done him by extending his life so that he can repent in his lifetime itself? Certainly, he must bestir himself with all of his powers to repent of his sins and to study Torah always, or, at least, to set aside a specific time for Torah study and not be swayed by those who would turn him from this.]

Chapter V

In this chapter there will be explained the greatness of the obligation to support Torah scholars and the greatness of the reward for this

From all of our discussion of the greatness of the Torah, which is the foundation of all, we can understand the greatness of the obligation of upholding the Torah that it not fall. And this holds not only for those who are busy with worldly affairs, who must certainly at least bestir themselves in this great enterprise in order to rescue themselves from the bitter punishments for neglect of Torah study, as Rabbeinu Yonah wrote in *Iggereth Hateshuvah*: "If one wishes to rescue himself from the bitter punishment and this great sin, let him occupy himself with the needs of the Torah scholars and the Rabbis, etc., so that they remain in his city and occupy themselves in Torah by his support." And Chazal have observed that the verse in *Mishlei* 3:18: "It [Torah] is a tree of life for its upholders" speaks not of "learners," but only of "upholders," who *support* Torah scholars and Rabbis — Even those who are themselves Torah scholars and fulfillers of mitzvoth in Israel have a great obligation to *support* Torah, and if not, they are in the category of "Cursed," G-d forbid, as Rabbeinu Yonah wrote in *Sha'arei Teshuvah*, Gate 3:19, in the name of the *Sifrei* on *Devarim* 27:26: "Cursed is he who does not uphold the words of this Torah to do them" — "If one learned and reviewed and taught others and fulfilled the Torah and is in a position to strengthen those who occupy themselves with Torah and mitzvoth but does not do so, he is in the category of "Cursed is he who does not uphold, etc."

Come and see the greatness of the eminence of one who upholds the Torah, and benefits a Torah scholar with his possessions and draws close to him, Scripture considering it as if he [thereby] cleaved to the Shechinah. As Chazal (*Kethuvoth* 111a) say on the verse (*Deuteronomy* 4:9): "And you that did cleave to the L-rd your G-d are all alive this day." Now is it possible for a man to cleave to the Shechinah? Is it not written (*Ibid.* 24): "For the L-rd your G-d is a consuming fire!" The intent is, rather, if one weds his daughter to a Torah scholar, or does business for a Torah scholar, or benefits a Torah scholar with his possessions, it is accounted to him as if he cleaved to the Shechinah." And they stated further (*Ibid.* 10b): "All who lodge Torah scholars in their homes and offer them of their fare are regarded by Scripture as presenters of daily ['continual'] sacrifices." And (*Ibid.* 63b): "R. Nechemiah opened [his discourse] in honor of the host, expounding (I *Samuel* 15:6): 'And Saul said to the Keni: Go, depart, go down from the midst of Amalek, lest I destroy you with him — and you have done lovingkindness with all the children of Israel': Now does this not follow *a fortiori*? If Yithro, who befriended Moses only for his own honor had this accorded [to his descendants, the Keni], then one who is host to a Torah scholar, and feeds him, and gives him to drink, and treats him of his possessions, how much more so!'... R. Elazar b. R. Yossi Haglili opened [his discourse] in honor of the host, expounding (II *Samuel* 6:11): 'And the L-rd blessed the house of Oved-Edom… because of the ark of G-d' [which he kept in his house]. Now does this not follow *a fortiori*? If the ark, which did not eat and did not drink — because they swept and sprinkled before it, thus [were they rewarded], then one who is host to a Torah scholar, and feeds him, and gives him to drink, and treats him of his possessions, how much more so!'" And in *Midrash Rabbah, Koheleth* 2: "R. Meir was an expert scribe and earned three *selaim* a week. With one, he fed himself; with one, he clothed himself; and with one, he fed Torah scholars."

And we find in *Midrash Rabbah, Shir Hashirim* 6:11: "I went down to a nut garden": "R. Yehoshua b. Levi said: 'Israel is compared to a nut. Just as a nut is cut and replaced, and is cut for its good — Why so? For it replaces itself like hair and nails — so, all that Israel "cut" from their labors and give to those who labor in Torah in this world, is for their own good. They cut, and it [(what they cut)] is replaced for them and adds to their wealth in this world and [gives them] goodly reward in the world to come.'" And, what is more, he [(his beneficiary)] is called "his friend," who learns in his name, and he shares in the reward for his Torah, as we learn in *Sotah* 21a, in respect to Shimon the brother of Azaryah, and as is known from [the partnership between] the tribes of Yissachar and Zevulun. As we find in *Midrash Rabbah, Parshath Kedoshim* 25a: "R. Huna and R. Yirmiyah said in the name of R. Chiyya b. Abba: 'The Holy One Blessed be He is destined to make shade and canopies for the men of mitzvoth [i.e., the upholders of Torah] next to the Torah scholars in Gan Eden. And there are three verses to this effect: one, (*Koheleth* 7:12): "For in the shade of wisdom [Torah], the shade of money"; (*Isaiah* 56:2): "Happy is the man that does this [Torah] and the son of man, who upholds it"; (*Mishlei* 3:15): "It [Torah] is a tree of life to those who uphold it." "Shimon, the brother of Azaryah, said in his name, etc." (*Zevachim* I, *Mishnah* 2): "Now was Shimon not greater than Azaryah? But because Azaryah did business and supported Shimon, therefore, the *halachah* was written in his [Azaryah's] name." Similarly, (*Devarim* 33:18): "Rejoice, Zevulun in your going out, and Yissachar, in your tent [of Torah]." Now was Yissachar not greater than Zevulun? But because Zevulun left the settlement to engage in business and returned and supported Yissachar and was given reward for his toil, the verse is written in his [Zevulun's] name, viz. "Rejoice Zevulun in your going out." And even in *this* world he [Zevulun] loses nothing by this [(supporting Yissachar)], as we find in *Midrash Rabbah, Parshath Tetzaveh* (*Shemoth* 36) on *Mishlei* 6:23: "'For a mitzvah is a lamp and Torah is light.' What is the intent of 'For a mitzvah is a lamp'? Anyone who does a mitzvah is like one who lights a lamp before the Holy One Blessed be He, and he vivifies his soul, which is called 'a lamp,' viz., (*Mishlei* 24:27): 'The lamp of the L-rd is the soul of a man.' And what is the intent of 'and the Torah is light'? Often, one thinks of doing a mitzvah and the *yetzer hara* within him says: 'Why do a mitzvah and losr your possessions? Before giving to others, give to your sons.' And the *yetzer tov* says: 'Give for the mitzvah. See what is written: 'For a mitzvah is a lamp.' Just as a lamp, when it is burning, even if thousands upon thousands light from it, its light remains in its place, so, all who give for a mitzvah do not lose their possessions, wherefore it is written: 'For a mitzvah is a lamp and the Torah is light.'"

And, similarly, in the holy *Zohar, Parshath Vayechi*: "Why does Zevulun always precede Yissachar in the blessings? Is Yissacher's occupation not in Torah, which takes precedence in all instances? Why, then, does Zevulun take precedence in the blessings? His father placed him first and Moses placed him first. But Zevulun merits this because he took bread from his own mouth and placed it in the mouth of Yissachar, wherefore he was placed first in the blessings. From here we learn that one who supports a Torah scholar receives blessings from above and from below. And, what is more, he merits 'two tables,' which others do not merit. He merits riches, that he be blessed in this world, and he merits a portion in the world to come."

[And we can hereby understand the verse "Rejoice Zevulun in your going out, and Yissachar, in your tents." That is, even though the merchant is not wont to rejoice in leaving his home for trade, but only when he returns home, lest the Holy One Blessed be He not prosper him and his toil be in vain — especially if he must sail on the sea, which is a place of danger — Moses, our teacher, therefore, says: "You, Zevulun, may rejoice in your going out to sail in boats (see Rashi there); for Yissachar dwells in your tents, which you have bequeathed him for Torah and for heritage. If so, the Holy One Blessed be He will prosper you" (as the holy *Zohar* writes)]

And one also merits because of this [support of Torah] that good and holy sons issue from him, as we find in the holy *Zohar, Parshath Metzora* (*Mishlei* 3:18): "It is a tree of life to those who hold fast to it, and its supporters are fortunate, etc." These are the placers of "stock" into the pockets of Torah scholars. For those who do so support Torah from the head until the end of the body. And our entire faith is dependent upon and supported by this. And he merits sons who are worthy of being prophets of truth.

[And, in truth, just as we find that the Holy One Blessed be He sanctified the tribe of Levi and exhorted Israel not to forsake it, as it is written (*Devarim* 16:19): "Take heed unto yourself lest you forsake the Levite all of your days upon your land," so, it is, likewise, the will of the Blessed L-rd that we support men who separate themselves from the affairs of the world in order to serve the L-rd. For this is certainly not inferior to supporting the Levite in this regard. As Rambam writes (*Hilchoth Shemitah Veyovel*, Chapter 13 *Halachah* 12 and 13): "Why did the Levite not merit inheritance in Eretz Yisrael and in its spoils with his brothers? For he was singled out to serve the L-rd, to minister unto Him and to teach His just ways and righteous judgments to the people, as it is written (*Devarim* 33:10): 'They shall teach Your judgments to Jacob and Your Torah to Israel.' Therefore, they were separated from the ways of the world. They do not wage war, as do the rest of

Israel, they do not inherit, and they do not merit things for themselves with the strength of their bodies, but they are "the army of the L-rd," as it is written (*Ibid.* 11): 'The L-rd bless his [Levi's] strength.' And the Holy One Blessed be He bequeaths [things] on them, as it is written (*Numbers* 18:20): 'I am your [Levi's] portion and your inheritance.' And [this applies] not only to the tribe of Levi alone, but to every man of all those who enter the world, whose spirit moves him, and who understands of himself to be separate, to stand before the L-rd, to minister unto Him and to serve Him, to know the L-rd and to walk justly, as G-d made him. And he divests himself of the many "accountings" that men seek, he is sanctified as "holy of holies," and the L-rd becomes his portion and his inheritance for ever and ever. And He bequeaths to him in this world what suffices him, as He did to the Cohanim and the Levites. As David, may peace be upon him said (*Psalms* 16:5): 'The L-rd is the portion of my inheritance.'" Until here, his (Rambam's) beautiful language.]

And also in the category of supporting Torah scholars is wedding one's daughter to a Torah scholar. As Chazal have said (*Kethuvoth* 111b), that [if one weds his daughter to a Torah scholar], it is as if he were to cleave to the Shechinah. And, as written in *Pesachim* 49a: "One should [if necessary] sell everything he has and wed the daughter of a Torah scholar and wed his daughter to a Torah scholar, so that if he dies or is exiled, [at least] his sons will be Torah scholars."

And in our times, in our many sins, in many places the horn of Torah has descended to the dust, and the number of Torah scholars is dwindling, and no one takes them into their homes to make a match with them. And it is sometimes easier to find a proper match for a commoner than for a Torah scholar. How great has this stumbling block grown! For through this, Torah will expire, G-d forbid, when they [the Torah scholars] see that no one supports them. It is also a great shame for Torah when its learners are bereft and desolate and not taken into homes. Woe to that shame! Woe to that humiliation! How will we answer the Holy One Blessed be He in the future, when we are brought to judgment for shaming of the Torah! As we find in *Zohar Chadash* "(*Malachi* 3:19): 'Behold, the day is coming which shall burn as an oven, etc.' This is the day when Moses, our teacher, is destined to claim the shame of the Torah." And the Gaon, R. Yehonathan, raised an outcry over this in his book *Ya'aroth D'vash*.

And all of this comes from the deception of the *yetzer*, which entices a man to say that his daughter will not achieve success or high station if she weds a Torah scholar, which would not be the case if she married this and this man. And, in truth, this is not so. For the Holy One Blessed be He, the G-d of the world and Provider of sustenance for all of His creatures, viz. (*Psalms* 136:25): "He gives bread to all flesh" — Would He withhold sustenance from a man, G-d forbid, because he learns Torah and fulfills its mitzvoth? Woe unto him who thinks thus of the Blessed Creator!

And I am not speaking of those men upon whom the light of Torah did not shine, who do not exert themselves to make a match with a Torah scholar, who did not taste of "the honey of its words," and did not see its sweetness. But I am amazed at the householders, the men of Torah, who recognize its great worth, but who neglect this! From this, there will also result great harm to those who are indifferent to making a match with a Torah scholar.

And, in truth, how much should one exert himself with all his strength to cleave to a Torah scholar, even if he must sacrifice many of his possessions [to do so]. As Chazal have said (*Pesachim* 49b): "One should sell everything he has and wed the daughter of a Torah scholar, and wed his daughter to a Torah scholar, etc.; and one who gives his daughter, etc."

And in our times, the obligation is even greater. For when one makes a match with a Torah scholar there sprout from him afterwards generations of fearers of the L-rd and fulfillers of His mitzvoth. Not so, if he does the opposite. Who knows what will become of his descendants? As we see before our eyes, in our many sins, in these times, that whoever is richer [than his neighbor] finds it more difficult to rescue himself from the wiles and stratagems of the *yetzer*. Therefore, one must see to it to bring himself closer to Torah and to those who study it; and "the Torah defends and saves," as Chazal have said (*Sotah* 21a).

Chapter VI

This chapter, too, speaks of the great obligation to strengthen Torah.

We have said all this about seeing to the needs of Torah scholars to enable them to occupy themselves with the Torah of the L-rd. How much more so is it a great mitzvah, in every city, for those who are able, to exert themselves to establish yeshivoth of Torah for youths who have not yet become "learners," so that [the study of] Torah not decline, G-d forbid. For "if there are no kids, there will be no goats." How much more so in our times, when the horn of Torah has descended almost to the dust in our many sins must we strengthen it so that it not fall, G-d forbid, entirely.

And in our many sins, we see with our own eyes that there are many youths who could have been *poskim* in Israel, but who, because they have no teacher, remain absolute ignoramuses. And there are some of them who also become corrupt. And even those towns which have yeshivoth are declining, for there is no one to be found to support them in supplying their needs. Woe to our eyes that see this! And there is no one to find a solution for this, that Torah not expire, G-d forbid. And how shall we answer before the Blessed One's throne when the shame of Torah is claimed from him!

And the brunt of the responsibility lies in the city dignitaries, who have the power to protest and to amend, as Chazal have said on the verse, *Vayikra* 4:21: "It is the sin-offering for the assembly," followed by (*Ibid*. 21): "If a leader sin," to teach us that the sin of the assembly is the sin of the leader, in that he is held responsible for not seeing to it to correct matters.

But the counsel of the *yetzer* is known in this, that when a mitzvah of this kind presents itself to him he assumes a cloak of humility, saying: "I am the least of [those in] the city, and my words will certainly not be heeded. Why should I waste my breath?" But when a man reflects upon himself, he will see that this is only the counsel of the *yetzer*. For if, in the midst of his speaking, someone would in the least "touch" his honor, his mouth would "sling torches" at him, and he would arouse men to defend him against the other. But when the honor of G-d is at stake, he suddenly becomes humble and lowly. This is nothing other than the *yetzer hara* changing the man, as the leopard, its spots. [This is what Chazal (*Berachoth* 61a) intimated (in saying) that the *yetzer hara* lies between the two chambers of the heart, having no fixed place, as the *yetzer tov* does, to the right. But he varies his enticements, all according to the situation.]

Therefore, the man whose heart has been touched by fear of the L-rd will see to it to exert himself in supporting Torah, so that payment not be exacted of him in the future for the blood of Israel, as it is known, that because of the sin of neglect of Torah, sons die, as we find in *Tanna d'bei Eliyahu*: "Whoever is in a position to protest, but does not do so, and to return Israel to the good, but does not do so, all of the blood spilled in Israel is on his hands alone, as it is written (*Ezekiel* 33:7): 'But you, [Ezekiel], son of man, I have made you a watchman for the house of Israel, and you have heard a thing from My mouth, and you must warn them,' [and if you do not]… he [the wicked] one shall die in his sin and I will demand his blood from your hand." And, likewise, if one stands up for the honor of the L-rd and His holy Torah, which have been desecrated now in our sins, there is no end for his reward, as we find in *Yerushalmi* in the last chapter of *Berachoth*: "If you have seen a generation which is neglectful of Torah, arise and strengthen it, and you will receive the reward of all of them."

And even though it is known to all that today, because of our declining influence, in our many sins, and [because of] other reasons, it is not easy for one to exert himself to bring this to fruition, still, he should not be lax in this, for "according to the expenditure is the reward." And even if some men shame him because of this, he should not pay heed to this at all. And he should know that because of this his reward will be greater, for having suffered shame for the Holy One Blessed be He. And thus do we find in *Yerushalmi*, the last chapter of *Peah* (8:6), in respect to charity collectors: "R. Elazar was a charity collector. Once, he came home and asked: 'What did you do [in my absence]?' They answered: 'A group [of people] came and ate and drank and prayed for you.' R. Elazar: 'I have no goodly reward [from this].' Another time [after returning from an absence], he asked: 'What did you do?' They answered: 'A different group came and ate and drank and shamed you.' R. Elazar: 'Now I have goodly reward.'"

And, in *Avoth d.R. Nathan*: "Better one time with suffering than a hundred without suffering."

And conversely, the greatness of the punishment of one who does not support Torah is explained in the holy *Zohar, Parshath Vayishlach*, viz.: "If one occupies himself with Torah study and no one supports him, and no one puts "stock" into his pocket to strengthen him, because of this, the Torah is forgotten in every generation, and the power of Torah is weakened every day; for those who occupy themselves with Torah have nothing to support them, and the kingdom of the idolators strengthens itself every day. Come and see what this sin causes, because there is no one to support the Torah as it should be supported: Those [higher worlds which are called] "supporters" (*somchim*) are weakened and cause him [i.e., the primal serpent] who has no thighs and legs to take strength and stand."

(*Bereshith* 3:14): "And the L-rd G-d said to the serpent: 'Because you have done this, you are more accursed than all the beasts… On your belly shall you go…" What is the intent of 'On your belly shall you go?' That its "supporters" would be broken and its feet would be cut off and it would have nothing to stand on. And when Israel do not want to support the Torah they give it [(the serpent)] supports and thighs to stand on and prevail." (Thus far, the holy *Zohar*.)

And know further that it is found in the holy books that one who supports learners of Torah, even if he is an ignoramus in this world, he merits knowing the Torah in the world to come. And, in truth, it is obvious [that this is so], for since he has a share in the Torah of the one he supported, and it is known that the great pleasures of Gan Eden are inherent in the very spirituality of Torah, he must, as a matter of course, know the Torah.

And if so, let every man reflect how [much] he must support the learners of Torah. For, in this world, if they asked a man who was not a Torah scholar [or — even if he were —) but he had not yet learned the tractate that his friend, the poor Torah scholar, was now learning: "How much would you give to be expert, by heart, in this tractate or in the *Yoreh Deah* or in the *Choshen Mishpat*, he certainly would answer: "I would give whatever I could, even for one chapter; how much more so, for an entire tractate." And this, even in this world, where we do not recognize the greatness of the holiness of the Torah and the greatness of its worth. How much more so, in the world to come, where all will see before their eyes the greatness of the holiness of the Torah and sense the exaltedness of its worth — (And it is known from the holy *Zohar* that "one who inherits one tractate inherits one world") — how much will he rejoice afterwards in the portion of Torah that he will find set aside for him, which he had not toiled for in this world, but [had attained] only for the little that he had set aside from his labor while yet living! And if a man reflected upon this always, in his lifetime, he would pursue the Torah scholars and desire to cleave to them and to strengthen them, much more than one would pursue another to take him into partnership in the affairs of this world!

Chapter VII

In this chapter there will be explained the greatness of the reward of one who supports his sons in Torah study, and, the converse, the greatness of his punishment, G-d forbid, [if he does not do so]

And in our many sins, how many grow lax in Torah and give no thought to the great punishment that is destined for neglect of Torah study, as they said in *Midrash Mishlei, Parshah* 10: "R. Yishmael said: Come and see how sore is the day of judgment, when the Holy One Blessed be He is destined to judge all the world. If one comes who has learned Scripture, but not *Mishnah*, the Holy One Blessed be He turns His face away from him, and the throes of Gehinnom grow in him, etc., and they take him and cast him into Gehinnom. If one comes who has learned two or three orders [of the six orders of *Mishnah*], he is asked: 'My son, why did you not learn *all* the *halachoth*?' If one comes who has learned the *halachoth*, He asks him: 'My son, why did you not learn *Torah Cohanim*? Why did you not review it? For it contains all, etc.?' If one comes who has learned *Torath Cohanim*, the Holy One Blessed be He asks him: 'My son, why did you not review the five books of Torah, which contain the *Shema*, *tefillin*, and *mezuzah*?' If one comes who has learned the five books of Torah, the Holy One Blessed be He asks him: 'My son, why did you not learn *hagaddah*, etc.' If one comes who has learned *hagaddah*, the Holy One Blessed be He asks him: 'My son, why did you not learn *Talmud*? etc.' If one comes who has learned *Talmud*, the Holy One Blessed be He asks him: 'If you have learned *Talmud*, have you contemplated the Divine Chariot? etc., My throne of glory, how it stands? etc., how many ways it revolves? etc.'"

And, more than this, they do not even support their sons in Torah, and they send them to school only until they know a little *Chumash*. Woe unto us that things have come to such a pass in our days! Do we not know what is ruled in *Yoreh Deah* 245:6, that where the father has the means it is incumbent upon him to pay for his son's being taught until he knows *Mishnah*, *Gemara*, *halachoth* and *aggadoth*?

And I know their excuses, that the times are difficult, etc. But, in truth, if they searched their souls they would know that the *yetzer* is only deceiving them. For in other things, which are only of physical benefit to their son, does not each one of them assist his son with all of his strength, even more than he is able? And sometimes, he even places his life in danger because of him, doing things which are against the *din*, both between man and his neighbor and between man and the L-rd. And he blesses himself in his heart, saying: "All will be well with me, for I am doing charity at all times by feeding my family." But when he must support his son in Torah, to know how to serve the L-rd, bringing both his son and himself to eternal life, as we shall adduce below from the *midrashim* of Chazal, he says that times are hard! And this is as Scripture states (*Isaiah* 93:2): "And not *Me* did you call upon, Jacob; for you grew weary with Me, O Israel" — "with *Me*," specifically.

As we find on this verse in the *Midrash, Esther Rabbah* 3: "All day he is busy working and does not become weary; he prays, and he becomes weary!"

And, in truth, the expenditures for the Torah study of his sons are outside of the expenditures for sustenance fixed for him on Rosh Hashanah, as Chazal have said (*Beitzah* 16a): "All the sustenance for man is fixed for him from Rosh Hashanah until Yom Kippur, except expenditures for Shabbath, ...and expenditures for his sons' Torah studies, which, if he gives less, he is given less [by Heaven], and if he gives more, he is given more." Come and see what Chazal have said (*Kiddushin* 30a): "If one teaches his son's son Torah, Scripture reckons it unto him as if he had received it on Mount Sinai, viz. *Devarim* 4:9: 'And you shall impart them [(words of Torah)] to your sons and to the sons of your sons," followed by (*Ibid.* 10): 'the day you stood before the L-rd your G-d in Chorev.'" Also, through this, he merits long life for him and his sons, it being written (*Ibid.* 11:19): "And you shall teach them to your sons," followed by (*Ibid.* 21): "So that your days be prolonged and the days of your sons, etc."

Also, through his son's Torah learning, he merits being rescued from Gehinnom, as we find in *Tanna d'bei Eliyahu Zuta* 12: "Ignoramuses who have had their sons taught Scripture and *Mishnah*, are rescued by them from that shame and that humiliation and that mortification and from the *din* of Gehinnom."

And sometimes they also merit thereby to be numbered among the *tzaddikim*, as we find in *Midrash Hane'elam, Ruth*, chapter 2: "When R. Zmira went to Kfar Ono, he saw pillars of flame rising in the clefts of the mountains of Ararat. Inclining his ear, he heard voices, and an Arab told him: 'Come with me and I will show you wonders hidden from men.' He went with him behind a rock and saw other clefts with flames rising on high and heard other voices, at which the Arab said to him: 'Incline your ear here, etc.' He did so and heard voices saying: 'Woe! Woe!' at which he said: 'This place is certainly one of the places of Gehinnom,' and the Arab left him. In the meantime, he bent down in a different place and saw a man screaming and being taken and placed into a different depth into which he disappeared and was seen no more. At this, he fell into a dream in which he saw that man and asked him: 'Who are you?' He answered: 'I am a sinning Jew, who has not left undone any sins in the world.' R. Zmira: 'What is your name?' The other: 'I do not know. Those sentenced to Gehinnom do not remember their names.' R. Zmira: 'Where do you come from?' The other: 'From upper Galilee. I was a butcher, and because of the many evils I did there, they sentenced "that man" [i.e., me] to three times [of punishment] in the daytime and three times at night.' R. Zmira rose from there and went to upper Galilee, where he heard a child's voice saying (*Mishlei* 2:40: 'If you seek it as silver, if you search for it as hidden treasure, then you will understand the fear of the L-rd.' He went to another house of study, where he heard the voice of a different child saying (*Zephaniah* 2:3): 'Seek righteousness, seek humility. Perhaps you will be concealed' [from His wrath]. He went and sought that wicked man, and questioned a child, who said to him: 'Rebbi, may this and this come upon that man, who did not leave undone any evils or sins in the world. May it be thus with that wicked man and to the nurse who gave suck to him.' R. Zmira: 'Did he have a son in the world?' The child: 'Yes, he left one son, and he is wicked like his father, and he is the child that goes to the slaughterhouse.' He [R. Zmira] sought him out and took him and occupied himself with him in Torah until he had taught him reading, prayer, and *Shema*, after which he taught him *Mishnah, Talmud, halachoth* and *aggadoth*, until he grew very wise — and he is R. Nachum Hapakuli. And why did they call him "Hapakuli"? As it is written (*Isaiah* 28:7): "*paku pliliyah*" — [homiletically,] "he released [his father from] the *din* [of that world]." And many sages of the generation descended from him, who were called "Pakuli." That man [the butcher] came to him in a dream and said to him: 'Rebbi, how much you have comforted me — so may the Holy One Blessed be He comfort you. For from the day that my son knew a single verse, He released me from my *din*. Once he recited the *Shema*, they manumitted my *din* both by day and by night, by one time. Once he read in school, they annulled my *din* altogether. On the day he grew so wise that they called him "Rabbi" they placed my seat among the *tzaddikim* in Gan Eden. And every day that a Torah novelty is cited in his name they crown me with the highest crown that the *tzaddikim* are crowned with. Because of you I have merited all this honor. Happy is the lot of him who leaves a son who toils in Torah in this world!'"

And similarly, in *Tanna d'bei Eliyahu Zuta* 17: R. Yochanan b. Zakkai said: "Once, I was walking on the road, when I found a man collecting wood, and I spoke to him, but he did not answer me. Afterwards, he came and said to me: 'Rebbi, I am dead and not alive.' And I said to him: 'If you are dead, why do you need this wood?' He answered: 'Rebbi, listen to this one thing that I will tell you. Once, when I was alive, my friend and I were involved in sin in my palace. And when we came here, they decreed death by burning upon us. When I collect wood, they burn my friend; and when he collects wood, they burn me.' And I said to him: 'Until when is your *din*?' He answered: 'When I came here, I left my wife pregnant; and I know that she is pregnant with a male. Therefore, I beseech you to take care of him when he is born until he is five years old and [then] take him to school to [learn to] read. For when he says: 'Let us bless the blessed L-rd,' they will raise me from the *din* of Gehinnom.'"

Also, all of the reward we wrote of above in respect to one who supports Torah scholars obtains also with one who supports his son for Torah study. And he also merits thereby that he finds favor in the eyes of the Holy One Blessed be He, as we find in *Tanna d'bei Eliyahu Zuta* 23, in respect to the query of the attribute of *din* as to why He favors Israel when it is written (*Devarim* 10:17): 'The great G-d... who does not show favor,'; and the Holy One Blessed be He answers: 'But do they not show *Me* favor, etc. And, furthermore, they teach Torah and set up groups to occupy themselves with Torah and pay a wage to the teachers to teach their sons Torah!'"

And, conversely, the punishment of one who deprives his son of Torah study is explained in the holy *Zohar, Parshath Pekudei* 256: "...two pillars on the western side, etc." These are appointed to proclaim in all the heavens about all those who deprive their sons of Torah and remove them [from it] so that they not occupy themselves with it: 'Woe unto Ploni, who deprived his son of Torah. Woe unto him, for he goes lost from this world and from the world to come, and from [his] portion in the world to come!'"

And this is an open rebuke to those who deprive their sons of Torah study when they are yet youths of fourteen or fifteen, and through this they remain [callow] youths, "shaken out" of Torah and mitzvoth, whose only desire is to wear fashionable clothing and to broaden their horizons with silver and gold. Woe to the shame of that father when his time comes to return to G-d!

And there are some who rationalize thus: "What good will it do him to be a [Torah] learner? Is he gong to be a Rabbi?" (the implication being that if he is *not* going to be a Rabbi, a Jew need not know how to serve the L-rd, G-d forbid!) Let there not be such in Israel. Are we not familiar with the verse (*Psalms* 19:9): "The mitzvah of the L-rd is clear, enlightening the eyes," which is understood to mean that a man, without Torah to guide him, is like a blind man, walking by himself on a road full of pits, whose danger is extremely great, and whose failure is certainly nearer than his escape. So, exactly, is a man devoid of Torah. Not only will he be lacking many hundreds of mitzvoth because of this [ignorance of Torah], not knowing at all if what he is doing is a mitzvah or not, but he will commit in their stead many hundreds of transgressions which he thought to be mitzvoth. And, even more, the mitzvoth that *will* remain with him, aside from most of them being performed without joy, without love, and without fear, will themselves be imperfect and defective, for he will not know how to perform them according to the *din*.

By way of illustration, consider two mitzvoth that are observed by all Jews, *tefillin* [and the recital of *Shema*]: *Tefillin* — Has he taken care that they be [perfectly] square, according to the *din*? And that the straps are black? For all of this is a "*halachah* to Moses from Sinai." And also that the *tefillin* be placed on the head and not on the forehead? And also that the hand phylactery be placed entirely on the biceps and not [even] slightly below? Quite understandably, anyone who is not a learned person will be likely to transgress these things.

And so with the recital of the *Shema*: Has he taken care to accept upon himself the yoke of the kingdom of Heaven according to the *din*? And, likewise, to make [his recitation] audible to his ears and to enunciate correctly, as explained in *Shas* and in *Shulchan Aruch*. And also to recite it in its prescribed time, in summer and winter, for all this is a *din* of the Torah. And, also, [to observe] many details of the *dinim* obtaining with these mitzvoth. And from these, one will reason, *a fortiori*, to those mitzvoth that Jews are not accustomed to — that he will certainly lack them without a knowledge of the Torah.

And everyone will recognize this lack when the Holy One Blessed be He is destined to proclaim that they all come to accept their reward for the mitzvoth, as Chazal say (*Vayikra Rabbah* 27): "A Heavenly voice is destined to resound in the mountain peak, proclaiming: 'Who wrought with G-d, let him come and take his reward!'" Then, each one will "feel" his mitzvoth and recognize the greatness of his deficit in mitzvoth, which he suffered through his lack of knowledge of the Torah. And this is the intent of "enlightening the eyes," the Torah enlightening the eyes of a man in the fulfillment of the mitzvoth.

And now, let us reflect and take *mussar* from the earlier generations, that preceded us these several hundred years (as in the times of the Maharshal, the Maharsha, the *Maharam Shif*, the *P'nei Yehoshua*, and the Tzelach, who were all heads of *Methivtoth*), who sent their children to school, and who, if they did not have the means to hire a private teacher would send their sons to a yeshivah to learn until he became a man. Shall we say that every father thought that his son would be a Rabbi or a *posek* in Israel. Do we not know what Chazal (*Koheleth Rabbah* 7) say on the verse (*Koheleth* 7:28): "One man of a thousand have I found" — "A thousand embark upon Scripture, and from them emerge a hundred men of *Mishnah*; from them, ten men of *Talmud*; and from them, one who is worthy of being called "a man," and to pronounce ruling in Israel." But the clear truth is this: A father who sent his son to a school and a yeshiva reasoned thus: "If the L-rd finds me worthy of having a son who will be a man of *Talmud* and a teacher in Israel, how goodly is my portion! But if I do not merit this, but only that he know a little of *Gemara*, or, in any event, *Mishnayoth*, this is also good. For when the Holy One Blessed be He grants him a trade — no matter what trade it be — he certainly will set for himself a fixed study session for himself in *Gemara* or *Mishnayoth* or, in any event, in *aggadoth chazal*. And even if, G-d forbid, he has no time on the weekdays, on the Holy Sabbath he certainly will go into the house of study and learn some pages of *Gemara* or *Mishnayoth*. And for this, too, all my exertions for him will have been well worth it, both in my lifetime and in my death" (As we know, a son who learns Torah accords merit to his father and releases him from Gehinnom. And even if he is in Gan Eden, he merits ascending through him.)

If so, why should we be "smarter" than the earlier generations? For, in truth, in this regard, we have been "without field or vineyard" more than eighteen hundred years, and, in spite of this, our G-d has not forsaken us. This [(reluctance to further the Torah education of our sons)] can only be due to the fact that the *yetzer hara* deceives the father into believing that he is being compassionate to his son by removing him from Torah and subjugating him to the affairs of the world. But, in truth, when he considers this well, he will see that he is being cruel to him in this and not compassionate. As we find in *Sifrei* on *Devarim* 11:19: "'And you shall teach them [(words of Torah)] to your sons to speak in them.' From this they have taught: When the child begins to speak, his father speaks the holy tongue with him and teaches him Torah. And if he does not do so, he is fit to be buried, as it is written: 'And you shall teach them to your sons to speak in them… (*Ibid.* 21): so that your days will be lengthened.' If you teach them to your sons your days will be lengthened, and, if not, your days will be shortened." For thus are words of Torah expounded: From the negative you infer the positive; and from the positive, the negative. (And the *Sifrei* speaks not only of very young children; but so long as his son is under his authority, it is incumbent upon him to teach him Torah [For does the verse specify "minors"?]) And thus have Chazal said (*Shabbath* 32b), that a man's sons die because of neglect of Torah. Therefore, let each man see to it to strengthen his son in Torah, and he will thereby lengthen his days — he and his sons. And the Holy One Blessed be He, who gives bread to all flesh, will certainly not withdraw His eyes from the *tzaddik*.

Chapter VIII

More on the subject

There are some today who use a different rationalization: Why should we work for naught to teach him Torah? "Perhaps he will have to go to the army when he reaches twenty, and it is better to teach him other things which will make his service easier."

This can be compared to [the instance of] a man who must make a long sea voyage and despairs of buying food, preparing nothing, out of fear that what he buys will not suffice.

[And, in truth, how much should we be ashamed! For if two good, useful business opportunities presented themselves to a man, so that if he took one he would have to leave the other, he would look with a sober eye to determine which is certain and which is uncertain. And how much more so [would he choose the first] if it [the second] is only a possibility of a possibility. He would also look with a sober eye to determine which is better and more useful and which lasts a longer time. For sometimes, even if one is better than the other, if the second lasts for a longer time, he will choose that. How much more so if it is intrinsically better than the other. But when it comes to choosing between the service of the L-rd and the affairs of the world, the *yetzer* entices us to abandon the service of the L-rd, which is better and more useful in itself than all the affairs of the world, as the *tanna* has said (*Avoth* 4:14): "Better one moment in the world to come, etc.", and it is also eternal, as opposed to all the affairs of this world, which is only as a passing shadow. And also, the eternal reward that comes from serving the Blessed L-rd is a certainty than which nothing is more certain — and the *yetzer* entices us to leave all this because of the possibility of a possibility of [benefit in] this world! And this is what we say in the confessional service [of Yom Kippur]: "We have turned away from Your mitzvoth and from Your goodly judgments, and it was not comparable to us." That is, the eternal good was not [even] comparable in our eyes to the transitory good of this world. The proof: We have rejected the certain before the uncertain! And one who wishes to be saved from the enticement of the *yetzer hara* will reflect constantly within himself and consider the greatness of the pleasure of the reward that the Holy One Blessed be He will give him for [the observance of] His mitzvoth. As the GRA has written, that it is for this reason that the Holy One Blessed be He has created the eternal world with all that is necessary for the reward for fulfillment of Torah and mitzvoth and did not give His reward in this world. For even if a man were given all of this world and its pleasures for one mitzvah it would not suffice for the pleasure he deserves for the mitzvah. And if a man reflects upon this, he certainly will not reject the certain, eternal good for the possibility of the possibility (of pleasure) in this world.]

And, in truth, we should be ashamed and humiliated before our fathers of the earlier generations, who lived a few hundred years before us. How will we answer them when they ask us: "Why were you so lax in Torah study and in fulfillment of the mitzvoth? Don't you know of all the decrees and all the suffering that passed over us? [Don't you know] that they subjected us to all kinds of tortures to annul Torah and mitzvoth, in spite of which we stood firm and strengthened ourselves with what little strength remained in us to stand watch over the Torah for the honor of the L-rd, the G-d of heaven and earth, not to transgress even any of the "fences" of Chazal? And you, with the help of the L-rd, who were protected by kings of lovingkindness, who allowed you to fulfill all of the Torah and the mitzvoth, were neglectful in fulfillment of the Torah! For, in truth did the king prevent us from sending our children to a school and teach them Torah so that they would know how to serve the L-rd? Do not the kings in our days believe in the L-rd and accord honor and glory to His Torah? This [has happened] only because the *yetzer hara* has outsmarted us with his deceits to remove from us the honor and the fear of the King of kings, the Holy One Blessed be He."

And I will "raise my parable" and say: Two rulers were battling each other and they set a time of four days for the war. On the first day the first ruler overpowered the second and slew many of his foes. On the second day they warred again and the second overpowered the first. On the third day they again went out to war and the first again overpowered the second. At night, when they took counsel, one said to his neighbor: "Let us try to find some stratagem to defeat them. For what good is it if we win again tomorrow? Perhaps if we go out to war again tomorrow the second ruler will again overcome us as on the second day." The other answered: "I have a good plan. The place where they keep their shields and weapons is outside the camp. They are protected by just a few guards and not the whole army. At night let us fall suddenly upon them and take them." The plan was approved by the other, and they did so. On the morning of the fourth day the men of the first ruler trumpeted as a signal for the onset, at which the men of the second ruler ran to don their armor — but they found nothing and were forced to surrender and to take upon themselves the yoke of their foes.

So, exactly, is our situation. It is known that the *yetzer hara* is a man of war, who battles constantly against Israel. Sometimes he defeats us and sometimes we defeat him. And the *yetzer* says in his heart: "I have no way to defeat Israel. I will see to it to take their shields and weapons with which they fight me (the Torah, which alone defends Israel against the *yetzer hara*) and *it* is the weapon with which they fight me" (as Chazal have said [*Kiddushin* 30b]: "I have created a *yetzer hara*, and I have created Torah as its antidote," and without it, it is impossible to escape it, as we have written about at length elsewhere.) And so do we see with our own eyes in our time. For this is the way of the *yetzer hara*, to overcome us by arguments to keep us from learning the holy Torah.

I shall copy what I have said on a verse in the *Song of Songs*, and then we shall return to our subject. (*Song of Songs* 1:7): "Tell me, You whom my soul loves, how will You graze Your flock? How will you make them lie down in the afternoon, etc." Rashi explains that the congregation of Israel hereby says before the Holy One Blessed be He, as a wife to her husband: "Tell me, You whom my soul loves, how will You graze Your flock, [Israel], and how will You make them lie down in the afternoon, in the exile of the idolators, which is a time of suffering for them as the [hot] afternoon is a time of suffering for the flock?" And the Holy One Blessed be He answers (*Ibid*. 8): "If you do not know, you fairest of the women, [Israel], then go out in the footsteps of the sheep," which Rashi explains: "If you do not know, My congregation and My assembly, the fairest of the women among the other nations, how you will graze and rescue yourselves from those who press you to stay among them, so that your sons not go lost, reflect upon the ways of your forefathers, who received My Torah and kept My 'keeping' and My mitzvoth, and walk in their ways, and, also, in reward for this, you will graze your kids, among the princes of the peoples. And thus did Jeremiah say (*Jeremiah* 31:24): "Make road markers for yourself… set your heart to the path, etc." Now, as to the answer of the Holy One Blessed be He, does Israel not know [by themselves] that it is a mitzvah to walk in the path of our forefathers? But, in truth, this is a deep matter. The congregation of Israel asked for counsel, what to do at this time, when we are without influence and steeped in many troubles and the *yetzer hara* entices us to remove from ourselves the yoke of Torah, so that thereby the yoke of the idolators might be eased from us. Therefore the term "grazing" is used, which connotes influence, and "how will You make them lie down," as explained by Rashi. The Holy One Blessed be He responds: "If you do not know, you fairest of the women, go out in the footsteps of the sheep." That is, reflect upon the ways of your fathers. For it is known that Israel's invocation of the L-rd's remembrance of "the merit of the fathers" in almost every prayer is contingent upon our walking to some extent in their ways. And though we will not be able to achieve even a fraction of a fraction of their holy ways (not to speak of "walking in their ways"), as Scripture said (*Joshua* 14:15): "the greatest of the giants," concerning which Chazal have said [*Bereshith Rabbah* 14:6] that this refers to Abraham and the other forefathers (apparently also in this regard) — in any event, if we see to it to attain what our intellects *can* attain of their holy ways and to grasp a little of their holy conduct, then their exalted merit will avail us to bring us to all good — which will not be the case if we "turn a shirking shoulder" and refuse to walk in their ways at all, in which instance, the remembrance of their merit will not be to our honor.

I shall adduce one instance, which is not even a fraction of a fraction of their holy ways: Why did the Holy One Blessed be He exalt Abraham so greatly because of the *akeidah* [the binding of Isaac]? Is it not true even in our days that if the Holy One Blessed be He commanded one to sacrifice his son as a burnt-offering he would not refuse? But the truth is, as Rambam writes, that his [greatness in his] trial was his acquiescence in it with absolute love. Witness his rising for it early in the morning, splitting the wood by himself, and waiting three days until the place [of the sacrifice] appeared to him. And there were several [other] trials included in this, as we find in the *Midrash*: that the Satan appeared in the form of a river, which Abraham had to cross on the way to the *akeidah*, walking neck-deep in the water and crying: "Save, O L-rd, for water has come to soul!" and the [apparition] vanished, all of this indicating his perfect love for the L-rd and his complete acquiescence [in His command].

And now let us reflect for awhile. What if Abraham had to give his son to a king for military service and he had several ways of easing that service, such as keeping him from Torah study for several years and teaching him some other subjects which would afterward lighten his load — and then, the Holy One Blessed be He appeared to him and said: "Do as you have always done; teach him Torah and mitzvoth, and then *I* will do as *I* want" — would not Abraham acquiesce in this in full love, even more than he did in the *akeidah*? And even *much* more so, for in this he would not even need the commandment of the L-rd, [but would do so himself]!

And now, how should we not be ashamed of ourselves, knowing that we also, bless the L-rd, are believers in the L-rd and in His Torah, and we remember always the merit of the *akeidah* of Israel, Abraham's son; and yet, when we find ourselves in the same situation, we immediately sacrifice Torah and mitzvoth — just to rescue him from military service! And the *yetzer hara* entices us, [telling us that] in this we are pitying our son. But, in truth, this is not pity, but cruelty to his soul (as mentioned above in *Sifrei*) and to all his future generations.

And, also, in most cases this will also cause him bodily harm; for he will be trained from his youth to fulfill his lusts, and when he cannot adequately satisfy them, he will injure men in all the ways that he can — through theft, robbery, and violence. "His hand will be against all, and the hand of all, against him" (*Bereshith* 16:12).

And now let us consider the other forefathers. It is known that Isaac, our father, was thirty-seven years old at the time of the *akeidah* (*Bereshith* 29:20). And if he had not acquiesced in the *akeidah*, the aged Abraham could certainly not have forced him into it. But, certainly, Isaac did this with full acquiescence, as it is written (*Bereshith* 22:8): "And the two of them went *together*" — with one heart. And Isaac, who acquiesced in this, would certainly not flout the will of the Holy One Blessed be He for [relatively] minor considerations. If so, we, who always bring his merits to remembrance [(for our sake)], how much should we walk in his ways, not to abandon Torah and mitzvoth for anything!

Chapter IX

More on the same subject

And now we shall speak of Jacob, our father, may peace be upon him. It is known that when he went from his father's house to Canaan, he was sixty-three years old, as Rashi explains. And he was seventy-seven when he came to the house of Lavan. What happened to the fourteen intervening years? Chazal say (*Bereshith Rabbah* 68:5) that he was with Shem and Ever and learned there in their house of study.

Now, ostensibly, this raises a question about our father, Jacob, may peace be upon him. Was this the time for Torah study? Was he not sixty-three years old and without children? And [this is] especially [puzzling] in view of the fact that only he, and no other man, was fit for the procreation of the holy nation of Israel which was destined to appear upon the earth. And all this was known to our father Jacob, as Rashi comments on (*Bereshith* 29:21): "For my days [of waiting] have been completed," "and when will I procreate the twelve tribes?" If so, it was a great mitzvah that he go immediately to the house of Lavan, as Isaac had told him and marry a woman and not to delay and separate himself for Torah study for fourteen years.

To answer all this, it would seem that Jacob knew that obviously Lavan would not agree to give him his daughter without receiving a great gift, as it is written (*Ibid*. 31:15): "Does he [Lavan] not regard us [his daughters] as strangers"? [see Rashi] And it is known that our father Jacob became impoverished by Elifaz [the son of Esav] on the way. If so, he would certainly have to do slave labor for him in order to marry his daughter, as Isaac had commanded him, and as, indeed, occurred in the end. And Jacob was afraid to go down to him and to remain there. For he knew that Lavan was a deceiver, and that he would also want to drive him from the world, as the Torah testifies about him at the end, that he pursued him and desired to kill him, lest the G-d of Abraham aided and rescued him (viz. *Ibid*. 31:42). And [he knew that] his house, too, was full of idols and that he could not withstand such impurity without the merit of the holiness of Torah, and that in the house of Lavan it would not be possible for him to cleave to Torah.

Therefore, anticipating this, he fled to Shem and Ever and studied Torah there with great diligence for fourteen years. For all of these years he did not once lay down to sleep a full sleep, as Scripture testifies about him (*Ibid*. 28:11): "And he slept in *that* place," as Rashi explains there. And, with such learning, though he remained in the house of Lavan afterwards for several years, nothing could harm him. [According to our words, the figure of fourteen years is very apt. For since they were meant to offset the years that he would have to remain in the house of

Lavan, and it is known that this would be fourteen years, Jacob knowing that he could not return to his house so long as Joseph had not been born, he [Joseph] being as "flame" and Esav as "straw" [see *Ovadiah* 1:18], and as it is written (*Bereshith* 30:25): "And it was, when Rachel bore Joseph, that Jacob said to Lavan: "Send me away, etc."", (as Rashi explains), and it is known that Joseph was in the fourteenth year, as it is written (*Ibid.* 31:41): "I served you fourteen years for your two daughters, etc." — therefore, Jacob first learned Torah fourteen years without interruption, so that the merit of these fourteen years would stand for him in the house of Lavan, as mentioned above.]

Now we, who always bring to remembrance the merit of the fathers [on our behalf] must walk, likewise, in the footsteps of Jacob our father, may peace be upon him. And every father must see to it to habituate his son to Torah and to mitzvoth so long as he is at his table; that is, until he is twenty-one years of age. And then, even if his lot falls to serve his majesty, the emperor, and he certainly will not be able to study Torah at that time, still, there will not depart from him the holiness of the Torah that he had learned until then. [And certainly the Holy One Blessed be He will prosper him and will incline the hearts of the king and his counselors and his princes to him for the good, as it is written in regard to Joseph (*Bereshith* 39:21): "And the L-rd was with Joseph, and He conferred grace upon him, and He granted him favor, etc."] And also, at the end of his term of service, when he returns home, all of his deeds will be done with integrity and his father will not be ashamed of him, and the Holy One Blessed be He will prosper him for this in this world, as he did with Jacob our father at the end of his term of service with Lavan, as written in the Torah. And also, in the celestial world, when he merits standing before the throne of honor of the Blessed One, he will be one of the "holy ones" of the L-rd in the merit of having singled out the L-rd to be his G-d, as it is written (*Devarim* 16:17-19): "The L-rd did you single out this day to be to you as a G-d, and to walk in His ways, and to keep His statutes, and His mitzvoth… And the L-rd did single you out this day… and to be a holy people to the L-rd your G-d, etc."

But, if he [the father] will seek to remove from him the yoke of Torah and mitzvoth in his youth in order to lighten the load of his military service, so that he will have to serve only a short time, then he will be a shame to his father in his beginning in this world and source of humiliation to him in the end, in the upper world, for he will have traded an eternal world for a temporal one.

And because it is known that the *yetzer* always stirs up a man to think only of temporal success, the *tanna* has given us a balm for this, saying (*Avoth* 2:1): "Weigh the loss of a mitzvah against its gain, and the gain of a transgression against its loss." That is, let one appraise the smallness of the loss that he incurs in this world by performing a mitzvah against the vastness of the eternal, spiritual reward that he will gain in the upper world. And if the *yetzer hara* invites him to perform a transgression for some pleasure, let him appraise the smallness of the pleasure that he will enjoy from it in this world for a minute time against the vast punishment and eternal suffering that it will cause him.

And the same applies in our case. In order to overcome the *yetzer* and those who incite him to incline his son from the path of good to that of evil, let one put before his eyes the eternal reward and punishment, respectively, that a man derives from his sins, and then the *yetzer* will relax its grip on him. For this is the language of the holy *Zohar* in *Parshath Bechukothai* 115: "(*Malachi* 1:6): 'A son will honor his father, and a servant his master.' A son will honor his father, as it is written: 'Honor your father and your mother,' which they explained: 'with food and with drink and the like.' This, during the life of his father. Now lest you say that after his father dies, he is exempt from this, this is not so, for [in this respect, too,] it is written: 'Honor your father.' For if the son walks in crooked paths, he certainly shames his father; he certainly humiliates him. But if that son walks in a just path and corrects his misdeeds, he certainly honors his father. He honors him in this world before people; he honors him in the world to come before the Holy One Blessed be He. The Holy One Blessed be He pities him [the father] and places him in his seat of honor. Happy are the *tzaddikim*, who merit holy sons, holy offspring, of whom it is written (*Isaiah* 61:9): 'All who see them will defer to them, for they are seed blessed of the L-rd.'"

And, what is more, even if this [disreputable] son of his dies, and he [the father] has already merited through his deeds to sit in Gan Eden, even so, there will accrue to him [the father] great suffering from him. For they will take him from Gan Eden to Gehinnom to witness the suffering of his son, as Chazal have said. And the GRA has adduced this idea on the verse (*Mishlei* 29:17): "Chastise your son and he will give you peace, and he will give pleasures to your soul": "When your son, etc."; and, furthermore, he will give you peace from Gehinnom, 'and he will give pleasures to your soul' in Gan Eden, as in the episode of R. Akiva, who learned Torah with a wicked son and rescued him [the father] from Gehinnom; and, what is more, even a *tzaddik*, if he has a wicked son, is taken from Gan Eden to Gehinnom to witness the suffering of his son. And this is the meaning of 'Chastise your son, and he will give you peace' in your place, and he will also give you pleasures, etc."

And when he reflects constantly and weighs the smallness of the reward of transgression in this world against its eternal loss, the father will certainly not pay heed to the voice of the "whisperers" and will choose life, to strengthen his son in the Torah of the L-rd, which is the true life, as it is written (*Mishlei* 3:18): "It is a tree of life to those who hold fast to it." And if he eats of its fruits, he lives forever, as Chazal have formulated for us in the blessing "And eternal life did He plant in our midst." And then he will merit eternal life, he and his seed, as it is written: "And he will give pleasure to your soul," and, as it is written in the Torah (*Devarim* 30:19): "And choose life, so that you live, you and your seed."

And also in this world, his affairs will prosper, as Chazal have said (*Avodah Zarah* 19b): "Whoever occupies himself with Torah, his affairs prosper," as it is written (*Psalms* 1:2-3): 'but in the Torah of the L-rd is his desire,… and all that he does shall prosper.'"

And all this is alluded to in short in the answer of the Holy One Blessed be He to the congregation of Israel (*Song of Songs* 1:7): "How will you *graze*?", which connotes "influence." How will you make them lie down in the *afternoon*?", which connotes the severity of the time. "If you do not know, etc.… in the footsteps of the sheep," which alludes to reflection upon the ways of our forefathers — Abraham, Isaac, and Jacob. If we walk in their ways, He will grant us influence, as our fathers had, and there will be attenuated for us the severity of the times in all of our dwelling places.

And, with the help of the L-rd, I have found, similarly, in the holy *Zohar* that this verse alludes to strengthening our sons in Torah, whereby we will have strength to protect our sons and whereby we shall endure among the nations, viz. *Zohar, Parshath Balak*: "If you do not know *for you*, you fairest of the women, etc." Why "for you"? [The meaning is:] If you do not know how to strengthen yourself in exile and how to gird yourself with power to defend your sons, then "go out *for you*," to strengthen *yourself* "in the footsteps of *the sheep*," the children in their teacher's house, who study Torah." From them you will take strength to protect your sons.

Chapter X

*In this chapter there will be explained what Chazal have said, that
"a man without Torah is like a fish without water"*

And let a man not err, saying: "What is all this fuss about removing my son from Torah? Can't he be a Jew, like other Jews, without it?" But, in truth, it is not so, my brother, for it has already been proved from what Chazal have said in *Berachoth* 71b and in several other places, and from what has occurred in our times, too, in the crucible of experience, that a Jew taken from Torah is like a fish taken from the water. Though it may have some life left in it, it will surely die in the end. It is possible for a fish to live a few hours so long as the water is yet on its body; but when it dries up, it will die immediately, for its life-element has expired.

The same is true of the essential holiness of the L-rd which hovers over His people, Israel, through which they will merit to endure forever, as it is written (*Devarim* 4:4): "And you who cleave to the L-rd your G-d are all alive today, etc.", concerning which Chazal have said that this is only through the agency of Torah. And when men separate themselves from Torah, so long as the "moistness" of Torah is still upon them they still occupy themselves somewhat with its mitzvoth, to which they were accustomed in the past. But with the passage of time, as the moistness begins to dry, they also begin to forsake mitzvoth, and who knows to what this can lead.

And, in truth, this is the intent of the verses in *Parshath Bechukothai* (*Vaykira* 26:14-15): "And if you do not hearken to Me (to toil in Torah, etc., as Rashi explains there), and you do not do all these mitzvoth (If you do not learn, you will not do), and if (as a result of not doing) you despise (the doers of) My statutes, and if your souls repel (the exemplifiers of) My ordinances, (the sages), not to do (i.e., preventing others from doing) all of My mitzvoth (i.e., if you deny that they are '*My*' mitzvoth) to break My covenant" (i.e., to deny *Me* — seven transgressions, the first leading to the second, etc., all this as explained by Rashi according to *Torath Cohanim*.)

And I have hereby explained what we say each day in the second section of the *Shema* (*Devarim* 11:13): "And it shall be if you hearken… to love… (*Ibid*. 16): Pay heed unto yourselves… and you shall serve other gods, etc." For is it not the way that when a man exhorts his son to follow the right path, he does so in accordance with his [the son's nature]? If he [already] walks on that path, he exhorts him to summon up more strength and not depart from it; and if he walks waywardly according to the whims of his heart and desires to leave him, he commands him at the least not to depart from the way of the L-rd altogether, G-d forbid. And if he would do the reverse, and command his son who walks in the right path not to depart from the way of the L-rd and change his faith, G-d forbid, this would be neither to his honor nor to his son's. And here does the beginning of the section "And it shall be, etc." not speak of men who fear the L-rd and love His name with their whole heart and soul, as it is written "to love, etc."? How, then, can we understand "lest your heart be enticed, etc." And, furthermore, the phrase "and you turn astray" (*vesartem*) would seem to be superfluous.

But the truth is according to its plain meaning. For in the beginning of the section it is written (*Ibid.* 13): "and to serve Him with all your heart," concerning which Chazal have said (*Ta'anith* 2a): "What is service of the heart? Prayer." And, therefore, Scripture states: "Pay heed unto yourselves lest your heart be enticed." That is, lest the *yetzer* entice you to say: "Why should I study Torah if I already love the L-rd, and, thank G-d, I pray every day? This is enough, and what of it if I do turn away now completely from Torah [study] or if I turn my son away from it? Does he not pray every day?" Therefore, Scripture comes and apprises us that the end of turning away from Torah will be "and you will serve other gods," as we wrote in the beginning, that this is comparable to a fish's being taken from water, in which instance his very life will depart in a short time. So with the Jew who departs from Torah [study] completely and swerves from the path of *mussar* to a different path. He is not far from the service of other gods. (And this is obvious, for thus is it found in *Sifrei* on this verse: "lest your heart be enticed, and you turn astray, and you serve, etc." — once a man separates himself from Torah, he immediately cleaves to idolatry.

And that is why Scripture says afterwards (*Ibid.* 18): "And you shall place these, My words, upon your heart." That is, let these words of Mine — that when a man turns aside from Torah [study], he will come, G-d forbid, in the end, to idolatry — enter your heart. And, therefore (*Ibid.* 19): "You shall teach them to your sons, etc." and not be satisfied with your son's fulfilling the mitzvah of prayer alone. And for this reason, Scripture concludes (*Ibid.* 21): "So that your days be prolonged and the days of your children on the earth," as Chazal say in *Perek Chelek*: "The exiles are gathered in only in the merit of Torah."

All this [applied] even in the earlier generations; how much more so, in ours, when so many have strayed from the way of the L-rd by separating from the Torah. This is certainly "a time to do" for [the sake of] the L-rd, and to strengthen our sons in Torah and tradition.

And this is the language of the holy *Zohar* in *Parshath Terumah* on *Psalms* 129:126): "It is a time to act for the L-rd," viz.: "So long as the Torah endures in the world and men occupy themselves with it, the Holy One Blessed be He rejoices in the work of His hands and rejoices in all of the worlds, and the heavens and the earth remain standing. What is more, the Holy One Blessed be He gathers all His tribunal and says to them: 'See the holy people that I have on the earth, by whom the Torah is adorned. See My handiwork, about which you have said: 'What is man that You remember him?'" And when they see the joy of their Master in His people, they immediately open [their mouths] and say (I *Chronicles* 17:21): 'Who is like Your people, Israel, one nation in the land?' But when Israel neglect Torah, His strength, as it were, weakens, wherefore "it is a time [for *you*] to act for the L-rd.' These are the *tzaddikim* who are left. They must gird their loins and perform good deeds, so that the Holy One Blessed be He will strengthen Himself to rejoice with the *tzaddikim* and with His camps and battalions. Why so? (*Psalms, Ibid.*): [For] 'they have violated Your Torah,' and the men of the world do not occupy themselves with it as is fitting."

And especially in our times, when we see with our own eyes in our many sins that the youth who have departed from the Torah have also abandoned the observance of Shabbath and other observances, it certainly devolves upon every father to strengthen his sons in the Torah of the L-rd and to train him in His mitzvoth, as it is written (*Mishlei* 22:6): 'Train the youth, etc.' And his reward for this will be very great, far greater than that of the preceding generations, as we find in *Avoth d'R. Nathan* 3:6: "Better a hundred times with suffering than one time without suffering," and (*Ezekiel* 44:15): "But the Cohanim - the Levites, the sons of Tzaddok, who kept the keeping of My sanctuary when the children of Israel strayed from Me — they shall draw near to Me to serve Me, etc."

What emerges for us from all of these chapters is that each one must see to it to sanctify his faculty of speech with the holiness of Torah and to strengthen the pillar of Torah, and by doing so, we will merit the coming of the Redeemer, speedily, in our days, Amen.

Conclusion

Wherein will be explained more matters relevant to Gates One and Two

Chapter I

In this chapter it will be explained how by guarding his tongue one will merit distinctive eminence in the world to come.

Chazal have said (*Bava Bathra* 165a): "The majority [transgress the sin of] theft; the minority, illicit relations; and all, the "dust of *lashon hara*." From this, one can reflect upon the greatness of guarding his tongue. For do we not see it to be the nature of all men to take pride in something which mirrors his eminence? If he is extremely wealthy, he will exert himself greatly to have a magnificent courtyard; if a homeowner, to have a beautiful home; and even if he is a servant, he will see to it to have a beautiful uniform for Shabbath and Yom Tov so that he is not embarrassed before his friends. Now, if this is so in this transient world, whose pleasures and honor are only vanity and emptiness, then how much more so is it so in the eternal world.

Is it not known that because a man cleaves to the service of the Holy One Blessed be He to fulfill His mitzvoth there is created there in his honor a holy sanctuary for him for his pleasure, as stated in *Midrash Koheleth*, that each *tzaddik* is given a distinct dwelling for his honor. And if this is so, the man who guards himself in his lifetime from illicit relations, though his reward will also be great for this and he will be given a place readied for eternal pleasure, still, this kind of sanctuary and its pleasure are found for a minority of Israel in Gan Eden, and his eminence is not distinctively recognized, for do not only a minority stumble in illicit relations? And if he guards himself against theft, and a minority also guard themselves from this transgression, if so, they have a sanctuary like his. But if he guards himself in the trait of guarding his tongue, in all its details, the eminence of his sanctuary created by this mitzvah will be recognized by all in Gan Eden. For do not *all* stumble in the "dust of *lashon hara*" (if not one who bestirs his soul not to be lax in this), so that there is no other sanctuary like this one.

And, especially, one who scrutinizes carefully the introduction to the *Chafetz Chaim*, and, the first two gates of all of its chapters will see that in fulfillment of the trait of guarding his tongue there will be deducted from him every year several hundreds and thousands of sins and added to him in exchange many hundreds and thousands of mitzvoth. For even if there only be deducted from him through this ten words of improper speech each day, that he has muzzled his mouth from speaking, it would still amount to over three thousand per year (And in this way I have explained what Chazal have said (*Arachin* 15b): "All who speak *lashon hara* increase sins until the heavens," the meaning being that if one is habituated to this sin, then from this itself his sins increase greatly), and those [muzzled] words would be reckoned as mitzvoth for him in the world to come. As Chazal have said (*Makkoth* 23b): "If a man sits [idle] and does not commit a sin, he is rewarded as one who has done a mitzvah, and, for every moment that he muzzles his mouth, etc." And he will also arrive, as a matter of course, at many holy traits, as I have written in the Second Gate of this work.

Chapter II

In this chapter there will be explained the value of guarding one's tongue, for him who sets times for Torah

And, especially, if one has a time set aside for Torah in the house of study, how much will the trait of guarding his tongue avail his learning that it not be disturbed! For failing that he runs the risk of losing learning every day, and his learning itself will be fragmented. And the greatness of the punishment for this is well known. As Chazal have said (*Avodah Zarah* 3b): "If one interrupts his Torah study to engage in talk, he is fed broom-coals, as it is written (*Iyyov* 30:4): 'Those who interrupt *maluach* [(homiletically) "words written on the *tablets*" (*luchoth*)] with [idle] talk, broom-coal roots are their bread.'" And this is measure for measure. For if one studies Torah, his soul endures forever by the light of the holy Torah, which does not consume the soul (G-d forbid), but, to the contrary, sustains it eternally, as bread sustains his body in his lifetime. For this reason, Torah is called "bread," as it is written (*Mishlei* 9:5): "Come, eat of My bread, etc." And if he stops in the middle of his learning, he indicates that he does not want that bread, wherefore, he is fed there — instead of the food of the soul, the light of Torah — the light [i.e., the fire] of broom-coal roots.

Why broom trees, specifically? Because those coals made from a broom tree do not burn out for twelve months, as Chazal have said (*Bava Bathra* 74b), to teach us that he is judged for this like a *rasha* [a wicked one], whose punishment in Gehinnom lasts for twelve months. And this is the language of the holy *Zohar* in *Parshath Shelach*: "If one interrupts words of Torah for idle talk, his life is 'interrupted' from this world and his judgment awaits him in the world to come."

[And, in truth, it would seem to me as good counsel for one who would like to guard his mouth and his tongue from forbidden speech, to teach himself not to speak at all in the house of study or the house of prayer. For aside from this being a great mitzvah in itself because of the sanctity of the place, as the holy books write, it is also of great avail to us in other respects 1) that the Torah one studies in the house of study and his prayers be complete, not lacking any answering of "*Amen*" and "*Amen yeheh shmer rabbah*" and "*Barchu*", 2) that through this there be in the accounting of the days of his life about ten years free of forbidden speech. For a Jew is found during the day in the house of study for his prayers and for some time after his prayer, for at least four hours a day, especially if he also has a set time for Torah study every day in the house of study for about two hours. Attending to this, about one-fourth of the full day is spent by him in Torah and prayer. If so, how good it will be for him when a fourth part of the days of his life will be added in which there will not have been any forbidden speech, but only Torah and prayer, 3) that though through this it becomes easier for him every day, too, to guard his faculty of speech, having taught himself every day to suppress it five or six hours all the time that he sat in the house of study.]

Chapter III

In this chapter there will be explained that one must exert himself in particular for a mitzvah that lacks "patrons"

In *Sefer Charedim* we find that even though one is obligated in all of the mitzvoth he must still hold fast to one of them, with great strength and constancy, that he does not transgress all the days of his life. For the generality of Torah, comprised of the 613 mitzvoth, is called a tree of life, viz. (*Mishlei* 3:18): "It is a tree of life to those who hold fast to it." And one who holds fast to one branch of a tree holds all of them, all being one body, following after that branch. But if he tried to hold on to all of the branches together, he could not do so. And this is the intent of *Shabbath* 118b: "R. Nachman b. Yitzchak said: 'May it [(reward)] so come to me that I fulfilled [the mitzvah of] the three Sabbath meals.' ...R. Sheheth said: 'May it so come to me that I fulfilled the mitzvah of *tzitzith*!' R. Yosef asked R. Yosef b. Rabbah: 'Which mitzvah is your father most scrupulous in?' He answered: 'The mitzvah of *tzitzith*. One day he was going up a ladder when one of his fringes tore, and he would not come down until he had repaired it.'" And Rashi explains "I fulfilled the mitzvah of *tefillin*" as his not having walked four ells without *tefillin*. Similarly, with *tzitzith*... See the *Sefer Charedim* there, who adduces proof for his words from the *Yerushalmi*, too, that because of this, one's days will be enhanced and lengthened in the world which is entirely good and long.

And we, too, shall say about our subject, that in our times, when, in our many sins, the [mitzvah of avoiding] the sin of *lashon hara* and *rechiluth* has been entirely abandoned by some people, if one would strengthen himself always to guard his tongue against *lashon hara* and *rechiluth*, how much reward would be his because of this! For is it not known what is written in *Sefer Charedim* that a mitzvah that has no "patrons" is like a *meth-mitzvah* [a dead man with no one to bury him (whom the finder must bury)], and "a mitzvah that has no 'chasers' — run after it to do it," because the mitzvah cries out, saying: "How lowly I am, to have been abandoned by all!" And the greatness of [the mitzvah of] *meth-mitzvah* is already known from what is stated in *Berachoth*, that even the high-priest or a Nazirite or one who was going to slaughter his Pesach offering or to circumcise his son — who are not permitted to render themselves unclean for relatives [(through dead-body uncleanliness)] — *do* render themselves unclean for a *meth-mitzvah*, so that it not lie in shame [(unburied)].

And now let us see: Is not a *meth-mitzvah* mere matter, without life, spirit, or soul, in spite of which, because this matter was once the receptacle of a living Jew, the Torah was so concerned about its shame and permitted [its burial] even to the high-priest or to a Nazirite, and [permitted one] not to slaughter the Pesach offering or to circumcise his son, to render himself unclean for it [the dead body] and to see to its needs — *a fortiori*, with the holy Torah, which is more precious than pearls, and which is the "plaything" of the Holy One Blessed be He, as it is written (*Mishlei* 8:30): "And I [Torah] was His plaything every day" — if one of its mitzvoth, G-d forbid, lies in shame, how much more so are we obligated to strengthen ourselves in it, so that it not cry out against us in Heaven!

And see, my brother, the greatness of the abandonment that lies in *this* [(speaking *lashon hara*)] to one who is accustomed to it and does not consider it [as transgression of] a negative commandment at all. For even if he speaks evil of his neighbor and demeans him to the depths of degradation, if you ask him: "Why did you speak *lashon hara* and *rechiluth*," he will give you a hundred rationalizations as to why this is not in the category of *lashon hara*. And if you prove to him that it is *absolute lashon hara*, he will retract his original statement and say that even if it *is* in the category of *lashon hara*, the Torah certainly did not intend the interdict to apply to such a man, whom he has seen doing this and this wrong, and who is a flatterer, whose wrongdoing it is a mitzvah to denounce. In short, the more you want to show him the greatness of the sin in what he has said about him until now, the more he will speak *lashon hara* and *rechiluth* and remove him from the category of "your fellow man," saying that he is not a Jew, according to the parameters of his *yetzer hara*. Is there anything like this in all the transgressions in the world? For example, if we saw someone eating *neveilah* [carcass] or *treifah* [torn living flesh], and we reproved him for having transgressed the Torah of the L-rd and not having taken heed to avoid it — is it conceivable that he would take yet another piece of *issur* before his reprover and eat if before him! (Unless he be a heretic, G-d forbid, who had left the congregation of Israel, or one who had removed his sons from religion — and we are not speaking of such as these.) And in *this* bitter sin, which also carries a negative commandment of the Torah, and whose punishment is extremely severe, as we have explained many times from *Shas* and *Poskim*, we see, in our many sins, that the more we rebuke a man for having spoken *lashon hara* or *rechiluth* against his friend, the more he will demean him in the future! This can be for no other reason than that by force of habit this thing [the mitzvah against *lashon hara*] has become *hefker* [abandoned]. And even those who are not given to this sin, still, with many of them, their heart is not embittered so much by this sin as by [transgression of] the other negative commandments in the Torah. If so, there is no greater *meth-mitzvah* than this!

And, in truth, how much should the speaker of *lashon hara* be ashamed of himself because of this. For if he were called up to the Torah and found the verses there to concern the *issur* of speaking *lashon hara* (such as *Vayikra* 19:16: "Do not go talebearing among your people," or *Devarim* 27:24: "Cursed is he who smites his friend in secret," or *Ibid*. 24:9: "Remember what the L-rd your G-d did to Miriam," or *Shemoth* 23:1: "Do not bear a false report," and the like) and the point of a *yod* were missing in some place, he would refuse to make the blessing on the Torah, saying that the Torah of the L-rd must be perfect, as the Holy One Blessed be He gave it to us, and not defective. He believes, then, in truth, in the Blessed L-rd and in His holy Torah, in all of its letters, but when that *subject* comes to hand, immediately the verses of the Torah are abandoned by him, and he does not think it a sin at all! Remember, my brother, what we find in *Tanna d'bei Eliyahu Rabbah*, Chapter 28: "If one recognizes words of Torah and 'passes them by,' he is an absolute evildoer."

Chapter IV

In this chapter there will be explained the abundance of reward that is found in guarding the tongue and the merit of benefitting the many

Therefore, the understanding man must strengthen himself in this [(guarding his tongue)] constantly, and then he will be fortunate in this world and the next. For even with other mitzvoth, if one strengthens himself never to transgress them, his reward is very great, as we wrote above; how much more so with this.

For is it not written (*Mishlei* 2:4-5): "If you seek for it as silver, if you search for it as hidden treasure — then you will understand the fear of the L-rd." And it is well known that everyone would prefer having a steady income even with less profit than a chance income with greater profit. How much more so with this ["income" of guarding one's tongue], which is a steady income with great profit. For with this mitzvah one can earn both when he is sitting in his house or when he is in the house of prayer or the house of study, and also when he goes to the market and sees people speaking what they should not be speaking (and distancing himself from them.) As Chazal have said (*Kiddushin* 39b): "If one sat and did not transgress, he is rewarded as the doer of a mitzvah." In sum: With this mitzvah one can "earn" from the time he rises from his sleep [in the morning] until the time he goes to sleep in the evening, effortlessly, and with great profit. For, for every moment of muzzling his mouth he merits the "secreted light," as Chazal have stated.

And [the above is] especially [true] in view of Chazal's statement (*Yoma* 9b, *Gittin* 57a) to the effect that the second Temple was destroyed because of the sin of vain hatred and *lashon hara*. If this sin had the power to destroy what was built, it undoubtedly has the power to prevent the rebuilding of what was destroyed, G-d forbid.

Therefore, the man who strengthens himself in guarding his tongue with all of his power and also spurs others to do so for the honor of the L-rd and His Torah, so that its mitzvoth not be abandoned, G-d forbid, his merit will be very great. For, in truth, the congregation of Israel are in the status of *k'sheirim* [righteous] and *tzaddikim*, but [they are remiss in guarding their tongues] because they are deficient in the knowledge of the *dinim* in this area; and many also lack the counsel to escape the *yetzer* in this area, all of which we have discussed in the Second Gate. Therefore, if someone were found to awaken them to this, his words would certainly be accepted and the merit of the many would redound to him.

And this is the language of *Zohar Chadash* in *Parshath Lech Lecha*: "R. Avahu said: 'Come and see how great is the man who causes another to repent.

Whence do we know this? From *Bereshith* 14:18: "And Malki Tzedek, king of Shalem" R. Chiyya Rabbah taught: 'When the soul of the *tzaddik* who causes others to repent leaves his body, Michael, the great prince, who presents the souls of *tzaddikim* before his Creator, goes out and greets that *tzaddik*, as it is written: "And Malki Tzedek" — this is Michael, the chief of the keepers of the gates of righteousness; "the king of *Shalem*" — this is the Heavenly Jerusalem. (*Ibid.*): "brought out bread and wine" — he came forward to him and said: 'Come in peace.'"

And in 62b: "The herald proclaims each day: 'Happy are those who occupy themselves with Torah and those who enable others to learn Torah, and those who "overlook their traits."'"

And this [(abstention from *lashon hara*)] will certainly help hasten the coming of the Redeemer, speedily, in our days, as this itself furthered the redemption from Egypt, that there was not among them the sin of *lashon hara*. As we find in *Midrash Rabbah, Parshath Emor*: "Because of four things Israel was redeemed from Egypt: They did not change their names; they did not change their language; they did not speak *lashon hara*; and not one of them was found to be licentious." (As to the problem posed by *Shemoth* 2:14: "In truth, the thing has become known," the commentators have already discussed this.)

Chapter V

In this chapter it is explained why we must set our hearts upon the road that our forefathers trod

We must walk upon the road that our forefathers trod, as it is written (*Jeremiah* 31:20): "Place your heart upon the road that you [i.e., your forefathers] trod. As stated by *Tanna d'bei Eliyahu Rabbah* 23: "When Israel were in Egypt and in the desert, they were wholehearted, etc. And when they were in Egypt, they all gathered and dwelt together, because they were all together in one bond, and they made a covenant together that they would do lovingkindness with each other, and keep in their hearts the covenant of Abraham, Isaac, and Jacob and serve their Father in Heaven alone and not forsake the language of the house of Jacob, their father, and not learn the language of Egypt so as [not to follow] the ways of the idolators. How [did this manifest itself]? When Israel served their Father alone in Egypt, and did not change their language, the Egyptians said to them: 'Why do you not serve the gods of Egypt, so that his [Pharaoh's] labor be lightened for you?' Israel answered: 'Now did our fathers, Abraham, Isaac, and Jacob forsake our Father in heaven that their children after them should forsake Him?' They answered: 'No, etc.' And they circumcised their sons in Egypt and the Egyptians said to them: 'If you do not keep [this practice] and do not circumcise, perhaps the hard labor will be lightened for you,.' And Israel said: 'Did our fathers forget the covenant of our G-d in heaven that their children after them should forget it?' The Egyptians: 'No.' And Israel: 'Just as our fathers, so we shall not forget forever.' A variant: When Israel circumcised their sons in Egypt, the Egyptians asked them: 'Why do you circumcise your sons? After a short time won't they be thrown into the river?' Israel: 'We will circumcise them, and afterwards, do with them as you like.' And when Israel would make the seven-day [wedding] feast, the Egyptians asked: 'Why… After a short time won't he be taken out to back-breaking labor?' Israel: 'We will make the… feast, and afterwards, do with us as you like. The dead will die and the killed will be killed and the born will live.' With all of this, the Egyptians would revile Israel, and smite them, and beat them, and intimidate them, and Israel could not flee from them, as it is written (*Psalms* 42:14): "You make us a shame to our neighbors, a mockery and a scorn to those around us… (18): All this has befallen us, but we have not forgotten You, and we have not belied Your covenant, etc.""

If so, we, too, will set our hearts to that road, and we shall see to it to do lovingkindness with one another and keep the covenant of Abraham, Isaac, and Jacob to serve our G-d in heaven alone and not incline our hearts to the enticement of the *yetzer hara* and its claims, just as Israel did not incline their ears to the claims of the Egyptians even though they offered to lighten their burdens. And for this let there be fulfilled in us the verse (*Michah* 7:15): "As the day of your [i.e., your fathers'] going out of the land of Egypt, I will show it [Israel] wonders," speedily, in our days, Amen!

Chapter VI

In this chapter there will be given wondrous counsel for rescuing oneself from
lashon hara and from other sins between a man and his neighbor
a telling analogy for this

And now, let us conclude the book as we began, with the verse (*Psalms* 34:13): "Who is the man who desires life, who loves days to see good?", by introducing my explanation of the verse (*Psalms* 140:12): "The man of the tongue will not be established on the earth. The man of violence — evil will hunt him to his downfall." We shall preface this by a general introduction to this work.

In sum, one who truly wishes to guard his mouth and his tongue, in order not to come to *machloketh* [contention] and *lashon hara* and cursing and "whitening of the face" will acquire for himself with full payment the trait of patience, to "overlook his traits" in all regards. That is, to acquiesce within himself that for this holy trait he will expend every year about four or five silver rubles. And, for a richer man, a larger sum, as will be explained.

We shall explain our words: For the most part, the *issur* of *machloketh* and *lashan hara* and *rechiluth* comes about through a small thing which makes one think that Ploni has offended him, and he follows "the line of *din*," not to overlook his traits and yield at all. And, as a matter of course, this leads to agitation and contention. But if he resolved always (that is, before the provocation occurred) that for this trait of "overlooking one's traits" (which is itself a trait of guarding one's tongue, as I have written above) he must expend some money every year, as for all of the other mitzvoth, he would not take offense at all! Think of some other mitzvah, such as that of *tzitzith* (if we had *tcheleth* [the blue string[in our time), or if it were impossible to obtain an ethrog or the like in our time unless one spent four or five silver rubles on it (even if he were not wealthy; and if he were, even more than that), certainly no man in Israel would be suspected of foregoing the mitzvah because of this unless he had nothing at all, G-d forbid.

So should one act in regard to the trait of overlooking one's traits, and, in doing so, he would be rescued from many severe sins, even though this is not a positive commandment, but only a good trait in general. Is it not known that because of the smallness of our minds it is very difficult for us to know the *din* of the Torah clearly as to when it is permitted to take offense against one's friend and quarrel with him. For very often it may [only] *seem* to one that Ploni has offended him in something (for we are not speaking of outright robbers or the like, who would pick our pocket). And also because "a man is close to himself" and "a man does not see a fault in himself," one who does not overlook his traits is always liable to come to the *issur* itself of theft, *machloketh*, and *lashon hara*, and the like;

and certainly these *issurim* are greater than that of foregoing a positive commandment alone.

And I know the "rebuttal" of the *yetzer* — that if so, he will constantly have to spend four or five silver rubles for these things; and this is impossible. Therefore, I shall explain myself: If one bethinks himself well of the accounting for one week, he will see himself that many of the offenses and quarrels and [episodes of] *lashon hara* and the like are over small things, his feeling that Ploni has wronged him over some *zahuv* [a coin] or the like. For we are not speaking of wealthy persons, but of plain ones. Therefore, if one will resolve within himself to expend for [the cultivation of] this trait four or five silver rubles every year, he will avoid thereby in any event a thousand words of forbidden speech, [the avoidance of] which is well worth four or five silver rubles, and "one who comes to cleanse himself is helped [by Heaven]." And, in the end, he will merit the attainment of this trait in completeness (and, as a result, he will come to the attainment of the great trait of *chesed* [lovingkindness] (see next chapter)

But if he does not do this, but always takes offense at every small thing, he must know that he will certainly come in the end to many forbidden things, and that he is very likely to become impoverished thereby, G-d forbid, (as I have written above in the Gate of Remembrance, Chapter VI, in the name of *Sefer Hakaneh*, that through *lashon hara* one is reduced to poverty).

I shall elucidate this with a telling analogy: There was once a great miser who never shared his bread with the poor, and scrounged for many years with every household expense, whereby he accumulated several hundred rubles of silver. This miser was always contemplating new possibilities of saving, and he finally decided that he would begin to be sparing of the bread that he ate, and so he did. The first month he habituated himself to doing without a quarter of a litre of bread every day. By doing so, his pocket became fuller and he rejoiced greatly in this as was his wont; and he felt no frailty of heart because of this. And, in the third month, when he had become accustomed to this, he began to scrimp on another quarter of bread, until, with the passage of days, he began to feel frail of heart and went to a doctor, who said to him: "You are suffering from emaciation, and there is almost no cure for this; however, I have a certain drug, which may cure you, but it will cost you two hundred silver rubles." When the miser heard this, he fled from the doctor's house. But his condition worsened every day, and he saw that his end would be terrible, so he went again to the doctor, and begged him: "Give me that drug that you spoke about and I will give you whatever you want, for 'my soul is at the gates of death.'" The doctor replied: "I will have to know the source of your disease to know how to prepare the drug." The miser turned to him and said: "I must admit that I myself am the cause of it." And he told him the whole story. The doctor responded: Silly man, all together you have saved about four or five rubles, and you have endangered your life. And who knows for a certainty that this drug will help you! What is more, you must now spend fifty times your profit!"

So, exactly, in our instance. One who guards his honor and every cent of his money to such an extent that on the slightest suspicion he will not allow anyone to touch it will not escape every week from *lashon hara* and *machloketh*; and beyond a doubt there will accumulate in the course of a year, many hundreds of words of forbidden speech and *machloketh* because of this. And it is quite possible that when on the Day of Remembrance he comes for judgment before the L-rd, he will find that because of this his sins are more than his mitzvoth, for they will create the majority. And because of this he will emerge liable for death by the *din* of Heaven, as Chazal have said (*Rosh Hashanah* 16b): "Absolute evildoers (i.e., those with a majority of sins, according to Rashi) are inscribed and sealed immediately for death." But the Hoy One Blessed be He in His abundant mercies redeems him from death (as we find in *Tanna d'bei Eliyahu*, Chapter One), and He transmutes the punishment of death to one of poverty, and, as a result, he falls from his status.

Now when we delve into the cause of most of the sins which have led to this, we find it to lie in five or six silver rubles. For he may have once spoken *lashon hara* against his friend and also quarreled with him, suspecting him of having touched his *zahav* (money), and had stood up against him like a pillar of iron, both to his face and in his absence until he had proved his point. And sometimes the entire sum in question could have been g.p. (a type of coin) or even less than that, so that in sum he may have profited about five or six silver rubles. And what did he gain by all this? Several hundred sins of forbidden speech (aside from the occasional intermixture of the "dust of theft" in his pocket, which, in itself has the power to finish him and his possessions). And because of this there remained only a step between him and death, so that, in the end, he fell from his ["high"] estate.

And this is the intent of (*Psalms* 140:12): "The man of the tongue will not be established on the earth." That is, he will have no basis or foundation on which to solidly establish his position, but he will be driven from one state to another, as the verse concludes, "Evil will hunt him to his downfall."

Therefore, let a man not act in this manner, but let him "overlook his traits" in all matters, and he will thereby merit being remembered for life when the Day of Remembrance arrives and will remain in his former position. And on Rosh Hashanah the Holy One Blessed be He will certainly add to the influence he had lost through the trait of overlooking one's traits. And this is the intent of the verse (*Psalms* 34:13): "Who is the man who wants life, who loves days to see good?" (That is, he wants both, life and good) "Guard your tongue, etc." For if he does not, he must lose one (even in this world) either life or good, as mentioned above. But if he guards his tongue from evil, he will be remembered for life and also for good, as we find in *Midrash Mishlei*, that when it is a man's way to speak good, the angels above also speak good of him.

Chapter VII

In this chapter there will be explained the greatness of the trait of *chesed* [lovingkindness] and the value of a society for *gemiluth chasadim* (the doing of *chesed*)

And, in truth, how great is this mitzvah in the eyes of the Blessed L-rd, it being written (*Michah* 6:8): "He has told you, O man, what is good, and what the L-rd requires of you — but to do justice and to love *chesed*, etc." And Chazal have said (*Succah* 49b): "'to do justice' — this is *din*; 'and to love *chesed*' — this is *gemiluth chasadim*." And he also fulfills in this the mitzvah of (*Devarim* 29:9): "And you shall walk in His ways," as we find in *Sifrei* on the verse (*Ibid.* 10:12): "'to walk in all His ways' — these are the ways of the Holy One Blessed be He, as it is written (*Shemoth* 34:6): '*Hashem, Hashem*, the G-d who is merciful and gracious, slow to anger, and abundant in *chesed*, etc.'" And Chazal say (*Bava Metzia* 30b): "R. Yosef taught (*Shemoth* 18:20): 'And you shall apprise them of the way' — this is *gemiluth chasadim*."

And through this, one awakens the trait of *chesed* above. As Chazal say: "The Holy One Blessed be He says: 'Now these, [human beings], who themselves need *chesed*, do *chesed* with one anther; I, who am full of *chesed* and mercy, how much more so must I do *chesed* with My creations!'" And thus do we find in the holy *Zohar, Parshath Emor*: "We learned: 'With the deed below, the deed above is awakened.' If one does something below, the power above is awakened correspondingly. If a man does *chesed* in the world, *chesed* is awakened above and reposes on that day and it [the day] is crowned in it for his sake. And if one acts with mercy below, mercy is awakened on that day, and it is crowned with mercy for his sake. And then, that day stands for him to be a shield for him when he needs it, etc. Happy is he who manifests a deed which is *kasher* below; for he thereby awakens the corresponding force above. With that trait with which one measures, it is measured unto him."

And it [*gemiluth chasadim*] is one of the three things on which the world stands, as we find in *Avoth, Chapter* 1: "The world stands on three things: on Torah, on *Avodah* (the sacrificial service), and on *gemiluth chasadim*." And it is equivalent to sacrifices. As stated in *Avoth d'R. Nathan* (4:4): "Whence do we derive this for *gemiluth chasadim*? It is written (*Hoshea* 6:6): 'For I desired *chesed* and not sacrifice.' The world, *ab initio*, was created only with *chesed*, as it is written (*Psalms* 893): "For I said: 'The world will be built through *chesed*.'" Once, R. Yochanan b. Zakkai went out of Jerusalem and R. Yehoshua went after him and saw the Temple in ruins, at which he said: "Woe unto us, the place where our sins were atoned is in ruins!," at which R. Yochanan responded: "My son, do not despond. We have an atonement equivalent to it. Which? *Gemiluth chasadim*, as it is written: 'For I desired *chesed* and not sacrifice!'" (See *Succah* 49b, to the effect that [according to R. Elazar) charity is greater than sacrifices; how much more so, *gemiluth chasadim*!)

It [*gemiluth chasadim*] is greater than the mitzvah of *tzedakah* [charity], as R. Elazar said (*Succah* 49b): "Greater is lovingkindness than charity, as it is written (*Hoshea* 10:12): 'Sow for yourselves by charity; reap by lovingkindness.' If one sows, it is not certain whether or not he will eat; but if he reaps, he will assuredly eat." "The Rabbis taught: 'In three respects, lovingkindess is greater than charity: Charity [is conferred] with one's wealth; lovingkindness — both with one's wealth and one's body. Charity — to the poor; lovingkindness — both to the rich and the poor. Charity — to the living; lovingkindness — both to the living and the dead.'" And it is one of the things, the fruit of which one eats in this world, with the principal remaining for the world to come, as we find in *Peah* I.

Chazal have said further (*Yalkut Tehillim*): "*Chesed* stands up for a man until the end of all the generations, as it is written (*Psalms* 103.:17): 'And the *chesed* of the L-rd is from world unto world to those who fear Him, etc.'" And this trait is one of the three goodly traits implanted in Israel — shamefacedness, mercy, and lovingkindness, as Chazal have stated (*Yevamoth* 79a).

And if one averts his eyes from this mitzvah, his sin is very great. As Rabbeinu Yonah writes (*Sha'arei Teshuvah* 67) on the verse (*Devarim* 15:9): "Take heed unto yourself lest there be in your heart a base thing, to say: 'The seventh year has drawn near, the year of *shemitah* [release], and your eye be evil against your brother the pauper, and he cry out against you to the L-rd, etc." — this is his pure language: "We have hereby been taught that one who refrains from lending to the poor transgresses two negative commandments ("take heed" and "lest"). If we have been exhorted not to desist from lending at the approach of the seventh year for fear of the institution of release, how great must be the sin of one who refrains from lending when there is no danger of his suffering such a loss. Because of the greatness of the transgression, the Torah refers to the thought of one who is averse to lending as 'a base thing.'" And, in *Midrash Shir Hashirim*: "R. Yehudah says: 'If one denies [the mitzvah of] *gemiluth chasadim*, it is as if he denies the Deity. But King David, may peace be upon him — what would he do? He would do lovingkindess, with all, etc.'"

Therefore, because of the greatness of this mitzvah, they were accustomed in all the diaspora of Israel to have societies for *gemiluth chasadim* to lend a man in time of need. Now, in truth, why is this holy society superior to the *gemiluth chasadim* that one does by himself? For several reasons:

There is no comparing many doing a mitzvah to [just] a few doing it, as Chazal have said. And even though, because they are many, his [i.e., each individual's] money does not cover the whole loan but only a [small] part of it, still, it seems clear that the Holy One Blessed be He considers each one as if he alone were the giver of the loan; for without his small amount, the poor man could not secure what he needed. [This is similar to our saying (regarding the forbidden Sabbath labors) (*Shabbath* 3a): "[Only] one who does the whole labor [is responsible], and not one who does [only] part of it," notwithstanding which if each one by himself cannot carry the load, the *Mishnah* rules that [each] is responsible. The reason is that this is not called "part" of the labor; for since without him it is impossible for the labor to be done, it is considered as if he himself did the entire labor.]

And [(another reason for the superiority of *gemiluth chasadim* societies)] is that it is a mitzvah which one spends money for and which does not come without expenditure, its reward being far greater because of this, as written in the holy *Zohar, Parshath Terumah*. Also, the mitzvah [(of the society)] can be performed even when he is at work or sleeping. And aside from all these, it is well known what *Midrash Koheleth* says, that if a man pines for mitzvoth and has no permanent mitzvah for the generations, what pleasure can he have? But one who has a part in a mitzvah of the many, such as the one we are discussing, or one who leaves over money to support yeshivoth of Torah study — even if he is sitting in Gan Eden there is reposed upon his soul sweetness and light through the mitzvoth that are constantly fulfilled through the monies he left distinctly to this end.

And know, my brother, that the mitzvah of *gemiluth chasadim* is the highest level of the eight levels of the mitzvah of *tzedakah*, as Rambam wrote in *Hilchoth Matnoth Aniyim* 10:7, viz.: "There are eight levels of charity, one above the other. The very highest is supporting a Jew who has fallen [into poverty] and giving him a gift or a loan or entering into partnership with him or providing work for him in order to uphold him so that he need not appeal to people. Concerning this it is written (*Vayikra* 25:35): 'And you shall uphold him, [even if he be] proselyte or sojourner, and he shall live with you.' That is, so that he does not fall and become dependent upon others." (see *Yoreh Deah* 249)

And how fitting and right it is to conduct oneself as I have seen done in some holy towns in Israel where there have recently been established a holy society for this purpose, which is called "the support of the fallers," which supports and upholds the fallers so that they not collapse entirely, G-d forbid. And this is what they do: They lend out for a specified amount of time a sum of money as indicated in their regulations and allow the repayment to be made in easy weekly installments. They appoint a man (either gratis or for a wage) from the society who goes each week to collect the monies from the borrowers in such a way that there is almost never any money missing from the fund. Now see how many advantages there are in this arrangement. Aside from fulfilling at the time of the loan the positive commandment of "And you shall uphold him," which is the highest level of the mitzvah of *tzedakah*, as mentioned above, he further does *chesed* with the borrower in the manner of repayment. And the formulation of Chazal (*Succah* 49b) is well known: "R. Elazar said: '*Tzedakah* is rewarded only according to the lovingkindness within it."

May the L-rd strengthen our hearts to emulate His *chesed* so that the greatness of His lovingkindness not depart from us. As Chazal have said (*Vayikra Rabbah* 36): "If you see the merit of the fathers and the merit of the mothers 'tottering,' cleave to *gemiluth chasadim*, as it is written (*Isaiah* 54:10): 'For the mountains will depart and the hills will totter, but My *chesed* shall not depart from you'" — this is *gemiluth chasadim*. (*Ibid.*) 'And the covenant of My peace shall not totter' — this is [i.e., refers to] one who makes peace between a man and his wife and between a man and his neighbor." For this, too, is *gemiluth chasadim*. And may there be fulfilled in us (*Ibid.* 14): "With *tzedakah* will you be established, etc."

Part Two

Chapter One

In this chapter it will be explained that if one "abandons" his mouth, he is likely to lose all of his mitzvoth

It is written in *Mishlei* (13:7): "There are those who enrich themselves and have nothing, etc." It is known that *Mishlei* consists of analogies (*meshalim*). [In the above instance, the analogy is as follows:] *Just as* in monetary matters, it is possible for one to heap up riches, and yet, when it comes to the accounting, he may find that the great profits in his business are offset by many damages, so that when one is set against the other, he is seen to be left with nothing— *so*, in matters of eternity, it is possible for a man always to do mitzvoth and good deeds and yet to have an evil nature, which prompts him to slander his fellows. A man like this, when he comes to the higher world, will find that he has nothing, that all of the vines and plants that he planted in Gan Eden through his deeds have been covered with thorns and nettles, and the vines below are not visible, as it is written (*Ibid*. 24:31): "I passed by the field of a lazy man, and by the vineyard of a man lacking a heart, etc." That is, there are two types of people: one is too lazy to acquire Torah and good deeds for his soul. This is [what is intended by] "the field of *a lazy man*," one who did not learn, or who forgot through his laziness; and the second lacks a heart. He has Torah and good deeds, but his heart lacks concern for them [to see to it] that they endure. About the first, Solomon writes (*Ibid*. 24:30): "and, behold, it was all grown over with thorns"; i.e., instead of beautiful words of Torah there grew thorns and briers of idle speech. And, about the second, (*Ibid*.): "nettles had covered its face." In our context this is understood as meaning that every word of Torah and holiness that he had spoken and that could have produced "glorious fruit, holy to the L-rd," was covered and overlaid from above with the spirit of uncleanliness of his forbidden speech.

As we find in the holy *Zohar, Parshath Pekudei*: "And in this evil spirit there are found other inciters of *din*, which are designated to seize upon evil or filthy speech that a man utters with his mouth, that is followed by words of holiness. Woe to them and woe to their lives! Woe to them in this world and woe to them in the next world! For those unclean spirits take that unclean word, and when he subsequently utters words of holiness, those unclean spirits come forward and take that unclean speech and defile [with it] the holy speech, so that the speaker is not credited with it, and, the holy power is weakened, as it were."

And, King Solomon, may peace be upon him, said in a similar vein (*Mishlei* 13:3): "One who widens his lips— it is 'breaking' for him," which the GRA explains: "One who widens his lips [in *lashon hara*], though he has a good soul, and though he has done many mitzvoth and [built] many 'fences,' his mouth will break everything."

The verse (*Ibid.* 24:31) ends: "and its stone wall was broken down." That is, in the course of time, even a strong stone fence will break down, and the vineyard will be trodden underfoot by every wayfarer and will be worth nothing. So is it with the man that does not look to what leaves his lips, which are, [as it were,] "abandoned" by him. All of the strong fences which he had built in the beginning around his conduct will be destroyed. Therefore, the man of heart, who wishes to amend his deeds, must first of all build a fence for his vineyard; that is, he must put an extra-strong guard upon his mouth and his tongue so that they not bring him to grief again.

As to Solomon's using the word "vineyard," aside from the fact that all of Israel is considered a vineyard, viz. (*Isaiah* 5:7): "For the vineyard of the L-rd of hosts is the house of Israel," and every Jew has a portion in this vineyard— aside from this, everyone has a distinct vineyard in Gan Eden, as it is written (*Koheleth* 12:5): "A man goes to *his* eternal house." And he must take especial care with it, to plant it with pleasing growths and to guard it that it not spoil.

He must also root out *thorns* and *briers* from his vineyard. That is, people to whom he has caused a loss with his tongue or whom he has shamed or grieved. He must conciliate them with his mouth, and he must also confess before the L-rd for having transgressed His will as stated in the Torah. For all sins between man and his neighbor are also sins between man and his Maker, as is well known. And even if he spoke against them not to their face and his words had no effect, in any event, he must repent before the L-rd, and thus the thorns will be removed from his vineyard, as will the spirit of uncleanliness that covered its face (see Part One, *The Gate of Torah*, where we expanded on this.)

[The end of the (opening) verse (*Mishlei* 13:7): "and [there are] those who impoverish themselves and have great wealth": It is known that if one repents out of love [of the L-rd], all of the sins that he committed in the beginning become merits for him; so that it emerges that the more he had sinned in the beginning and had become impoverished, the wealthier he becomes afterwards. This can be understood according to its plain meaning: One who repents out of love is certainly embittered over each sin he has committed, and grieves over how his heart could have permitted him to transgress the will of the Creator, who gives life to all of the creation in His lovingkindness and His goodness. As a result, his sin is uprooted from the beginning, and he fulfills thereby the positive commandment of repentance. It emerges, then, that for every sin he committed in the beginning, there is now in its place the positive mitzvah of *teshuvah*.]

Chapter II

More on this Subject

Our sages (*Yoma* 39a) have said on the verse (*Vayikra* 11:43): "And do not make yourselves *unclean* by [eating] them [*sheratzim* (creeping things)], that you be rendered *unclean* by them"— If one makes himself unclean a little, they make him unclean a lot; [if he makes himself unclean] in this world, they make him unclean in the world to come." Rashi explains there: "They *permit* him to become unclean a lot," but this does not accord with "they *make* him unclean."

However, according to the aforementioned holy *Zohar*, this is understood plainly, viz.: "Through his forbidden words, the spirit of uncleanliness comes to rest upon them, after which the *chitzonim* [the "external," profane forces] take these forbidden unclean words and defile through them all the [subsequent] words of holiness, so that they cannot ascend above as a gift before the Blessed L-rd, the spirit of uncleanliness reposing upon them. And this is the intent of Chazal's 'they make him unclean a lot,' and 'from below— they make him unclean from above.' That is uncleanliness is drawn down from above upon the source of his soul, too."

As to their saying "They make him unclean in the world to come," that is, when he dies and his soul returns to G-d, who gave it [to him], to render there *din* and accounting (and he will certainly wish that they bring it to Gan Eden), the destructive agents will forestall it and clothe it in a despicable, unclean vestment created by its sins (and who can conceive of the greatness of the shame and mortification this vestment will cause it), and it will be compelled thereby to descend to Gehinnom, a place of darkness and shadow, to cleanse itself there of the filth of its sins.

To what may this be compared? To a groom who is being brought by his groomsmen to the marriage canopy, and, on the way, is accosted by some empty fellows who bespatter him with mud and mire from the soles of his feet until his head. When the groomsmen shout at them: "Empty ones, where did you get so much filth?" they show all [who are assembled there] that the groom is one of their companions and that he himself prepared all the mud and mire. So is it, exactly, in our instance. A man himself, through the filth of his sins, creates this revolting, unclean vestment, and, perforce, dons it and cannot rid himself of it, since he himself prepared it. As Scripture states (*Isaiah* 50:11): "Walk in the flame of your fire and in the brands that you have kindled. By My hand has this come to you." And Chazal have said, similarly (*Avodah Zarah* 20b): "Let a man not think [lewd thoughts] in the daytime and come to uncleanliness at night." They have hereby taught us that if he had not first put the thought into his mind, the spirits of uncleanliness could not have cleaved to him and defiled him.

And all of this was alluded to in the verse concerning Yehoshua ben Yehotzadak, the high-priest, viz. (*Zechariah* 3:1): "And He showed me Yehoshua the high-priest standing before the angel of the L-rd. And the Satan was standing on his right, to accuse him... (4) ...Remove the dungy vestments from him [Yehoshua]." The "dungy vestments" connote the uncleanliness of transgressions, which are as repulsive as dung. And "Remove ... from him" indicates that he was clothed in them against his will. And this is what Scripture tells us tersely in (*Vayikra* 11:43): "Do not make yourselves unclean in them, lest you become unclean through them."

And Scripture states (*Ibid*. 49): "And you shall make yourselves holy, and you shall be holy, concerning which Chazal say (*Yoma* 39a): "If a man sanctifies himself a little, they sanctify him a lot; from below, they sanctify him from above; in this world, they sanctify him in the world to come." And now, everything is plainly understood. The Holy One Blessed be He, being the source of the good and of *chesed*— when a man suppresses his *yetzer* and draws himself a little to the side of holiness— the Holy One Blessed be He confers upon him "a lot" of holiness, a "full handful." As Chazal say (*Shir Hashirim Rabbah* 5): "The Holy One Blessed be He said: "Open before Me an opening like that of a [fine] needle, and I will open for you an opening like that of an entrance hall." "from below, they sanctify him from above." That is, holiness is drawn down from above upon the source of his soul. "in this world, he is sanctified in the world to come." That is, when he ascends above and has to stand before the throne of the L-rd, he is clothed in vestments of the majesty and glory of sanctity (as it is written of Yehoshua ben Yehotzadak (*Zechariah* 3:4): "And I have dressed you with festive garments.")

And this is the intent of (*Bamidbar* 15:40): So that you remember and do all of My mitzvoth and you will be holy to your G-d." Now, ostensibly, "so that you remember and do all of My mitzvoth" is superfluous, for it is written [just] *before* (*Ibid*. 39): "and you will remember all the mitzvoth of the L-rd and you will do them." And it should have been written *there* "and you will be holy to your G-d." But, the verse [39] intimates to us something essential, i.e., *when* are the mitzvoth of so much avail that through them a man will be "holy to G-d"? When he takes heed not to go astray after the thoughts of his heart and the sight of his eyes. As Chazal have said on this verse, (*Berachoth* 12): "'After your hearts' — this is heresy;" 'and after your eyes' — this is adultery.'" And the *Chinuch* writes that included in "heresy" are all of the thoughts that run counter to the perspective of Torah, and included in "adultery" is pursuing the lusts of the world.

To what may this be compared? To one whose house is full of mud and mire. Even if he will bring into his house the finest golden vessels, it will not be beautified thereby. He must first remove the mud and mire and then bring in the vessels. And so is it in our instance. The Jew has been given the power through his cleaving to Torah and mitzvoth to root in his soul the holiness of the L-rd, as it is written (*Bamidbar* 35:34): "I, the L-rd, dwell in the midst of Israel." But when is this? When he does not allow the *yetzer* to reside there through his false ideas or filthy thoughts. And this is the intent of "And you shall not go astray after your hearts and after your eyes, after which you stray." (That is, [this will occur] only if you guard yourselves in the future against your straying). "so that you remember and do all of My mitzvoth, etc." That is, if you are careful not to go astray, as mentioned above, the great result will follow that through the doing of the mitzvoth you will be holy to the L-rd. (As the Men of the Great Assembly have formulated for the blessing over a mitzvah: "who sanctified us with His mitzvoth." ["so that" refers to "and you will be holy" (i.e., "*so that*, in remembering and doing My mitzvoth, *you will be holy* to your G-d")]. But if, G-d forbid, you *do* go astray, the mitzvoth will not avail for your becoming holy. And this is the prophet's intent in (*Jeremiah* 4:3): "Plow for yourselves a furrow and do not sow upon thorns." Happy is he who reflects upon this. It will be good for him in this world and in the next.

[And in this manner I have explained the verse in *Psalms* 81:10: "There shall not be in you a strange god and you shall not bow down to a foreign god. (11) I am the L-rd your G-d who brought you up from the land of Egypt. Open wide your mouth and I will fill it." Now, ostensibly, it should first have been written "I am the L-rd your G-d, etc." and only then "There shall not be in you a strange god," as it is written in the Torah. Why is the order reversed? But, Chazal have told us (*Shabbath* 105b): "Which is the strange god in the body of a man? The *yetzer hara*." (In the beginning it incites him to commit transgressions which are not so severe; but, in the end, "transgression breeds transgression," and it permits him even to bow down to idols.) And the intent of the verse [in *Psalms*]: "I am the L-rd your G-d, etc." is: Have I not brought you up from the land of Egypt so that you receive the Torah, as it is written (*Shemoth* 3:12): "And this is the sign for you [Moses] that I have sent you. When you take out the people from Egypt, you will serve G-d on this mountain." For this [the receiving of the Torah] is the purpose of the exodus, as Rashi explains. Therefore, "open wide your mouth and I will fill it." This is like a rabbi's telling his disciple: "Open up your mouth and let your words shine forth." For the Holy One Blessed be He wishes to give each Jew a great share in the Torah. However, in truth, everything is dependent upon the power of the recipient, wherefore He says: "Open wide your mouth." That is, ready yourself to receive much, and I will fill it according to your widening. But this is prefaced by: When will this be fulfilled in you? When "there will not be in you a strange god," when the *yetzer hara* will not be a guest in your body. Then you will be able to open wide your mouth to Torah, and I will fill it. For it is to this end that I brought you up from the land of Egypt (As it is written (*Ibid.* 13:9): "And it shall be a sign upon your hand... so that the Torah of the L-rd shall be in your mouth.") But if there is a strange god in your body— that is, if it is full of lewd thoughts, G-d forbid, I will not be able to fulfill your wish to widen your mouth with Torah.

But still, one should not despair, even one for whom it is difficult to cleanse his thoughts and to entirely remove lewd thoughts from his heart. For if so, even His mitzvoth and his Torah would not avail to sanctify his soul, and how would he ever attain his end? But the major element here is Chazal's formula: "If one comes to cleanse himself he is helped [by Heaven]." And if he desires with his whole heart to remove lewd thoughts from it, he will certainly be aided by Heaven to do this, and he must not, G-d forbid, nullify any mitzvah or Torah, even though his thoughts are not entirely pure. In this connection Chazal have said (*Pesachim* 50b): "Let one always occupy himself with Torah and mitzvoth, even *lo lishmah* [not for the sake of Heaven], for from *lo lishmah*, *lishmah* [for the sake of Heaven] will follow." That is, the holiness of the Torah and the mitzvah will help him, so that it will be in his power to do and to learn for the sake of Heaven, too. And this is what is alluded to in the above verse itself. For, in the beginning it is written (*Bamidbar* 15:39): "And you will remember all the mitzvoth of the L-rd and you will do them." "the mitzvoth *of the L-rd*," implying for the *sake* of the L-rd, is written only in respect to remembering, but not in respect to doing, his not yet having attained purity of thought in the *doing* of the mitzvoth. In any event, the doing of these acts will bring him to remove the [impure] thoughts of the heart and to overcome his lusts, after which he will reach the level of (*Ibid.* 40): "and you will *do* all of *My* mitzvoth," the doing, too, being exclusively for the sake of the L-rd; and this will bring him to the level of holiness— "and you will be holy." However, all of this obtains only with one who comes to purify himself and strengthens himself to remove the lewd thoughts and to keep himself from [the gratification of] his lusts. (Only) then does "He who comes to purify himself" obtain.]

Chapter III

In this chapter there will be explained several of the sections of the
Torah which speak of this [(*lashon hara*)]

First of all, the episode of the serpent, who spoke *lashon hara* of the Holy One Blessed be He and thereby brought death to the world. And (*Bereshith* 29:20): "If G-d will be with me and guard me," concerning which Chazal have said: "if He will guard me against *lashon hara*." And the episode of Joseph (*Ibid.* 37:2): "And Joseph brought their evil talk to their father," this being the catalyst of the descent of the Jews to Egypt. And (*Shemoth* 2:14): "In truth, the thing has become known" (see Rashi there and what we shall write below). There, too, (4:1) Moses our teacher, may peace be upon him, says: "But they will not believe me," and the Blessed L-rd counters (*Ibid.* 2): "What is this in your hand?" ... (3) ...and it became a serpent." Also there (6): "And, behold, his hand was leprous as snow." And (*Ibid.* 17:2): "And the people quarreled with Moses... (7) ...over the quarrel of the children of Israel, etc." followed by (8): "And Amalek came and warred with Israel, etc." And (*Ibid.* 23:1): "You shall not bear a false report, which applies to both the speaker and the receiver [of *lashon hara*] (as we find in *Makkoth* 23a), followed by (2): "Do not be after many to do evil." And, in reference to the *me'il* [the outer robe of the *ephod*] (*Ibid.* 28:32): "A border shall there be to its mouth roundabout," and the entire section. And (35): "And its sound will be heard when he comes to the sanctuary, etc." And the entire section of *Tazria* and *Metzora*: the plague-spots of houses, the plague-spots of clothing, the plague-spots of men, (*Vayikra* 13:46): "Solitary shall he sit"— even outside of the camp of Israel. And his atonement— "chirping" birds. And (*Ibid.* 19:16): "Do not go talebearing among your people," (*Ibid.* 17): "Reprove, shall you reprove your neighbor, but you shall not bear sin because of him." And (*Ibid.* 25:17): "You shall not wrong, one man, his fellow," which relates to verbal wronging, which is also in the category of evil speech. And (*Bamidbar* 5:1): "And they shall send out of the camp every leper"— even if he were as great in Torah as Doeg. And (*Ibid.* 12:1): "And Miriam and Aaron spoke against Moses, etc." And the entire section of *Shelach Lecha*, which speaks about the spies. And (*Ibid.* 21:5): "And the people spoke against G-d and against Moses." And (*Devarim* 23:10): "When you go out as a camp against your foes, guard yourself against every evil thing [*davar ra*]," concerning which Chazal have said: "*davar ra*" may be read as "*dibbur ra*" [evil speech]. And in *Tetze*, the "giving out of an evil name [*motzi shem ra*]," and (*Ibid.* 24:9): "Remember what the L-rd your G-d did to Miriam, etc." And (*Ibid.* 27:24): "Cursed be he who smites his friend in secret," which refers to *lashon hara*. And it is known that all of the "cursings" were preceded by blessings; and they opened with blessing, saying: "Blessed is he who does not smite"— whence we derive that one who is heedful in this is blessed.

Chazal have said (*Sanhedrin* 26b) that the Holy One Blessed be He said to Doeg, the wicked one: "When you reach the section concerning the speakers of *lashon hara*, what do you expound?" The meaning is: When a man commits a transgression, by nature he is ashamed and aggrieved to come upon the relevant section in the Torah. Because of this *Eliyahu Rabbah* writes (end of 138): "One who is blind or lame should not be called to the Torah for the section [that discusses these defects]. Similarly, one who is suspect of illicit relations should not be called for that section, or the like." If so, in our instance, we have demonstrated above that a great portion of the Torah speaks of these things [(*lashon hara*)] and a man who broadens his lips and abandons his speech in whichever direction his *yetzer* desires, will certainly in the course of his life transgress each thing many tens of times, and how his soul will storm when they show him in time to come that in the few days of his life he has transgressed many tens of sections in the Torah. It is known what Chazal (*Chagigah* 5b) have said on the verse (*Amos* 4:13): "For He that forms the mountains and creates the winds and tells a man what his speech is"— "even a man's lightest converse is related to him at the time of his judgment." How much more so will he be reproved for these grave forbidden matters [of *lashon hara*] and have them laid before his eyes, as it is written in *Psalms* 50:20: "You sit and speak against your brother. Against your mother's son you utter slander ...but I will reprove you and set it in order before your eyes." And it is known what the GRA has written, that for every utterance of forbidden speech (such as *lashon hara* and *rechiluth* and the like) one must descend to the very depths of Sheol, and it is impossible to visualize the throes and afflictions one suffers for one such utterance.

And even in the end, when he is cleansed of his sins through the multitude of afflictions that he suffers, and merits because of his mitzvoth taking his portion in Gan Eden, how will he be shamed there forever when he comes to these sections (for every soul in Israel will merit there to bask in the light of the Torah that he learned in his lifetime), and like a mute will not open his mouth in them [(the words of Torah)], and this, not for a year or two; but for thousands upon thousands of years. Whenever he comes to these sections he will moan for his soul— how could he have allowed himself to abandon such a great portion of this holy, awesome Torah scroll! For there he will see for himself how all the holy angels sweat and tremble at the word of the L-rd, and he, a small, lowly, dark creature contemptuously ignored the words of the L-rd hundreds and thousands of times in his lifetime! Happy is the man who reflects upon these things when he is still in this world! How happy and blessed will he be in this world and the next!

It is known what is written in *Sefer Chasidim*, that a mitzvah that has no "patrons" is like a *meth mitzvah* (see Part One, Conclusion, Chapter III). And *that* mitzvah accuses and laments: "How unfortunate I am, that all have forgotten me!" And this applies to even an isolated mitzvah; how much more so, (as we have demonstrated to the reader) to one that occupies a great portion of the Torah, that deals with exercising care with the faculty of speech. And it is understood, then, that when men are not careful of this, but unleash their tongues as they desire, a great part of the Torah lies in shame. How great is the reward of those who are heedful of this, not to transgress in this area. He honors these mitzvoth, and about him Scripture has written (I *Samuel* 2:30): "For those who honor Me, I shall honor."

[And see, now my brother, that according to the epitomization of Chazal (*Bava Bathra* 165a), that all [men stumble] in *lashon hara*, there is no *issur* in the world that is as "abandoned" as that of *lashon hara*. For in theft, only the majority stumble; but in *lashon hara*, all! And even though they have said that this applies only to the "dust" of *lashon hara* and not to *lashon hara* itself, Rambam of blessed memory has already written: "Would that we guarded ourselves from the *issur* itself!" If so, there is no other mitzvah that has been abandoned to this extent. And one who strengthens himself in it, in truth, accords honor to the mitzvah, and it will ascribe merit to him above for doing so.]

And it is known that Chazal have said that one who fulfills a mitzvah, though we have been commanded to do so by the Blessed L-rd, is regarded by the Holy One Blessed be He as if he himself had originated it. And this is so with even an isolated mitzvah; how much more so with one which occupies such a great portion of the Torah. If one strengthens himself to fulfill them [(all the aspects of this mitzvah)], it will be accounted to him in time to come as if he himself had conceived of all these holy things that are written in these sections. How much greatness and honor he will be accorded in time to come because of this! And how much will his heart rejoice in this! In this man there will be fulfilled (*Psalms* 105:3): "The heart of the seekers of the L-rd will rejoice!"

Chapter IV

In this chapter there will be explained that through the sin of the tongue a man's sins are publicized on high and he harms himself and the entire world

It is written in the Torah (*Shemoth* 2:14): "And Moses was afraid, and he said: 'In truth, the thing has become known,'" concerning which Rashi says that Moses wondered why Israel was smitten more than all the other peoples, and now he saw why they deserved this [i.e., because there was *lashon hara* among them.] Now is it not written in *Ezekiel* 20 that they were guilty of great sins, [among them] idolatry, an extremely grave sin, in spite of which he wondered at [the severity of] their afflictions! How is it, then, that because the sin of *lashon hara* was added to this that his wonder was allayed?

[This is resolved, however,] through the holy *Zohar*, viz.: When one speaks *lashon hara* he arouses the Great Adversary against Israel, which brings death, sword, and slaughter to the world. This is the language of the holy *Zohar* in *Parshath Pekudei*: "There is a certain spirit that stands over all those who speak *lashon hara*, and when men, or one man, stir up *lashon hara*, then there is stirred up that unclean spirit above called Sachsucha ('contention'), and it comes to repose upon that awakening of *lashon hara* initiated by men, and it ascends on high, and the stirring up of *lashon hara* causes death, sword, and slaughter in the land. Woe to those who stir up this evil agent and do not guard their mouths and their tongues and are not concerned about this, and do not realize that on the lower arousal is dependent the higher arousal, both for good or for evil, etc. And all conspire to awaken that Great Serpent to condemn the world. And all because of that awakening of *lashon hara* which is initiated below."

We have explained elsewhere that without the sin of the tongue, it would not be granted the power to make known on high the abominations of men and to demand *din* for them. [And now] all is clear. For Moses our teacher, too, may peace be upon him, knew that in Egypt there were many great sins [among the Jews], but in the beginning he thought that there was not among them the sin of the tongue, so that, as a result, the Satan could not condemn. [As Chazal have said (*Vayikra Rabbah* 26): "The generation of Achav, even though they were guilty of idolatry, would go to war and win, because there was no *lashon hara* among them. The generation of David {in the days of Saul), though there were among them children who were versed in the forty-nine facets of the Torah, would go to war and fall, because there was *lashon hara* among them"] But when Moses saw that there was *lashon hara* among them, he said: "In truth, the thing has become known," saying as it were: "In truth, now the "known" thing, the sin of idolatry, has become known above and has been publicized, and all of their sins are heaped up upon them, for which reason they are so greatly smitten.

And from all this a man can reflect on how careful he must be in guarding against this sin, that he not harm himself, [for when he speaks *lashon hara* against his friend, he is punished measure for measure, being spoken against above (as Rabbeinu Chaim Vital of blessed memory wrote in *Sha'ar Hakedushah*: "When you mention the evil of your friend, they will relate your sins")], and that he not harm the entire world, as mentioned above in the name of the holy *Zohar*.

We find in the Torah that if one stole from his friend, his amendment is to return the stolen object to its owner, and if he grieved or shamed him, to conciliate him and be forgiven by him. But one who habituates himself to *this* sin [*lashon hara*] certainly stirs up the Great Adversary to condemn the world. Who knows how many were impoverished because of him [the speaker] and how many died because of him? And though by the laws of man he cannot be punished for this, still, by the laws of Heaven, even though this is *gramma* [(an act of indirect causation)], he is not absolved of this. Therefore, one who heeds his soul should take great heed of this.

Chapter V

In this chapter there will be explained the greatness of the blemish on high, arising from the sin of the tongue

We find in the Torah that when a man commits a sin whose intentional transgression requires a sin-offering, that the blood of the sin-offering is sprinkled on the outer alter and that if the anointed priest committed the sin, its sprinkling must be on the inner alter and the holy *parocheth* [(the curtain separating the Holy from the Holy of Holies)]. The reason is as follows: For every sin that a man commits, the "blemish" rises on high in the holy world according to the greatness of his soul. And it is known (see *Ta'anith* 5a) that everything we see in this world has its counterpart above. There is a Jerusalem below and there is a Jerusalem above. There is a mountain of the L-rd, the Temple Mount, below and a "mountain of the L-rd" above. There is a place called the "camp of the Shechinah," the court of the tent of meeting, below, and also, above, concerning which Scripture says (*Psalms* 29:3): "And who will stand in His holy place?" When a man sins, he brings uncleanliness above into the holy place, the court of the tent of meeting above. Therefore, here he must sprinkle on the outer altar, whereby the uncleanliness above is removed. But the blemish of the anointed priest, whose level of holiness is extremely great, reaches the highest place, the tent of meeting above, wherefore, here, too, he must sprinkle on the tent of meeting.

Now we sometimes find, even with a plain person, that because of the greatness of his misdeed, his sin reaches on high in the holy, awesome place, opposite the holy of holies, wherefore the Torah commanded to sprinkle for him opposite that place. We find this in the instance of [the cleansing of] a leper, as it is written in the Torah (*Vayikra* 14:16): "And the Cohein shall dip... and he shall sprinkle of the oil with his finger seven times *before the L-rd*." And we find in *Torath Cohanim* (and in Rashi): "opposite the holy of holies." The reason: Because of the greatness of his misdeed [(*lashon hara*)], his sin reached above, into the holy of holies, wherefore the sprinkling must be, likewise, opposite that place, in order to cleanse him.

How much must a man shudder when he remembers that his sins have reached until the holy of holies. And, in truth, we find the likes of this in *Tanna d'bei Eliyahu*, that the *lashon hara* that a man speaks rises until the throne of glory, as it is written (*Psalms* 73:9): "They have set their mouth in the heavens, and their tongue walks the earth."

More than this, we can see something wondrous and awesome. When the high-priest entered once a year into the holy of holies, his first service, prior to receiving the blood of the bullock and its sprinkling was the smoking of the incense, as written in the Torah. And we find (*Yoma* 49a) that the incense atoned for the sin of *lashon hara*, as they say there: "Let a thing done in silence [(the smoking of the incense)] come and atone for an act [(*lashon hara*)] done in silence." From here we can understand the greatness of the harm of the tongue, which reaches until the holy of holies, completely within. And this (service) requires the high-priest, the holiest man in all of Israel, and he must atone there "before the L-rd."

And reflect further, my brother, that even though the high-priest was permitted to enter completely within, once a year, he was permitted to do so only with the incense cloud, to remove the sin of *lashon hara*. (Without it, he was liable to death.) And, afterwards, the sprinkling of the blood. It is seen, then, that this sin holds up all the atonement of the inner service. "'*Chukah*' [a statute] is written in that respect." (*Yoma* 40a)

All of us can also learn proper conduct from this: that when one comes to amend his actions and to repent before the L-rd for his sins, he should first see to it to correct this sin of *lashon hara*, after which his repentance will be accepted. As we see with the high-priest, that before he came to atone for the sin of defiling the sanctuary and its holy things, though it, too, is punishable by *kareth*, the Torah still commanded him to atone for the sin of *lashon hara* by means of the incense.

Chapter VI

In this chapter it will be explained that one who does not guard his faculty of speech, even if he does not speak lashon hara and rechiluth, itself, will, in the future, be lacking a great portion in Torah thereby

One who values the days of his life must take care not to lose them voluntarily, but, in our many sins, we are not heedful of this. Let us explain ourselves. Is it possible for someone to give to another the days of his life? And even if it were, it is known that no one would agree to do so, not even to give him a month or a week of his time — and rightly so. For there is nothing so precious as time. For in the limited time that the Holy One Blessed be He has given a man in His lovingkindness, he can inherit eternity for himself. But with our own eyes we see that one who does not guard his faculty of speech wastes every day, wittingly and willingly, much of his time. Sometimes, several hours, or, at least, one hour a day go to waste, in which he speaks with people of things which do not even affect his work, prattle in general. Now, indeed, I know that one who would want to contend with me will say that this is not so. But if one would give some thought to himself to add up all of his talk of the day which was not vital, he would find that he had wasted an hour or two a day, or thirty hours a month, or, in a yearly accounting, even if we reckon only one hour a day, he would have accumulated more than three hundred and fifty hours that had gone to waste. And, certainly, he would not have gained the next world by this, nor even this world, and only this profit — that there would have gone lost to him in this time a great portion of Torah (the Blessed L-rd having allotted to each man a portion of life sufficient for is needs, his Torah, and his [future] world, as the *Chovoth Halevavoth* has written, and that he would have diverted that portion to idle maters [(aside from there certainly having been included in them *lashon hara*, *rechiluth*, verbal wronging and other (forms of) forbidden speech.)]

But, conversely, one who acquiesces in guarding his faculty of speech (and such a man will certainly not go to any gathering of men, for there it would be impossible for him not to stumble into forbidden speech of his own or, in any event, into hearing *lashon hara*, *rechiluth*, *leitzanuth* or other [forms of] forbidden speech [as I have explained in Part One], or (if he resolves) that if he meets someone, he will not speak about any man) — a man like this will certainly add [to his life] several tens of hours a week which are free for studying Torah or fulfilling [other] mitzvoth.

And this is the intent of the verse (*Koheleth* 9:9): "See life with the woman that you love all the days of the life of your vanity, for that is your portion in life." "the woman that you love" alludes to Torah ["that you love" — for "one learns Torah only in the place (i.e., the subject) that his heart desires" (*Avodah Zarah* 19a)] And Scripture has exhorted us not to miss one day of Torah, for that is our portion in life. "your vanity" alludes to one who gives thought to himself to guard all of the days that he lives on the earth, not to waste one day, realizing that this world is a world of vanity, and that he has been sent here only to do the embassy of the Master of the world, to attain his portion in the Torah and in the fulfillment of mitzvoth in order to shine in the light of life in the world to come. About such a man we can hope that he will guard his days, that not one day will go to waste.

In sum, just as the men of great wealth, who possess notes of great value, guard them vigilantly, each one of them representing a portion of their wealth, so, exactly, must the man of heart guard his days and hours, each of them being his portion in life. The maxim of the sage is well known: "There is no loss like the loss of time." For if a man loses a dinar from his pocket, he can hope to find it or that the Holy One Blessed be He will grant him a different one instead. But if a certain hour goes to waste, he will never find it again. And he will be made to face this when he comes for his accounting in time to come and they set out before him how he had spent his days and hours, as it is written (*Psalms* 50:21): "I shall reprove you; I shall set it out before your eyes." Chazal have said: "They illumine all of his deeds before him. Then he will bemoan himself over his conduct, but who will be able to help him then?" Happy is he who bethinks himself of all this while he yet lives!

To the man who guards his speech there is yet another constant profit. For whenever he wishes to speak and he reflects that this might involve some *issur* of *lashon hara* or verbal wronging or *leitzanuth*, or the like, and he suppresses himself and does not speak, it is reckoned for him above as if he had actively fulfilled a mitzvah, as Chazal have said (*Makkoth* 23a): "If a man sat and did not commit a transgression that presented itself before him, he is given reward as if he had performed a mitzvah," and there will thus be added to him [who guards his mouth] many thousands of mitzvoth!

Chapter VII

In this chapter it will be explained that one who is careful to avoid this grave sin assists in the building of the Temple to be

The apothegm of Chazal (*Yoma* 9b) is well known, that the generation of the second Temple possessed Torah and mitzvoth and its destruction was due to the sin of *sinath chinam* [vain hatred] and *lashon hara*. And the Rishonim write that if there was power in this sin to destroy a house that was already built, how much more so would it prevent its rebuilding. And this is intimated in Chazal's apothegm: "Any generation in whose days the Temple is not rebuilt is [like one] in whose days it is destroyed." And if so, we must perforce strengthen ourselves to correct this sin; that is, to take care not to stumble in it. For, how long will we remain in exile?

But, in truth, let us reflect who can correct this sin? The plain person can certainly not do so correctly, since he does not know what *lashon hara* is and what *rechiluth* is and what enters into their categories. So that their fundamental correction depends upon one who is a Torah scholar. *He* can reflect upon their *halachoth* and take care to fulfill them.

Chazal have said (*Yerushalmi Sanhedrin* 2:6): "When King Solomon married the daughter of Pharaoh, transgressing (*Devarim* 17:17: 'And he [a king] shall not multiply for himself wives,' the *yod* of 'and he shall not multiply' [*lo yarbeh*] ascended before the Blessed L-rd and said: 'A deed of gift which is nullified partially is nullified entirely.' If Solomon nullifies me, who will fulfill me?' [That is, this mitzvah applies only to a king.] The Holy One Blessed be He answered: 'Solomon and a thousand like him will be nullified, but a letter of My Torah will not be nullified!' — whence it is seen that the Holy One Blessed be He is categorically opposed to one letter of the Torah being *hefker* ["abandoned"] to all. And if we ask ourselves what in the Torah has been abandoned, we find that the sin of *lashon hara* is *hefker* [i.e., not considered a sin] in the eyes of those who have not tasted the taste of Torah.

[And in our many sins, even one who can understand the *dinim* of the Torah does not find this sin as stringent as the others. A proof of this is that if it happened to someone that somehow kosher meat were mixed up with meat that was *neveilah* [carrion] or *treifah* [lit., "torn"], and he stumbled in this [i.e., he ate the latter], his heart would be bitter within him, and it would literally pain his soul, and he would fast over it and all his life remember that he had stumbled in the sin of *neveilah* and *treifah* — but not with *this* sin! Even if he had stumbled in verbal wronging or in whitening one's face [with shame] or in *lashon hara* or *rechiluth* itself — for all of which there are explicit negative commandments in the Torah — and even if he had done all of them together, if he had instigated a quarrel in which there were verbal wronging and whitening of the face and *lashon hara* and *rechiluth* combined, his heart would not be in too much of a turmoil because of this. And even if after the quarrel it dawned upon him that he had caused all this himself, still his soul would not be so troubled by this that he would go to a sage to seek counsel for this as he would for *neveiloth* and *treifoth* and the like. Another proof: He would remember it for only a few days, after which it would be forgotten entirely, as if he had never tasted the taste of these sins in all of his days. All of this is clear proof that the *yetzer hara* prevents even the man of heart from applying his eyes and heart to these things.]

If so, how much must a Torah scholar, at least strengthen himself to be careful of these *issurim* relating to the faculty of speech [i.e., *lashon hara*, *rechiluth*, verbal wronging and whitening of the face] so that the words of the L-rd not be as *hefker*.

Now according to what we have explained above, there is dependent upon this the building of the future Temple [And the *sefarim* (the sacred books) have written in the name of the holy *Zohar* that if [even] one synagogue observed the trait of *shalom* correctly, we could merit the coming of the Messiah. If so, the coming of the Messiah is in our hands, (but we must first take care to avoid *sinath chinam* and *lashon hara*)]. And all who strengthen themselves to correct this sin will have a share in the future Temple; for without them, the Temple would be in ruins forever, G-d forbid.

Now if we were authorized to build the Temple and money were required, it is well known that each Jew would willingly contribute all that he could, so that he, too, would have a share in the Temple. Now, in our case, money is not required at all! Only to strengthen ourselves and to distance ourselves from the grave sin of *lashon hara* and *sinath chinam* and to hold onto the trait of *shalom*. By doing so, the sin will be corrected and we will merit the coming of the Messiah and the building of the Temple.

And how exalted will be the name of that man who was the cause of the rebuilding of the Temple, as we find in *Nechemiah* (Chapter 3), where are recorded for all time the names of those men who donated a portion of the wall of Jerusalem. How much more so, [one who gives] for the Temple itself!

Chapter VIII

Exhortations to soul-accounting

We learned (*Bava Bathra* 78b): R. Shmuel b. Nachmani said in the name of R. Yonathan (*Bamidbar* 21:27): "Therefore, the rulers say: 'Let us come to Cheshbon, etc.': 'the rulers' — these are the rulers over their *yetzer*. 'Let us come to Cheshbon' — Let us come and make the world's accounting ['*cheshbon*' = account], the loss [entailed by the performance] of a mitzvah against its reward; and the reward of a transgression against its loss." The plain meaning is well known: this [the reward of a mitzvah] is forever, and this [the "loss" of a mitzvah] is temporal. Also, this [the "reward" of a transgression] is a negligible pleasure, and this [the reward of a mitzvah] is awesome. For "one moment of pleasure in the world to come is greater than all the pleasures of this world," and the opposite for transgression.

It also seems to me that one should imagine that the two bases of a balance scale are standing before him. On one is written the loss that he will suffer by the performance of a mitzvah, and on the other, the reward. He will *see* that the reward far outweighs the loss, so that the loss can hardly be seen, and, thereby [i.e., by this visual aid] the *yetzer* will be smitten. Likewise, with transgressions. Let him imagine that on one side he will see the "reward" of the transgression, and on the other side, the destructive agents, plotting his tortures with sore, bitter afflictions.

(*Bamidbar*, *Ibid*.): 'You will be built up and established' — [If you do thus,] you will be built up in this world and established for the world to come." Now when we reflect upon this [we ask]: Why did R. Shmuel b. Nachmani juxtapose this *mussar* with this verse? How are they related? This would seem to be resolved by what Chazal say (*Chagigah* 15a): "The *tzaddik* takes his portion and the portion of his neighbor [the *rasha*] in Gan Eden; the *rasha* takes his portion and the portion of his neighbor [the *tzaddik*] in Gehinnom." Ostensibly, this is difficult. Is He not a G-d of truth and a righteous Judge? Also, to which *tzaddik* is this portion given? It would seem that the explanation is as follows: The two are living in one city. The *rasha* always mocks the conduct of the *tzaddik*, his Torah and his *avodah* [Divine service], and slanders him to the populace. And the *tzaddik* strengthens himself and bears his shame and does not enter into a quarrel with him, and continues walking in the way of the L-rd, in His Torah and in His *avodah*. When they come for judgment in the world to come, the *rasha* loses his portion of merit. For aside from nor desiring to serve the L-rd, he mocked one who *did*, and thereby also "cooled off" Divine service in the eyes of men. To whom, then, do all his merits revert? To his neighbor, the *tzaddik*, whom he mocked and whom he caused shame and humiliation, and who was constantly constrained to strengthen himself so as not to slacken in his service. [This is the purport of: "He (the *tzaddik*) takes his portion and the portion of his neighbor (the *rasha*) in Gan Eden."]

As to: "The *rasha* takes his portion and the portion of his neighbor [the *tzaddik*] in Gehinnom," this may be understood as follows: By his constant mockery and ridicule of the *tzaddik* he causes defects in his [the *tzaddik*'s] Divine service, for which the *rasha*, being the cause of these defects, must take the punishment upon himself.

And now we return to the verse. It is known that in the beginning, the cities belonged to Moav. And the governors say to Sichon and his soldiers: "Let us come to the city of Cheshbon and it will be regarded now as the city of Sichon." And the [*mussar*] analogue in our instance: The aspects of *tikkun* [amendment] wrought in Gan Eden by the acts of the *reshaim* will revert to the *tzaddikim*, who governed their *yetzer* and served the L-rd and paid no regard to the *reshaim*, who shamed them and their service.

They also expounded "the city of Sichon" in a different fashion, viz. (*Ibid.* 28): "For a fire has gone forth from Cheshbon, a flame from the city of Sichon. It has consumed Ar of Moav, the possessors of Arnon" — If a man makes himself like a young ass [*ayir* - similar to *ir*, "city"], which docilely follows the cajoling talk [(*sicha*, intimated by "Sichon") of its driver], in this case, the *yetzer*, "A fire will go forth from Cheshbon" — from those who reckon the account of the world, "a flame from the city of Sichon" — the *tzaddikim*, who are referred to as "sprouts" [*sichin*, intimated by "Sichon"], and it shall consume those who make no reckoning of their end." The explanation (in my humble opinion) is, according to the other phenomenon of which Chazal apprise us, that the *rasha* takes his portion and the portion of his neighbor [the *tzaddik*] in Gehinnom. This is the intent of "for a fire has gone forth from Cheshbon" — that is, the fire of Gehinnom, created by the sins of the *tzaddikim* will go forth from them, i.e., it will not prevail over them. And over whom *will* it prevail? Over the *reshaim*, who make no reckoning of their end. And thus, the conclusion of the verse: "It has consumed Ar of Moav" — intimating that it will consume the lusters, (viz. [*Ibid.* 25:1]: "And the people began to lust after the daughters of Moav"). (*Ibid.* 21:28): 'the possessors of the heights of Arnon' — the haughty of spirit."

Chapter IX

Bereshith

We learned (*Arachin* 15b): "R. Yochanan said in the name of R. Yossi b. Zimra: 'If one speaks *lashon hara*, it is as if he would deny the Deity, viz. (*Psalms* 12:5): "who have said: 'with our tongue will we be mighty; our lips are with us. Who is lord over us?'"'" The intent is: One whose tongue is like "a drawn-forth arrow" to praise himself before people always and to say: "When I just open my lips against him, I shall finish him with my tongue, and he will be trodden down before all. Who can overcome my tongue? And even if this time I don't finish him off, are not our lips with us, and I can defame him before men and he will be despised by all." And he does not reflect at all that there is One above all, whose eyes range over all the earth.

And, in truth, in all of the sins, there are some that come from lusts and some that come from desire for wealth, that gain ascendancy over him, wherefore he stumbles and transgresses — as opposed to speaking *lashon hara* against one's friend, where there is no pleasure, as it is written (*Koheleth* 10:11): "And there is no advantage to the man of the tongue." This [i.e., one's speaking *lashon hara*] stems only from the word of the L-rd being *hefker* in his eyes, and his not being solicitous of the Creator's command at all, wherefore they have considered him a denier of the Deity. Another reason written in "the books of the fearers" [of the L-rd]: It is known that one who wishes to speak *lashon hara* looks around on all sides to see if anyone is looking, making it appear that the eye of Heaven does not see, G-d forbid, as Chazal say in respect to a thief, (who steals at night).

When we reflect further upon this, we find that the first *lashon hara* that came to the world came through the serpent, and through denial of the living G-d, the snake saying to Eve (*Bereshith* 3:5): "For G-d knows that on the day you eat from it, your eyes will be opened" (as Rashi there interprets it in the name of the *Midrash*: "Every craftsman hates his competitors. He ate from this tree and created the world. *You* eat from it and your eyes will be opened, and you will be like gods, creators of worlds.") And this brought death to all the world, and all hate it and wish to kill it, as Scripture says (*Ibid.* 15): "And hatred shall I place between you and between the woman... He will crush your head, etc." [aside from its other punishments: its legs were cut off, viz. (*Ibid.* 19): "On your belly shall you go"; and its food is dust, viz. (*Ibid.*): "And dust shall you eat"; and its faculty of speech was removed.

And so, with the man of *lashon hara*. When his evil nature is revealed, all hate him, and guard themselves from him, lest he make them objects of shame and humiliation. And even if he merits rising for the resurrection, he will be like an absolute mute. As Chazal have said (*Devarim Rabbah* 6): "The Holy One Blessed be He is destined to cut off the tongues of the men of *lashon hara*, as it is written (*Psalms* 13:4): 'The L-rd will cut off all "smooth" lips, the tongue that speaks boastful things.'" The reference is to the time of the resurrection. Who can fathom the greatness of the suffering of that man and his eternal shame! For then all will know the nature of that man, that he was an evildoer, who, with his smooth lips stirred up hatred between man and his friend, as Scripture states (*Koheleth* 12:13): "The end of the thing, all is heard," which Onkelos translates: "All the deeds of men are destined to be revealed, etc." For this reason [i.e., that he was a man of *lashon hara*] this punishment came upon him, that all men rose living and with their speech intact as of yore, and this man, as an absolute mute. From this a man can reflect upon the gravity of the sin, which reaches to his very soul in this world and the next.

And know, further, that just as the serpent was punished in its food, as it is written: "And dust shall you eat all the days of your life," so the man of *lashon hara* is punished with poverty, as it is written in *Sefer Hakanah*: "See and understand that all who utter *lashon hara* are punished with leprosy," and he concludes: "One who does not become a leper is punished with poverty, which is equivalent to leprosy, and he becomes a pauper, beholden to men."

And, in truth, this is a wonder in my eyes. For it is the nature of a man to seek remedies and blessings from great men for success in [earning] a livelihood. And how will all the remedies and blessings help them if, G-d forbid, they are habituated to the sin of *lashon hara* and *rechiluth*, which is subject to an explicit curse [*Arur*] in the Torah (*Devarim* 27:24): "Cursed [*Arur*] is he who smites his friend in secret," which, according to Rashi, refers to *lashon hara*. And Chazal have said (*Shevuoth* 36a): "'*Arur*' — in it lies a curse; in it lies excommunication." And this [*Arur*] was not uttered by one man alone, but in consensus with all of Israel, in addition to the Cohanim and the Levites, as stated in Scripture. And this one [(by speaking *lashon hara*)] *voided* his blessing!

Had they [the remedy seekers] listened to me, I would have apprised them, rather, to be especially careful in guarding themselves against this sin, and, in particular, not to *actively* harm their friend in the area of theft, robbery, cheating, and the like. [(For these are certainly a potent force in eroding one's possessions and causing them to go lost, as we have written in the booklet, *Sefath Tamim*, in the second and third chapters, adducing verses and citations from Chazal.)] For then his possessions would certainly be blessed, more than by all the "remedies." As is well known, all the *arurim* were preceded by blessings, e.g., "Blessed is he who does not smite his friend, etc." And all of Israel answered "Amen" to this. And this blessing will certainly be fulfilled.

Chapter X

Noach

(*Bereshith* 9:22): "And he [Cham] told his two brother outside": The Torah hereby tells us his sin, that aside from not covering him [Noach] himself, he also told of it outside; that is, in the market, as Onkelos says, paying no heed to his [Noach's] state, not to shame him before people — wherefore he [Noach] cursed him.

Vayetze

(*Ibid.* 28:20): "And He guards me on the way that I will go": We find in the *Midrash*: "And He guards me from *lashon hara*." And thus have Chazal said in *Sifrei* on *Devarim* 23:10: "When you go out as an encampment against your enemies, then you shall guard yourself against every *evil thing*" that this alludes to *lashon hara*. And it is obvious that when a person goes to a place of danger he needs special guarding, as it is written there (*Ibid.* 15): "For the L-rd your G-d walks in the midst of your camp to save you, etc." And it is known that because of the sin of *lashon hara* the Shechinah departs from Israel, and there is no one to protect it. And so with Jacob when he went to Lavan, which was a place of danger, as we know from the end of the episode when he pursued him to kill him had the Holy One Blessed be He not saved him, as it is written (*Devarim* 26:5): "An Aramean (Lavan) would destroy my father [Jacob]" — wherefore Jacobour father prayed that he not stumble in this (*lashon hara*).

Chapter XI

Vayeshev

The Torah expanded greatly on the episode of Joseph and his brothers, which resulted in our descent to Egypt and had many other awesome consequences, so that everyone should take *mussar* from this on how to guard his mouth and his tongue.

In *Avoth* 1:13 we find that Hillel used to say: "If I am not for myself, who will be for me, etc." This apothegm is highly comprehensive. Its plain meaning relates to zeal in the service of the L-rd, saying: "If a man himself does not bestir himself while he is yet alive and while he still has strength, who can help him?" As Scripture states (*Koheleth* 9:10): "All that your hand finds to do, in your strength do it" — "in your strength," specifically. We have already expatiated upon this elsewhere. For a man can depend but very little upon his sons, and his principal (task) is to prepare "provender for his destined abode." And it is in this regard that Hillel says plainly: If a man himself does not benefit his soul, who can do it for him?

But he also alludes hereby to an awesome phenomenon. And that is: If a man does not do evil to himself, who can do evil to him? For the truth is that everything that happens to a man in this world, both for the good or for the bad, is brought about by the man himself. As it relates to our subject, the descent to Egypt, its first cause was Abraham's saying [to the Holy One Blessed be He] (*Genesis* 15:8): "How do I know that I will inherit it?" and His responding (*Ibid.* 13): "You will surely know, for your seed will be a stranger in the land [Egypt], etc." And Chazal have said (*Shabbath* 89b): "Jacob should have gone down to Egypt in iron chains, but his merit availed him to be honored by being brought honorifically to his son who reigned in Egypt.

And the reason that Joseph reigned and his other sons humbled themselves to him stemmed from Jacob our father himself. Because he became angry with Rachel upon her saying to him (*Bereshith* 30:1): "Give me sons," he was told by G-d (as related in the *Midrash, Bereshith Rabbah* 71:10): "Is this the way to answer those who are oppressed? Upon your life, your sons will stand before her son [Joseph]!"

In sum, one must be extremely careful in his words, for he thereby affects his fate, whether for the good or for the bad, G-d forbid.

(*Ibid.* 37:2): "And Joseph brought evil report of them (the sons of Leah) to their father": He told him that they called their brothers [the sons of the concubines] "servants," and that they were suspect of illicit relations, and of *eiver min hachai* [(eating a limb torn from a living animal)]. The verse tells us that he told no one else but their father, and this, only in order that he reprove them — in spite of which he should not have done so, for he should first have reproved them himself; for the *din* of reproof applies even from a disciple to his teacher, and he should not have revealed it to his father. [(And perhaps he did reprove them first and they admitted to him that they should not have called them servants. For, in truth, before Jacob had married them, he had freed them and taken them as wives, as the verse states in respect to them (*Ibid.*): "the wives of his father." Or perhaps they had contested the suspicion itself saying that it was not true, i.e., that they had *not* called them servants. As to his suspecting them of illicit relations, this was an error on Joseph's part, for by means of the *Sefer Yetzirah* they had created a *golem* in the form of a woman.)]

And Chazal say concerning this in the *Midrash* (*Midrash Rabbah*): "(*Mishlei* 16:11): 'A scale and just balances are the L-rd's' — for all of them he was punished measure for measure. For 'they call their brothers servants' — Jacob was sold as a servant. For 'they are suspect of illicit relations' — all of Egypt suspected him with the wife of Potiphar. For 'they are suspect of *eiver min hachai*' because he did not see them perform *shechitah* — this was a mistake, and Scripture thus apprises us (*Bereshith* 37:3): 'And they slaughtered a kid of goats' (after having sold him) and did not eat it live."

(*Bereshith* 37:3): "And Israel loved Joseph more than all of his sons, for he was the son of his old age.": Scripture hereby apprises us that Jacob did not accept the *lashon hara* that Joseph brought to him, and loved him only because he was the son of his old age.

(*Ibid.* 5): "And Joseph dreamed a dream... (8) ...Will you reign over us?": Scripture expatiates upon the dreams to rationalize somewhat the extreme hatred of the brothers to Joseph to the point of wanting to remove him from the world: They assumed that he desired to reign over them, for which reason he had brought "evil report" of them to their father, so that he should remove them from his presence [as Rashi explains (*Ibid.*): "for his dreams and *for his words*" — "for the evil report that he had brought to their father." And the robe that his father made him served as "supporting evidence" that he had accepted his report], and that perhaps, G-d forbid, he would agree with Joseph, so that he [Joseph] would be a "master" over them, as in Isaac's blessing to Jacob (*Ibid.* 27:29): "Be a master to you brothers, and your mother's sons will bow down to you." Or, [they thought,] G-d forbid, that he [Jacob] would banish them altogether, as Noach said (*Ibid.* 9:25): "Cursed is Canaan; a servant of servants shall he be to his brothers." Therefore, they took counsel on how to rid themselves of him.

(*Ibid.* 14): "And he [Jacob] sent him [Joseph] from *Emek* Chevron" — "from the *deep* [(alluded to by "*Emek*")] counsel of that *tzaddik* [Abraham] buried in Chevron, in fulfillment of what was stated (*Ibid.* 15:13): 'for your seed will be a stranger in a land that is not theirs.'" The meaning here (in my humble opinion) is that Egypt was the "nakedness of the land," an extremely impure place, for which reason it was ordained in the beginning that one of the sons of Jacob would come to publicize there [in Egypt] belief in the Divine providence, as it is written (*Ibid.* 41:25): "What G-d is to do He has shown to Pharaoh." For a similar reason Joseph commanded afterwards that they [the Egyptians] circumcise themselves — all to weaken the power of impurity, so that it would be fit afterwards for Israel to sojourn there.

(*Ibid.* 37:15): "And a man found him, and, behold, he was straying in the field, etc." Scripture expatiated on this so that one not ask: How could this great calamity have been brought about through "the embassy of a mitzvah," Joseph having gone there to fulfill the bidding of his father! Also, how could all of this have been initiated through our father Jacob? Therefore, Scripture tells us that the embassy was completed in Shechem, and his going farther was of his own volition.

(*Ibid.* 17): "For I heard them [the brothers] saying: 'Let us go to Dothan [*nelchah dotainah*],' which Rashi interprets: 'to seek against you *nichlei datoth* [legal devices (suggested by '*nelchah dothainah*')] to kill you with." The explanation: It was decided by them that Joseph was a man of *lashon hara*, who provoked their father to hate them. And who knows how much contention he would stir up among them? They, therefore, sought some pretext to rid themselves of him in a way which would not make them "murderers" legally. As far as his being killed indirectly through them, this did not concern them. And as to their saying (*Ibid.* 60): "Let us go and kill him," this was meant in the same indirect sense. As stated in the well known *Gemara, Makkoth* 23a): "If one speaks *lashon hara*, he is fit to be cast to the dogs, it being written (*Shemoth* 23:1): 'You shall not bear a false report,' preceded by (*Ibid.* 22:39): 'To the dog shall you cast it.'" And we find in the *Gemara* (*Bava Kamma* 24b): "If one sicked a dog against someone, he is not guilty [of murder]." And even though by the law of Heaven, he is certainly liable for "indirection," too, they thought that in this instance they would not be liable by the law of Heaven because Joseph was a man of *lashon hara* and contention.

(*Ibid.* 22): "Throw him into this pit in the desert. ...in order to rescue him from their hand, to return him to his father": His [Reuven's] counsel proved to be to Joseph's benefit (for it rescued him from their hand), but, in any event, casting him there was dangerous; for there were snakes and scorpions there. (He [Reuven] did not know about this, however, for if he did, this would be actual "murder," it being stated in *Yevamoth* 121b): "If one fell into a pit full of snakes and scorpions, it may be testified about him that he is dead." (Below we shall explain the "measure for measure" in this.)

(*Ibid.* 25): "And they sat down to eat bread": Scripture here apprises us that they wronged him in this. For even the greatest sin, which incurs the death penalty, requires abeyance of judgment, it being incumbent upon them that night to deliberate upon the judgment itself and not to preoccupy themselves with eating. We shall explain below the suffering they experienced because of this, "measure for measure."

(*Ibid.*): "…and, behold, a caravan of Ishmaelites …going down to take it to Egypt": Scripture hereby apprises us that by the same means with which one wishes to harm his neighbor the blessed L-rd contrives to benefit him. And here, when he was sold to the Ishmaelites, he was brought to Egypt to the house of Potiphar, where he underwent and withstood the trial [with the wife of Potiphar], in the merit of which he ascended to greatness.

(*Ibid.* 26): "And Judah said to his brothers: 'What profit if we kill our brother? (27): Let us go and sell him to the Ishmaelites.'": On the one hand this resulted in great benefit to Joseph, his being saved from death; and, on the other, in great harm, their agreeing to sell him as a slave.

(*Ibid.* 28): "And they sold Joseph to the Ishmaelites for twenty pieces of silver… (34): And Jacob rent his garments … and he mourned his son many days."

From here on, Scripture begins to relate the punishments and the mortifications that they suffered for this, all "measure for measure." First of all, Judah was punished, who was the immediate cause of the sale. He became a mourner over his sons, and certainly also rent his garments over them, according to the *din*. And his brothers, too, were not exempt from the punishment of "rending" [*k'riyah*], for they, too, rent their garments on their day of woe [viz. *Ibid.* 44:13]. And because he [Jacob] mourned his son "many days," therefore, (*Ibid.* 38:12): "And after 'many days,' the daughter of Shua, Judah's wife, died." And because he deceived his father with a kid of goats, dipping Joseph's robe in its blood, they deceived him, too, with a kid of goats, as we find in the *Midrash*. And because they said (*Ibid.* 37:32): "Recognize, now," he, too, was punished through Tamar with (*Ibid.* 38:25): "Recognize, now, whose are this signet and cloak and staff? Who can imagine the greatness of the shame and the mortification that he suffered then!

In any event, we can see [from here] the greatness of the lovingkindness of the Blessed L-rd. for as soon as he said (*Ibid.* 38:26): "She is right [*Tzadkah*], [She is with child] by me," and he accepted the *din* upon himself, a Heavenly voice came forth and said: "*Tzadkah*, from Me came forth secret things!" The essential idea is that the entire episode is Divine Providence (see Rashi there). As we find in the *Midrash*, the angel appointed over lust invested him at that time — whence it is seen that from this very shame decreed upon him, much good shone upon him, Tamar conceiving two righteous sons, from which the kingdom of the house of David emerged.

We find the same with respect to Na'ami. 'It is written (*Ruth* 1:19): "And the entire city was astir over her. And they said: 'Is this Na'ami?'" Rashi comments that all had gone out to bury the wife of Boaz, and all of them said: "See what happened to her because she left Eretz Yisrael!" Indeed, why did it happen? The truth is that it is "measure for measure." For certainly when she and her husband left Beth Lechem at the time of the famine because of [all] of the paupers who had converged [upon them for food], undoubtedly all cried out, saying: "Who will support us now in the time of the famine?" And because of this it was decreed upon her that when she returned to Beth Lechem all the city would be astir and would say: "See what happened to her!" — until she herself accepted the *din* upon her by saying (*Ibid.* 20): "Do not call me Na'ami ("sweet"), call me Mara ("bitter") for the Almighty has sorely embittered me."

But if we reflect further, we see the greatness of the goodness of the Holy One Blessed be He, that the punishment itself results in great good. For a place was prepared for her to restore her tranquility and to sustain her old age. For in the death of the wife of Boaz, it was ordained by Heaven that he marry Ruth, as it is written (*Mishlei* 19:14): "And from the L-rd, an understanding wife." And through this Oved was born to her, who, as it is known, was Machlon, as the Kabbalists wrote, wherefore it is written (*Ruth* 4:17): "A son was born to *Na'ami*" [(and not "to Ruth," Machlon having been the son of Na'ami [viz. *Ibid.* 1:2])].

In sum, a man must believe that "from the mouth of the Almighty evil does not emerge, and if suffering does result we must know that good lies in it.

And now we shall speak about what transpired with Joseph. First of all, the Torah apprises us that even though it was decreed upon him that he be a slave for having said about his brothers that they called their brothers servants, still, the mercies of Heaven were upon him, that his success grew there, his being appointed the overseer of Potiphar's house.

(*Bereshith* 39:6): "And Joseph was beautiful in from and in appearance": As Rashi explains it, once he saw himself elevated, he began preening his hair, at which the Holy One Blessed be He said to him: "Your father is in mourning and you preen your hair! I will incite the 'bear' against you," whereupon (*Ibid.* 7): "And it was, after these things, that the wife of his master, etc." and Heaven contrived to have him placed in the prison house.

It is known, according to our sages of blessed memory that he worked in the house of Potiphar only one year, and that he sat in the prison house for twelve years, [for he was driven out of his father's house when he was seventeen years old and he stood before Pharaoh when he was thirty], and we find in *Shemoth Rabbah* 3 that he had to sit in the prison house for ten years for having spoken *lashon hara* about his ten brothers, and because he said to the chief butler (*Bereshith* 40:13):

"For if you *remember me* ... and you *remember me*," it was decreed upon him [that he sit there] another two years — but when the time was completed, he did not remain there an extra moment, as it is written (*Ibid.* 41:14): "And they 'hastened' him out of the pit," and not "And they *took* him out of the pit," for then he would have remained there a few superfluous moments.

From all this, we see the gravity of the *issur* of *lashon hara*, twelve months for each man having been decreed upon him, corresponding to the [time of] the judgment in Gehinnom. And while he sat there all of Egypt spoke about his being suspect [with Potiphar's wife], as Rashi explains on the verse (*Ibid.* 40:1): "And it was after these things that there sinned, etc.", and this [(his being suspected)] was because he had suspected his brothers. But after his punishment was completed, the Holy One Blessed be He remembered his righteousness and raised him higher and higher until he was publicized throughout the land of Egypt in glory and renown as a holy man of G-d, as it is written (*Ibid.* 41:38): "Can there be found such a one! a man invested with the spirit of G-d?"

Chapter XII

Continuation of *Vayeshev*

(*Bereshith* 42:9): "And Joseph remembered the dreams ... and he said to them: 'You are spies, etc.'" In all of this his intent was to secure atonement for their sins," as it was [his intent] in (*Ibid.* 25): "And Joseph commanded that their vessels be filled with grain, that their money be returned, each to his sack, etc." And, in truth, the money caused them much grief in the beginning of their [return journey], when (*Ibid.* 27): "the one [Levi (according to Rashi)] opened his sack (28) ... and their hearts went out, and each trembled to his brother, saying: 'What is this that G-d has done to us?'" And also at the end, when they came to their father (*Ibid.* 35): "And, as they emptied their sacks, behold, each (found) his money bundle in his sack, and they saw their money bundles, they and their father, and they were afraid." And also (*Ibid.* 43:18): "And the men were afraid, for they were brought into the house of Joseph ... and they said: 'It is because of the money which was returned to our sacks, etc.'" They suffered greatly because of the money; this, to atone for them because of the money they had taken for him [in selling him as a slave].

And it was, therefore, brought about by Heaven that the first to open his sack and find the money was Levi, as explained by Rashi. For he was the first who said to his brother Shimon (*Ibid.* 37:19-20): "Behold this dreamer of dreams is coming, and now, let us go and slay him."

(*Ibid.* 42:37): "And Reuven said to his father: 'You may kill my two sons if I do not bring him [Benjamin] back to you... (38): And he said: 'My son shall not go down with you.'" The *Midrash* relates that Yaakov said about him [Reuven]: "He is a foolish *bechor* [(first-born)]. Are they his sons and not my sons?" The words of Reuven must, indeed, be understood, but, essentially, this is the explanation: Whatever issues from a man's mouth [(aside from what relates to fear of the L-rd, which is a function of man's free will)] is brought about by Heaven. This is the thrust of Chazal's statement: "All is in the hands of Heaven except the fear of Heaven." And the *Midrash* tells us that this ejaculation of Reuven's [("You may kill my two sons, etc.")] was fulfilled in his sons, [i.e., descendants], Dathan and Aviram [(in the episode of Korach)]. And, in truth, he [Reuven] himself was the cause of this, by saying (*Bereshith* 27:32): "Cast him into this pit which is in the desert." The *act* was extremely evil, for which reason they [Dathan and Aviram] descended, living, to Sheol, to the midst of the pit. As to his *intent*, being good, as it is written (*Bereshith, Ibid.*): "in order to rescue him from their hands to return him to his father," he merited that one of his descendants, On ben Peleth, be saved, by returning in repentance to His Father in heaven (wherefore he was called "On," his being in *aninuth* ["mourning" (for his sin)] all of his life, as Chazal have stated.

And Judah said (*Ibid.* 43:9): "If I do not bring him [Benjamin] to you and present him to you [alive], I shall have sinned against you all the days," Judah going surety both in this world and the next, and through this, experiencing great suffering, more than all of the other brothers, as written in *Parshath Vayigash*. The reason for this is that he caused Joseph's being sold as a slave. In truth, Judah was the most eminent of the brothers, and he should have strengthened himself to return Joseph to his father, wherefore he was punished by Heaven by having to go surety for a different brother [Benjamin], to bring him to his father. And in this, he strengthened himself with all his power, and he also acquiesced in prostrating himself before the lord of the land to be taken as a slave, so that his brother could return home to his father. And all the other brothers who acquiesced in the sale were made to undergo great sorrow by acquiescing in becoming slaves themselves, as it is written (*Ibid.* 44:9): "And we, too, shall be slaves to my lord." And also (*Ibid.* 50:18): "And his brothers also went, and they fell before him [Joseph] and they said: 'Behold, we are your slaves.'"

Another awesome thing which befell Judah: Our sags of blessed memory have said (*Sotah* 7b): "All those years that Israel was in the desert, the bones of Judah were 'rolling around' in his casket, until Moses arose and implored mercy for him. He said... (*Devarim* 33:7): 'Hear, O L-rd, the voice of Judah' — at which his limbs reunited. But he was not yet brought to the Heavenly synod, at which Moses said (*Ibid.*): 'and to his people shall You bring him.' But he could not engage in halachic converse with the sages there, at which Moses said (*Ibid.*): 'Let his hands do battle for him', etc." All this befell him because he had said (*Bereshith* 43:9): "If I do not bring him [Benjamin] to you and present him to you [alive], I shall have sinned against you all the days." __ But he *did* bring him! But, "the curse of a sage is fulfilled even if the condition [(in this instance, bringing him back)] is fulfilled" (*Makkoth* 11b). And we have already said that whatever issues from a man's mouth is by Divine providence, so that the L-rd's will was being enacted here. It seems to me that the explanation is as follows: It is known that they [the brothers] placed a ban on anyone who would reveal this [(the sale of Joseph)] to our father Jacob, and they included the Shechinah in this ban, wherefore the Holy Spirit [of prophecy] was removed from our father Jacob (until the end [of the episode], where it is written (*Ibid.* 45:27): "And the spirit of Jacob their father revived," which Onkelos translates: "And the Holy Spirit [again] reposed upon him.") And because of this ban it was decreed upon him [Judah] that holiness depart from him entirely, (as any man who is excommunicated), wherefore Judah was constrained to accept excommunication upon himself, as it is written: "And I shall have sinned against my father all of the days."

And see further that the Holy One Blessed be He does not withhold [any] reward [that is due]. We have already mentioned above that in the counsel of Judah there was also great good for Joseph, for he rescued him from death. It was in this regard that Jacob said about him (*Bereshith* 49:8): "Judah — you, will your brothers praise" (see Rashi there). Our sages of blessed memory have said that because he saved Joseph from death the L-rd pitied the kingdom of the house of Judah, not destroying their seed until the destruction of the Temple, unlike the other kings of Israel, who were all temporary. When one finished his [allotted] time, another arose and killed him and his entire household, not leaving a trace — as opposed to the kings of the house of David, of the seed of Judah.

And see another extremely awesome thing which unraveled itself in the course of time, measure for measure. For Joseph stumbled in the sin of *lashon hara* [against his brothers] as related in the Torah. And his brothers did not want, by any means, to forgive him, relating to him in the extreme of *din*, saying (*Bereshith* 37:20): "Let us go and kill him (that is: "Let us sic the dogs on him" and the like,) and they wished to sell him as a slave because of this, though Judah defended him and did not allow them to kill him, as it is written (*Bereshith* 37:26): "What profit if we kill our brother, etc." Still, he by no means wanted to forgive him, saying (*Ibid.* 27): "Let us go and sell him." And because of this, in the succeeding generations, when one of the seed of Judah stumbled in the *issur* of accepting *lashon hara*, the distinctive one of the seed of Joseph would by no means forgive him. And who is it that stumbled in this way? No less than our lord, King David, may peace be upon him, who believed the evil that Tziva spoke of Mefibosheth, and said (II *Samuel* 19:30): "You [Mefibosheth] and Tziva shall divide the field" — at which a Heavenly voice came forth and said: "Rechavam [of the seed of Judah] and Yaravam [of the seed of Joseph] shall divide the kingdom." And, as it is written in Scripture, that after the death of Solomon, Yaravam and all of Israel came to Rechavam and besought him to ease somewhat his yoke upon them and they would serve him, and he answered them (I *Kings* 12:14): "My father [Solomon] chastised you with whips, but I will chastise you with scorpion-thorns" — whereupon all of them answered (II *Chronicles* 10:16): "Each to your tents, O Israel," and they crowned Yaravam. And the underlying cause was David's acceptance of *lashon hara*. As our sages of blessed memory said: "If David had not accepted *lashon hara*, the kingdom of the house of David would not have been divided and Israel would not have served idolatry, and we would not have been exiled from our land." And all of this is "measure for measure," as we have written.

And now let us see the suffering that came to them from Heaven because of the bread, their sitting down to eat bread [(before selling Joseph)]. For when they brought Benjamin and stood him before Joseph, they thought that they had thereupon satisfied his demand, and that he would permit them to return home. But it was not to be so, as it is written (*Bereshith* 43:16): "And Joseph saw Benjamin with them, and he said to the overseer of his house: 'Bring these men into the house, and [see to it] to slaughter something (for a meal) and prepare it, for with me will these men dine.'" And, later, (*Ibid.* 25): "…for they heard that they would eat bread there," and (*Ibid.* 18): "And the men were afraid, for they were brought into the house of Joseph. And they said: 'It is because of the money that was returned to our sacks … and to fall upon us, and to take us as slaves." And (*Ibid.* 31): "And he said; 'Place bread.'" (*Ibid.* 33): "And they sat before him, the first-born according to his seniority, etc." And, similarly, the entire episode of the goblet, everything centering around the meal, where they saw the goblet by which he divined. For if he had not invited them to dine with him and to see the goblet, they could not in the end have been suspected of theft, and undergone the great suffering [which followed] whereby they all consented to become slaves.

But, in truth, all this was "measure for measure." Because of their sitting to eat bread when Joseph was in the pit, it was decreed upon them to also sit and eat bread under terrifying circumstances, until Judah himself said (*Ibid.* 44:16): "What shall we speak and how shall we justify ourselves? G-d has found out the sin of your servants." [And he, taking upon himself the *din* of Heaven, as it were,] — "Behold, we are slaves to my lord, etc." And with this, he averts the essential *din* for the selling [of Joseph]. [And though Joseph is not yet reconciled in this *parshah* and says (*Ibid.* 17): "The man in whose hand the goblet is found — he shall be my servant. And you, go up in peace to your father," Judah does not agree to this, viz. (*Ibid.* 18): "And Judah drew near to him," until the end of the episode, (*Ibid.* 45:1): "And Joseph could not restrain himself, etc."]

And from all of this awesome episode we can understand how much one must guard his tongue and his deeds. And also, from [the account of] Joseph, we can understand his holy trait, viz. (*Ibid.* 45:5): "And now, do not be grieved, and do not vex yourselves that you sold me here." And, similarly, at the end of the *parshah* (*Ibid.* 50:21): "And he comforted them and he spoke to their hearts." And witness further the greatness of Joseph, who did not tell his father what had been done to him, until it was revealed to him prophetically before his death, as it is written [(Jacob speaking)] (*Ibid.* 49:23): "They [the brothers] embittered him and they antagonized him and they hated him, etc." And, more than this, we find in the words of Chazal that Joseph took care not to be alone with his father, so that his brothers not suspect him of telling his father what he had suffered at their hands.

Chapter XIII

Shemoth

(*Shemoth* 2:14): "And Moses was afraid, and he said: 'Indeed, the thing has become known.'" (see above, Chapter IV)

(*Ibid.* 4:1): "And Moses answered and he said: 'But they will not believe me, and they will not hearken to my voice; for they will say: 'The L-rd did not appear to you.'" (*Ibid.* 2): "And the L-rd said to him: 'What is this in your hand?' And he said: 'A staff.'" Why did G-d hold this against Moses? Should he not have questioned as he did? I heard from the Gaon, R. Eliyahu Schick, of blessed memory, that He took exception to the words "But '*Hen*' they will not believe me," stated categorically. He *should* have said "*Perhaps* they will not believe me." [This explains what our sages of blessed memory said: "When the Holy One Blessed be He said to Moses (*Devarim* 31:14): "*Hen* your days have drawn near to die," Moses replied: "With '*Hen*' did I praise You (viz. *Ibid.* 10:14): "*Hen*, to the L-rd your G-d are the heavens and the heavens of the heavens, etc.") and with '*Hen*' do You answer me?" The L-rd replied: "But you also said: 'But *Hen* they will not believe me.'" Ostensibly, this is unexplainable; but, according to the above interpretation, the meaning is clear: The Holy One Blessed be He said to him: "'*Hen*' your days have drawn near to die" — categorically. This was very difficult for Moses to accept, and he answered: "But I praised You with '*Hen*,'" and do You answer me with '*Hen*'!" And to this the L-rd replied, that this is "measure for measure" for his also having said '*Hen*' [categorically].

And, (in my humble opinion,) it is possible to answer that Moses' saying "They will not believe me" may have led some to come to doubt his prophecy, as in the episode of Korach. [For, although in the end, the truth of his prophecy was evident to all — as it is written (*Devarim* 11:2): "For it is not [with] your children [that I speak now], who did not know and who did not see the chastisement of the L-rd your G-d... (6): And what He wrought against Dathan and Aviram, the son of Eliav... (9): ...but with *you*, whose eyes have seen the entire great deed of the L-rd, that He has wrought" — still, in the beginning, he suffered sorely at the hands of Korach, Dathan, and Aviram.

(*Shemoth* 4:2): "What is this in your hand? And he said: 'A staff.'" (see Rashi, to the effect that He said to Moses: "*Mizeh* ["From this"] that is in your hand, you deserve to be smitten" [for having wrongly suspected the innocent]. From this we can understand that in all instances of *lashon hara* — it being known from *Tosefta Peah* that punishment is exacted for them in this world, with the principal remaining [for punishment] in the world to come — there is no necessity of adducing a distant cause for his punishment, but [it can readily be understood] as proceeding from what is immediately "at hand."

And, even according to the second explanation in Rashi, it can be understood as His saying to him: "Is it not evident to all that it is [only] a staff, and that it cannot cause any great harm? I shall show you how 'the dread of death' can proceed from it." And, the analogue (along the same lines), that through *lashon hara*, a seemingly small thing can lead to "the dread of death."

(*Ibid*. 3): "And he threw it to the ground and it became a serpent" (see Rashi). It is also possible to say that He intimated to him that by words of *lashon hara* there was created the serpent that "prosecutes" man above, desiring to "bite" him.

(*Ibid*. 4): "Stretch out your hand and *hold its tail*." He thereby intimated to him that by merely fleeing it he had not yet rescued himself from it — until he had accepted his punishment [for speaking against Israel].

(*Ibid*. 5): "And he stretched out his hand and *grasped* it." It is not written "and *held* it" (as commanded), but "and *grasped* it," indicating that Moses did as the L-rd had commanded, and even more, for grasping it makes it more dangerous. But as soon as he had acquiesced [in his punishment], it was removed from him.

(*Ibid*.): "And it became a staff *in his hand*," specifically, to intimate that when one accepts upon him the suffering that is brought upon him, *immediately*, the *din* of Heaven departs from him.

And this will explain what we find in *Avodah Zarah* 16b: "The rabbis taught: When R. Eliezer was seized by the heretics, he was taken up to the scaffold for "judgment." The archon said to him: "An old man like you to engage in such frivolity!" He replied: "The Judge has my faith!" The archon thought that *he* was meant (when he had intended his Father in heaven), and he said to him: "Since you have taken on the faith of Dimus [(the idolatry of the archon)], you are free!" The idea is that since R. Eliezer had accepted G-d's judgment upon him, the *din* departed from him *immediately* and it entered the mind of the archon that *he* was meant, and he freed him!

(*Shemoth* 4:6): "And the L-rd said to him again: 'Put your hand into your bosom, etc.'" (see Rashi). In this instance, He also intimated to him that he had spoken *lashon hara*, and that because of this he would be stricken with leprosy. And even though in the beginning, he had already received his punishment in dread of the serpent, *this* ["Put your hand into your bosom, etc."] was because of the *second* thing he had said, i.e., "And they will not hearken to my voice." And, in truth, it was not so [i.e., that they did not hearken], it being written afterwards (*Ibid.* 31): "And the people believed, and they hearkened, etc."

(*Ibid.* 7): "And He said: 'Return your hand to your bosom'" — to show him that it was not the bosom which caused the leprosy, but the sin, and that when the sin was removed, the bosom itself would effect the cure of his hand.

Chapter XIV

Beshalach

(*Ibid.* 17:7): "And he called the name of the place Massah and Merivah because of the "quarrel" (*riv*) of the children of Israel and because of their "proving" (*nasotham*) the L-rd, saying: 'Is the L-rd in our midst or not?'" This is followed by (8): "And Amalek came and warred, etc." From the juxtaposition of the verses we learn that the sin of Merivah also contributed to bringing Amalek upon them. The same holds true for other idolatries — wherefore one must take great care to avoid *merivah* (quarreling).

Mishpatim

(*Ibid.* 23:1): "Do not receive a false report," concerning which our sages have said (*Pesachim* 118a): "All who speak *lashon hara* deserve to be cast to the dogs, it being written 'Do not receive [*tissa*] a false report,' which may also be read 'Do not spread [*tassi*] a false report.' And this is preceded by (22:30): 'To the dog shall you throw *it* [which can also be read "him"].'" This is easily understood. For it is the way of the dog always to bark and sometimes even to bite one who walks by him, even if he does so "innocently." So is it the way of the man of *lashon hara* to harm everyone with his "bark." He finds fault with all men and shames them. It is only fit, then, that he be cast before the dogs and that they affright and bite him, "measure for measure."

The Maharal of Prague gives another reason. The dogs guarded themselves when necessary [at the exodus] from barking, as it is written (*Ibid.* 11;7): "And against all the children of Israel a dog will not sharpen its tongue." Yet *he* [man] whom the L-rd has accorded understanding and knowledge cannot keep his *yetzer* from doing so — wherefore he is worse than they!

The *Sefer Charedim* writes in the name of he Kabbalists that sometimes Heaven reincarnates his soul in a dog, and this is intimated by "He deserves to be cast to the dogs."

Juxtaposed with this is (23:2): "Do not incline after many [wicked men] for evil." The commentators explained this to mean that even if one sees that many have habituated themselves to a certain sin he should not follow them. And so, in our instance. Even if one sees that many of his friends and acquaintances stumble in this sin of *lashon hara*, he should not be enticed into following them.

Chapter XV

Tetzave

We learned (*Arachin* 16a): "The *me'il* (the robe of the high-priest) atoned for *lashon hara*, the Holy One Blessed be He saying: 'Let that which produces a sound [(the bells on the robe)] atone for the sound of the *voice*' [i.e., *lashon hara*]." And this is so, only if his acts [of *lashon hara*] were not of avail [to produce quarrels and the like]; but if they were, plague-spots come upon him." With the help of the Blessed L-rd, we will explain the relevant section in the Torah, word by word:

(*Shemoth* 28:31): "And you shall make the *me'il* of the *ephod* [i.e., belted by the *ephod*] entirely of *blue wool* [*tcheleth*]." It would seem that *tcheleth* was necessary because of what our sages of blessed memory have said about *tzitzith* (*Menachoth* 89a), that *tcheleth* is reminiscent of [the color of] the sea; the sea, of the firmament; and the firmament, of the Throne of Glory. That is, he shall remember thereby that he will come before the Throne of Glory. Similarly, in our instance. It is stated in *Tanna d'bei Eliyahu*, that the *lashon hara* that one speaks ascends opposite the Throne of Glory, as it is written (*Psalms* 73a): "They have placed their mouths in the skies, and their tongue walks the earth." Since he is clothed in *tcheleth*, he will remember and reflect upon whither his words ascend, and he will guard himself against this.

(*Shemoth* 28:32): "And the mouth of its head shall be [folded over] within it." This intimates what Chazal have said on the verse (*Job* 26:7): "'He suspends the earth on nothingness [*blimah*]' — On whom does the earth depend? On him who clamps his mouth shut [*bolem piv*] in a time of quarrel." That is, he suppresses all his speech then, that it not go forth.

(*Shemoth*, *Ibid.*): "A border shall there be for its (his) mouth roundabout, the work of a weaver": That is, he should imagine that on his mouth roundabout there is the work of a weaver, his lips being woven one to the other, so that he cannot open them.

(*Ibid.*): "As the opening of a suit of armor shall it [its neck-opening] be for it, so that it not be torn." Why need the Torah add "as the opening of a suit of armor"? Is it not sufficient to have stated "And the mouth of its head shall be [folded over] within it. A border shall there be for its mouth"? It must intimate, then, that just as one dons armor for protection, that he not be harmed by the arrows shot at him, so, if one clamps shut *his* mouth, it affords him protection against his antagonist, and, in the end, it serves to silence him by giving him no answer. If he answered him, however, the quarrel would widen and he would come to blows, as it is written (*Ibid.* 21:18): "And if men quarrel, and a man strike his neighbor with stone or fist, etc." And the Holy One Blessed be He is also his Protector because of this, because "the earth depends upon him," as mentioned above.

(*Ibid.* 33-34): "And you shall make on its (lower) hem pomegranates of purple ... and golden bells in their midst roundabout [one bell between every two pomegranates]. A golden bell and a pomegranate [next to it], a golden bell and a pomegranate, on the hem of the *me'il* roundabout. The allusion here would seem to be to what Chazal have said (*Chullin* 89a): "What is a man's 'trade'? Let him make himself a mute. I might think, even to words of Torah. It is, therefore, written (*Psalms* 58:2): 'Righteousness shall you speak.'" It is found, then, according to this, that whenever one has time, he should not remain idle, but he should learn Torah. And the learning should not be silent, as we find in *Eruvin* 54a. And when one cannot learn Torah, whatever the reason might be, he should make himself a mute, who cannot open his mouth. And for this reason there were on the hem of the *me'il*, "a golden bell and a pomegranate, a golden bell and a pomegranate," alluding to the study of Torah, as mentioned above. And, in the midst of this, when he cannot learn, he should embrace the trait of silence [as our sages of blessed memory have said (*Avoth* 1:16): "R. Shimon ben Gamliel said: 'All my life, I grew up among the wise, and I found nothing better for the body than silence.'"] And this is alluded to by the pomegranate next to the bell; that is, like a pomegranate, that makes no sound. And, if one conducts himself in this manner, the Torah assures us (*Ibid.* 35): "and its sound will be heard when he comes to the sanctuary." That is, the sound of his prayer and his Torah will be accepted on high, which will not be the case if he does not guard his faculty of speech and mixes his speech with *lashon hara*, *rechiluth*, and the like, in which case the forbidden speech will defile his words of holiness and they will not be accepted on high, as mentioned above in Chapter I.

And (*Shemoth, Ibid.*): "...and when he leaves and he will not die" is to be understood in the same vein. That is when his time to leave the world arrives, he will find there everything that he said "before the L-rd," as we find in the holy *Zohar*: "Even a solitary breath that leaves a man's mouth is not lost." "and he will not die": That is, through this, he will have eternal life, as it is written (*Vayikra* 18:5): "And he shall live through them."

Chapter XVI

Tazria and *Metzora*

In these *parashiyoth*, the Torah wrote at length about the greatness of the uncleanliness of the *metzora* [one afflicted with *tzara'ath* (leprosy)] and of his cleansing. And the *Gemara* in *Arachin* is well known, that *tzara'ath* afflicts one who speaks *lashon hara*, as stated there (*Arachin* 15b): "If one speaks *lashon hara*, he is afflicted with plague-spots, viz. (*Psalms* 101:5): 'He who slanders his neighbor in secret, him *atzmith*,' and (*Vayikra* 25:30): '*latzmituth*,' which the *Targum* renders '*lachalutin*'; [that is, that he be a *metzora muchlat*], concerning which we learned: 'The only difference between a quarantined leper and a confirmed [*muchlat* (similar to '*lachalutin*')] leper is disheveling of the hair and rending of the clothes" [(these obtaining with the second, but not with the first)]. As to (*Arachin* 16a): "Plague-spots come for seven things, etc.", the Maharsha writes that there, it is possible that *tzara'ath* atones for him, for he is subject to quarantine — as opposed to the sin of *lashon hara*, where he is a *metzora muchlat*.

See the greatness of the uncleanliness of a *metzora*. For one who enters his tent, as soon as his head and most of his body enter, he is unclean. And this is so even if the *metzorah* is sitting under a tree and a clean person passes under it.

There are three types of uncleanliness: dead-body uncleanliness, *zivah* [genital discharge] uncleanliness, and *metzora* uncleanliness. The [one affected with the] first is sent only outside the camp of the Shechinah; the second, outside two camps, and the third, the *metzorah*, outside [all] three camps, as it is written (*Vayikra* 13:46): "Solitary shall he sit; outside the camp in his dwelling." That is, even the other unclean ones may not sit with him. And our sages of blessed memory have said. What is different about the *metzorah* that he sits alone? He [by his *lashon hara*] separated a man from his wife, a man from his neighbor — "Solitary shall he sit."

And it is written further in the Torah (*Ibid*. 95); "His clothes shall be rent and his hair shall grow long." The reason may be that *lashon hara* stems primarily from pride, one's fancying himself a distinguished man among men, whereby his heart prompts him to demean his friend. For if he recognized his own shortcomings, he would not seek another's blemishes. This is attested to by Scripture's writing concerning his cleansing (*Ibid*. 14:4), that he is to take cedar-wood, hyssop, and a tongue [lit. worm] of wool [dyed] scarlet. Rashi explains: "If he has grown proud as a cedar, let him lower himself as a worm and as hyssop and it will be forgiven him." Therefore, Scripture writes that his clothes shall be rent and his hair shall grow long, in order to abase him, that he appear to all as despised, and his heart not grow proud to speak against others.

It would also seem, according to what is known, that through the mitzvoth there are created precious vestments to clothe one's soul when it ascends, as we find n the holy *Zohar* (and as the GRA explains *Koheleth* 6:8: "At all times let your clothes be white.") And it is also known that through *lashon hara* the spirit of uncleanliness is drawn down on all the words of holiness that he utters afterwards, and they do not accrue to him, as we find in the holy *Zohar*, *Pekudei* 263: "And from this evil spirit there issue forth other 'arousers of *din*,' which are appointed to seize upon the evil or filthy speech that a man utters with his mouth, after which he utters holy words. Woe unto them [such men]! Woe unto their lives! Woe unto them in this world! Woe unto them in the world to come! For those spirits of uncleanliness take that unclean word, and when he thereafter utters holy words, those spirits of uncleanliness come forward with that unclean word and defile [with it] the holy speech [that follows], and it does not accrue to him. If so, if one speaks *lashon hara* and then fulfils the positive commandment of reciting the *Shema* or of praying or of reciting grace after meals, or other blessings of the one hundred daily blessings, which certainly create vestments for the soul — when the unclean words draw down upon them the spirit of uncleanliness, they are immediately sullied and defiled and no longer fit to clothe the soul, wherefore the Torah writes (*Vayikra* 13:46): 'His *clothes* shall be rent,' intimating the vestments of his soul."

(*Ibid.* 45): "And [the hair of] his lips shall he cover": Because he certainly said in the beginning (*Psalms* 12:5): "Our tongues shall we strengthen. Our lips are with us. Who is master over us?", the L-rd commanded that now he be covered over his lips.

(*Ibid.*): "And 'Unclean! Unclean!' shall he cry" to keep people away from him. Because it was his way in the beginning to reveal the shame of his friend before others, therefore, he is now compelled to reveal his own shame before others.

Now when we come to assess the greatness of the sin of *lashon hara*, the damage one can do with his tongue, we find ourselves powerless to do so. For it permeates all of *Torah, Prophets, Writings*, and the apothegms of our sages of blessed memory. And, in general, one knows that he undermines thereby [the processes of] the upper worlds, [strengthening thereby the *Sitra Achara* (the "Adversary") and giving it power to incriminate the entire world.] And, below, he spoils the entire creation and himself, [for he thereby draws down the spirit of uncleanliness on all the fibers of his soul, as we find in the holy *Zohar*, *Metzora*.] And he harms others, as our sages of blessed memory have said (*Arachin* 15b): "The third tongue [i.e., the tongue of the talebearer, which is the third between a man and his neighbor, to reveal secrets to him] kills three: the speaker [of *lashon hara*], the accepter, and the object." And, in general, they said (*Ibid.*): "All who speak *lashon hara* magnify sin until the heavens, as it is written (*Psalms* 73:9): 'They set their mouths in the heavens when their tongues walk the earth.'" The plain explanation is that they thereby arouse the great Prosecutor against Israel, and bring death, sword, and slaughter to the world, as we find in the holy *Zohar* (see Chapter

III). And we can say that apparently "All who speak *lashon hara*" applies to one who is habituated to it and does not take it upon himself to guard himself against it. And there is always someone who finds someone to speak about every day. And even if we do not reckon many words, but only four or five a day, that is, about thirty words a week, and, in the course of a year, about fifteen hundred words, even if we consider *lashon hara* only one negative commandment, [he violates] fifteen hundred negative commandments a year! For certainly, just as in words of holiness, every word in itself is [fulfillment of] a positive commandment, so, in forbidden speech, every word is an *issur* in itself. And if he conducts himself in this manner his whole life, he accumulates about eighty thousand or more. And it is known that from every transgression a "prosecutor" is created, as we find in *Avoth* 4:11: "Anyone who commits one transgression acquires for himself one prosecutor" [How much turmoil must grip one's heart when he reflects that he has massed against himself a great army of such prosecutors!] All this, by a reckoning of four or five words a day, which are common to many men. How much more will there be found, among the notorious speakers of *lashon hara*, more than two hundred [such] words a day. This is the intent of "All who speak *lashon hara* magnify sin until the heavens."

And let one not think: "Do I not say every day: 'Forgive us, our Father, for we have sinned'?" This would avail if one considered this [*lashon hara*] a sin and took it upon himself to guard himself against it. For penance requires, at least, absolute regret [for the past] and also acceptance [for the future]. And, in our many sins, one who is habituated to *lashon hara* does not consider it a sin at all. And even on Yom Kippur, when one says: [Forgive us] "for the sin that we have sinned before you with *lashon hara*," he does not accept upon himself 'guarding' for the future. And even if we say that he does, is this not among the sins between man and his neighbor, for which Yom Kippur does not atone until he conciliates his neighbor? (see *Yoma* 85b). And, a man like this — has he not certainly harmed several tens of men with his tongue? He has hurt this man by verbal wronging, and that one with *lashon hara*, and the other, with "whitening of the face" and the like. About such a one our sages of blessed memory have rightly said that a man by his *lashon hara* magnifies sin until the heavens. Therefore, a man must set his heart and his mind to this, that he not be "entrapped" above in this sin. They have also said "If one speaks *lashon hara*, he and I cannot live [together] in the world, as it is written (*Psalms* 10:15): 'He who slanders his neighbor in secret, him will I cut down... him will I not abide.' Read it not: '*him* will I not abide,' but '*with* him' will I not abide."

And see further that in all places we find that we must be solicitous of men's honor and not reveal their shame; but they were not solicitous at all of the honor of a person like this [(an inveterate *lashon-hara* speaker.)] To the contrary, they saw to it that the name of this man should be publicized, and all, so that he be humbled and receive atonement. For in the past, when one had to bring libations for the offerings, he had to go with his money to the keeper of the seals (*Shekalim* 5) and tell him for which offering he required libations [(for the cost of the libations was not the same for all offerings.)] He would give him the seal, with which he would go to the keeper of the libations, who would give him what he needed. On the seals there was written: "calf," "male," "goat," "sinner" [i.e., "*metzora*"], so that he would know how many libations he needed to take. We see, then, that they were not solicitous of the honor of the *metzora* at all and wrote "sinner" on his seal, so that he would know how many libations he required for his offerings.

And see further that from his cleansing we can reflect upon the greatness of his sin. For Scripture required the Cohein to place what remained of the oil on his palm or on the head of the one to be cleansed, something that we find in no other place. And this, because he must also have sinned in the *acceptance* of *lashon hara*. And the *issur* of the acceptance of *lashon hara* stems from his believing the *lashon hara* absolutely in his *mind*, whereby he transgresses the negative commandment of (*Shemoth* 23a): "You shall not bear a false report," as we explained in *Chafetz Chaim*, in the name of the Rishonim. If so, his *mind* is full of blemishes and faults vis-à-vis many men, wherefore the Torah required him to cleanse his *head*, so that henceforward he will follow this path no more and will judge every man in the scales of merit.

Chapter XVII

Kedoshim - Behar

It is written (*Vayikra* 19:16): "Do not go talebearing among your people." This negative commandment includes both *rechiluth* and *lashon hara*, as we find in *Yerushalmi*. [*Rechiluth* (talebearing)] is one's saying to his friend: "Ploni said this about you" or "did this and this to you." *Lashon hara* is one's telling his friend something demeaning of another, or other things which cause him (the other) bodily, monetary, or emotional harm.] And this negative commandment also includes *lashon hara*, as our sages of blessed memory have said in explanation of this verse: "Do not be as a merchant [*rochel*], who takes his wares from one to another." And it is known that this negative commandment obtains even if what is said is the truth, as all of the commentators have written. For if it is false, it is in the category of *motzi shem ra* [giving out a bad name], and is far more severe than *lashon hara* in general.

Preceding the aforementioned verse is [*Ibid.* 15): "...In righteousness shall you judge your neighbor," concerning which our sages of blessed memory have said (*Avoth* 1:5): "Judge every man in the scales of merit." This also applies to our subject, implying that even if you see something demeaning in him, still you must seek some merit in him, viz.: Perhaps he spoke or did this thing unwittingly, or he did not know that it is forbidden to do or say this thing, or perhaps he has already regretted [what he did or said], and the like. Therefore, Scripture commanded that you not bear tales about him and not tell others the demeaning things that you know about him. All the details of *lashon hara* and *rechiluth*, and the greatness of the reward of him who takes care to avoid it, and the punishment for the transgressor are explained in *Chafetz Chaim* and *Shemirath Halashon*, Chapter I.

(*Ibid.* 16): "You shall not stand by the blood of your neighbor," which Rashi explains: "to watch him die, if you are able to save him, as in the instance of one drowning in the river or being attacked by animals of robbers." See *Sanhedrin* 73a, to the effect that if he cannot save him himself, he must exert himself to hire others to save him. This precedes "Do not go talebearing," apparently to teach us that if he transgressed by severe *rechiluth* against a man, injecting great anger in the heart of Ploni against him to the extent of endangering his life, [(as Doeg did before Saul against David)], he must thereafter see to it to remove the danger. And if he cannot do so by himself, he must get others to try to save him. The verse concludes; "I am the L-rd," which Rashi understands as "trusted to reward" one who is careful to avoid *rechiluth* and who exerts himself to save his friend from danger, and "trusted to exact punishment" of one who does the opposite, as we find in *Peah* 1:2: "For three transgressions punishment is exacted of a person in this world, with the principal remaining for him [for punishment] in the world to come: idolatry, illicit relations, murder — and *lashon hara* over and against all."

(*Ibid.* 17): "Reprove shall you reprove your neighbor, but do not bear *sin* because of him"; that is, do not "whiten his face" in public, even by way of reproof; how much more so, otherwise. If one whitens the face of his friend in public, his sin is too great to bear. As we find in *Bava Metzia* 58b: "If one whitens his friend's face in public, it is as if he sheds blood." And (*Ibid.* 59a): "It is better for one to cast himself into a fiery furnace than to whiten his friend's face in public. Whence is this derived? From [the instance of] Tamar, viz. (*Bereshith* 38:25): 'She was taken out [to be burned], and she sent to her father-in-law, saying, etc.'" It is apparent from this that even if the man [spoken against] is, indeed, liable, still, great care must be taken not to shame him. And it emerges from the *Gemara* that if one is accustomed to whiten his friend's face in public, he has no share in the world to come.

(*Vayikra* 25:17): "And you shall not wrong, one man, his fellow.": Here, the Torah exhorted against verbal wronging; that is not to hurt his fellow with words. And, in *Bava Metzia* 58b: "Verbal wronging is worse than monetary wronging, for the first is directed against his person, and the second, against his possessions; and the second allows of restitution, whereas the first does not." And it is stated there: [With the destruction of the Temple,] "all the gates [to the L-rd] are locked except the gates of wronging." [i.e., they are open to the wronged one to cry out and] to exact punishment of the wronger. And verbal wronging also is in the category of *lashon hara*, as we find in *Yoma* 44a.

Chapter XVIII

Beha'alothecha

(*Bamidbar* 12:1): "And Miriam and Aaron spoke against Moses, etc." From this *parshah* we learn several things [concerning *lashon hara*]:

1) The *issur* obtains even if the one spoken against is humble and lowly of spirit and does not take offense at what is said about him. [For this reason this is juxtaposed with (3): "And the man Moses was exceedingly humble."

2) [The *issur* obtains] even if he [the speaker] benefited him [the one spoken about] greatly, as when he [the second] were in dire straits and he [the first] greatly exerted himself for him and rescued him [(as when Miriam rescued Moses from the Nile)]

3) The *issur* of *lashon hara* obtains even if he does not speak about him before several persons, but only before one, and [even if] that one is his relative, who will not go and tell others.

4) [The *issur* obtains] if one says about an eminent personage that his conduct is not suited for him, that it *would* be if he were the paragon of his generation; but since he is not, but only on par with the other eminent men, his conduct is too pretentious. This, too, is absolute *lashon hara*. Their mistake [(that of Aaron and Miriam)] was that they compared Moses with other prophets and with the forefathers, as we find in *Sifrei*, wherefore it was a cause of wonder with them that he separated from his wife. Did they, too, *not* separate? Therefore, the Holy One Blessed be He said to them (*Ibid.* 6): "If your prophets be … (7) Not so My servant Moses, etc.," who was on a higher level than all of them, being *constantly* receptive to prophecy — wherefore he *had* to separate.

(*Ibid.* 10): "And Aaron turned to Miriam, and, behold, she was leprous." For through the sin of *lashon hara*, plague-spots come, and his [the speaker's] punishment is to be a *metzorah muchlat* [a confirmed *metzorah*], as we find in the *Gemara* (*Arachin* 15b): "If one speaks *lashon hara*, he is afflicted with plague-spots, viz.: (*Psalms* 101:5): 'He who slanders his neighbor in secret, him *atzmith*,' and (*Vayikra* 25;30): '*latzmituth*' which the *Targum* renders '*lachalutin*'; [that is, that he be a *metzora muchlat*] concerning which we learned: 'The only difference between a quarantined leper [*metzora musgar*] and a confirmed [*muchlat* (similar to '*lachalutin*')] leper is disheveling of the hair and rending of the clothes" [(these obtaining with the second, but not with the first)]. And the prayer of Moses availed her, but not entirely — only to change her from a confirmed leper to a quarantined leper.

Chapter XIX

Shelach

How great is the power of *lashon hara*! For when we were in the desert, many times we rebelled against the L-rd, as in the episode of the golden calf and the like, and still their decree was sealed only because of the *lashon hara* of the spies alone. And we find there (*Arachin* 15a) that verbal imputation of an [illicit] act ["*motzi shem ra*"] is worse than the act itself. For one who ravishes a virgin pays a fine of only fifty silver shekels, while one who imputes an evil name [to her] is fined a hundred silver shekels, it being written (*Devarim* 22:19): "And they shall fine him a hundred [shekels of] silver… for he has given out an evil name [(of licentiousness)] about a virgin of Israel." And he [the imputer of the evil name] also receives stripes because of this, as it is written (*Ibid*. 18): "And they shall chastise him [with stripes]."

And now we shall explain in brief the episode of the spies. For, on the surface, it is cause for great wonder: What is it that caused them to sink to such depths and to mislead Israel? More than that — even Sanhedrin erred in this, it being written (*Bamidbar* 19:1): "And the entire congregation [the Sanhedrin (Rashi)] lifted their voices, etc." And more than this, they said (*Ibid*. 13:31): "For they are stronger than He," which our sages of blessed memory interpreted as: "He is unable, as it were, to rescue His vessels from there." How could they speak such nonsense?

But, when we reflect upon this well, we find that we, too, have this kind of *yetzer hara* which befuddled the spies. (We shall explain this at the end.) But first let us speak about the spies, who went to spy out the land. For Moses our teacher, may peace be upon him, said (*Ibid*. 18): "And see what the land is like," which Rashi interpreted: "There is a land that 'grows' warriors, and there is a land that 'grows' weak men. There is a land that grows populaces and there is a land that reduces populaces." (*Ibid*. 20): "And what of the land? Is it fat or lean, etc.? …And you shall take of the fruit of the land": For it is a great advantage to see the land producing fruits that are big and good. Likewise, when we see it producing strong, tall men. Anda large population is a sign of very good air. But all this, [is the perception of] those who believe in the words of the L-rd, who promised to give us the land; and, certainly, "He is not a man, to retract [His word]." But if one wavers in this, and begins to doubt and to think that to defeat warriors so strong as these and a populace as large as this, great merit is required, that all must be righteous and holy, and that we lack men of this kind, the more he sees the men of the land to be numerous, strong, and so tall as to defy conventional measurement, all of this is overwhelming to him, and he is crestfallen.

And it is known that it is the way of the *yetzer* to vary its stratagems, for which reason it sits at the two openings of the heart (*Berachoth* 61a). That is, sometimes it instills pride into a man's heart to make him think that he is one of the fearers of the L-rd, and perhaps, even one of his lovers. And when it beholds a man who wishes to strengthen himself in something for the honor of the Blessed L-rd, in the manner of a true lover, it casts sadness upon his heart, so that he thinks that this mitzvah or this mode of conduct does not become him, but only "the holy ones who are in the land," not one so small as he. And it reawakens in his thoughts mean acts that he did in the days of his youth. And even though sometimes he regrets and is embittered over this, it causes him to forget this and to remember only things that suit his situation, as he thinks, in order to vex and humble him so that he will have no desire for that mitzvah.

Here, too, when they came to spy out the land, the *yetzer* intensified itself over them, causing them to say: "To defeat men so numerous and so strong requires great, awesome merit which we do not possess. For we have just made the golden calf and [eaten] flesh of lust. [(This, although they had already repented and had wept profusely (for their sin), as we find in *Pirkei d'R. Eliezer*, that on the last of the forty days of Moses' ascent to the mountain, when they knew that on the morrow he would descend from the mountain all of Israel spent the night fasting and went the next day to receive him, weeping profusely, and it was told them that the Holy One Blessed be He had forgiven them, so that [this day] was instituted for them for forgiveness for future generations)]. For this reason they said (*Ibid*. 27): "We came to the land to which you sent us, and it is, indeed, flowing with milk and honey, and these are its fruits (28): but the people are strong, who dwell in the land… and also the children of the giant did we see there (29): Amalek dwells in the lands of the south, etc." This, as if to say: "We need the merit of Moses our teacher, as of yore"; as if to say: "Who knows if he will live until then?" (For they had an intimation from the prophecy of Eldad and Medad (*Sanhedrin* 27a, 29a) [that he would die before then]). And, aside from this (*Ibid*.): "And the Chitti and the Yevussi, etc." That is, to defeat all of them *before* we come to Eretz Israel requires great merit. How much more so to come to the people in Eretz Israel and overcome them there!

(*Ibid*. 30): "And Calev silenced the people towards Moses": As Rashi explains. "He said: 'Is it this alone that Moses has done to us? Did he not split the sea for us and bring down the manna for us, etc.?'" His intent was: If the Holy One Blessed be He had come against us with *din*, He would not have split the sea for us and He would not have brought down the manna for us. For at the sea, too, they [Israel] were not as they should have been, as it is written (*Psalms* 106:7): "And they rebelled at the sea, by the Sea of Reeds." And also with the manna, in the beginning there was complaint. And, indeed, in all that period, until now, [as Moses our teacher said afterwards (*Bamidbar* 14:19): "Forgive, I pray you, the sin of this people in the greatness of Your lovingkindness, and as You have forgiven this people from Egypt until now."] And now, too, "we will go up" to Eretz Yisrael, "and we shall inherit it," as Moses said, when we come there.

(*Ibid.* 13:31): "And the men who went up with him said: 'We shall not be able to go up against the people [(that is, we will not even be able to *go up*, as they said before (30): "Amalek dwells in the land of the south, and the Chitti, etc.")], for they are stronger than He.'" That is, when does the Holy One Blessed be He drive out a people? When He finds another that is better than it, He gives them power to destroy them and to inherit their place. But for people such as we, who were great sinners with the golden calf and with the flesh of lust, He will not drive out such great peoples. As to His promising us to give us the land, this is only on condition that we merit it, as *tzaddikim*. [Then,] He would drive out the foe before us and would grant us permission to destroy them.

Now, when the spies saw that the people were wavering, and that some of them were inclining to the view of Calev, they spoke *lashon hara* against the land, saying (*Ibid.* 32): "The land which we passed through to spy out, etc." That is, we examined it closely and we saw that its air is very bad and harms people and that only men of unusual strength were left in it. [They intimated thereby: When you come to the land, which is very holy (you will find that) the attribute of *din* reposes there. For there is no comparison between one who does not do the will of the King outside the palace and one who does not do it inside the palace. Therefore, only absolute *tzaddikim* can survive there. And we are not on that level, and the land is not fit for us.] (*Ibid.* 33): "And there we saw the giants... and we were in our eyes like grasshoppers.": That is, our hearts melted, and you, too, when you come there, your hearts will melt with fear. And, as a result, the "higher guarding," too, will depart from you, for, as it is known, His "guarding" is a function of a man's trust in Him, as is well known.

(*Ibid.* 14:1): And the entire congregation [(the Sanhedrin, according to Rashi)] lifted their voice and clamored, etc." For, in truth, the greater the man, the more he recognizes his lowliness. As we say each day: "Are not all the strong ones as naught before You, and the men of name as if they never were, and the wise, as lacking knowledge, and the understanding, as lacking intellect, etc.?" Therefore, he [the great man] is especially lowly in his eyes, as David said (*Psalms* 22:9): "And I am a worm, and not a man, the shame of men and the despised of people." Therefore, when the spies put it to them that their generation was not significant in the eyes of the L-rd because of the evil of their acts and the stiffness of their necks, and was not worthy that a miracle be performed for them to overpower these giants, this seemed very reasonable to them.

And these two claims were countered by Joshua and Calev in short: As to your claim that you made a careful inspection and found its air to be bad, we, too, toured it and inspected closely, and we found that (*Ibid.* 7) "the land is good, extremely good."

And, as to the first claim, that the L-rd's promising the land was contingent upon our being *tzaddikim*, this is rooted in error. The Holy One Blessed be He is not so exacting with a man as to say: "I will help you only if you are a *tzaddik*"; but He does say: "I will *not* help you if you rebel, G-d forbid." Therefore, Joshua and Calev concluded [their argument with] (*Ibid.* 9): "Only against the L-rd do not rebel." And so long as a man does not rebel against the L-rd to deliberately uproot His mitzvoth, he may hope for all good. As to your frightening the people that there are men of imposing stature there and giants, (*Ibid.*): "Do not fear the people of the land, for they are our bread." If a man chanced upon a great bread for eating, one hundred ells long, would he be afraid to come near it? Does it not lack the spirit of life to war with him? To the contrary, it has been presented to him to eat and to enjoy. Here, too, (*Ibid.*): "Their (protective) shade has departed from them," for the L-rd has filled them with awe and fright, and they are ours for the eating, as it is written (*Devarim* 7:16): "And you will eat all the peoples." For the giants, with all their might and strength — their heart is humbled more than the rest of the people, and they hide in the mountains and in the fortified cities, as it is written (*Joshua* 11:21): "And Joshua came at that time, and cut off the giants from the mountain, from Chevron, from Devir, from Anav and from all of Har Yehudah." And, similarly, (*Judges* 1:10): "And Judah went… and they smote Sheshai, Achiman, and Talmai."

And now we shall explain what we wrote in the beginning, that this type of *yetzer* of the spies is found with us, too. That is, if we come to a Jew and ask him: "Do you believe that there is great reward for observers of the Torah?", he will answer: "Certainly, I believe with perfect faith that one moment of pleasure in the world to come is worth more than all the life in this world." And if you ask him: "If so, why are you lax in Torah study, which inevitably results in great laxity in mitzvah observance?", he will answer: "True, happy is he who attains to Torah study and mitzvah observance and thereby merits the great pleasure of the world to come. But who can merit this if not very special individuals? For this requires the expenditure of all one's bodily powers, and his life will be entirely worthless to him. For he will have to separate from all the affairs of the world and sit in the house of study day and night, and all his thoughts will have to cleave to the L-rd and to His Torah. And such a regimen requires a holy man. A man like this merits Gan Eden, but not plain men like me."

But, in truth, this is an error from the outset. The Torah did not require a plain man to learn day and night and not ply an occupation at all, but to ply an occupation and to set aside times for Torah study. And, indeed, the Torah commanded that this be done with faith and without deceit, as our sages of blessed memory have said (*Shabbath* 31a): "A man is asked [when he is brought to judgment]: 'Were you honest in your dealings? Did you set aside times for Torah study?'" And thus with all of the mitzvoth. When we reflect upon it, we find that the Torah was not at all exacting with a man, as it is written (*Michah* 6:3): "My people, what did I do to you and how did I tire you? Answer Me." The main thing is that he take care not to be a rebel, G-d forbid, against the King of the world. That is, not to deliberately violate the positive or negative commandments of the Torah. But if he is not a rebel, he is certainly eminently meritorious above.

And when the *yetzer* sees that in this way it cannot entice a man, he begins to entice him in different ways, viz.: "True, the Holy One Blessed be He accepts a man if he only sets aside times for Torah, but know that when you come for the accounting on high, before the Throne of Glory, there they are very exacting in the *manner* of Torah study [and, likewise, in the *manner* of performance of mitzvoth], [to determine] if they were done correctly and without any ulterior motive; and, also, in the *manner* of Torah study. [They will ask you] if you stopped in the middle for idle talk, and other such strong questions. And you know that the G-d of the heavens is a G-d of truth. Who, then, can emerge meritorious in judgment other than absolute *tzaddikim*?" With all such arguments the *yetzer hara* comes against a man in order to make him despair and to belittle him, so that he be lax in the service of the Blessed L-rd. Now, even though, in truth, all of these arguments are justified, the *yetzer hara* causes a man to forget that the Holy One Blessed be He, who loves lovingkindness and wishes to benefit his creations, created to this end repentance, which preceded the [creation of] the world. Therefore, if one finds himself not to have done the mitzvah or to have learned as he should have, he must immediately regret this and take it upon himself to conduct himself correctly in the future.

Chapter XX

Korach

We learned (*Arachin* 15a) that for the sin of *lashon hara* one is afflicted with plague-spots. And the *Gemara* asks: "But did R. Anani bar Sasson not say that the robe atones for *lashon hara*? ...Let that which produces a sound [(the bells on the robe)] atone for the sound of the voice [i.e., *lashon hara*]?" And it answers: "There is no contradiction: In one instance, his deeds avail; in the other, his deeds do not avail. If his deeds avail, plague-spots come upon him; if his deeds do not avail, the robe atones." And the *Gemara* asks: "But did not R. Shimon say in the name of R. Yehoshua ben Levi that *lashon hara* is atoned for by the incense? For R. Chanina taught: We learned that the incense atones, it being written (*Bamidbar* 17:12): 'And he [Aaron] put on the incense and he atoned for the people.' And the school of R. Yishmael taught: 'For what does the incense atone? For *lashon hara*. Let what is done in secrecy [(the offering of the incense on the silver altar)] come and atone for an act [*lashon hara*] committed in secrecy.'" And the *Gemara* answers: "There is no contradiction: *Here* [(the incense atones)] when it [the *lashon hara*] is spoken secretly; *there*, [(the robe atones)] when it is spoken in public." What emerges from this is that when his deeds avail, he is afflicted with leprosy, even if it were spoken secretly, and when they do not avail, a distinction must be made, viz.: If it were spoken secretly, the incense, (which was also offered secretly, all men having to remove themselves) atoned; and if it were spoken in public, the robe atones [(the sound of its bells being heard when he left the sanctuary)].

This seems to contradict "And he put on the incense and he atoned for the people." For there the *lashon hara* was in public, it being written (*Ibid.* 6): "And the entire congregation of the children of Israel railed on the morrow against Moses and against Aaron, saying: 'You have put to death the people of the L-rd.'" It may be that for this reason Aaron had to bring the incense to the people, in public, and to atone there for them, the daily incense offering brought in secret not sufficing, since the *lashon hara* was in public.

As to the atonement not sufficing through the robe, in which Aaron was clothed, it is possible that since the *lashon hara* was directed to Aaron himself, he could not be atoned for by his robe.

[It seems more apt to say that here, where they said: "You have put to death the people of the L-rd," their act is "of avail." For Rashi explains "of avail" as "leading to quarreling," so that "not of avail" would refer to *lashon hara* which does not lead to quarreling. And this obtains only with *lashon hara* where one shamed a man not in his presence and no harm was caused the man because of this. But in an instance of verbal wronging, where he shames and hurts one [(for this, too, is in the category of *lashon hara*, as we see from the episode of Avdan (which shall be adduced below) and from Rashi (*Yoma* 44a — "*al lashon hara*")], it is not possible to say that his act does not avail, for this [the verbal wronging] *itself* avails, for he shames and hurts him. This is proved by the instance of Avdan (*Yevamoth* 105b), who shamed R. Yishmael b. R. Yossi, saying to him: "Are you worthy of learning Torah from Rabbi?" We are told there that at that moment Avdan became a *metzora*, and Rashi explains there that the punishment for "*lashon hara*" is plague-spots.

As it applies to *our* instance, Moses and Aaron were told to their faces "You have put to death the people of the L-rd." This is [obviously] an instance of their act "availing," and for this the robe is certainly of no avail, as we see in the *Gemara* (*Arachin* 15a), nor the merit of the daily incense offering.

Why did the Holy One Blessed be He say (*Ibid.* 10): "And I will consume them [(who spoke *lashon hara* against Moses and Aaron)] this instant"? Would it not have been sufficient to punish them with plague-spots? It is possible that this may be because they spoke *lashon hara* so audaciously against *Moses our teacher*, may peace be upon him [(who was "trusted in the whole house of the L-rd," and did nothing without being told to do so by the L-rd)], and against Aaron, the "holy one" of the L-rd, saying that they had killed the people of the L-rd. If so, they deserved to be put to death by the hands of Heaven, G-d forbid. Therefore, it was decreed against the speakers that they die in the plague, which is much more severe than the punishment of plague-spots. And only after many people were killed in the plague, the rest were protected (against their *lashon hara*) by the merit of the incense that Aaron offered up in public, as mentioned above.

In this vein we can understand what is written in the Torah, that Miriam was afflicted with leprosy because she spoke wrongly against Moses our teacher, may peace be upon him. Did she not speak privately with Aaron, and not in public, in which instance she should have been protected in the merit of the incense, which atones for *lashon hara* spoken in secret? Perforce, we must say, as in the above instance, that *lashon hara* spoken against the "lord of the prophets" is far graver, and is not atoned for by the incense but only by plague-spots. But, in any event, her punishment was attenuated by the prayer of Moses. For it is known that the punishment of plague-spots for *lashon hara* is to be a *confirmed* leper, as explained in the *Gemara*, but her punishment was attenuated, only to be quarantined for seven days (see end of Chapter XVIII).]

Chapter XXI

Chukath

(*Bamidbar* 21:4): "And they journeyed from Hor Hahar by way of the Red Sea to go around the land of Edom, etc." It is known that this took place later, when "the dead of the desert" had already died out and they were close to entering Eretz Yisrael. But because of their making a detour of the land of Edom, who did not allow them to pass through their land, they thought, that G-d forbid, this might take many more years. This is what caused them to speak out and to be punished severely for it.

All this is an intimation of the end of the exile, when there will be found people who will also speak after this manner, and will, likewise be punished severely for it. Therefore, the man of heart will take great care in this regard, not to speak wrongly of the L-rd, G-d forbid.

(*Ibid.* 5): "And the people spoke against G-d and against Moses, etc." There are many questions here: 1) First it is written "against *Elokim* and against Moses," and then (7):"because we spoke against *Hashem*." 2) (*Ibid.* 6): "and they bit *the people*." This always connotes the *inferior* ones," and this is followed by "and a large number died of *Israel*," [connoting the superior ones]. 3) (*Ibid.* 7): "And let Him remove from us *the snake*." Should it not be the *snakes*? Was there only one snake? 4) Why did the prayer of Moses not avail to remove them entirely? 5) (*Ibid.* 8): "*whoever* was bitten": This implies, even one who was not so eminent. And this is followed by (9): "if the snake had bitten *a man*," [connoting an *eminent* man]! Also, in the beginning (8), *re'iah* ["seeing"] is written; and, afterwards, (9) *habatah* [gazing (intently)] is used.

We shall answer the questions in order: As to their saying "against *Elokim* and against Moses," they emulated in this, the primal serpent, who also spoke against the Holy One Blessed be He, who said that the reason the Holy One Blessed be He did not permit eating from the tree of knowledge was (*Bereshith* 3:5) "For *Elokim* knows that on the day you eat from it... you will be like *elohim*" [which Onkelos translates 'great ones'], wherefore He withheld this good [of eating] from you. Here, too, in giving you manna, He gave you "faulty bread," and He is destined to exact punishment of you through it [see Rashi], that your bowels will burst, when you are not meritorious; for He wishes to conduct himself with you according to the attribute of *din*. And, in truth, it was not so. For it was in His mercy and lovingkindness that He gave them bread from heaven, which contained no waste, the like of which he had not even given to our holy forefathers, as it is written (*Devarim* 8:3): "And He fed you the manna, which you did not know, and which your forefathers did not know, to make it known to you that not through bread alone shall a man live, but by all that issues from the mouth of the L-rd shall a man live." And he also wished to spare them exertion. For is it not known that the cloud of the L-rd dwelt among them, because of which it is written in the Torah (*Devarim* 23:13): "And a place shall there be for you outside the camp [outside the cloud of glory], and you shall go out there outside." Therefore, He gave them manna to eat, which produces no waste and which is absorbed into the organs, so that they would always be clean and pure, wherefore it is written thereafter (7): "because we spoke against *Hashem*" [connoting "mercy"], who gave us manna in His mercies.

(*Ibid.* 6): "And the L-rd sent against the people the fiery serpents [(which burn by their venom)]. This is because in their speaking they roused the primal serpent, who "prosecuted" them, as we find in the holy *Zohar, Pekudai* 26:9): "There is a certain spirit which stands over all those who speak *lashon hara*, and when men stir up *lashon hara* or when one man stirs up *lashon hara*, then there is roused that unclean spirit above, which is called *sachsuchah* ("contention"), and it comes to repose on that rousing of *lashon hara* initiated by men, and it ascends above andthereby causes death, sword, and slaughter in the world through this rousing of *lashon hara*. Woe to those who awaken that evil spirit and do not guard their mouths and their tongues and pay no heed to this. They do not realize that upon this lower arousal there is contingent that higher arousal above, both for good or for bad, and all conspire to rouse that great serpent to prosecute the world — and all because of that rousing of *lashon hara* below." That is why *Hashem* [(connoting "mercy")] sent among them the fiery serpents, to atone by their deaths for their speaking against Him and to have a portion in the world to come. And though, even without this, they were in a desert in which fiery serpents were found, as it is written (*Devarim* 8:15): "in the great, awesome desert of fiery snakes and scorpions," still, with all this, Divine Providence was with them that they not be touched by them. Not so now. For not only were they not guarded against them, but He incited them against them. And the incitement was only against the [common] "people," who were the principal speakers [of *lashon hara*], but there was no incitement against those who were in the class of "Israel." However, in any event, because of the great "prosecutor" above, protection was removed from all of them, and "a large number of Israel [also] died." This resolves the second question.

We shall now come to explain "And let Him remove from us *the snake*." They reflected that by their words they had aroused against themselves "the great prosecutor," the great snake, and [they said to Moses:] "Pray to the L-rd that He remove *it* from us," so that the plague cease entirely and the protection return as it was. And Moses heeded their words and prayed for them.

(*Ibid.* 8): "And the L-rd said to Moses: 'Make for yourself a fiery serpent, etc.' That is, as to your asking that it be removed entirely, (that they be protected as at first and the snakes not touch them), it is impossible to seal its mouth altogether, that they be guarded as at first. But your prayer will avail for this: that from now on,

I will not incite the snakes against them. And though they are nevertheless dangerous, "make a fiery serpent for yourself and place it on a high pole," that they can always reflect that it was their speech that aroused the serpent on high to prosecute them before the throne of glory, [as we find in *Tanna d' bei Eliyahu*, that the *lashon hara* one speaks ascends until the throne of glory, as it is written (*Psalms* 73:9): "They have placed their mouths in the heavens, etc."], and through this they will be humbled before the L-rd and He will have mercy upon them. This resolves the fourth question.

And now we shall come to explain the end of the verse, "*Whoever* was bitten will *see* the snake and live." It is well known that the words and acts of a man who is not very significant can cause harm only relative to the significance of his soul, as opposed to the words and acts of an eminent man, where the defect ascends to the higher worlds. This is the intent of "*Whoever* was bitten"; a man who is not significant, and is only in the category of "*people*," in which instance "if he *sees* it, he will live." That is, "seeing" alone and moderate reflection are sufficient for him. But, if the serpent bit "a *man*," an *eminent* man, who went astray [through *lashon hara*], and he thereafter *gazed* with *intent* and with deep reflection upon the fiery serpent on the pole, then, (a snake not biting in vain, so that he must have sinned [through *lashon hara*]), if he asks forgiveness of the L-rd, and takes upon himself not to repeat his offense in the future, "he shall live."

Chapter XXII

Tetze

(*Devarim* 22:13): "If a man takes a wife and he comes upon her, and he hates her, (19): and he libels her and gives out about her an evil name, and he says: 'I took this woman and I drew near to her, and I did not find virginity in her'... (22:18): and the elders of the city shall take the man and *they shall chastise him*." Our sages of blessed memory have said that he receives stripes, having transgressed "You shall not go talebearing."

(*Devarim* 22:19): "And they shall fine him a hundred (shekels of) silver... for he has given out an evil name about a virgin of Israel." (*Arachin* 15a, *Mishnah*): "We find that one who speaks [(*lashon hara*)] with his mouth is worse than one who commits the act." [For one who ravishes or seduces must give only fifty shekels and, also, is not liable to stripes, as opposed to one who gives out an evil name (*motzi shem ra*).] And this may be the intent of (*Amos* 4:13): "For He forms the mountains and creates the wind and tells a man what his converse is." That is, a man, when he reflects sometimes about his affairs, thinks only of his deeds, and not at all of his words, saying to himself: "What harm can my words do? Are they not insubstantial?" But, in truth, it is not so. For the effect of his words on high can be much worse than that of his deeds. And this is the intent of "He tells a man what his converse is." That is, at the time of judgment they will set out before him and show him to his eyes [(as it is written (*Psalms* 50:21): "I will reprove you and set it out before your eyes")] what damage he had done with his converse. It is not written "what his *speech* is," but "what his *converse* is," "converse" connoting light, simple talk. As our sages of blessed memory have said (*Chagigah* 5a): "Even slight converse between a man and his wife is related to him at the time of judgment." Not even one word is lost that is not written down, as Scripture states (*Koheleth* 10:20): "For the bird of heaven will carry the voice, and the winged one will tell the thing." As it is known, "the winged one" is the angel Gavriel, who proclaims above, everything that is done in this world. As to "will carry the voice," this is as the naturalists write, that every article of speech — the voice, with every letter that issues from his mouth — is found in the air, not even one letter being lost. And this is what happens when a man speaks with his friend. The voice and all of its letters reach the ears of his friend. And along these lines they said (*Bava Metzia* 58b): "R. Yochanan said in the name of R. Shimon b. Yochai 'More severe is verbal wronging than monetary wronging (i.e., cheating)' [even though monetary wronging is by deed and verbal wronging only by speech]; for of the latter it is written (*Vayikra* 25:17): 'And you shall fear your G-d,' and of the former it is not written 'And you shall fear your G-d.'" R. Elazar said: "*This* [(verbal wronging)] is with his body; the other is [only] with his money." R. Shmuel b. Nachmani said: "*This* [(monetary wronging)] is subject to restitution; *that* [(verbal wronging)' is not subject to restitution." And if he caused his face to "whiten" [with shame] thereby, his sin is too great to bear. As we find there: "If one causes his friend's face to whiten in public, it is as if he has spilled blood."

(*Devarim* 23:14): "And a peg shall there be for you *al azenecha*": Bar Kappara expounded: Read it not "*al azenecha*" ["among your implements"], but "*al aznecha*" ["upon your ears"]. If one hears something unseemly, let him place his fingers in his ears? [That is, if he understands that they are going to speak of such things, or if he does not want to hear anymore.] This is as R. Elazar said: "Why are a man's fingers like pegs? So that if he hears something unseemly, he can place his fingers in his ears." It was taught in the school of R. Yishmael: "Why is the ear itself stiff, and the lobe soft? So that if one hears something unseemly, he can place his lobe in his ear." The Rabbis taught: "Let one not permit his ears to hear idle talk, for they are the first to be 'burnt' of all the organs."

(*Ibid.* 24:8): "Be heedful of the plague-spot of leprosy, to take great care, and to do according to all that the Cohanim, the Levites, teach you… (9): Remember what the L-rd your G-d did to Miriam on the way when you went out of Egypt." And, in *Sifrei*, "Remember what the L-rd your G-d did to Miriam on the way, etc.": "I might think: [Remember] in your heart. But this is already stated. How, then, am I to understand "Remember"? That you should say it with your mouth." It is clear, then, that they understood "Be heedful, etc." as be heedful not to *contract* [leprosy], and, [if you do,] "to do all that the Cohanim, etc."

"Remember what the L-rd your G-d did to Miriam" — "Mention it with your mouth always" [Ramban]. And he writes there that this is an explicit positive commandment, just as (*Shemoth* 20:8): "Remember the day of Sabbath to sanctify it," (*Ibid.* 13:3): "Remember this day that you went out of Egypt, etc." And this, too, just as the former, is a positive commandment, to mention the great punishment that the L-rd brought upon the *tzadeketh*, the prophetess, who spoke only of her brother, the "redeemed of her soul," whom she loved as her soul, and who did not speak thus to his face, to embarrass him, and not in public, but only in private, to her holy brother [Aaron] — and all of this did not avail [to save her from leprosy.] You, too, if 'you sit and speak against your brother; if you slander your mother's son,' (*Psalms* 50:20), you will not be saved."

Chapter XXIII

Tavo

Aside from all of these *parshiyoth* mentioned above, which speak of the *issur* of *lashon hara*, the Holy One Blessed be He gave a special blessing to one who guards himself from this sin, and, conversely, about the man of *lashon hara* it is written *Arur*, ("Cursed"), viz. (*Devarim* 27:12): "These shall stand to bless the people on Mount Gerizim, etc." For all of the eleven *arurim* opened with *Baruch* ("Blessed") for one who guarded himself against it, and all of Israel answered "Amen." And then they [the Levites] said (*Ibid*. 24): "Cursed is he who smites his neighbor in secret," which refers to *lashon hara*, as we find in *Sifrei*; and all of Israel would answer "Amen." How much must one take care to guard himself against this sin, for which he is cursed by all of Israel. And happy is he who guards himself against this sin, for which he is blessed by all of Israel together!

(*Devarim* 26:17): "The L-rd did you single out this day to be to you as a G-d, and to walk in His ways, and to keep His statutes, and His mitzvoth, and His judgments, and to heed His voice." From this verse we learn the greatness of strengthening oneself to walk in the ways of the traits of the Holy One Blessed be He, to be merciful, gracious, and the like. For Scripture mentioned this quality ["to walk in His ways"] before keeping the statutes, the mitzvoth, and the judgments, whereby we infer that it takes precedence to the others [(as we find in *Berachoth* 41b on the verse that speaks in praise of Eretz Yisrael (*Devarim* 8:8): "a land of wheat, barley, grapevine, etc." — "That which precedes (in the verse) precedes for the blessing."] And one must greatly strengthen oneself in this — whence we learn in our instance to guard greatly against the *issur* of *lashon hara*. For this is one of the ways of the traits of the Holy One Blessed be He, as our sages of blessed memory said (*Sanhedrin* 43b) concerning the deed of Achan, who violated the ban, because of which Israel was defeated in the war. (*Joshua* 2:6): "And he [Joshua] fell on his face to the ground before the ark of the L-rd... (10): And the L-rd said to Joshua: 'Arise, why do you fall on your face... they have also stolen; they have also denied... (12): I will not be with you if you do not destroy the *cherem* [(the forbidden property] from your midst.'" Joshua said to Him: "Who has sinned?", to which He answered: "Am I a slanderer? Go and cast lots and it will be known to you." Even for something that it was a mitzvah to clarify, such as the act of Achan, where they were obliged to destroy the *cherem*, even so, since it could come to light of itself, it should not be spoken.

And, in truth, since the Holy One Blessed be He created a man in His image, as written in the Torah, he must liken himself to the Blessed Creator in every way that he can. And it is because of the greatness of this trait ["to walk in His ways"], which is the fundamental principle in the service of the Blessed L-rd, that Scripture singled it out (in *Devarim* 19:9) — "and to walk in His ways all of the days." That is, it is not sufficient that one be adventitiously a good man, merciful, gracious, abundant in lovingkindness and the like, but "all of the days" he must take care to cultivate this holy trait of walking in His ways. And as to the rest of the mitzvoth, even though he must keep them, too, all of the days, Scripture did not single out each mitzvah by itself [(for "all of the days")], but spoke of them only collectively, in (*Devarim* 29:28): "The hidden things are for the L-rd our G-d, but the revealed ones are for us and our children forever, to do according to all the words of this Torah." The reason is as we have written.

I have shown, before the eyes of all, the abundance of *parshiyoth* in the Torah which speak of and exhort against forbidden speech. And there are many tens of verses in *Prophets* and *Writings*, which abominate the man who abandons his mouth to everything that his *yetzer* desires. Happy is the man who is solicitous of the honor of the Torah of the L-rd and takes care not to transgress it. Of his portion may our portion be, and of his lot, our lot!

Chapter XXIV

In this chapter it will be explained that even he who was remiss in the guarding of his tongue for a great part of his life can, notwithstanding, strengthen himself in his remaining days

Know further that even if one did not guard his mouth and his tongue for a great length of time, he can still strengthen himself for the future in the remaining days that the Blessed L-rd will vouchsafe him that they not be spoiled. To what may this be compared? To a man who hired a caretaker to tend to his vineyard for all the days of the summer. He did not take care of it for several months, and it deteriorated greatly, thieves breaching its fence and stealing most of its growths. Is it conceivable that the owner will now abandon it entirely and leave it to the ravages of the animals? To the contrary, he will now add "guarding to his guarding" and fix its fence and set his eyes and heart upon it that he not lose even one fruit. So, in this instance, exactly, as it is written in *Mishlei* (24:30-31): "I passed by the field of a lazy man, and by the vineyard of a man lacking a heart. And, behold, it was all grown over with thorns; nettles had covered its face, and its stone wall was broken down." And his counsel for his vineyard is that he fix his fence and root out its thorns and nettles and keep his eye upon it that it not deteriorate even further.

And in our instance, the remedy for the future, likewise, is that he make fences for himself, that he distance himself from the company of men and that he not speak about any man, and that if he had hurt anyone by his tongue, by shaming and insulting him, he should conciliate him. And he should guard his tongue the remaining days of his life, that his speech be only in words of holiness and in words of Torah [except for what is needed for some exigency or for his livelihood]. And then he can say about himself; "Happy is our old age, that has atoned for our childhood."

Chapter XXV

Purity of Thought

Until now we have spoken about setting to rights the faculty of speech, the first fundamental, the demarcation between "man" and "animal," for which reason Scripture gives it precedence, viz. (*Devarim* 30:19): "For the thing is very near to you, in your mouth and in your heart [i.e., your thoughts] to do it." And now we shall speak a little about the faculty of thought, which resides in a man's heart, viz.: "and in your *heart* to do it." Scripture writes (*Psalms* 24:3-4): "Who shall ascend the mountain of the L-rd, etc.? ...The clean of hands [i.e., one who is clean of theft] and the pure of heart." We learn from this that a man's thoughts must be pure and not intermixed with vanity. We say every day: "Make our hearts one, to love and to fear Your name, and let us not be ashamed, forever." This means what it says. It is known that what resides in a Jew's heart always, is faith in the L-rd, the G-d of the heavens and His Torah, this being the essence of holiness [as intimated in *Bamidbar* 35:39: "I am the L-rd who dwells in the midst of the children of Israel."] For this reason we ask the Blessed L-rd that He make our hearts one, to love and to fear His name, and that there not be intermixed in this another love. For if in his heart, the locus of thought, there also is planted a love for the vanities of the world, in the end, he will be shamed and mortified by it forever.

For it is known that all of a man's affairs — both his acts and his thoughts, all will ascend above, before the L-rd, as we say in the Rosh Hashanah prayer: "For the remembrance of every creation comes before You, the acts of a man, etc., the thoughts of a man and his stratagems." And all will be set forth before the man, as it is written (*Psalms* 54:21): "I shall reprove you and I shall set it before your eyes," and the man will be greatly shamed.

To what can this be compared? To [the instance of] a wealthy man, a merchant in precious gems, who, journeying from home, asks one of his companions to take care of his possessions, permitting him first to see his beautiful gems. Upon opening the chest, he sees them, and, beside them rotted earth. At this, he says to himself: "This wealthy one is a fool! How can he leave rotted earth together with such beautiful jewels!" The analogue is self-explanatory. Is it not obvious that all the dead things of the world, in the course of years, all turn to dust, both he himself and all the things he yearned for in his lifetime, as it is written (*Koheleth* 3:20): "All came from dust and all returns to dust." And he will be astonished at himself forever. How could he have combined in his chest [i.e., in his heart] two loves together? Love of the L-rd and His Torah, the true gems, more desirable than gold and fine gold, and the love of dust — together! Did he not know in his lifetime that in the end all would return to dust? Therefore, one must take great care to drive out of his mind, thoughts of lust for the desires of the world. This is the intent of "And make our hearts one ... and let us not be ashamed, forever."

And this is the intent, in the recital of *Shema*, of (*Devarim* 6:5): "And you shall love the L-rd your G-d with *all* your heart, etc."

Chapter XXVI

In this chapter it will be explained that a man is obliged to exert himself in Torah and the fear [of G-d] together

It is written in *Mishlei* (9:18): "The beginning of wisdom is the fear of the L-rd." This indicates that the beginning of wisdom for the man who seeks to be wise is to acquire fear of the L-rd. Yet, another verse in *Mishlei* states (4:7): "The beginning of wisdom is to acquire wisdom." This would seem to indicate that the beginning of all for him who desires to acquire wisdom is to reflect upon wisdom [that is, the wisdom of the Torah]! But, in truth, there is no contradiction. Solomon, may peace be upon him, desired to teach us that both are necessary, that one without the other is not worth anything [(as per the *Tanna* in *Avoth* (3:17): "If there is no fear, there is no wisdom; if there is no wisdom, there is no fear")]. That is, if one would seek to place all his toil and reflection upon acquiring fear of the L-rd and think to acquire wisdom afterwards, King Solomon, may peace be upon him, advises us that it is not right to do so. For to acquire fear as befits a Jew, he must seek it as silver, as Scripture states (*Mishlei* 2:9): "If you seek it as silver, …then you will understand fear of the L-rd." And the seeking of silver is not for one day or one week or one month; but silver is always on his mind. So, the man who wants to acquire fear of the L-rd. He must always reflect upon His greatness and upon the goodness which He confers upon him each day and increase fear of the L-rd in his soul. And if he waits to reflect upon the wisdom of Torah until he becomes a fearer of the L-rd in truth, this will take a long time, so that all of that time that his heart is void of wisdom, his fear is worth nothing. For if there is no wisdom there is no fear, and (*Avoth* 2:5): "A boor does not fear sin."

Let us illustrate a little: Even if one were eager to fulfill the will of the Creator with the mitzvah of *tefillin*, so long as he did not know the locus of the *tefillin*, whether on his head, specifically, or whether his forehead also sufficed. And so, the hand phylactery, whether on the biceps, specifically, or even below that. And so, if they must be perfectly square or even a little rounded. And what must be his intent in putting them on, and the like. Let us say that he did not know the *halachoth* of *tefillin* — he would be many years without [the mitzvah of] *tefillin*. And so with many mitzvoth. Therefore, as soon as he realizes that his purpose in this world is to attain fear of the L-rd, he must see to it immediately to meditate in Torah, so that it show him the way in which to walk and thereby come to know the Holy One Blessed be He.

And so, conversely: If he desires to steep his mind in wisdom; that is, the wisdom of the Torah alone, and to dispense with the fear of the L-rd, his wisdom is worthless. And this is the intent, in *Avoth*, of "If there is no fear, there is no wisdom." That is, if he does not fear the L-rd, and, as a result, all of His mitzvoth are not fixed in his mind to fulfill them — And so with his faculties, that of speaking and that of hearing — if they are free to speak and to hear whatever he wishes — whether *lashon hara* or *rechiluth* or verbal wronging or levity or the like, then, "everything goes" with him.

[And this is the intent of *Mishlei* 4:7: "The beginning of wisdom is to acquire wisdom," and, the end of the verse: "and with all of your acquisitions, acquire understanding." This is self-explanatory: "Wisdom" connotes what is apparent, first principles, what one learns from others; and "understanding," what one reflects upon thereafter by himself, to understand one thing from another. Therefore, he says that first one must acquire wisdom, and then he must strengthen himself to understand one thing from another. As they said (*Shabbath* 31a): "At the time of judgment they ask a man: 'Did you discourse in wisdom? Did you understand one thing from another?'" As to "and with all your acquisitions, acquire understanding," this is understood according to *Midrash Shir Hashirim* 8 in the episode of R. Chiyya b. Abba and R. Yochanan, who were walking on the way and came upon a field, at which R. Yochanan said: "This was mine, but I sold it to toil in Torah," and thus, until the last field. At this, R. Chiyya began to cry, and said to him: "What will you leave over for your old age?" R. Yochanan answered: "Why does this disturb you? I sold something that was created in six days, as it is written (*Shemoth* 20:11): 'For six days the L-rd made, etc.', and I bought something which was learned in forty days, as it is written (*Ibid.* 39:28): 'And he was there with the L-rd for forty days.'" And this is what Scripture intimates to us in "and with all of your acquisitions acquire understanding." It is right that one give all he possesses to acquire understanding. That is, that he grow wise in all matters of Torah in order to understand one thing from another.]

And our sages of blessed memory have said, that in time to come all of a man's acts will be "lit up" before his face. And so, with his speech. Nothing that he said in the world will be lost; not even one thing will go unrecorded. Even the idle talk that he spoke in this world will be repeated to him at the time of judgment. And it is known what the holy *Zohar* says: "...And from this evil spirit there arise other arousers of *din*, which are assigned to seize upon evil speech or filthy speech which issues from a man's mouth and then is followed by holy words. Woe to them [the speakers]. Woe to their lives! Woe to them in this world! Woe to them in the world to come! For those spirits of uncleanliness take that word of uncleanliness, and when he thereafter speaks holy words, those spirits of uncleanliness come forward and take that unclean speech to that holy word, so that it does not accrue to his [(the speaker's)] merit, and the power of holiness is thereby attenuated." [see Chapter II on *Vayikra* 11:43]

Now if this man had learned every day Scripture and *Mishnah* or *Gemara*, and he knew that at the time of judgment they would present before his eyes all the *Mishnah* and *Gemara* that he had learned, how great would be his yearning for this [presentation] at all times — Would that this [moment] arrived and they cited this to his credit! However, when they thereafter bring all those books [that he studied] and he sees that on every page the spirit of uncleanliness resides because of the forbidden speech that he spoke in the beginning or in the middle [of his learning], and that they [(the holy words)] are worth nothing, how great will be his grief then when he reflects upon himself, how he himself, with careless abandon, made his Torah go lost!

To what may this be compared? To one who bought from his friend a complete *Shas*, bound in fine leather, without looking inside, relying upon its fine binding. He pays for it and the seller goes on his way. When he goes to his house [and opens it], he sees that the entire *Shas* is besmirched with fats and grease that had spilled out upon it and that not even one tractate is intact. How embittered he is at having been deceived by that seller, who had praised it before him — and he had not opened it himself to see what he had bought!

So, in our case. If one's mouth is perpetually open, and he takes no care [of what he says], then even if he has learned all six orders of the *Mishnah* and the entire *Shas* several times, when he comes on high [for judgment], he will find not even one *Gemara* that will defend him. For each one will be overlaid with the spirit of uncleanliness and will be disgusting to look at. Therefore, the wise man, whose eyes are in his head, before he begins to grow wise in Torah and to fulfill "The beginning of wisdom is to acquire wisdom" must fulfill "The beginning of wisdom is the fear of the L-rd." And then he will be happy and it will be good for him in this world and in the next. For his Torah will be much beloved by the Blessed L-rd, their being no blemish in it. A man like this must bestir himself and heap up as much wisdom as he can. And if he wastes one moment of Torah, this is a great loss. For "a servant who does needlework cannot be compared to one who strings pearls."

Chapter XXVII

In this chapter it will be explained why every man must exert himself to fulfill all *of the mitzvoth, with no exceptions to the rule*

Until now we have spoken about the beginning of the verse (*Psalms* 34:13-15): "Who is the man who wants life, etc., Guard your tongue from evil, etc." And now, with the help of the L-rd, we shall explain the end of the verse: "Depart from evil and do good," as it applies to the beginning of the verse. It is well known what our sages of blessed memory have said about this, viz.: "Who is the man who wants life" — in the world to come, "who loves days to see good" — in this world. "Guard your tongue, etc. Depart from evil and do good." We shall precede [the explanation of this verse] with what is said in the name of the GRA on the verse (*Isaiah* 3:10-11): "Say of the *tzaddik* that [he is] good, for the fruits of their deeds shall they eat. Woe to the *rasha* [the wicked one], for he is evil. For the recompense of his hands shall be rendered him," viz.: If one fulfills the mitzvoth between a man and his Maker, the essence of his reward is in the world to come; and so, his punishment, when he transgresses them. And for the mitzvoth between a man and his neighbor, where he benefits his fellow men, he receives his reward in this world, too. Similarly, if he transgresses them, aside from the punishment awaiting him in the world to come, he is punished in this world too, for by his acts he also causes suffering to men. The terms "*tzaddik*" and *rasha*" apply to the relationship between a man and his Maker, and the terms "good" and "evil," to that between a man and his neighbor.

And the verse is now resolved, viz.: "Say of the *tzaddik* that [he is] *good*," i.e., that by his acts he benefits also his fellow men — "for the fruits of *their* deeds [(those of the *tzaddikim*)] shall *they* [(their fellow men)] eat." "Woe to the *rasha*, for he is *evil*," i.e., even in the area of "between man and his neighbor" — "for the recompense of *his* [the *rasha*'s] hands shall be rendered *him* [his fellow man]." And now, the aforementioned verse is also resolved, viz.: "Who is the man who wants life" — in the world to come; "who loves days to see *good*" — even in this world. "Depart from [doing] *evil* and do *good*," i.e., also the mitzvoth between a man and his neighbor, to do good to his fellow man, and through this to see good, even in this world.

Now, "Depart from *evil*" includes all aspects of evil: theft, violence, wronging, interest, cheating, "whitening" one's face, and the like. And "do good," includes all aspects of good: charity, lovingkindness, supporting the indigent, burial of the dead, visiting the sick, welcoming guests, returning lost objects, returning a pledge, paying a hired worker on time, and many other such mitzvoth between a man and his neighbor. A man must set his heart on all of them and spur himself to fulfill them. As we have seen with the mitzvah of shofar, that all run to fulfill it, so should it be with all mitzvoth, to pursue them and to rejoice in their fulfillment. As we say every day: "Therefore, O L-rd our G-d, in our lying down and in our rising, let us speak in Your statutes and rejoice in the words of Your Torah and in Your mitzvoth forever." [And, in our many sins, we say to the Holy One Blessed be He that we shall do this, but we transgress it. And in us there is fulfilled what our sags of blessed memory have said (*Berachoth* 6b) on the verse (*Psalms* 12:9): "...when the vile are exalted over the sons of men" — "these [i.e., mitzvoth] are the things that stand at the height of the world, and the sons of men cheapen them."]

In sum: One must take care to fulfill the words of the Torah, both those things between man and his Maker and those things between man and his neighbor. For they are all the word of the L-rd, as it is written (*Devarim* 32:46-47): "...which you are to command your children to keep and to do — all the words of this Torah. For it is not an empty thing for you. For it is your life." For just as with the body there is life in every limb, and all [of the limbs] are required by it, so, in every mitzvah there is life for a man's soul and all [the mitzvoth] are required by it. This is the intent of *Koheleth* 12:13: "The end of the matter — all has been heard. Fear G-d and keep His mitzvoth. For this is the whole man." That is, through the fear of G-d, not to transgress any negative commandment and to fulfill all of His positive commandments — this is the whole man. That is, *then* the man is called "complete," which is not so if some mitzvah is minor in his eyes, G-d forbid, in which instance he is lacking in his soul.

And how fitting is the homily of our sages of blessed memory on the verse (*Shemoth* 32:16): "And the tablets [*luchoth*] are the work of G-d.": "'*Luchoth*' is written [without the *vav*] to show that they [the tablets] were both the same; that is, they looked like one tablet. For it is known that on one tablet, on the right, there were written those things between man and his Maker, and on the second tablet, that begins (*Ibid.* 20:13): "You shall not kill," "You shall not commit adultery," until the end of that tablet, there were written those things between man and his neighbor. That is, one should not think about any one of them that it is only superficial, to "beautify" a man. For this reason they are written in great proximity, to show that one is not superior to the other. And they also looked like one tablet, to intimate that just as one is considered a "man among men" only when he is whole in his limbs; but if he is missing any part of his body, he is lowered in the eyes of men and also in his own eyes, so is it with the soul. When is he the "complete man"? When all the words of the L-rd are beloved of him, which is not the case, G-d forbid, if he belittles any of the words of the L-rd, whether in the area of man and his Maker or in that of man and his neighbor. Then he is not a "man."

It is public knowledge to all of Israel, both young and old alike, that the Torah is read, with the sanctity of a *sefer* Torah, only when it is entirely written without even one letter missing. Only then is it called (*Psalms* 19:8): "The Torah of the L-rd is complete." But if a letter is lacking, it does not possess the sanctity of a *sefer* Torah, but only the sanctity of *parshiyoth*. So is it with the Jew. When is he included in the congregation of Israel, having a share in the world to come? Only when he believes that the entire Torah was given by the L-rd from heaven. But one who denies it — even one letter of it — is not in the congregation of Israel (see *Sanhedrin* 99a; *Rambam, Hilchoth Teshuvah* 3:5; *Yoreh Deah* 158).

Now, in truth, all of Israel are believers, children of believers, that all of the Torah was given from heaven by the word of the L-rd to Moses, His servant. If so, if one believes that every mitzvah was given by the Blessed Creator, how can he allow himself to treat lightly anything in the Torah? In truth, this does not arise, G-d forbid, from heresy, but from his having transgressed it several times and in his having come to feel it as permitted. As our sages of blessed memory have said; "Once a person commits a transgression and repeats it, it feels permitted to him." But this itself is an egregious sin, allowing oneself to transgress anything of the words of the L-rd (as expanded upon by Rabbeinu Yonah in *Sha'arei Teshuvah*). Therefore, one must be extremely heedful in this and it will be *good* for him.

Chapter XXVIII

Great awakening to the severity of the sin of theft

In our many sins, there are many men who are very heedful of observing the Torah according to the *din*, but who make light of the *issur* of theft, cheating people with all kinds of stratagems, being habituated to this and not knowing that it strikes at their very being and that they thereby leave the category of "your neighbor" and "your fellow," in addition to invalidating themselves from giving testimony. A proof: Our sages of blessed memory have said that grazers of small cattle, [who are used to grazing in the field of others] "are not pulled out and are not put down." That is, if they have fallen into a pit, they are not to be taken out, even though for other Jews there is a negative commandment against this, viz. (*Vayikra* 19:16): "Do not stand [idly] by the blood of your neighbor," one being obliged to pull him out and even to hire others to do so. But, in this instance, because of his wickedness, he is not to be taken out.

We shall expand somewhat on the severity of theft, which, when one reflects upon it, will make him tremble. The *Midrash* writes: "Lest you say that I have given you the Torah for your evil — I have given it to you only for your good." Now this obviously presents a question: How could one [even] suspect that the Holy One Blessed be He, the source of good and lovingkindness could give us the Torah for our evil? But the explanation is as follows. There are in the Torah several sections on punishing sinners — with death, stripes, or monetary payment — which might lead one to believe that the Holy One Blessed be He is angry with the sinner, wherefore He prescribed these punishments for his evil. But, in truth, this is not so. The Holy One Blessed be He brings punishments upon him to cleanse him. For our sages have said (*Makkoth* 23a) about one who is liable to stripes because he has transgressed a negative commandment of the Torah: (*Devarim* 25:3): "And your brother shall be demeaned before your eyes" — "Once he has been demeaned [by receiving stripes], he is like your brother." And, similarly, even with one liable to the death penalty, we tell him: "Confess, for all who confess have a share in the world to come." And this serves as a paradigm for all such things in the Torah, as in the instance of a thief (*Shemoth* 22:2): "If he lacks [the money to return], he should be sold for his theft," in order to return the money to the owner, so as to cleanse himself of the sin of theft, even though through this he descends from his sanctity. For *ab initio*, a Jew is forbidden by negative commandment to wed a handmaid, it being written (*Devarim* 23:18): "And there shall be no harlot from the sons of Israel"; but after he is sold by *beth-din* he descends from his sanctity and weds a handmaid, and his children are slaves forever. In any event, the Torah descends to "the end of the matter," that this is preferable for him rather than having the sin of theft remain upon him and returning and coming to Gehinnom as a *gilgul* [(a reincarnation)].

Chapter XXIX

In this chapter there will be explained the exertion and the zeal required for the attainment of Torah and mitzvoth

(*Avoth* 1:13): "He [Hillel] used to say: 'If I am not for myself, who is for me? And if I am [only] for myself, what am I? And if not now, when?'" If the *tanna*, Hillel, was wont to say this, there are certainly found in it principles and foundations to spur a man to his acts and ways in this world to bring him to his eternal happiness. And there are certainly included in his words lofty thoughts and varied explanations. We have explained this at length elsewhere. But, in its plain sense, I have come to explain now that the *tanna* comes to remind us of the great zeal required by a man for Torah and good deeds day by day.

For, in the way of the world, if we see a man not working day after day, and ask him: "What is this? How can you feed your wife and your family if you do nothing?" he can answer in one of three ways:

1) He has a factory with many workers and supervisors from which he receives enough for his livelihood, so that he finds the time to sit idle.

2) His line of work is very lucrative — diamond polishing, pearl stringing, and the like, so that with a few hours of work a day he brings home enough for his livelihood, and, in the rest of his time, he sits idle.

3) His work demands only a few weeks a year, the time of the market, where he journeys every year, and where he earns enough to last him for the whole year. And the rest of the time he sits idle.

And the *tanna* comes to remind us here that for the work of Heaven, which is the work for his soul in eternity, not one of the above answers can justify one who is lax in his work, the work of holiness.

1) "If I am not for myself, who is for me?" He has no workers and helpers to supply him with his soul's livelihood. But only he himself can provide for its happiness and its life. "If I am not for *me*," for what pertains only to *me*, the essence of man, his enduring soul — If I myself do not exert myself for it to attain its requirements — Torah and good deeds — who will bring me life and happiness for it? For this cannot be acquired by any act of acquisition except the toil of the man himself for his soul [As to his attaining a portion of his Torah by his support (of others who learn), does he not also attain that by his own acts, supporting them by his wealth?]

2) As to the second answer of the idler that he need not work a whole day for a livelihood, but that a few hours suffices, the *tanna* says that for the needs of his *soul*, this is not sufficient, for "the time is short and the work is long." For even if all of his work and toil all the days of his life were devoted to the needs of his soul — the acquisition of the Torah of the L-rd and the fulfillment of His mitzvoth — of what account is his toil in his scant days for the needs of the life of his immortal soul in eternity? And this is the intent of "And if I am for myself" — If I devote myself entirely to my [immortal] *self*, that is, to my *soul*, the [essential] selfhood of a man, "what am I?" Of what account is my work in [such] scant days for [such] a long road? As Mar Ukva said when he saw the account of his charities on high: "A long road and a light load." For, given the length of the road, his "sustenance" was of no account; and, furthermore, he had wasted "half of his money."

How much more so, when a man reckons the account of his lifetime, will he see that only a minute portion of his toil was for himself, and most of it for vanity. If so, how will he justify to his soul not giving heed, at least to the hours that he is not working, to attain in them Torah and mitzvoth, the acquisitions of his *self*?

The man who works for his livelihood, for his wife and for his small children — how much more so for their Torah tuition — the man who works for this does not work in vain. And not only his fixed Torah times, but all of his toil is for doing the will of the Holy One Blessed be He, and his toil will show fruits. But if a man works a whole day for a *lavish* livelihood, for spacious homes and beautiful clothing, beyond the requirements of his station, then certainly his toil is not his. For what will he show for it?

How much more so if he squanders the wages of his toil for educating his children in the "new ways," teaching them foreign studies and removing them from the Torah of the L-rd. Is his toil not "not for him"? To the contrary, he must yet render judgment and accounting for having removed his children from the Torah of the L-rd. And, similarly, if he toils until old age in order to leave a blessing [i.e., an inheritance] for his sons after him, this, too, is not for him. As Resh Lakish, who left over for his sons a *kav* of saffron, said about himself (*Psalms* 99:11): "And they leave their wealth to others." (*Gittin* 47a).

And for all of these [reasons] Hillel came to spur men on to prize their time that it not go to waste. And one must not fool himself, saying: "My modicum of Torah and [Divine] service is sufficient for myself." It is not so. For even if he devoted all of his toil to himself alone, of what account is he? And, especially, when most of his toil is not for him, "what is he?"

"And if not now, when?" This is directed at the third answer given by those in the world who do not labor, that their primary source of livelihood is "market day," the great fair, which allows them to live lavishly the whole year. This claim itself dictates even greater zeal. For if we see this man idle on "market day" itself, spending his time on nothingness, the great question becomes: "If you didn't work even on 'market day,' won't you starve a whole year?"

Yes, my brother, is this world not "market day," when one must buy the wares to feed his soul all the days of his long life in the world that is entirely long? And if now, on "market day," he luxuriates in laziness and shirks his labor, will his soul not starve in the world of eternal life? This is the intent of "If not now, when?" And thus, in *Koheleth* (9:10): "And all that your hand finds to do, do with your power." That is, do not work lazily, but to the limits of your power. For only *now* is the time of doing, for (*Ibid.*): "there is no doing or reckoning or knowledge or wisdom in Sheol, whither you are going." For the days of labor will already have ended, and only from what is prepared for him by his toils in the days of his life in this world will his soul live there. As written in the Torah (*Devarim* 7:11): "…today to do them [the mitzvoth]," and not tomorrow to do them, but only to receive their reward. (*Eruvin* 22a)

And, in truth, "And if not now" implies "every hour and every day." One must think "If not *now*" — that the Holy One Blessed be He determines for a man every day what he is to attain of the Torah of the L-rd and His service. As to the *yetzer*'s enticing him that tomorrow he can make up for today, this is an error. For tomorrow is an obligation in itself, and he will not be able to make up the time that he lacks now. And only from day to evening [of the same day] do we find in Chazal: "One may borrow [of his time] in the daytime and make it up [in Torah study] at night." And this is the intent of (*Devarim* 4:9): "And lest they depart from your heart *all* the days of your life." And thus, (*Koheleth* 9:9): "And see life… *all* the days of your vanity" — that is, that not one day go lost. And thus, (*Rambam, Hilchoth Talmud Torah* 1:10): The verse "And lest they depart from your heart all the days of your life" implies that one may not be idle in the Torah of the L-rd for even one day — until his last day. And this is intimated in the verse (*Mishlei* 3:28): "Do not say to your friend: 'Go and return, and tomorrow I will give you,' if you have it with you [today]." "your friend" is the *good yetzer*, a man's *true* friend, who counsels him as to what will be good for him forever.

[In sum, one must know that he has come to this world only for a specified time, for Torah and mitzvoth, and that he is destined to return to the higher world to receive his reward. As it is written (*Devarim* 7:11): "which I command you today to do them," concerning which our sages of blessed memory have said: "Today to do them, and tomorrow to receive their reward." But, the *yetzer hara* entices a man in his youth, that he yet has many years to live, and, in truth, this is an error, as we have written above. For each day is given him by the Blessed Creator with exact accounting, as it is written (*Job* 7:1): "Does a man not have an allotted time upon the earth?" And he cannot exempt himself from this day in anticipation of the next day. A man in this world is like one who has come to sojourn in a distant land for a specific time, as it is written (*Psalms* 119:19): "I am a sojourner in the land; do not hide Your mitzvoth from me." He must pity each day, that it not go to waste.

I have adduced a telling analogy for this: A man, because of his poverty, leaves his land to travel in a distant land (Africa and the like) in order to provide for his family. He is extremely lazy and he always goes about idle. Once, one of his acquaintances from his city meets him and asks him: "Why are you going about and doing nothing, and not seeking a job. Was not that your purpose in coming here?" "Why do you wonder about this? I still have time. For from the time I came here only twenty years have passed?" His friend replies: "Are you out of your mind? Even if you were born here and you constantly went around idle, this is not the right way for a man to act, as everyone knows. How much more so that you are only sojourning here and have left the land of your birth only to earn a little and return to your land. You should have looked around every day to find anything you could to earn something by, and you should have allowed no day to be wasted. And you answer that you are only here twenty years? This answer befits a fool, not a man!"

The analogue is self-explanatory. A man's soul, when it descends to the earth is an absolute sojourner [not a "settler" as he is in heaven, (as it is written (*Psalms* 39:13): "I am a sojourner with You, a settler, like all of my forefathers")], who has come to sojourn here to attain Torah and mitzvoth. For in heaven he can earn nothing, and he has been given an allotted time for this, to return afterwards to its source above and to be bound up there in the bond of life with the L-rd his G-d. And he must reflect upon every day and every hour from the day he becomes a man to ascertain that his sojourn in this world not be in vain. This is the intent of (*Psalms* 119:19): "I am a sojourner in the land; do not hide Your mitzvoth from me." And the man who answers "I am only twenty, or thirty and I have time" is like the idle sage mentioned above.]

Chapter XXX

In this chapter there will be explained the essence of the faculty of speech, hearing, and seeing, and the great obligation of guarding them

I have further undertaken to awaken men to guard their faculties while yet in this world, to realize that the faculties of speech, hearing, and sight are implanted in the soul. The *soul* hears; the *soul* sees; the *soul* speaks. The material [component], which is flesh and blood, does not see or hear or speak at all. It is just that the Holy One Blessed be He has implanted [the faculties in such a way] that sight, hearing, and speech are mediated by the surrounding flesh. Sight [which proceeds from the soul in the brain, as Chazal say: "Just as the Holy One Blessed be He sees but is not seen, so, the soul sees but is not seen"] (is mediated by) the eyes; hearing, by the ears; speech, by the tongue. But all of these are faculties of the *soul*.

It emerges, then, that even when a man's matter disintegrates and becomes dust, and his soul returns to G-d, as it is written (*Koheleth* 12:7): "And the dust will return to the earth, as it was, and the spirit will return to G-d, who gave it," it retains all of these faculties — sight, hearing, and speech — for these will not have been annulled by the separation of matter from it [the soul]. For matter is only the garment of the soul, as it is written (*Iyyov* 10:11): "With skin and flesh did You clothe me." Now if one removes his garment, will his soul be annulled thereby?

Now this is known to all, that when one lacks one of these three faculties, he is not considered a "man among men." That is, if he is blind, he is perceived as dead. And if he is deaf, not hearing at all; and, more so, if he is an absolute mute, not hearing and not speaking, he is not reckoned at all among [other] men. And, especially if he must sit in some kind of gathering and he is blind or deaf, how much suffering is his lot!

And one should also know that all of these faculties — sight, hearing, and speech — which the Holy One Blessed be He implanted in a man's soul, as essential as they are to a man in this world, as is known to all, they are even more essential to his *soul* [in the next world]. That is, to *see* the glory of the L-rd, and with his ears to hear the words of G-d in Gan Eden. As we find, in *Midrash Tavo*, that the Holy One Blessed be He is destined to learn Torah with Israel in time to come, to speak in words of Torah in Gan Eden.

Now it is known that of all the hope of a man, ennobled by the name "Israel," the primary hope is to merit life in the world to come, the greatest delight of all the delights of the world. As stated in *Avoth* 4:17: "Better one moment of pleasure in the world to come than all the life of this world." And it is also known what has been written in many *sefarim*, including the GRA, on (*Mishlei* 13:13): "He who cheapens a thing will be injured by it," viz.: When a man cheapens a mitzvah, he injures *himself*. For every thing in his organs receives its vital force from a mitzvah. For the 248 positive commandments correspond to the 248 organs of a man, as we find in the *Midrash*, so that there is thereafter found [(by the cheapening of a mitzvah)] an injury in the soul in [the area of] the corresponding limb.

Accordingly, if one is not heedful in his lifetime of his faculty of sight, and permits himself to gaze at what the Torah forbade, he should know with certainty that in time to come he will be like a blind man, unable to gaze upon the light of the L-rd, just as one who is sick in his eyes cannot see by the light of his soul. And the degree of the injury to his eyes is proportional to the degree of his [self-abandonment].

And how much bitterness will one suffer because of this in the end, that for one minute of pleasure that the *yetzer* has fed him with its seductions, it has corrupted his eyes and darkened them, by drawing down upon them each time the spirit of uncleanliness of the spirit of harlotry.

And the eye is the first entrance of the evil inclination, for through it there enters the heart the power of desire and lust against which we were exhorted at Mount Sinai, and as our sages of blessed memory said: "The eye sees, the heart desires and the instruments of action consummate." And, concerning this it was intimated (*Eichah* 3:51): "My eye scalds my soul more than all the daughters of my city." "my city" alludes to the powers of the body (which is also called *guf* [body]), as in *Nedarim* 32b: "'a small city' — this is the *guf*." The verse intimates that the eye has corrupted his soul more than all the other powers of the body, all of them coming to consummate only what his eyes have begun.

And now we shall speak about the faculty of hearing. Hearing, in itself, is good, as it is written (*Isaiah* 55:3): "Hear, and let your souls live." And (*Mishlei* 15:31): "The ear that hears the reproof of life, in the midst of the wise will it reside." And hearing works on a man to cause him to satisfy [an obligation] by hearing as if he had performed it himself. A proof may be adduced from the reading of the *Megillah*, the blowing of the shofar, and other such things, such as [the recitation of] Kiddush and the grace over meals, where one makes the blessing and all the listeners satisfy the obligation. Similarly, all of the receiving of the Torah was through hearing. All this, for good things. The reverse is true for bad things, G-d forbid. Hearing [bad things] also greatly affects a man's soul. It is well known what our sages of blessed memory have said (*Kethuvoth* 5b): "The Rabbis taught: 'Let a man not allow idle speech to be heard by his ears, for they are the first of the organs to be "burnt."'" How much more so [does this apply] to one who intends to cause *rechiluth* to be heard by his ears, this being proscribed by a negative commandment in the Torah, viz. (*Shemoth* 23:1): "You shall not bear a false report," or to one who hears, with intent, *lashon hara* and other forbidden things, or frivolous speech or *leitzanuth* (levity), in which instance his sin is too great to bear. And our sages of blessed memory have said about the scoffer (*Avodah Zarah* 18b) that suffering comes upon him, as it is written (*Isaiah* 28:22): "Do not scoff, lest your bonds be strengthened." And they have also said (*Shabbath* 33a): "Even he who *listens* [to obscenity] and remains silent [is condemned], it being written (*Mishlei* 22:14): 'The abhorred of the L-rd will abide there' [next to the speaker of obscenity.]"

In sum, just as in hearing good things one fulfills many tens of mitzvoth each day, (e.g., answering Amen, *yeheh shmei rabbah*, *Barchu*, *Kedushah*, and answering all of the amens [in the *Amidah*]), so, hearing bad things affects a man's soul very adversely.

Returning to our subject, if a man in his lifetime constantly degrades his faculty of hearing, employing it for forbidden things, let him know that in time to come he will not have the power in his ears to hear the words of the living G-d.

And now we shall speak of the faculty of speech that the Holy One Blessed be He implanted in a man's soul, which distinguishes him from all the other animals. And He gave him the *power* of speech whereby a man can merit speaking before the Holy One Blessed be He and meditating in his Torah, which is the end of the creation. As Scripture states (*Jeremiah* 33:25): "If not for My covenant [of Torah] day and night, the statutes of heaven and earth, I would not have made."

[It is clear, then, from Scripture, that day and night were created for the sake of the Torah. And I have hereby explained (*Menachoth* 29b): "Dammah, the son of R. Yishmael's sister, asked R. Yishmael: 'May one such as I, who have studied the entire Torah, study Greek wisdom?' — whereupon he pronounced over him (*Joshua* 1:8): 'This book of the Torah shall not depart from your mouth, and you shall study it day and night.' Go and find an hour which is neither of the day nor of the night and study Greek wisdom in it!" I have explained this by analogy. A certain tailor had a great deal of work and had to hire a worker for a month to come to his house to finish the work. This he did, and he paid him. After this the worker brought some of his own work to do there — whereupon the tailor said to him: "Until now, when you did *my* work, I had to give you my table and all of my tools to work at it. But now, when you are doing your own work, why should I give you my table and all of my tools?" The analogue: The Holy One Blessed be He created time, day and night, to do *His* work, and you now want to learn Greek wisdom on *His* time! Go out and find an hour which is neither day nor night and learn it then!]

And through every word of Torah, holiness is added to a man's soul. For with every word he fulfills the mitzvah of *talmud* Torah, as written in the *sefarim*. And through each mitzvah a man's soul is sanctified, as it is written (*Bamidbar* 15:40): "So that you remember and do all of My mitzvoth; and you shall be holy to your

G-d." And there is no mitzvah performed by the organs, where a man has mitzvoth added to him as profusely as that of speech [of Torah] granted him by the L-rd. For whatever mitzvah one does with his organs, he must allocate to it [at least] several minutes, and in this time, if he were learning Torah, he could utter hundreds of words of Torah. Therefore, a man is not permitted to leave off Torah study if the mitzvah can be performed by others. And this is what is intimated by *Mishlei* 14:4: "Wealth adds many friends," which the GRA explained: Through the wealth of Torah many friends are added to a man. For with every word of Torah with which one fulfills the mitzvah of Torah study, there is created for him one defender, and these [defenders] are the true friends of a man.

In sum, speech is a man's happiness and his success if well used. But, conversely, if he uses it incorrectly, there is no organ among all the others that he can be harmed by [as much as by] the tongue. For, certainly, from every forbidden word there is created a prosecutor against him, and in one hour he can speak several hundred forbidden words of falsehood, levity, *rechiluth*, and *lashon hara*.

And, in general, in the instance of other transgressions, regret and repentance obtain, as opposed to sins of speech, where they do not obtain. And even though he says in Confession: "We have spoken *lashon hara*," it does not occur to him that what he spoke is *lashon hara*, and that he must take it upon himself not to repeat it in the future. He does not think at all about this. Where, then, is his repentance?

And where there is no repentance from below, there is no forgiveness from above. And sin is added to sin almost without number. [And even on Yom Kippur, when he says; ("Forgive us) for the sin that we sinned before You with *lashon hara*," it does not occur to him to think: "What will be the end, with the multitude of 'prosecutors' that arise against me through my faculty of speech, which I was not careful with until now and because I did not seek counsel to strengthen myself against recurrences of these things?" And, in truth, not one word has been lost. As our sages of blessed memory say on *Amos* 4:13: "He relates to a man what his converse is" — "Even the light talk between a man and his wife is related to him at the time of *din*."] And this is (the intent of) what our sages of blessed memory have said: "All who speak *lashon hara* magnify sin until the heavens."

And, worst of all, if one habituates his mouth always to speak forbidden things, in time to come the faculty of speech is taken from his soul. And, in truth, how is he better than a beast in having been given the faculty of speech if with it he angers the Holy One Blessed be He? All of this is intimated in the words of our sages of blessed memory, viz.: "The Holy One Blessed be He is destined to cut out the tongue of the speakers of *lashon hara*, as it is written (*Psalms* 12:4): 'The L-rd will cut out all smooth lips, the tongue that speaks great things.'" That is, there will be taken from his tongue its faculty of speech. And how much shame and mortification will he suffer in Gan Eden, even if he merits a portion there through his mitzvoth — still, he will be reckoned a mute there, without the faculty of speech.

What emerges from all of our words is that one must guard his soul in his lifetime in all of these three faculties — sight, hearing, and speech, that they not be defective, and he must take it to heart that they are essential to him for eternity.

And if it happens, for any reason, that they are spoiled, he must see to it to repent before the L-rd with true repentance, with strong resolution not to repeat his offense in the future. And he must make fences for this, not to come to this folly again and to amend each one accordingly. As our sages of blessed memory have said (*Shemoth Rabbah* 23:3): "*Tzaddikim*, in *that* through which they sin, they are conciliated," and then, [life is] happy and good for him — in this world and the next.

Conclusion

Chapter I

Great impetus to congregational prayer

In our many sins, people in our times have begun to breach the holy practice which was observed until now by *all* of the people of Israel. Even though some may not have merited to learn Torah, still, the prayer ritual, in its holiest form, was observed by the entire populace. That is, all spurred themselves to rise early in the morning, to go to the synagogue, to pray with a *minyan* (ten Jews), and to hear the Torah reading — all according to the *din*. And, as a matter of course, there were some who got together after praying to study *Mishnayoth*. But, in our many sins, today, the *yetzer* has greatly intensified, so that aside from strengthening itself to annul Torah learning from the children of Israel, young and old alike [(and even from schoolchildren, the breath of whose mouth is very precious, as is well known)], it strengthens itself further, little by little, to annul also the mitzvah of prayer and *tefillin*, from the children of Israel. First of all it persuades one, because of his preoccupations, not to go steadily to the house of prayer for *mincha* and *ma'ariv* [(the afternoon and evening prayers)], but only at intervals. And, in the course of time, the thing [(i.e., not going)] becomes permissible to him, so that even when he is entirely free in his house, he is too indolent to go to the house of prayer. And through this he abandons his Torah session, whether it be in *Chayei Adam* or *Ein Yaakov*. And after this the *yetzer* begins to entice him to absent himself occasionally from *shacharith* [(the morning prayer)], and not to attend regularly, but only on Mondays and Thursdays to hear the Torah reading. And, in the course of time, the thing becoming permitted, the Torah reading, too, is not significant in his eyes and he comes only on Shabbath, for prayer. Soon, he does not come on Shabbath either, but only on Shabbath Rosh Chodesh, when the cantor sings. Then the *yetzer* further intensifies and entices him to go in the way of his wicked friends and sometimes omit the mitzvah of *tefillin*, the glory of our heads. In sum, the *yetzer* strengthens itself to take from the people of Israel all of its pride and glory.

I have, therefore, undertaken to set forth the importance of congregational prayer. But first, let us explain the great *obligation* thereof. The formulation of our sages of blessed memory — "four mils to prayer" is well known. Many of the Rishonim explain this as meaning that if one is walking on the road and he knows that four mils further on he will find a *minyan*, he must wait [to pray] until he comes there. As far as going back, if he knows that he will find a *minyan* within the distance of a mil, he must go back. From this we can understand that certainly, if he can find a *minyan* in the city, even if it is almost a mil away, he must go there. And our sages of blessed memory have already said (*Berachoth* 8a): "Whoever has a synagogue in his city and does not frequent it for prayer is called 'a bad neighbor.'"

Now we come to detail the great difference between praying alone in one's house and praying with a *minyan*:

1) First of all, one is rewarded for *going* to the synagogue *in itself*, as we find in *Avoth* 5:14: "There are four characteristics of those who go to the synagogue: If he goes and does not do [i.e., pray, (because of some accident)], he has the reward of going." And the reward is according to the number of steps. The more steps, the more reward (see *Sotah* 22a).

2) Very often, when one comes to the synagogue he also learns a chapter of *Mishnayoth* or a *halachah* or *Ein Yaakov* and the like. And our sages of blessed memory have already said (*Berachoth* 64b): "One who leaves the synagogue and goes to the house of study merits beholding the face of the Shechinah," which is not the case with him who prays alone in his house, who remains without Torah. This abuse is very commonplace in our days, in our many sins, with many mourners who want to bestow merit upon their fathers by making a permanent *minyan* in their house for the entire one-year mourning period. Immediately after praying each one goes to his house, so that all of those who pray there are left without Torah. This is not at all to the merit of their fathers. The major amendment for the soul of one's father is his son's strengthening himself to learn Torah every day and also to do lovingkindness — just as the major amendment for the atonement of one's sins when he is still alive is through Torah and lovingkindness, as it is written (*Mishlei* 16:6): "By lovingkindness and truth, sin will be atoned, as our sages of blessed memory have said: "'truth' — this is Torah, as it is written (*Ibid.* 23;33): 'Buy truth and do not sell it.'" So, the son who wishes to accord merit to his father, his major contribution is Torah and lovingkindness. (See *Ahavath Chesed*, Chapter XV, where we have elaborated on this.)

3) It is also known what the *sefarim* have written, that if one habituates himself to a certain bad trait and his friends emulate him and also do as he, he is punished because of them [see *Yoma* 86a, Rashi - "*kegon*"]. And it is known that G-d's reward for good is [proportionately] greater than His punishment for evil. It follows, therefore, *a fortiori*, that if one habituates himself to a mitzvah or to a good trait and his friends emulate him, he will be rewarded for them. As it affects our subject, it is known that if one habituates himself to go to the synagogue to pray with a *minyan* each day, many of his friends and his acquaintances emulate him, and he will receive reward for them, too.

4) The verse (*Mishlei* 2:4): "If you seek it [Torah] as silver… then you will understand the fear of G-d" is well known. And in monetary matters it is well known that if a business opportunity presents itself to a man, by which he can earn five gold pieces, and another opportunity, by which he can earn double, he will certainly choose the second. In our case, too, is it not known that there is no comparison between a few who occupy themselves with a mitzvah and many who

do so? As it is written (*Vayikra* 26:8): "And five of you will pursue a hundred, and a hundred of you, ten thousand" (see Rashi there). Therefore (as it concerns our subject) it is known that [in the synagogue] aside from the mitzvah of prayer, we fulfill other commandments of the Torah: a) the positive mitzvah of *tefillin*, b) the positive mitzvah of reciting the *Shema*, c) the positive mitzvah of remembering Egypt. If so, if one comes to the synagogue to pray with a *minyan*, and all fulfill all of these mitzvoth, each mitzvah rises [proportionately] in holiness, which is not the case with one who prays alone.

5) It is well known what we say every day (*Peah* 1:1): "These are the things whose fruits one eats in this world, with the principal remaining for the world to come, etc.... and coming betimes to the synagogue in the morning and in the evening."

6) This [(synagogue attendance)] leads to length of days, as we find (*Berachoth* 8): "When R. Yochanan was told that there were old men in Bavel, he wondered, saying: 'It is written (*Devarim* 11:21): "so that your days and the days of your children may be multiplied upon the land which the L-rd swore to your fathers" — but not outside of that land.' When it was told him, however, that they were morning and evening in the synagogue, he said: 'This is what stands in their favor'" (see there further.)

7) Every man, when he prays, hopes that it will be a time of [Heavenly] will, that his prayer be accepted. And it is well known what our sages of blessed memory have said (*Berachoth* 8a): "When is a time of [Heavenly] will? When the congregation is praying."

8) Our sages of blessed memory have said (*Ibid.*): "The Holy One Blessed be He does not reject the prayer of the many, it being written (*Job* 36:5): 'G-d is mighty, and will not reject [the many].'" This, as opposed to one praying alone, when each blessing is scrutinized for proper intent. As we find in the holy *Zohar* on the verse (*Psalms* 102:18): "He will turn to the prayer of the devastated one, and will not reject *their* prayer" [that of the many.] And it is well known that today there are many disturbances and it is almost impossible to find a man who prays one prayer with proper intent, unless he labors on it greatly. Now does not each man wish his prayer to be accepted above? If so, in any event, he must fall back upon this counsel, to pray with the congregation, of which it is written (*Job, Ibid.*) "G-d is mighty, and will not reject [the many]."

9) When one prays with the congregation, he has [the opportunity of saying] *Barchu*, *Kedushah*, and *Amen yehei shemei rabbah*, each of which, in itself, is awesome. For through "*Barchu*" we make a crown for the Holy One Blessed be He, as we find in *Midrash Konein*. And through *Kedushah* we fulfill (*Vayikra* 22:33): "And I shall be sanctified in the midst of the children of Israel." And through this,

holiness is conferred upon us, as the verse concludes: "I am the L-rd who sanctifies you."

And through "*Amen, yehei shemei rabbah*" one is forgiven for all of his sins, as our sages of blessed memory have said (*Shabbath* 119b): "If one says '*Amen, yehei shemei rabbah*' with all of his strength [i.e., with all of his intent], even if there is a trace of heresy in him, he is forgiven."

[And how much must a person strengthen himself to keep himself from omitting "*Kedushah* and *Amen, yehei shemei rabbah*!" For it is known what our sages of blessed memory have said, that on high there are several thousands of ten thousands of ministering angels, who say *kedushah* all day long with awe and fear. And we find (*Tanna d'bei Eliyahu* 16) that there are four hundred and ninety-six thousand ten thousands of ministering angels who stand before Him and sanctify His great name all day long, from sunrise until sunset, saying "Holy! Holy! Holy!" And, from sunset to sunrise, "Blessed is the glory of the L-rd from His place!" How much will a man be ashamed when he comes to the world on high and sees all this great tumult issuing from the mouths of ten thousands of holy angels, sanctifying and praising the name of the Holy One Blessed be He, who formed and created them with happiness and joy, when he remembers that when he was in the world of doing, the Holy One Blessed be He had given him, too, this great eminence of praising and sanctifying His great name at all times, like the host of heaven on high, and he, in his indolence, had abolished this by his perverse will. The principal thing is for a man to remember in his lifetime that the time will come [if he does not take heed] when he will want with all of his will to praise and sanctify the name of the L-rd, but will not be permitted to do so. For a man is permitted to occupy himself with Torah, and, likewise, to sanctify the name of the L-rd, only while he is still alive, in this world.]

And now, if we come to the count, let a man reflect upon the great zeal he should devote to this; that is, to strengthen himself and to pray with a *minyan* each day. For from one day alone, from the prayers of *shacharith* and *minchah*, he has thirty-eight Amens from nineteen blessings of prayer [i.e., the *Amidah*], respectively [(And our sages of blessed memory have said (*Shabbath* 119b): "If one is careful in the answering of Amen, the gates of Gan Eden are opened for him, as it is written (*Isaiah* 26:2): 'Open, you gates, and let there enter a righteous nation, keeper of *emunim* [faith].' Read it not "*emunim*," but "*Amenim*."'")], and eight times "*Amen, yehei shemei rabbah*," and another sixteen *Amenim* from the *Kadishim* and two *Kedushoth* and *Barchu*.

All this is in one day. Go and count how many there are in one week, in one month — in one whole year! Is there a count to the profusion of merits accumulating for a man through his habituation to praying with a *minyan*!

10) Add, especially, on Mondays and Thursday, when he also fulfills the mitzvah of reading the Torah, which is an ancient enactment from the days of Moses our teacher of blessed memory, as we find in *Bava Kamma* 82a. And in the time of the *Gemara*, the men of the villages would come to the city on Mondays and Thursdays to hear the recitation of the Torah, as we find in the beginning of *Megillah*. In our many sins, we must be ashamed before the men of the villages of the earlier generations, who did not hesitate even to ride from the villages to the cities for this; and among us it is customary to ride from the city early in the morning even on Mondays and Thursdays for a small thing, but not to hear the reading of the Torah.

We have set forth a little of the eminence of a man who is habituated to praying with a *minyan*, and the great increase of his mitzvoth and merits. The major thing here is that this mitzvah be a steady one, and not one that he slackens in. But if sometimes he performs it and sometimes slackens in it, G-d forbid, then he is in the class of (*Vayikra* 26:21): "But if you walk with Me by chance, etc." (see Rashi there). And thus have our sages of blessed memory said (*Berachoth* 6b), that when a man is accustomed to come to the house of study, and once does not come, the Holy One Blessed be He "inquires" after him as to why he has not come. And this is intimated in (*Isaiah* 50:10): "Who among you who fears the L-rd — who listens to the voice of His servant — has walked in the darkness, where it is not light for him?" (If he had gone to perform a mitzvah, it would have been light for him, but having gone on a mundane errand, it was not light for him) (*Ibid.*): "Let him trust in the name of the L-rd." Why has this befallen him" Because he should have trusted in the name of the L-rd and did not. R. Yochanan said; "When the Holy One Blessed be He comes to the synagogue and does not find ten men there, He becomes angry, viz. (*Ibid.* 2): 'Why, when I came, was there no man? when I called, was there no response?'" The intent is that even if a man were presented with an opportunity for profit at the time of his going to the synagogue, he should not pay heed to it, but trust in the name of the L-rd that what was set aside for him by Heaven will not be detracted from him. And, indeed, very often this is a test from Heaven for him. As our sages of blessed memory have said: "There is no man who is not subjected to tests. A rich man is tested; a poor man is tested, etc." And when a man reflects upon this, he sees this in his experience. He may sometimes stand a whole day in his shop and see very few customers, and when the time for the *minchah* prayer arrives [or on Sabbath eve before sunset], new customers come, whom he had never seen before, and beg him to sell to them — and all this, as a test, the Holy One Blessed be He testing him to see if his [Divine] service is dear to him [to be performed] with all of his heart and all of his soul.

And aside from all we have written in praise of prayer with a *minyan*, there is another great mitzvah that results from this; namely, initiating his sons also in the service of the L-rd. For when a son sees that his father regularly attends the synagogue and that this mitzvah is beloved by him, he, too, becomes accustomed to it and the honor of the Blessed L-rd is increased thereby. In truth, I have often wondered why it is that in our days we see only very few of the youths in the synagogue. But it has become clear that the son learns this from his father. When he sees that this mitzvah is not beloved by his father; for sometimes he goes to the synagogue and sometimes he prays at home (even when not forced to do so), he [the son] becomes even more proficient in this and does not go at all! It is found, then, that not only does he not fulfill the mitzvah of *chinuch* [(initiating his son in mitzvoth)], but, to the contrary, he effects the opposite — bad *chinuch* — removing his sons from the way of the L-rd; and he is liable in the future for them [(his sons)], too. The man of heart will take all of this to heart, and then, he will be happy and it will be good for him.

Chapter II

On the mitzvah of love of the L-rd

I have come, further, to awaken ourselves to what is written in the *Gemara* (*Berachoth* 14b): "Ulla said: 'If one recites the *Shema* without *tefillin*, it is as if he testifies falsely against himself.'" (For he says (*Devarim* 6;8): "And you shall tie them [the *tefillin*]," and he has not tied them.) And even though he intends to do so afterwards, this does not avail, since he does not tie them immediately. And, ostensibly, this is the *din*, too, with (*Ibid.* 5): "And you shall love the L-rd your G-d." He should see to it [at that time] to plant the love of the L-rd in his heart. And this is as the *Chovoth Halevavoth* writes in the Gate of the Love of the L-rd, Chapter III, that one should reflect upon the greatness of the Creator and His exaltedness, [His sustaining all the world], and, conversely, upon his own smallness and insignificance and the like. And then he should recognize the great good of the Blessed One to him in the continuation of His benefactions to him from the day of his birth, not according to his deeds, and hiding his sins from men and extending [his life]. And if it is difficult for him to do all this while reading the *Shema*, he should see to it in any event to reflect upon it at least once a day. Should it be that just because it is a constant mitzvah that is not dependent upon time that it should not be fulfilled even once a day? And it is good that he think about it after praying, before going home to eat, for it is similar to the other mitzvoth incumbent upon a man, like *tefillin*, or 'taking' the lulav and its species on Succoth, where one does not eat before he fulfills them.

Chapter III

Arousal to the study of mitzvoth, and the property of *tzitzith*

I have come, further, to awaken ourselves to [the significance of] something we say every day in the section of *tzitzith* (*Bamidbar* 15:39): "And you shall see it, and you shall remember all the mitzvoth of the L-rd." Our Rabbis of blessed memory have said concerning this (*Menachoth* 43b): "Seeing leads to remembering and remembering leads to doing." But when is this of avail? When he studies and knows the mitzvoth but is afraid that he might forget them. *Tzitzith* avails for this, that he will remember them and not forget them, and, as a matter of course, he will come to fulfill them. But if he does not know the mitzvoth, how will *tzitzith* avail him? Therefore, it is very desirable that one learn all of the book, *Mitzvoth Hashem*, or, at least, *Kitzur Sefer Charedim* which is included in *Zichru Torath Mosheh* of the Chayeh Adam. He will thereby know the mitzvoth and will fulfill correctly the mitzvah of *tzitzith*.

Now, in truth, *tzitzith* is comparable to a list that a man makes when he travels to buy merchandise and which he refers to several times so as to fix in his mind which merchandise to buy. But all this is of avail only when he knows and recognizes the types of merchandise. However, if he does not, then even if he looks at the list the whole day, he will not know what to buy. Therefore, it is well to do as we have written.

And the verse implies that the seeing of the *tzitzith* is of avail in spurring one [to do] the mitzvoth of the L-rd and not to go astray after his eyes. If so, how fitting it is to look at them several times a day, especially when some impure thought or some [kind of] anger enters his heart. It is then highly advisable to gaze upon the *tzitzith*, whereupon the *yetzer* will depart.

Chapter IV

On "You shall not covet"

I have also come to awaken ourselves to another thing that most men stumble in. It is well known that [the *issur* of] theft obtains both with others and with relatives, and even with one's father and mother, as we find in *Bava Kamma* 70a: "If one stole from his father, etc." And it is obvious that the negative commandment of "You shall not covet" also obtains with all. And see *Choshen Mishpat* that the negative commandment of "You shall not covet" does not obtain with desiring in the heart alone, but with one's being so profuse in blandishments of another that he finally consents to give him what he wants. Accordingly, if one joined another in a wedding agreement [*tenaim*] to wed his daughter to his son and they agreed what each would give [(For before they reach an agreement, each is entitled to ask whatever he wishes, stating that lacking this, he does not wish to sign)], and after this he heaped blandishments upon the other to extract more and more, apparently the negative commandment of "You shall not covet" obtains, and this with all such optional gifts [(as opposed to grants of charity)], where the other does not really wish to give but consents only under the pressure of the blandishments.

Postscript By the Translator

"מי האיש החפץ חיים אוהב ימים לראות טוב נצור לשונך מרע
ושפתיך מדבר מרמה סור מרע ועשה טוב בקש שלום ורדפהו"

(*תהילים לד: יג-טו*)

"Who is the man who desires life,
who loves days to see good?
Guard your tongue from evil, and your lips
from speaking deceit.
Turn from evil and do good, seek peace
and pursue it."

(*Psalms* 34:13-15)

Owed to the Chafetz Chaim

To you are owed the lust for life,
the love of days with goodness rife.
To you are owed the guarded tongue,
that will not move to utter wrong.
To you are owed the lips discreet,
that will not stir to speak deceit,
the heart that well has understood
to turn from evil and do good,
the will to see it and to do it,
to seek sweet peace and to pursue it.
Shine down on us from your abode;
for all of these to you are owed

by Shraga Silverstein

Printed in Poland
by Amazon Fulfillment
Poland Sp. z o.o., Wrocław